Gary F. Coombs

Counseling
Cross-
Culturally

Counseling Cross-Culturally

AN INTRODUCTION TO
THEORY & PRACTICE FOR CHRISTIANS

DAVID J. HESSELGRAVE

BAKER BOOK HOUSE
GRAND RAPIDS, MICHIGAN 49506

Contents

Foreword

Readers of his earlier books know that David J. Hesselgrave is a careful scholar who is in tune with current missionary trends and willing to tackle difficult issues in his writings. In producing a book on counseling he has dared to move into a new field and to call for an approach to helping that acknowledges the influence of Western therapies even as it recognizes that these can be irrelevant in other societies.

Within the past decade, the counseling profession has become increasingly aware of the cultural implications of counseling. Books, articles, and workshops have all addressed the issue of cross-cultural counseling, but in several respects these have been weak. Many of the leaders in this field, for example, have been professional counselors who have expertise in counseling theory and methodology but who often know little about social psychology or cultural anthropology. As a result, there sometimes is an insensitivity to the attitudes and perspectives of people in other societies; often there is an enthusiasm about applying counseling techniques with but little awareness of the need to first study and understand a culture before

5

attempting to make therapeutic interventions in other people's lives.

Most of the literature about cross-cultural counseling with which I am familiar is also limited to discussions of how to help people within the borders of the United States. There is emphasis, for example, on how white counselors can help blacks or Hispanics, how middle-class people can reach the poor, or how Western therapies can be adapted to Vietnamese or Haitian refugees. Much of this is of limited value to the missionary who moves into another society and seeks to give counseling or counselor training to nationals who are living and experiencing problems within the contexts of their own cultures.

Because of his personal experience in living and counseling overseas and his familiarity with the literature about missionary and cultural anthropology, Hesselgrave is able to go beyond much of the current secular work in cross-cultural counseling. He brings an evangelical viewpoint to a new field that to this point has been almost exclusively secular, and he discusses cross-cultural helping from a missionary anthropological perspective that focuses on helping people in countries other than one's own. The inclusion of case histories and vignettes adds interest and brings greater clarity to the concepts that are presented— all in a well-organized and clearly documented fashion.

Cross-cultural counseling is a growing area of interest, both in psychology and in missions. Hesselgrave's book is a pioneering work on which others will surely build. It summarizes much of the current thinking in the field and issues a call for further research. I think it will make a unique contribution to the growing missionary literature.

Gary R. Collins
Professor of Pastoral Counseling and Psychology
Trinity Evangelical Divinity School

Foreword

In one volume David J. Hesselgrave addresses four distinct needs of the serious student of Christian cross-cultural counseling.

He describes the history and development of missionary contributions of Western secular and Christian counseling to non-Western counseling situations.

Utilizing universals from counseling's basic sciences and Scripture, he courageously plots a course that leads from uncertainty, through a unifying philosophy, and toward a basic science of missiologic counseling and psychology.

He offers numerous descriptions of real problems and solutions in counseling on the mission field and in other cross-cultural situations.

The reader will find in Hesselgrave's work—an introduction to theory and practice—a complete reference guide, a broad stimulus to his own thought and commitment to missions, and a handy guidebook.

Of special importance are the universal concepts the reader gains from this volume. Drawing from clear scriptural truths and the basics of the counseling sciences, Hesselgrave presents a paradigm that serves as a base for understanding, development, and practice. One begins to appreciate the sameness among the seemingly most dissimilar peoples, and how this sameness actually aids cross-cultural understanding and counseling. Hesselgrave thus not only provides a stimulus to study a newly emerging field, but also offers a work that should facilitate the actual delivery of effective cross-cultural counseling. This final product will be the mark of this book's real achievement.

Gary L. Almy, M.D.
Chief of Psychiatry Services
Veterans' Administration Medical Center
North Chicago, Illinois

Associate Professor of Psychiatry
University of Health Sciences/Chicago Medical School

Preface

There was a time, and it was not long ago, when theology and philosophy in one form or another provided the raw material out of which the really important books on missiology were made. In more recent times missiological literature has evidenced a significant shift. Increasingly, contemporary writings in the area reveal a debt to such disciplines as anthropology, psychology, linguistics, communication, and even marketing. Of course, this fact of missiological life will not constitute news to most of my readers. But what I want to point out is that the shift is comparatively recent and that it has both good and bad aspects.

The "bad news" is that theology has been forced out of the driver's seat in much of contemporary missiology. That is both incongruous and indefensible. Without orthodox theology there can be no sound missiology. Every worthy book on the Christian mission need not concentrate on a theology of mission, but all must be true to it. Theology is still queen of the sciences.

The "good news" is that as the aforementioned and related sciences have developed we have become more and

more aware of the invaluable insight they hold out to all
of us who are vitally concerned with Christian mission.
No alchemy can create divine revelation out of human
discovery. But, as Augustine so aptly put it, "Gold from
Egypt is still gold."

As for my own perspective, to the degree that I am
qualified to profess any expertise whatsoever it is in the
areas of communication and cross-cultural research. I
studied theology formally for three years and have attempted to stay abreast of theological discussions for more
than thirty years since that time. But I am not a professional theologian. I have had basic formal studies in psychology and counseling, have researched the area on my
own, have team-taught with colleagues in that area, have
counseled and worked as a missionary in another culture
for twelve years, and for almost twenty years have worked
with internationals from a variety of cultures who are
studying in North America. But I am not a professional
psychologist or counselor.

This book grows out of that background and has prof-
ited from the constructive criticisms of colleagues spe-
cializing in missiology, theology, psychiatry, and counseling. It is motivated by a desire to fill a glaring lacuna
in Christian literature and thus aid the cause of Christ at
home and abroad. It undoubtedly has its full complement
of weaknesses. But if it causes us to think before exporting
too much of the purely Western ingredients of counseling
theory and practice; if it aids us in being more sensitive
to other ways of diagnosing and dealing with human problems; if it encourages the inauguration of courses in cross-
cultural counseling in the curricula of our Christian
schools and provides some of the material for consideration in those courses—if in some measure it accomplishes these purposes, it will have been worth the effort
that has gone into its writing.

The New International Version of the Bible has been

quoted throughout this book, except in those cases where some other version is indicated.

I have used the masculine pronoun and the word *man* in a generic sense rather than resorting to such contrivances as "he/she" or alternating "he" and "she" or regularly substituting "person(s)" for "man" and "men." This makes me vulnerable to the charge of using sexist language, but it seems to me that, given the limitations of the English language, this approach is a small price to pay for a more straightforward and simple style.

Among many who deserve special thanks I would like to mention Gary R. Collins and Gary L. Almy, who provided forewords and helpful criticisms; William T. Kirwan, David Dillon, and James O. Buswell III for encouragement and suggestions; Mrs. Joyce Griffin and Mrs. Jeanne Beckner, who typed the manuscript; Scott Moreau, who checked the references; and doctor of missiology students at Trinity who allowed the use of their accounts of cross-cultural counseling experiences. I also want to express my gratitude to Dan Van't Kerkhoff and the enterprising people at Baker Book House for their willingness to risk something in the belief that Christian cross-cultural personnel will not long lag behind their secular counterparts in preparing themselves to counsel cross-culturally, and for their faith that this book will make a contribution to that preparation. Finally, I am indebted to my wife Gertrude and my children, Dennis, Ronald, and Sheryl, who together have constituted the kind of family that has made Christian ministry in various cultures both possible and rewarding.

David J. Hesselgrave
Trinity Evangelical Divinity School—
    School of World Mission and Evangelism
Deerfield, Illinois

PART 1

Introductory Considerations

1

The Christian Conscience and Cross-Cultural Ministries

"Teacher, my brother Omodo is persuaded that Jesus Christ is the true Savior and that the Christian way is the true way. But he says that if he became a Christian and joined the church he would be forced to reject two of his wives. Then he could not care for his garden. Also he says it would not be right for them. Will you talk to him?"

"Sahib, many people in our village now know and worship the true God. We have peace with him. We are thankful for this. But we do not have peace with many unbelieving neighbors. They are angry. They say we neglect the gods of our people and bring much sickness and trouble to our village. We do not know what to do. Can you help us?"

"Mr. Santos, our church is very happy to have had the opportunity to sponsor you and your family so that you could come to live in our country. However, we know that you are having difficulty in your new job and we also hear that your children are having some problems at school.

15

May we talk and pray together concerning these problems? We want to help in any way we can."

"Please come quickly, Reverend Anderson. My oldest daughter Sheila is so ill. She sits in a corner of our house; her eyes are set in a glassy stare; she will not talk; and when we try to approach her she first screams and then moans. The medicine man told our neighbor that an evil spirit has possessed her because she refused the rites and started going to your church. Can you help her?"

"Dr. Brown, it is a privilege to study in your country. I enjoy your class very much. I understand much that is written in the textbook. I am very sorry to fail the examination last week. It is not very much like examinations in our country. I am sorry. What should I do?"

A Contemporary Challenge

These vignettes emanate from very different situations. Three occur on the mission field; two occur at home. Three involve professional missionaries; two do not. Some participants are adjusting to a new faith; others are adjusting to a new environment.

But there are commonalities in these situations also. We can assume that Christians are involved, either as counselors or counselees. None of the problems is easily resolved. In each case an understanding of a second culture will be required if wise assistance and counsel are to be given.

Christians are being called upon increasingly to care, counsel, and cure across cultural boundaries. There are more than one hundred thousand missionaries in the world who bear the name *Christian.* An increasing number of Christian clergy, professors, and laypersons travel, witness, and minister abroad for long or short periods of time. Currently, 263,940 foreign students study in the United

States.[1] Our country is now home for hundreds of thousands of refugees from various cultural backgrounds. This situation is fraught with tremendous problems and unparalleled potential. Personal experience bears out the truth of this statement.

An Uncommon Experience?

Shortly after World War II, the inner-city church of which I was pastor became sponsor for a displaced person, Mr. A, from eastern Europe. The contact had been made by the director of a mission organization. It was his opinion that this foreign brother would be able to make a large contribution to our inner-city ministry, but if not, he would be employed in the mission headquarters in another city. With no small amount of exhilaration and with genuine hospitality our congregation welcomed the newcomer to their country, community, and church. Problems soon became apparent, however. Mr. A did not speak fluent English, and although local people were outwardly kind, inwardly and perhaps unconsciously they tended to be frustrated and even impatient in communicating with him. A group in the church took an offering for Mr. A, who promptly spent most of the money on an outrageously expensive billfold. Frustration grew as a result. As pastor, I tried rather ineptly and altogether unsuccessfully to bridge the gap by counseling church leaders and especially Mr. A. In a few weeks Mr. A was invited to join the staff of the mission in another city. Members of the congregation expressed their relief.

Several years later our small family of four lived on the outskirts of Urawa City, the capital city of Saitama Prefecture and located some fifty minutes by train from downtown Tokyo. Our home was visited by numerous

---

1. *UNESCO Statistical Yearbook 1981* (Dunstable, England: United Nations Educational, Scientific, and Cultural Organization, 1981), sec. 3, p. 462.

Japanese—mostly teen-agers but some older folk as well—
every week. In those postwar years they came with every
kind of question and problem imaginable. We visited family members in hospitals and sanitariums. We witnessed
in prisons and schools. We stood by as Japanese doctors
administered shock therapy and blood transfusions. We
sat with the bereaved as the roaring flames of the local
crematorium claimed the body of a family member. We
sat on the *tatami* floor before pictures of those who had
died during the war and attempted to answer questions
which up to that time we had faced only theoretically if
at all. And most of all we counseled concerning Christian
conversion, the Christian life, and Christian service. How
insufficient had been our preparation for such a ministry!
Whatever small part we had in the planting of a church
that today meets in its more than two-million-dollar facility across from the prefectural capitol must be balanced
with a recollection of numerous failures occasioned, at
least in part, by cultural misunderstandings that aborted
wiser counsel. Many times I have looked back on our
years in Japan—especially those early years—and have
wondered how I could have been so blind to the cultural
implications of the solutions I proposed to the overwhelming problems of searching people emerging from
the night of a misguided and misplaced faith. Slowly—oh,
so slowly—over a long period of time, our counsel began
to reflect the cultural sensitivity that made it more understandable and Christian.

Now for almost twenty years I have had the privilege
of teaching students here at home, first in a secular university and then in a theological seminary. In both settings I have interacted with young people from a score or
more foreign countries. I have watched them and worked
with them as they have wrestled with not only the materials of their respective academic disciplines but also,
even more importantly, the vagaries of a foreign culture
and its sometimes enigmatic value systems and pedagog-
ical approaches. Some have given up and returned to their

home countries. Others have struggled to achieve their goals, with varying degrees of success. But in almost every case the major adjustments have been made by the students rather than by American instructors and friends. Even when we have set up structures and set aside personnel to help foreign students, we have often failed to be of great help in counseling and helping them and their families in respect to the basics of living and learning in the United States.

A Careful Evaluation

How will Christians respond? We are reminded of the reproachful words of our Lord to his sleeping disciples in Gethsemane: "The spirit is willing, but the body is weak" (Matt. 26:41). There is a willingness and often an enthusiasm to help those of other cultures and subcultures. What we lack is the ability—not so much in terms of resources as in terms of skills. A 1977 survey of counselor-education programs in this country revealed that fewer than 1 percent of the respondents reported any instructional requirements for the study of nonwhite cultures.[2] The situation in similar programs in Christian schools is not likely to be much better.

At a recent conference of psychologists and counselors in Vail, Colorado, a task group recommended that

> the provision of professional services to persons of culturally diverse backgrounds [by those] not competent in understanding and providing professional services to such groups ... be considered unethical. It shall be equally unethical to deny such persons professional services because the present staff is inadequately prepared. It shall therefore be the obligation of all service agencies to employ competent persons or to provide continuing education for

2. Derald W. Sue, *Counseling the Culturally Different* (New York: Wiley, 1981), p. 4.

the present staff to meet the service needs of the culturally diverse population it serves.[3]

If it is unethical for unprepared secular counselors to work with persons of different cultures, what does this say regarding the activities of thousands of missionaries in other cultures and church leaders in our own who by the very nature of their task are required to counsel the culturally different? And what does it say concerning professional training programs devoid of any cultural insight except that provided by the middle-class white perspective in which the discipline has flourished (as we shall see) and yet ostensibly prepares counselors from and for numerous diverse cultures? The word *conscience* comes from the Latin and literally means "to know with" someone. Insofar as possible, should we not "know with" our inquirers and hearers from other cultures? Is this not an ethical concern, a concern of conscience?

Increasingly, professional and lay Christians are being presented with the opportunity to help and even heal people from other cultures. Most Christian workers with extensive intercultural experience will admit that they have often lacked the ability to relate to problems and perplexities occasioned by cultural differences. Yet training in cross-cultural counseling per se is minimal at best and often nonexistent.

The situation calls for a new kind of willingness on the part of God's people to prepare to aid those of other cultures so that they might find Christ and live in harmony with his will and in fellowship with his people. All Christians who take the Great Commission seriously—and especially those in the helping professions having to do with counseling and curing—should be among the first to address themselves to the potential of relating to peoples of differing cultural and religious backgrounds in a biblical and culturally appropriate manner.

3. Quoted in Sue, *Counseling the Culturally Different*, p. viii.

Cross-Cultural Psychology and Counseling
A Timely Birth?

Embedded in the pursuit of knowledge in general, and in its Western expressions in particular, is a high degree of competitiveness. It is not difficult to find illustrations of this. Think of the departmental divisions in our colleges and universities and of the ways in which they compete for funds, students, and fame. Think of the overly technical vocabularies developed within the various disciplines which have the effect of reserving their respective expertise for the initiated. Think of the competition between "theoretical" and "practical" disciplines in our Bible schools and seminaries. And think of the mistrust that often poisons dialogue between theologians and scientists.

One is tempted to conclude that knowledge makes its most singular gains not when we discover a new truth or even when we rediscover old truths, but whenever we discover each other. Why? Because new truth is in very short supply and old truths are readily available for the price of investigation. But in discovering each other we

21

find knowledge that is new to us and thereby we find the potential for correcting both our ignorance and inefficiency. Of course, in discovering one another we find another's errors as well as one another's truths. A risk is therefore involved.

One of the areas in which Christian scholars need to discover each other and attempt to integrate knowledge and correlate skills is the area of cross-cultural counseling. Tens of thousands of North American missionaries minister abroad. Most of them have gained a high degree of sensitivity to cultural differences, a few of them have expertise in counseling, and hardly any of them possess both cultural sensitivity and counseling expertise, but all of them actually counsel the culturally different. Hundreds of thousands of foreign students and immigrants with cultural orientations vastly different from our own are finding their way to our shores and are ministered to by Christian teachers, counselors, and pastors who rarely possess the knowledge and appreciation of cultural differences necessary to counsel them effectively. Millions of members of North American subcultures, especially in our cities, are being evangelized, discipled, and trained by Christians whose cultural orientation (often white, Anglo-Saxon, middle class) is a far cry from their own.

The challenge to bring the cross-cultural perspectives of missiology and the interactional understandings of psychology and counseling together in a meaningful way is great. Our counterparts in corresponding secular fields have already embarked upon this task. We who have been given the Great Commission should no longer lag behind.

With this in mind, in the next few pages I propose to provide background information concerning the related disciplines, describe missionary psychology and counseling as a subject area, and discuss some of the advantages of introducing this new subject area in schools of missions, Bible, and theology.

The Development of Ethnopsychology and Cultural Psychiatry

According to Gregory Zilboorg's definitive *History of Medical Psychology,* a new orientation in psychological medicine (one that brought psychotherapy to the forefront) was inaugurated by Anton Mesmer in the eighteenth century.[1] (Mesmerism was a curious combination of medicine, magic, and mentalism.) Throughout the nineteenth century, the rise of numerous theories and practices associated with medicopsychological studies resulted in psychiatry becoming a separate branch of medicine and an important contributor to the cultural development of both Europe and the United States.[2] Some of the most important names associated with this movement are those of Jean Martin Charcot, Pierre Janet, Hippolyte Bernheim, Emil Kraepelin, Josef Breuer, Sigmund Freud, and Carl Jung.

Meanwhile sociology and anthropology emerged as independent disciplines. Calvin S. Hall and Gardner Lindzey write,

> While sociologists studied man living in a state of advanced civilization and found him to be a product of his class and caste, his institutions and folkways, anthropologists ventured into remote areas of the world where they found evidence that human beings are almost infinitely malleable. According to these new social sciences, man is chiefly a product of the society in which he lives. His personality is social rather than biological.[3]

Overdrawn though this conclusion has proved to be, interest in studying sociocultural as well as racial differ-

1. Gregory Zilboorg, *A History of Medical Psychology* (New York: Norton, 1941), p. 378.
2. Ibid., p. 379.
3. Calvin S. Hall and Gardner Lindzey, *Theories of Personality* (New York: Wiley, 1957), pp. 114–15.

ences also developed among psychiatrists and psychologists. Kraepelin noted that the behavior of mentally ill persons whom he observed in his native Germany and other European countries varied in different regions. He went to Java specifically to study the influence of culture on mental disorders. There, "he noted that manic-depressive psychoses were uncommon, and that depressive reactions, if they occurred, seldom contained elements of sinfulness."[4]

In 1911 Alfred Adler broke with Freud and became the father of a new school of psychoanalysis. Social forces, Adler posited, motivated man. In his view, a person strives for superiority to compensate for feelings of inferiority. Moreover, each person seeks experiences that promote his own social interest and lifestyle.

By the third and fourth decades of the twentieth century a kind of rapproachement had developed between anthropologists and specialists who studied personality. Scholars such as Ralph Linton, Abram Kardiner, Ruth Benedict, Margaret Mead, A. I. Hallowell, and Marvin K. Opler took a special interest in psychology and personality development from their perspectives (mainly anthropological). From the disciplines of psychology and psychiatry, Karen Horney, Erich Fromm, Harry Stack Sullivan, and others adopted the social-psychology outlook. A new field, variously called anthropological psychiatry, psychiatric anthropology, psychological anthropology, cross-cultural psychology, enthnopsychology, enthnopsychiatry, or culture and personality, was developing.

Scholars in other related disciplines have also made important contributions. Notable have been the research in culture and learning theory by the Swiss theorist Jean Piaget and Clark L. Hull and John Dollard at Yale; the

4. E. D. Wittkower, with the assistance of Hsien Rin, "Recent Developments in Transcultural Psychology," in *Transcultural Psychiatry*, eds. A. V. S. de Reuck and Ruth Porter (Boston: Little, Brown, 1965), p. 4.

studies of sociologist George Homans on the relation between group interaction and human behavior; and the in-
quiries of David Bidney, Clyde K. Kluckhohn, Alfred L.
Kroeber, Robert Redfield, and Milton Singer on such philosophically, anthropologically, and psychologically important subjects as values and world views.

In recent years a spate of studies and journals bearing
upon cross-cultural psychology, counseling, communication, psychiatry, and anthropology has been released. These
studies have been published within the context of the dis-
ciplinic interests of the authors and under the qualifying
adjectives *transcultural, intercultural, cross-cultural,* or
cultural. (The meanings, or at least the nuances, of these
qualifiers are different, but one should not expect to find
uniformity in their use nevertheless.) The most complete
review of these works relating to the present study is provided in a six-volume publication entitled *Handbook of
Cross-Cultural Psychology.*[5] One should not overlook relevant and practical volumes such as *Counseling the Culturally Different*[6] and *Counseling across Cultures,*[7] but it
should be noted that the emphasis in these books is upon
surmounting cultural differences in counseling members
of minorities *within the North American context.*

The Development of Pastoral Theology, Psychology, and Counseling

In another place I have dealt with the problem faced by
the brilliant Saint Augustine upon his conversion.[8] Very

5. Harry C. Triandis, gen. ed., *Handbook of Cross-Cultural Psychology: Perspectives,* 6 vols. (Boston: Allyn and Bacon, 1979–81).

6. Derald W. Sue, *Counseling the Culturally Different* (New York: Wiley, 1981).

7. Paul P. Pedersen, Walter J. Lonner, and Juris G. Draguns, eds., *Counseling across Cultures,* 1st ed. (Honolulu: The University Press of Hawaii for the East-West Center, 1976).

8. David J. Hesselgrave, "Gold from Egypt': The Contribution of Rhetoric to Cross-Cultural Communication," *Missiology: An International Review* 4 (October 1976): 83–192.

simply put, it was the problem of how to use (or whether to use) his secular knowledge of rhetoric in his ministry in the kingdom of God. His conclusion was that all truth is God's truth and therefore should be put to kingdom use. The use is not to be indiscriminate, however. It must be governed by three cautions which are sometimes explicit and always implicit in Augustine's writings:

1. Nothing in excess.
2. The amount of useful "pagan" knowledge is small when compared with that derivable from the Scriptures.
3. The Scriptures constitute the standard of truth.

The results of Augustine's approach are to be found everywhere in his works and, in the light of our present interests, should be examined in *On Christian Doctrine*,[9] which can be thought of as the first manual for the pastor on Bible interpretation and preaching.

In spite of tensions, the so-called age of modern science was born in the work of men who held to a unified approach to knowledge. For them, theological truth and scientific truth were complementary. Only later were these disciplines considered separate. As a result, Augustine's problem has been reintroduced in modern dress, and here and there resolved in more or less satisfactory ways— sometimes more, and sometimes less!

Pastoral theology has developed as an "operations-centered" branch of theology, as opposed to the more "logic-oriented" branches of the traditional disciplines.[10] James N. Lapsley holds that there are four essentials in a viable pastoral theology:

9. Augustine, *On Christian Doctrine*, trans. D. W. Robertson, Jr. (New York: Liberal Arts, 1958).

10. James N. Lapsley, "Pastoral Theology Past and Present," in *The New Shape of Pastoral Theology: Essays in Honor of Seward Hiltner*, ed. William B. Oglesby, Jr. (Nashville: Abington, 1969), p. 32.

1. a basic focus on the caring, helping, healing, and sustaining aspects of ministry;
2. a recognition of the pervasiveness of these aspects of ministry;
3. the theological character of the discipline;
4. the use of the tools of the science that study personality and related disciplines.[11]

Lapsley notes that although the term *pastoral theology* came into use in the middle of the eighteenth century, no works devoted to it in that century met these four criteria. In the nineteenth century, Friedrich E. D. Schleiermacher's *Pracktische Theologie* at least hinted at the scientific nature of the discipline while concentrating on its theological orientation. In England, prior to World War I, Clement F. Rogers published his *Introduction to the Study of Pastoral Theology.*[12] This work emphasized the scientific nature of the discipline. Probably the most generally recognized precursor of the pastoral-theology movement as we know it today, however, was Anton T. Boisen. He advocated the use of a case-study method which utilized psychological insights. Although he did not develop a systematic pastoral theology, he exerted a profound influence on the general discipline and, especially through his *Exploration of the Inner World*[13] and a program for seminarians at Worchester State Hospital in Massachusetts, gave impetus to the Clinical Pastoral Education (CPE) movement. A number of professors in the pastoral field with specializations in psychology and counseling (Paul E. Johnson, Carrol A. Wise, Wayne E. Oates, and Seward Hiltner) were nurtured in that movement.

11. Ibid., p. 33.
12. Clement F. Rogers, *An Introduction to the Study of Pastoral Theology* (Oxford: Clarendon, 1912).
13. Anton T. Boisen, *The Exploration of the Inner World: A Study of Mental Disorder and Religious Experience* (Chicago and New York: Willett, Clark, 1936).

During the 1930s and 1940s, evangelical schools usually entertained a mistrust of psychology in general and of the CPE movement in particular.[14] Criticisms of the movement were that personal experience seemed to take precedence over Scripture; the notions of humanistic psychology were borrowed too uncritically; and little consideration was given to conservative theology. Evangelical psychologists such as Clyde M. Narramore and Henry Brandt, however, demonstrated that a biblical approach to pastoral counseling is possible. Evangelical resistance gradually has broken down. Schools have inaugurated departments of pastoral psychology and counseling. Pastoral counselors such as Jay E. Adams and Paul D. Norris; professional counselors such as Paul Tournier, James Dobson, and Charles Solomon; theoreticians such as Wayne E. Oates and Gary R. Collins; and popularizers such as Bill Gothard, Tim LaHaye and Norman Wright have become well known. Christian counseling has, in fact, achieved a somewhat independent status, although in most theological institutions it is still a subcategory of pastoral theology.

The Development of Missiology and Cross-Cultural Psychology and Counseling

Although the word *missiology* is comparatively new and has only recently achieved widespread recognition as a term for a legitimate academic discipline, the theoretical and practical study of the mission of the church is almost as old as the church itself.

In the seventeenth and eighteenth century several attempts were made to establish distinctive Protestant training schools for missionaries. One such was set up by Anton Walaeus at Leiden University in 1622. Another was

14. Gary R. Collins, ed., *Helping People Grow: Practical Approaches to Christian Counseling* (Santa Ana, Calif.: Vision House, 1980), pp. 12–15.

the Collegium Orientale Theologicum, founded at Halle by A. H. Francke in 1702. However, apart from the insights of Francke's student Bartholomew Ziegenbalg, who was later a missionary to India, not much more was written during the early centuries of Protestantism to suggest the cultural perspective of missiology as we know it today. That perspective became clearer in the nineteenth century, particularly through the work of Gustav Warneck. The first to be officially appointed to a chair of missionary science, Warneck is often thought of as the father of the science of missions.

In the twentieth century numerous Continental and British scholars have contributed to the discipline, among them the Dutch missionary and missiologist J. H. Bavinck. Bavinck brought a keen interest in theology, philosophy, and (to a degree) psychology to the study of missions. His best-known work is entitled *An Introduction to the Science of Missions.*[15] His countryman Hendrik Kraemer should also be mentioned because of his contributions relating to adherents of non-Christian religious systems.[16]

It is perhaps in twentieth-century America that missiology has received the most significant input from the scientific disciplines. The now defunct Kennedy School of Missions at Hartford Theological Seminary; the contribution over the years of the journal *Missionary Anthropology* (and its successor, *Missiology*); numerous mission scholars trained in anthropology, linguistics, communications, the history of religions, and other related disciplines; and several outstanding contemporary schools of mission all witness to the development of missiology as a scientific as well as theological discipline.

15. J. H. Bavinck, *An Introduction to the Science of Missions,* trans. David Hugh Freeman (Grand Rapids: Baker, 1969).

16. Most notable of Kraemer's works are *The Christian Message in a Non-Christian World,* 3d ed. (Grand Rapids: Kregel, 1956); and *The Communication of the Christian Faith* (Philadelphia: Westminster, 1956).

Until comparatively recently, however, the secular disciplines of psychology, psychiatry, and counseling and their corresponding disciplines in practical theology have not been called upon to make a really significant contribution to missiology. Nor has missiology contributed significantly to the disciplines of pastoral psychology and counseling in our Christian schools. Numerous psychological concepts and theories such as Abraham H. Maslow's motivational pyramid, Leon Festinger's cognitive dissonance, and Marshall H. Klaus's and John H. Kennell's bonding are reflected in missiological literature. Some Christian psychologists and counselors have aided missionaries in developing strategies for maintaining one's well-being in the field and coping with culture shock and re-entry problems. But in general, training in psychology and counseling in our Christian schools has been confined to preparing workers for intracultural ministries. Those who would utilize those insights for cross-cultural ministries have found it necessary to make their own (often unsatisfactory) cultural integration and adaptations. It would appear that, unless something is done soon, we will repeat the mistake that we have made over and over in Christian missions: namely, the unwarranted and wholesale exportation of counseling texts and theories, seminars on this and that personality or societal problem, and organizations designed to perpetuate Western approaches to problem-solving. It is precisely this mistake that has given rise to charges of ecclesiastical imperialism and widespread criticism of "Western" evangelistic strategies, pedagogies, church structures, school curricula, and even theologies!

All of the indicators point to the birth of a new subject area, or even a new discipline. We might think of it as the second phase of a twin birth. Pastoral psychology and counseling is about to be joined by a new academic twin—cross-cultural (or missionary) psychology and counseling. Its birth has not been anticipated. A name has not been settled on. Few academicians or practitioners are fully prepared to act as midwives or nursemaids. The heads of our Bible institutes, Bible colleges, and theological seminaries can be expected to wring their hands and shake their heads. Budgets are already strained and older siblings make many demands. Doctors of psychology and counseling are already preoccupied with the first child and the difficulties posed by an increasingly challenging Western environment in which it must mature. The twin will be delivered and nourished and make its contribution to the world and the church. Or it will be stillborn—the victim of a sort of benign neglect occasioned by a culturally conditioned inability to attend its delivery.

What, then, is missionary psychology and counseling? Wherein does it differ from pastoral psychology and counseling? Why do we need it? What contributions will it make if properly attended and nurtured?

Cross-Cultural Psychology and Counseling: Its Definition, Distinctiveness, and Importance

The major distinction between secular cultural psychology, psychiatry, and counseling and their Christian counterparts is to be found in the place accorded the authoritative revelation of God given in the Old and New Testament Scriptures. The major distinction between Christian pastoral psychology and counseling and Christian missionary psychology and counseling is to be found in the biblical distinction between the roles of the pastor and the apostle.

Paul makes it clear that the resurrected and ascended Lord of the church gave "person gifts" to the church. They are apostles, prophets, evangelists, and pastors and teachers (if we agree that pastors and teachers constitute one category—pastor-teachers; Eph. 4:11). These person gifts were given so that the church might be planted and perfected; so that pagans might be transformed into priests (Eph. 4:12; 1 Peter 2:9)! The two person gifts with which we are presently concerned are the apostles and the pastors. Although everyone knows what pastors are and do, there is some confusion concerning the apostles.

There are two kinds of apostles in the New Testament—the "special apostles" who were personally sent forth by our Lord, and the "representatives [lit., apostles] of the churches" (2 Cor. 8:23) who were sent forth by Spirit-directed churches and church leaders.[17] Although the distinctions were not rigid (apostles might undertake a pastoral ministry and vice versa), the record is clear that apostles crossed frontiers to extend the kingdom (Christ's rule), make converts, and establish churches in new areas and among new peoples, whereas pastors shepherded congregations in specific areas. All Christians were to be witnesses (Acts 1:8) and were to constitute a holy priesthood (1 Peter 2:9), but not all Christians were to be missionaries any more than all were to be pastors.

It is common knowledge that the word *missionary* has come to us from the Greek word *apostello* (to send forth) through the Latin *mitto* (to send). Roman Catholics are correct when they refer to their missionary enterprise and personnel as the apostolate. Perhaps they have avoided a certain confusion by doing so. However, most Protestants, when they consider the authority granted to the twelve special apostles, hesitate to apply the same designation to others. (Note, for example, the various translations of *apostoloi* in 2 Cor. 8:23.) Of course, the church today does not have living counterparts to the Twelve. But we do have those who are sent by Spirit-directed churches to cross boundaries and minister among people of other places and backgrounds. I conclude that the missionary of today is the contemporary counterpart of those early apostles of the churches such as Barnabas, Silas, Mark, Timothy, Titus, Andronicus, Junius, and others, and that a distinctive

17. David J. Hesselgrave, *Planting Churches Cross-Culturally: A Guide for Home Foreign Missions* (Grand Rapids: Baker, 1980), pp. 137–41.

aspect of their ministry is that of going into all the world to disciple the *ethne.*

There was a time, and not too long ago, when Christians generally thought of the frontiers across which they sent their missionaries as being primarily geographical. With the advance of transportation and communication technology on the one hand, and of the social sciences on the other, missiologists now think of missionary frontiers in cultural terms. The primary challenge is not so much to send a missionary to Kenya or Kalimantan (political problems aside) as it is to care, communicate, convert, counsel, and cure across the barriers existing between the culture of the missionary and those of Kenya and Kalimantan!

The primary concern of missionary psychology and counseling, therefore, will be to aid missionaries in carrying out their cross-cultural task (just as the primary concern of pastoral psychology and counseling is to equip pastors to minister to people of their own culture and congregations). Inevitably there will be secondary concerns and benefits. The discipline will help us all to recognize ourselves as products of culture. It will help us understand the culture-bound aspects of the disciplines of psychology and counseling in general and pastoral psychology and counseling in particular. It will help missionaries adjust to new cultural situations and readjust to old ones. It will help pastors and other Christian workers to counsel those of other cultures and subcultures within their congregations. It will aid foreign national Christian counselors in adapting an essentially Western discipline to their own cultural situations.

Some forward-looking Christian psychologists have emphasized the importance of culture to Christian counseling. In discussing "The Future of Christian Counseling," Gary R. Collins suggests that cultural differences between the West and the Orient, for example, make for significant differences in effective counseling approaches.[18] He concludes: "Christian counselors have given very little consideration to crosscultural counseling, and any approach to biblically based counseling in the future must not neglect this significant area."[19]

One can only applaud this emphasis. At the same time, Collins' own taxonomy of integration within psychology and counseling and with other disciplines makes a large place for Christian professional, pastoral, and peer counseling and "people-helping" but has no special place at all for missionary counseling and people-helping."[20] Very understandably, the approaches of Christian psychologists and counselors in the West assume a greater difference among Christian professional, pastoral, and lay caring and counseling than they do between any or all of these and cross-cultural caring and counseling.

A rethinking at precisely this point is appropriate. In the light of the biblical distinction between the roles of the missionary, the pastor, and the Christian peers or "lay priests," the crucial role played by Western culture in the development of the discipline, and the importance of non-Western cultures in any successful application of its principles, missionary psychology and counseling becomes equally distinctive and important as pastoral psychology and counseling. That we have not seen this to be so is itself an accretion of our own cultural development.

How might the subject area of missionary psychology be briefly described? First, the relationship between mission and counseling must be made clear. Second, foundations in such areas as theology, psychology, anthropology, communication, and world religions should be

18. Collins, *Helping People Grow*, pp. 341–42.

19. Ibid., p. 342.

20. Collins differentiates professional psychology and counseling, pastoral people-helping, and peer people-helping. As concerns integration with other theological disciplines he thinks of the potential in Christian education for preventive people-helping, in homiletics for public people-helping, and in philosophy of religion for apologetic people-helping.

explored. Third, the concept of culture, the impact of enculturation and acculturation upon groups and individuals, and counseling theories and practices in Western *and* non-Western cultures require examination. Fourth, the outlines of biblical, culture-sensitive counseling approaches for "typical" foreign cultures should be attempted. Fifth, case studies involving proposals for interpreting and solving problems in a cross-cultural context and suggesting techniques for interaction might be undertaken. Finally, ways of encouraging and upgrading the practice of Christian counseling by nationals should be considered.

Cross-Cultural Psychology and Counseling as a New Subject Area

In general terms the need for introducing this new discipline has been discussed. Let us now consider the advantages of including it as an integrated subject in our schools.

First, tens of thousands of Christians are already involved in cross-cultural helping ministries among peoples of many and multiform cultures. During furlough thousands of them take advantage of opportunities for continuing education. Still thousands of others are preparing to join them on the field. Anything that can be done to enhance the ministry of this host of cross-cultural workers is in the interest of Christ's kingdom. It is possible, of course, for Christian teachers of psychology and counseling and teachers of missiology to instruct students of mission separately within the confines of their own disciplines, leaving students to solve the problems of integration as best they can. This approach will prove to be unsatisfactory. Only a few students can take advantage of course offerings in both areas. Even if they study both counseling and culture, how can we expect them to attain an integration that their teachers themselves have not achieved?

Instead, scholars in one or the other subject area must attempt to master enough of the other discipline to integrate the two. Or, better yet, psychologists and missiologists must collaborate to present an integrated course of study.

Second, pastoral psychology and counseling has come to play such an important role in Christian training and experience in the West that the discipline inevitably exports its theories and therapies to the rest of the world. Missionaries major in psychology and counseling and take their discoveries to other cultures. Christian students come from other lands, major in the subject in the West, and return to their respective countries with Western credentials and approaches. Professionals and popularizers take their approaches to Africa, Asia, and Latin America in person, through their publications, or via personal representatives.

What a mixed blessing! "One psychiatrist [from India] said that it took him five years in India to unlearn what he had learned in five years abroad."[21] We might argue that the biblical base of Christian psychology and counseling militates against duplicating his experience. But to argue thus would be naive, if not dishonest. Any fair reading of Christian counseling materials reveals them to be heavily culturally freighted, even those most consciously biblical in their orientation. Furthermore, the importance of a knowledge of the cultural context to even the communication of the biblical message has been amply demonstrated times without number.

Third, think of the advantage that will accrue to Christian psychologists and counselors if they and their discipline are informed by a study of non-Western cultures. Their sensitivities will be heightened and their under-

21. Norman D. Sundberg, "Research and Research Hypotheses about Effectiveness in Intercultural Counseling," in *Counseling across Cultures*, ed. Paul P. Pedersen et al., rev. ed. (Honolulu: The University Press of Hawaii for the East-West Center, 1981), p. 331.

standing widened. They will become better prepared to deal with the problems of minorities in their own culture and of those representatives of other countries who are coming to our cities and schools in great numbers.

But beyond those obvious advantages is still another that is not so obvious. There is some evidence that Western psychology is moving beyond so-called first-force (psychoanalytic), second-force (behavioristic), and third-force (humanistic) psychologies to so-called fourth-force transpersonal psychology, reflected in such concepts and techniques as holistic health, biofeedback, life after life, past-lives therapy, inner healing, and guided fantasy; and in such movements as Transcendental Meditation, Yoga, Esalen, Arica, and Rajneesh. This "move forward" is really a move backward to the psychology of the ancient East. It can be thoroughly understood only in the light of cultures—not just philosophies—very foreign to our own.

In spite of strong tendencies within academia toward exclusiveness and competitiveness, scholars and professionals in medicine, theology, and the social sciences have been able to cooperate with each other or at least complement one another's work with positive results. Among those results are a more culture-sensitive psychology and psychiatry in the secular sphere, and the disciplines of missiology and pastoral theology and counseling in Christian curricula. Although a large amount of relevant research has been available for some years, the counseling field has just begun to respond significantly to the need for cross-cultural emphases and applications. Christian educators are faced with the opportunity to enter this challenging and promising area at the ground floor. By so doing they will benefit the cause of Christ at home and abroad. Pastoral psychology and counseling should be complemented by the addition of cross-cultural psychology and counseling to the curricula of Christian training schools.

3

Where Do We Go from Here?

We have been discussing and describing a discipline that has not yet been defined in precise terms. Specifically, what is meant by referring to cross-cultural (or missionary) psychology and counseling in a Christian context? At first glance the answer seems to be implicit in the question itself because, presumably, everyone knows what psychology and counseling are and everyone can understand the modifiers *Christian* and *cross-cultural.* Upon reflection, however, it becomes apparent that each of these words has a range of meaning, so working definitions should be helpful.

In using the word *Christian* in this context the primary reference is not so much to that which is somehow associated with one or another branch or brand of Christianity, but rather to that which is Christian as informed by the Holy Scriptures, the Bible.

The term *cross-cultural* has reference to the attempt to bridge gaps or divisions that result from subcultural and large cultural differences.

Psychology generally focuses on the behavior and mental processes of organisms. In the present context, the word *psychology* refers to how human beings relate to God, themselves, other people, and their environment.

Finally, authors of book after book on counseling proceed to discuss various aspects, types, and techniques of counseling without pausing to define what counseling actually is. If there is a central focus that characterizes much of these books it is that of helping people achieve mental health and well-being. When this emphasis is primary, counseling becomes somewhat synonymous with psychotherapy. In its widest signification, counseling is thought of as helping people solve personal or group problems. Unless we are cautious in the present context, therefore, we might be tempted to think of counseling so narrowly as to include only the activities of a very few Christian experts, or so broadly as to encompass almost all Christian ministries to others. To avoid both extremes, let us think here of counseling as that activity in which a qualified person interacts with individuals and groups in order to solve problems and effect positive change. In the missionary context, dealing with presenting problems that have a spiritual dimension will usually be the primary concern.

As the discussions in chapters 1 and 2 have made clear, in this book the designation *missionary psychology and counseling* is often used to refer to the discipline because, as one of the most conspicuous and challenging aspects of the Christian missionary enterprise is the cross-cultural aspect, one anticipates that the subject matter will be of greatest interest and value to those involved in missions.

Every viable academic discipline has at least four essential components: a basis in certain preunderstandings, a set of objectives, a body of subject matter, and a way of proceeding. Of course, Christian cross-cultural counseling as it has been described and defined will also exhibit these four components. Briefly overviewing them at this juncture will prepare the way for that which is to follow.

Preunderstandings

A complete listing of assumptions or preunderstandings for any but the most elementary of disciplines or subject areas would be practically endless! Without numerous preunderstandings we would have to reconstruct a great part of our corporate learning experience as part of a prolegomenon to every course of study. Education would rapidly come to a standstill.

The list of preunderstandings for a study of Christian cross-cultural counseling includes all that has been communicated, whether explicitly or implicitly, to this point. Such things as a full commitment to (and a basic understanding of) Christian teachings as revealed in a fully authoritative Bible, a dedication to the missionary task of the church, a belief that a knowledge of the social sciences can aid us in that task, and a conviction that subject matter with which we are concerned is sufficiently important and unique to merit a place in the curricula of our Christian schools and on the agendas of Christian cross-cultural workers—these are primary preunderstandings.

We also begin with some other assumptions which, although of a different order than those already mentioned, are nevertheless important. They have to do with the types of counselors who might be expected to have an interest in this subject, classes of counselees whom they can anticipate counseling cross-culturally, and the broad categories of problems they will most likely encounter.

Three Types of Christian Counselors

It should be clear from the outset that one can distinguish three distinct types of Christian counselors. The importance of these distinctions will become clearer as we proceed, but the distinctions themselves must be emphasized here.

The Christian professional cross-cultural counselor. As an academic discipline and a therapeutic profession, counseling has become more and more prominent in North American society in recent years. There are various reasons for this. In the first place, psychological knowledge has increased tremendously in the twentieth century. In the second place, Western culture has become characterized by mounting tension and turmoil. An increasing number of people require professional help in order to cope with the challenges of contemporary life. Studies of the effectiveness of professional counseling are not altogether reassuring.[1] Nevertheless, given the Western emphasis upon counseling both within and without the church, it is inevitable that more and more Christians will take this knowledge and skill to the mission fields, and more and more Christian professional counselors will be asked to work with the culturally different at home. The problem is that academic and vocational requirements in the Western world demand that counselors master the science of psychology and the art of counseling but do not demand that they master the science of studying cultural differences and the art of cultural adaptation. The implications of this will become clear as we proceed. Suffice it to say that none of the professions is in greater need of an understanding of differences in cultures than the helping profession particularly when its members attempt to cross cultural boundaries, large or small.

Other Christian professional workers. As we shall see, the risen Christ has given special person gifts to his church in order to build up his people and equip them for service. Those who devote most time and energy to counseling are the missionaries ("apostles") and pastor-teachers (although, in my understanding, contemporary evangelists and "prophets" also should be occupied with counseling individuals and small groups concerning conversion and a committed lifestyle, not just with public teaching and

---

1. Hans J. Eysenck, "The Effects of Psychotherapy: An Evaluation," *Journal of Consulting Psychology* 16 (August 1952): 319–24.

preaching). Missionaries cross cultural boundaries in order to communicate Christ and plant Christian churches. Until recently—and in most societies even today—pastor-teachers minister to those of their own cultures and subcultures. Missionaries and pastor-teachers are, of course, professionals. But in most cases they are not professional counselors. Often their course of study will have included only a few courses in psychology and counseling. Still, a significant share of counseling in the United States is done by clergymen.[2] And anyone with prolonged missionary experience will know something of the types of demands that are made upon a missionary's time and effort—many of which can best be classified as demands for counseling. Usually, however, the pastor-teacher has limited training in counseling and no training in cultural anthropology; the average missionary has limited training in the science of cultural anthropology and little or no training in counseling. It is this imbalance which we should seek to rectify.

Christian peer counselors. Christians are called upon to build up one another in the faith. In fact, Peter wrote that Christians constitute a "chosen people, a royal priesthood, a holy nation, a people belonging to God" (1 Peter 2:9). What a valuable resource the church has in a twice-born membership! And if believers are both willing and prepared to help others, hurting people both inside and outside the church will often go to these Christian friends when they would be very reluctant to go to a professional. Furthermore, because of our pluralistic culture lay Christians are now coming into contact with a larger number of people from other cultures and subcultures. Vietnamese, Cubans, Chinese, Koreans, and many others are at our doors. Of course, as Christians we want to help whomever we can, wherever and whenever we are called

2. Gary R. Collins, ed., *Helping People Grow: Practical Approaches to Christian Counseling* (Santa Ana, Calif.: Vision House, 1980), pp. 12–15.

upon. However, the very best intentions often do not automatically result in the most meaningful solutions.

Happily, some Christian psychologists and counselors are now devoting some of their writings and ministries to aid Christian laypersons in the development of their supernatural gifts and helping skills.[3] The new situation encourages professional cross-culturalists to make a similar contribution to Christian laypersons. As long as the laity do not get the notion that they cannot become people helpers unless they have this special training, these efforts are all to the good.

Five Classes of Counselees

As is the case with intracultural counselors, intercultural counselors will be called upon to deal with five broad classes of people.

Unconvicted unbelievers. Approximately three out of every four persons in the world are non-Christians. Many of these are settled in a false faith or in no faith whatsoever. In non-Western societies particularly, the majority of these people will be attached to one or another of the great religions. This adds an entirely new dimension to the helping ministry. In cross-cultural situations the counselor must be prepared to deal with questions and problems occasioned by beliefs in local gods and spirits or the religious teachings of Buddha, Confucius, or Mohammed. Even when counselees are not well schooled in these teachings, they are usually enmeshed in the world view and value system of the predominant religion of their culture. The reaction of a non-Christian counselee to the untutored Christian counselor is predictable: "If you do not know anything about my faith or the faith of my people, why do you come to change it?"

3. Gary R. Collins, *How to Be a People Helper* (Santa Ana, Calif.: Vision House, 1976); and Paul Welter, *How to Help a Friend* (Wheaton: Tyndale, 1978).

Convicted unbelievers. Quite a different set of problems may be encountered in the case of those who are convinced that irreligion is not a good option; that some faith other than the "faith of the fathers" is needed; and that Christ is the true way to God. As the Word of God is made known, almost invariably some unbelieving members of a given society will become convicted. In fact, at times whole societies will come to the place where they are ready to reject their previous faith and embrace Christ. Oddly enough, missionary experience teaches us that we Christians sometimes are least prepared to give adequate counsel to this type of people. The world is well populated with people who have made a sincere move toward Christ but have received inadequate counsel as to what true faith means and entails, and have subsequently reverted.

Nominal believers. It may be that as many as two-thirds or three-fourths of the people in the world who call themselves Christians have no vital relationship with God through Christ. These people also present an unusual challenge to the Christian counselor because they take exception to the idea that they are not Christians, and yet they must come to this realization before they will make a true commitment to Christ as Savior and Lord.

Immature believers. Those whom we would designate as immature Christians, on the other hand, have truly accepted Christ and want to live in accordance with his will but are new in the faith or uninstructed and confused as to Christian doctrine and practice. It is difficult for them to analyze their situations in biblical terms because they lack a knowledge of the Scriptures. They need someone who will instruct, encourage, and advise them in the faith.

Mature believers. Finally, there are those believers who know the Word of God and are living in fellowship with Christ. Of course, this does not mean that they do not have problems, so it is the joy of the Christian cross-cultural counselor who is equal to the task to encourage them and lead them to new vistas of Christian understanding and spiritual fruitfulness.

Four Categories of Counseling Problems

The cross-cultural counselor will encounter four broad categories of problems among counselees:

problems relating to well-being;

questions relating to conversion;

issues relating to Christian growth and lifestyle;

questions concerning Christian service.

The problems subsumed under these categories are not unrelated to each other. Anxiety, for example, will normally be considered a part of the first category, but upon analysis may prove to be related to any of the other three. These categories are not unlike those confronted in the intracultural counseling situation. However, they do take on definite cultural aspects. The cross-cultural counselor must be prepared to deal with problems and questions in these categories that may be very different from those of his own culture. For example, the necessities of everyday life may have been in plentiful supply in his own culture, whereas subsistence living may be a problem of the first order in a receptor culture. Similarly, disorders that may be fairly readily denominated as mental or physical disorders in his own culture may be invariably classified as a manifestation of disaffection on the part of local spirits in another culture. Again, conversion may involve the forsaking of various false gods, a radical change in lifestyle, and rejection by society at large. Even problems relating to Christian life and service take on different aspects. For instance, the Christians at Corinth faced not only the transcultural problem of factionalism, but also the culture-specific problem of eating meat offered to idols.

The foregoing does not constitute the only way of categorizing cross-cultural counselors, counselees, and counseling problems. Nor is it necessarily the best way. It is, however, the way they will be categorized in this book.

Objectives

It will be apparent that our overall objective is to increase the effectiveness of Christians involved in cross-cultural ministries so that problems might be solved, positive change effected, and God glorified. That is certainly a Christian and noble objective, but it is general and needs refinement. We have categorized the Christian helpers and the types of people to be helped. What are the categories of projected change?

Caring, Counseling, or Curing?

It is no simple matter to state the objectives of the caring professions. Nor is it easy to draw clear distinctions between psychotherapy, counseling, and people-helping.

One psychotherapist who worked with the Plains Indians in the United States noted a number of problems in connection with the undertaking but concluded that the greatest problem had to do with the conception of health held by the therapist himself. He resolved the issue by saying that his goal was "to restore the patient to himself."[4] This resolution may have satisfied the secular psychotherapist, but it is both culturally biased and spiritually deficient. His Oriental counterpart could be expected to emphasize returning the patient to his community. And his Christian counterpart would want to help return the patient to a relationship with God as a first priority.

4. Julian Wohl, "Intercultural Psychotherapy: Issues, Questions, and Reflections," in *Counseling across Cultures*, ed. Paul P. Pedersen et al., rev. ed. (Honolulu: The University Press of Hawaii for the East-West Center, 1981), pp. 148–49.

Similarly, there is ambiguity about where to draw the line between the disciplines of counseling and psychotherapy or, to put it another way, between counseling and curing. Various attempts have been made. For example, some would say that counselors deal with normal people who have problems, whereas psychotherapists deal with those who are emotionally or mentally disturbed or ill. Many psychologists prefer to think of counseling as intervention in situations where a pathology is present. But it is difficult to arrive at theoretical distinctions that are acceptable to a majority, and more difficult still to apply the theoretical distinctions in pratice. Then, to confuse the issue even more, it is not easy to discover clear lines of demarcation between people-helping and professional counseling, and between caring and counseling. Sometimes, at least, it would seem to be more in the credentials of the helper than in the nature of the help itself.

No attempt will be made to draw a clear, decisive distinction between helping, counseling, and psychotherapy here. It is evident that differences arise out of the qualifications of the helper, the nature of the help, and the condition of the person who is being helped. But caring, counseling, and curing are not mutually exclusive. They are complementary. And each constitutes part of a continuum. Because counseling can be thought of as occupying a center position, and for the sake of convenience, the terms *counseling* and *cross-cultural counseling* are used in this book. But focusing on counseling does not exclude caring and curing.

Aspects of Change

From both theological and scientific points of view, Christian cross-cultural counselors can be described as agents of change. Christ's person gifts to the church are given so that man's weakness and wretchedness might be exchanged for God's power and blessedness; and so that babes in Christ might grow into spiritual maturity. The status quo is not the divine order. Ever since the fall of man, God's program has been one of change.

Change, of course, can be viewed in various ways. Much depends upon one's perspective. Some members of the helping professions consider all human problems to be of the nature of illness or sickness and therefore view change as healing. In *The Case for Unorthodox Medicine*, Brian Inglis deals with nonmedical healing, which he proceeds to place in three categories: those emphasizing the body (e.g., herbalism and homeopathic and chiropractic techniques); those emphasizing mind (e.g., psychotherapy, hypnotherapy, and autosuggestion); and those stressing the spirit (e.g., Christian Science and spiritual healing).[5]

Others think of man's nonmedical problems not as illness or disease, but as failure to live up to his responsibilities. Rather than emphasizing "healing" for body and spirit, they emphasize volitional change—the necessity of choosing to think, feel, and do that which is right. Paul Welter's "living channels," for example, are ways in which we respond to what we learn: by feeling, thinking, choosing, and doing.[6]

There is something to be said for both approaches. In some cases man is victimized by disturbances inside or forces outside himself. In many cases, he victimizes himself. Although some psychologies and counseling approaches emphasize one aspect at the expense of the other, it is well to keep both in mind. But it will be difficult enough for even Christian specialists in mental health and development programs to deal in depth with psychosomatic and environmental change cross-culturally. The best that most cross-cultural workers can usually expect to do is to help people in regard to what they think, feel, and do insofar as they have the ability to so choose, in depen-

5. Brian Inglis, *The Case for Unorthodox Medicine* (New York: Putman, 1965), cited in Jerome D. Frank, *Persuasion and Healing: A Comparative Study of Psychotherapy*, rev. ed. (New York: Schocken, 1974), p. 47.

6. Welter, *How to Help a Friend*, pp. 88–90.

dence on God. This type of change will occupy most of our attention here.

The Great Commission and Counseling

Thinking of Christian counseling as being more or less synonomous with people helping, Gary R. Collins writes,

> It does not appear that the Great Commission was limited to one geographical area or to one period of history. Neither is there any indication that the instructions of Jesus were limited to a few people, like pastors or other church leaders. Clearly Jesus intended all of his followers for generations to come to be involved in the business of making disciples—evangelizing and teaching new believers. Might it not be, therefore, that the Great Commission has relevance for people helping today? *Since being a disciple and making disciples is a requirement for all Christians, surely the discipling of others must be a part of Christian counseling—perhaps even its major goal.*[7]

There is a certain validity to this approach. Certainly the fulfillment of the Great Commission is a task that is incumbent upon all Christians, not just upon a select few. By virtue of their Christian identity, therefore, Christian counselors of all three types should be involved in winning people to Christ and building them up in their faith.

The really unique characteristics of the missionary enterprise are not confined to the discipling activity per se, however. What is also unique about missioning is that disciples are to be made among all the nations (*panta ta ethne*; Matt. 28:19). In that context the primary reference is to the non-Jewish peoples of the world. However, these people must be viewed not simply as members of political entities, but also as members of ethnic, linguistic, social, and cultural "families." When Christian workers attempt to bridge cultural gaps occasioned by ethnic, linguistic,

---

7. Collins, *People Helper*, p. 4.

social, and political differences in order to discipline people, they participate in an activity that is distinctively
missionary.

It is interesting that Paul B. Meier, Frank B. Minirth,
and Frank B. Wichern choose the apostle Paul as an. outstanding New Testament example of a wise counselor.[8]
By virtue of his birth, education, and experience Paul was
uniquely prepared to counsel in the pagan world of his
time. This he did, face to face and (as Meier, Minirth, and
Wichern point out) by letter. And if, as W. Graham Scroggie conjectures, Paul wrote hundreds or even thousands
of letters of the type we find in the New Testament, the
extent of his involvement with individuals and congregations in a variety of cultural situations is difficult to
imagine.[9]

In this connection, it is important to note that Ralph
D. Winter of the U. S. Center for World Mission has calculated that no more than about 17 percent of the world's
population can be reached by Christian "near neighbors."[10]
In other words, if the Great Commission is to be fulfilled,
83 percent of the people in the world must be reached by
those who are willing to cross boundaries that may indeed
be geographical, but are primarily cultural.

Sources of the Discipline

If we view missiology as the science of mission (a definition which is inclusive of a theology of mission but is
more comprehensive) it is apparent that we cannot afford

8. Paul B. Meier, Frank B. Minirth, and Frank B. Wichern, *Introduction to
Psychology and Counseling: Christian Perspectives and Applications* (Grand
Rapids: Baker, 1982), p. 298.

9. W. Graham Scroggie, *Know Your Bible: A Brief Introduction to the
Scriptures*, 2 vols. (London: Pickering and Inglis 1940), vol. 2, p. 95.

10. Ralph D. Winter, "The Highest Priority: Cross-Cultural Evangelism,"
in *Let the Earth Hear His Voice*, ed. J. D. Douglas (Minneapolis: World Wide
Publications, 1975), pp. 228–30.

to be anything but eclectic and integrative in our approach. After all, we are dealing with the collective experience of two thousand years, with numerous peoples and cultures very different from our own, with religious systems of other nations, and with spiritual forces that often defy our best human efforts to understand or countermand.

Viewed from the larger perspectives of either missiology or psychology and counseling, cross-cultural psychology and counseling participates in this wider experience and concern. As a part of the former it is already informed by diverse missiological interests of long standing. As a part of the latter it becomes an expression of the rapidly growing interest in personality development and in difficulties faced by individuals and groups in other cultures. The only real question has to do with the sources of relevant information. What sources hold the most promise?

It is at this precise point that misunderstandings may well arise. Obviously, when we are dealing with academic and professional interests so thoroughly researched and explicated (as is the case with psychology and counseling), the initial categories and content are already supplied. The new element is culture, and traditionally anthropology (especially cultural anthropology) has been the science of "man in culture" par excellence. Certainly we will want to draw heavily upon insights from the discipline of anthropology. But more must be said in this regard. As a discipline anthropology itself has been characterized by rather serious limitations. It has largely confined itself to a study of the more primitive and undeveloped (from a Western point of view) societies and cultures. Only recently have social anthropologists and urban anthropologists expanded anthropological interests to include developed societies and modern urban populations. Anthropology has also been characterized by deep divisions and charges that even prominent anthropologists have managed the evidence in one way or another to support preconceived theories. Anthropology is the most important source of cross-cultural data, but we must remember that its reputation is not unsullied.

Not a few theorists think of communication as being the essence of psychiatry and counseling.[11] Understandably, then, the expanding corpus of cross-cultural communication can be expected to contribute significantly to our subject.

Cross-cultural counseling will also draw upon a knowledge of the non-Christian religions. The great religious traditions provide alternative world views and value systems. They define human nature and its challenges very differently, and accordingly prescribe different solutions for the same problem. It is all but unthinkable that one could wisely counsel a monocultural Buddhist without some considerable understanding of ingrained Buddhist notions of no self, karma, and enlightenment.

All of these sciences—and, indeed, others as well—are important to cross-cultural ministry. One missionary-missiologist, Marvin K. Mayers, speaks of his "behavioral sciences conversion" as being a key to effective ministry.

> During our furlough we were privileged to attend the University of Chicago to pursue advanced studies in linguistics.... It was there that I came into contact, for the first time, with social anthropologists and the teaching of the British school of social anthropology. Resolutions to the various problems I had left behind in the field began to fill my mind. I experienced what I now call my "behavioral sciences conversion." I had gone to Central America as a change agent under the direction of the Spirit of God, but I had not been trained as a change agent, nor had I been given the tools that should have been given to one

11. See, for example, D. Corydon Hammond, Dean H. Hepworth, and Veon G. Smith, *Improving Therapeutic Communication: A Guide for Developing Effective Techniques,* Social and Behavioral Sciences series (San Francisco: Jossey-Bass, 1977); and Jurgen Ruesch and Gregory Bateson, *Communication: The Social Matrix of Psychiatry* (New York: Norton, 1951).

who was committed to changing another. Therefore the changes introduced into the total setting by my introduction of the gospel were partial, inconsistent, resisted, or modified in ways over which I had no control.

I do not suggest that my training in social anthropology was a cure-all for every problem, but I realized that many problems we had faced in our mission program were problems amenable to solution with the proper tools.[12]

I would underscore Mayer's emphasis. At the same time, we must always keep Augustine's dicta in mind. Were we forced to undertake cross-cultural Christian ministry without either a knowledge of the sciences or a knowledge of the sacred Scriptures, there can be no question but that we would choose to keep the Scriptures. In the final analysis, scientific knowledge cannot compare with biblical knowledge in significance. The Bible, then, provides the indispensible source of information about cross-cultural counseling. All else is to be evaluated in its light. And by it all else must be measured.

The Procedure to Be Followed

As we proceed it will become clear that the cross-cultural counselor will find it necessary to carry out three interdependent investigations. In the first place, he must have some understanding of counseling theories and practices in his own and other cultures. He must see these theories and practices as, in large measure, culturally derived—as having inherent potential for cross-cultural counseling but not having unquestioned validity and universal applicability.

In the second place, he must develop or adopt a theory of cross-cultural counseling. This theory should take into

12. Marvin K. Mayers, *Christianity Confronts Culture: A Strategy for Cross-Cultural Evangelism*, Contemporary Evangelical Perspectives series (Grand Rapids: Zondervan, 1973), preface.

account at least three levels of data—those which are (or are perceived to be) characteristic of men in every place and time; those that are culturally derived and applicable; and those that are attributable to individuals in their uniqueness.

In the third place, he must ready himself to analyze problems and promote change when counseling the culturally different. We will attempt to aid the practice of cross-cultural counseling by introducing typical problem areas and counseling cases in a variety of cultures—problems and cases having to do with well-being, conversion, the Christian life, and Christian service.

The plan in this book, then, is to introduce some Western and non-Western counseling theories and practices; to develop a theoretical approach to the study of cross-cultural counseling; and to encourage effective practice of cross-cultural counseling by means of an examination of problem areas and case studies representative of various cultures (see fig. 1).

In this chapter we have attempted to plot a way through the relatively uncharted waters of Christian cross-cultural counseling. Our Christian intentions, concerns, and commitment should be clear. The Swiss scholar Jean Piaget maintains that philosophy precedes science. As Henry W. Maier puts it,

> In professional helping, our orientation to the helping process, for that matter to life, precedes and determines the nature of our interventive activities. Moreover, what is intrinsic to the helper's basic orientation determines what he or she sees, hears, feels, thinks, and above all conveys or does in the initial encounters with clients. Thus the helper is in fact a philosopher-scientist.[13]

13. Henry W. Maier, "Piagetian Principles Applied to the Beginning Phase in Professional Helping," *Proceedings of the Seventh Interdisciplinary Conference*, vol. 1 (cosponsored by University Affiliated Program, Children's Hospital of Los Angeles and the University of Southern California Schools of Education and Religion, 1979), p. 3.

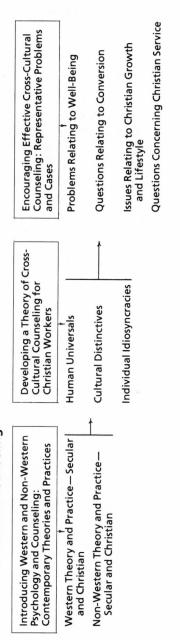

FIGURE 1 **Cross-Cultural Counseling**

Introducing Western and Non-Western
Psychology and Counseling:
Contemporary Theories and Practices

Western Theory and Practice—Secular
and Christian

Non-Western Theory and Practice—
Secular and Christian

Developing a Theory of Cross-
Cultural Counseling for
Christian Workers

Human Universals

Cultural Distinctives

Individual Idiosyncracies

Encouraging Effective Cross-Cultural
Counseling: Representative Problems
and Cases

Problems Relating to Well-Being

Questions Relating to Conversion

Issues Relating to Christian Growth
and Lifestyle

Questions Concerning Christian Service

There are various ways of expressing this principle. Often social scientists are much more proficient in recognizing the precommitments of others than they are in recognizing their own. When this is the case, precommitments are usually called biases or prejudices rather than philosophy. But whether these precommitments are called bias or prejudice or philosophy matters little in the final analysis. We all bring a certain precommitment (or precommitments) to our task. Ours is to Christ and his Word. But a Christian counseling the culturally different does not necessarily mean that the counsel itself is Christian. The counselor must be more than a Christian. He must be a knowledgeable Christian who draws upon God's truth wherever it may be found and who relies upon the power of the Spirit.

PART 2

Counseling in the Western and Non-Western Worlds

4

Secular Approaches to Individual Counseling and Therapy in the West

Counseling as we know it is a culturally prescribed way of human problem-solving. In one sense it is a Western phenomenon and a comparatively recent one at that. This refers, of course, to the kind of counseling in which therapists are in some way identified and certified through a process of formal education. If we think of counseling in larger dimensions—of seeking the advice of men and women made wise by virtue of long experience, or of availing oneself of the aid of those who evidence supernatural wisdom and power—counseling is as old as mankind and as pervasive as human society.

The Popularity of Counseling in the West

In spite of technological advantages, Western society is characterized by cultural malaise, social disintegration, and personality conflict. In spite of unprecedented learning opportunities, Western peoples search for meaning. In spite of a plethora of contacts, Western man experiences a poverty of relationships.[1] As early as 1960, researchers at the University of Michigan found in a landmark study of the "normal" adult population of the United States that 25 percent of all Americans admitted that they had felt themselves to be on the verge of a nervous breakdown at least once during their adult lives.[2] The same study revealed that counseling is considered to be one of the most important ways of resolving breakdown-inducing problems and that clergymen are among those from whom help is most frequently sought.

> Nearly one person out of every four indicated that he had a problem in which professional help would have been useful. *One out of seven* of all those interviewed had actually sought such professional help. Where have all these persons gone for help? *Forty-two per cent* had gone *to clergymen* and twenty-nine per cent to non-psychiatric physicians. Only thirty-one percent had gone to a psychiatrist, psychologist, or marriage counselor, either in private practice or in an agency setting. Fifty-four per cent of the Protestants who attend church at least once a week went to a minister when they sought personal help. Even among those who attend church less frequently, thirty-three per cent who went for help chose a clergyman. In the light of these findings, there is no doubt that *ministers occupy a central and strategic role as counselors in our society.* It is obvious that clergymen are on the front lines in the struggle to lift the loads of troubled persons![3]

These statistics may well have changed in the years that have intervened, but the church is obviously deeply committed to counseling ministries. The number of coun-

---

1. Howard J. Clinebell, Jr., characterizes our culture as a "touch-and-run" culture—a culture oriented toward interpersonal superficiality. Howard J. Clinebell, Jr., *Basic Types of Pastoral Counseling: New Resources for Ministries to the Troubled* (Nashville: Abingdon, 1966), p. 15.
2. Gerald Gurin, Joseph Veroff, and Shiela Feld, *Americans View Their Mental Health* (New York: Basic, 1960), p. 307; cited in Clinebell, *Basic Types of Pastoral Counseling*, p. 43.
3. Clinebell, *Basic Types of Pastoral Counseling*, p. 43.

seling courses in our seminaries has increased dramatically. The number of titles on counseling that occupy the shelves of the average minister's library is constantly on the rise. Ministers, particularly in the cities, devote large quantities of time to counseling people inside and outside the church. Many large churches employ professional counselors for their staffs. And books and seminars on peer counseling for Christian laymen are becoming common.

Culture and Counseling

Eric Berne speaks with an almost solitary voice when he says that cultural issues play little or no part in psychotherapy and that "principles learned in the treatment of young women in Connecticut or California were just as effective in the South Pacific."[4] A much more reliable statement is that

> the needs, the feelings, the vulnerabilities that we experience as people are the same the world over. Cues are different, values are different, styles are different, communication patterns are different, but the people are the same. . . . A rejecting mother, with no surrogates, will likely have the same pathological effect anywhere. Schizophrenia is as easily recognizable in Benares, Addis Ababa and Taipeh as it is in Chicago, even though there are still many questions about different etiologies in different cultures. . . . Psychological trauma is handled universally by mechanisms such as withdrawal, depression, regression, denial, and the like; however, what is traumatic and what defines withdrawal varies widely around the world. . . . The need for self-esteem is also universal, though the ways in which it is played out may vary greatly.[5]

4. Eric Berne, "The Cultural Problem: Psychopathology in Tahiti," *American Journal of Psychiatry* 116 (June 1960): 1076–81.
5. A. A. Alexander et al., "Psychotherapy and the Foreign Student," in *Counseling across Cultures*, rev. ed., ed. Paul P. Pedersen et al. (Honolulu: The University Press of Hawaii for the East-West Center, 1981), pp. 237–38.

We can also affirm Julian Wohl's statement:

Anthropology and intercultural psychiatric and psychologic students inform us that, in all societies which have been observed, procedures and practices are found that are the functional equivalents of our therapies. We have, however, no prior grounds for the belief that our forms are workable in those other societies.[6]

The peoples of the world live in an ocean of troubles and when one examines the floor of the ocean he finds that the contours are somewhat similar everywhere. Moreover, all societies exhibit institutions and persons for, and ways and means of, caring for troubled members. But after carefully examining cultural differences in caring, curing, and counseling, we will probably conclude that, although the principles of people-helping may have some cross-cultural validity, the outworkings of those principles will vary significantly from culture to culture.

Counseling as we know it is in large measure a Western way of dealing with human problems. Furthermore, inside and outside the church it mirrors the diversity of assumptions and approaches that is also characteristic of the West. Basic questions, which we will examine in part 2 of this book, present themselves to the cross-cultural Christian counselor.

First, what do we need to know about counseling in the Western world, especially as counseling is practiced in the United States and as it is understood in the Christian church?

Second, what are some alternative approaches to human problem-solving, particularly in the non-Western world?

6. Julian Wohl, "Intercultural Psychotherapy: Issues, Questions, and Reflections," in *Counseling across Cultures*, 1st ed., ed. Paul P. Pedersen, Walter J. Lonner, and Juris G. Draguns (Honolulu: The University Press of Hawaii for the East-West Center, 1976), p. 186.

Third, what are the implications of the foregoing in cross-cultural Christian helping relationships?

The Basic Idea in Counseling

The basic concept in counseling is that of "listening and responding in such a way as to bring about change in another person."[7] As we have come to understand it in the Western world, counseling can be thought of as occupying a more or less central position on a continuum that begins with lay people offering encouragement and advice and ends with highly trained professionals administering therapy (see fig. 2).[8] The crucial differentiating factors are the degree of education and expertise possessed by the helper, the kind of assistance given, and the degree of difficulty experienced by the person being helped.

It is not uncommon in our society for psychologists and psychiatrists to be denigrated as "head shrinkers" or "shrinks." Generally, however, they are held in high esteem and sometimes in awe. Actually, extreme reactions are not warranted. Almost everyone knows someone who has been significantly helped by a psychologist or psychiatrist. At the same time, the overall record of professionals does not reflect omniscience!

The contribution of lay volunteers, on the other hand, may be all too airily dismissed as insignificant. One of the pioneers in suicide prevention in the United States, Louis Dublin, insists that the role of the lay volunteer has been one of the most significant innovations in the fifty-year history of suicide prevention.[9]

7. David E. Carlson, "Relationship Counseling," in *Helping People Grow: Practical Approaches to Christian Counseling,* ed. Gary R. Collins (Santa Ana, Calif.: Vision House, 1980), p. 36.

8. The author is aware that not all theorists will agree at this point. For example, some see counseling and therapy as being significantly different.

9. Louis Dublin, "Suicide Prevention," in *On the Nature of Suicide,* ed. Edwin S. Schneidman (San Francisco: Jossey-Bass, 1969), p. 45.

64

FIGURE 2 The Counseling Continuum of the Western World

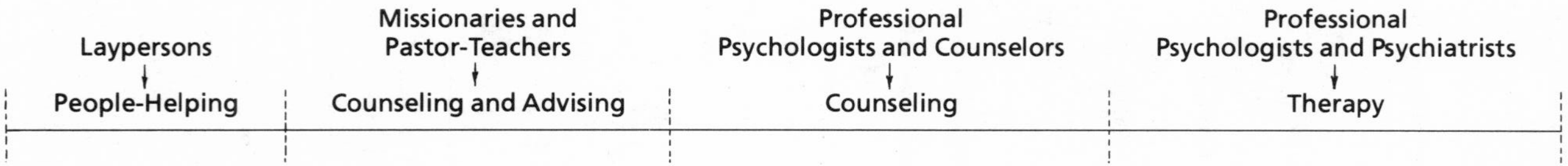

Laypersons	Missionaries and Pastor-Teachers	Professional Psychologists and Counselors	Professional Psychologists and Psychiatrists
People-Helping	Counseling and Advising	Counseling	Therapy

It is justifiable, therefore, to relate this discussion to the entire spectrum of people-helping, but the particular concern and focus here will be on the tens of thousands of Christian full-time workers who are occupied with helping numerous people who are culturally different from themselves.

Some Representative Approaches to Counseling and Therapy

Characteristic of most if not all counseling and therapeutic procedures in the West is the tendency to remove the individual from ordinary situations for a long or short period of time; to treat him or her in a specialized environment such as a therapist's office or a special residence or hospital; and to effect changes that will, it is hoped, be lasting as the patient returns to the "real world." The changes sought are cognitive, emotive, behavioral (thinking, feeling, acting), or, usually, a combination of these.

Beyond these similarities, however, there are numerous divergent approaches. We can but touch on some of the major emphases which may be helpful for our understanding in the present context. Students should refer to other works and the writings of the authors themselves for a more complete understanding of the theories involved.

The Psychoanalytic Approach

As developed by Sigmund Freud in the late nineteenth and early twentieth centuries, and carried forward by his pupils and a host of followers, psychoanalysis is based upon the idea that people are motivated by various instincts, of which the most basic is the sexual instinct. The realities of life, including moral restrictions, constantly circumscribe the gratification of instincts. There are three parts to the human personality: the id (instinctual needs), the ego (that part which is reality-oriented and attempts to satisfy the id), and the superego (the moral dimension;

the internalization of parents' standards and demands).
One's state of mental health is determined by his ability
to integrate the needs of these three aspects of his personality. In the attempt to suppress the id, one creates certain
defenses. But these are only partially successful and the
repressed instincts have ways of breaking through to the
surface in innocent actions or neurotic symptoms.

Of the various techniques used in Freudian psychoanalytic therapy some of the most prominent include the
following:

Free association. Clients are urged to express their
thoughts and feelings without any inhibitions or
embarrassment.

Dream analysis. Dreams are reported and analyzed as a
way of bringing the material of the unconscious to the
level of the conscious.

Behavior interpretation. Another way of analyzing the
unconscious is to interpret certain behaviors manifested
by the client.

Interpretation of resistance. An attempt is made to
understand any and all of the client's efforts to avoid producing the materials of the unconscious.

Interpretation of transference. Transference is the reliving of past conflicts and the imposing of the roles of people
involved in those conflicts on the persons involved in current therapy. The therapist uses this response to gain an
understanding of the client's unconscious feelings.

The Cultural Approach

Karen Horney and Harry Stack Sullivan were among
those who broke with Freudian theory. They became leaders in the "cultural school" of psychoanalysis. Each developed a theory and therapy that are somewhat distinct,
however.

In Horney's view, the basic drive is the search for security. When one's security is threatened, anxiety develops. As a consequence, the individual develops coping

strategies or patterns which differ according to his or her culture. These strategies are of three types: moving toward, against, and away from other people. Imbalances and inflexibility in resort to the three types result in neuroses and prevent the real self from emerging. Therapy aims at creating understanding of the idealized and actual selves, creating a balance in strategies, and enabling the emergence of the real self. Such techniques as free association and interpretation are used by the therapist, who is more directive than the analyst who uses Freudian techniques.

In Sullivan's opinion, the primary drives are for satisfaction and security. Drives for the former are largely physical. Needs for security, on the other hand, are culturally determined. Security results from the approval of others in society; insecurity results from disapproval. One's self-concept is based upon the perceived reaction of others. And these reactions can be correct or distorted. In therapy, the client is aided in seeing how relationships with others are based on distorted perceptions. The therapist takes the role of participant observer focusing on distortion-creating childhood experiences, an analysis of past distortions, and an analysis of any distortions that might occur between therapist and client. Because of the focus, Sullivan's approach is sometimes referred to as the interpersonal-relations approach.

The Existential-Analysis Approach

Introduced in the United States by Ulrich Sonnemann and Rollo May, existential analysis was first developed by two Swiss psychiatrists, Ludwig Binswanger and Medard Boss. Awareness of being is held to be the essence of human existence. To be human is to be a "being-in-the-world" and to be open to world-disclosing relationships. The readiness to accept all that is and can be is to be free as a human being. Human conscience constitutes a call to carrying out and fulfilling the possibilities of life. One is indebted to one's own existence and obligated to understand possibilities as possibilities.

May believes that the empty view of mental health implied in classical psychoanalysis led to the social-conformist approach of people like Horney and Sullivan. He sees the need for recognizing that the patient is self-centered and that neurosis, far from being a "failure of adjustment," is "a necessary adjustment by which centeredness can be preserved; a way of accepting non-being in order that some little being may be preserved."[10] Treatment involves an emphasis on the mutuality of freedom and responsibility; helping the patient face the guilt that has accrued from failure to live up to his potentialities; and assisting the patient in identifying and employing his own value system in the restoration process.[11]

Existential analysis is concerned not with the reasons for behavior but with the possibility of living more openly and fulfillingly. It is concerned not so much with recognizing problems as with seeing opportunities for new ways of living and relating. It is concerned not so much with classifying behavior as with removing restrictions. In spite of these basic differences analysts use such common techniques as discussion, free association, and dream analysis.

The Gestalt Approach

Frederick S. Perls and others have developed gestalt psychology (the term *gestalt* is German for "form" or "shape"; by implication, "meaningful whole") based on the idea that thinking, feeling, and acting must be integrated in a basic wholeness. If this unity of the self becomes "split," the resultant lack of unified experience in the self disturbs one's ability to relate productively to his environment. The goals of therapy are to achieve individual wholeness

---

10. Rollo May, *Psychology and the Human Dilemma* (New York: Van Nostrand Reinhold, 1966), pp. 116–17.

11. Ibid., pp. 180–81.

and productive, flexible interactions with the world. In therapy emphasis is placed on the client's acceptance of personal responsibility for what he does and feels. Assistance is given so that the client can understand his behavior, reintegrate disowned parts of the self, and live fully in the present. Two representative techniques used to accomplish these goals are reliving the past and taking care of its unfinished business (rather than simply talking about the past) and interpreting the clues to underlying conflicts offered by the so-called silent or body language of the client.

The Client-Centered Approach

The name most prominently identified with this approach is that of Carl R. Rogers. The basic assumptions are that humans have an innate urge to be "fully functioning" and self-actualizing. Progress in this direction is achieved when forces inimical to self-actualization are reduced or eliminated. When given proper encouragement, instruction, and reinforcement, people have the ability to accomplish this goal.

Rogers believes that at the heart of therapy is a change in the manner of the client's process of experiencing. The client moves away from a state in which feelings and experiences are remote, his self-concept is rigid, he is remote from people, and his functioning is impersonal. He moves toward fluidity, immediacy of feelings and experience, the discovery of a changing self, acceptance of feelings and experience, closeness of relationships, and integrated functioning. The most important factor in therapy is the quality of the interpersonal encounter between client and therapist. Rogers writes,

> I would like to share with you a conclusion, a conviction . . .—whether as a psychotherapist, teacher, religious worker, guidance counselor, social worker, clinical psychologist—it is the *quality* of the interpersonal encounter

with a client which is the most significant element in determining effectiveness.[12]

The qualities of which Rogers speaks are four:

Congruence. The counselor must be what he *is*; he must be genuine; he must openly express the feelings and attitudes that are flowing through him at any given moment in the process of therapy.

Empathy. The counselor must reflect an accurate, empathetic understanding of the client's private world.

Positive regard. The counselor must prize the client for what he is. Rogers says that this is love in the *agape* sense.

Unconditionality of regard. The counselor must avoid making judgments of any kind. He accepts the client just as he is. He does not impose his own values.

The Behavior-Therapy (Behavior-Modification) Approach

The classical conditioning theory developed by Ivan P. Pavlov and carried forward by Joseph Wolpe and others was based on the fact that a second stimulus (called a conditional or conditioning stimulus) can be used to produce the same response as the original stimulus. For example, a musical tone is associated with a light blow below a person's kneecap; the blow causes the knee to jerk. Eventually, hearing the musical tone alone will cause the patient to move his knee. Building on this type of research, B. F. Skinner developed his operant- (sometimes called instrumental-) conditioning theory: that is, that behavior can be modified by selecting and reinforcing voluntary responses on the part of the subject. For example, if a professor notices that each time he applies mathematics to a mechanical problem renewed interest is evi-

---

12. Carl R. Rogers and Barry Stevens, *Person to Person: The Problem of Being Human, a New Trend in Psychology* (Lafayette, Calif.: Real People, 1967), p. 89.

denced on the part of an apathetic student, he can effect that desirable behavior by reinforcing it in this way. This technique is called shaping.

Hand in hand with research and theorizing of this kind go behavior therapy (usually referring to outpatient therapy) and behavior modification (usually referring to inpatient therapy). The assumption is that maladaptive behavior can be corrected systematically by applying principles of learning. Behavioral change will result in appropriate changes in attitudes and feelings. Techniques are many and varied. They include counterconditioning, in which, for example, a phobia is overcome by replacing the fear with a response that contradicts fear, and operant conditioning, in which therapist and client together formulate a plan that entails rewards for engaging in desired behavior and punishment for engaging in undesirable behavior.

These approaches work quite well with certain clear-cut cases, but have often been criticized as involving unethical techniques and as securing primarily short-term improvement.

The Rational-Emotive Approach

Sometimes referred to as RET (rational-emotive therapy), this approach was developed by Albert Ellis in the 1950s when, he says, he became aware of the ineffectiveness of psychoanalysis.[13] One by one he eliminated the psychoanalytic techniques—free association, dream analysis, the compulsive use of transference relationships, and so on. He now believes that in spite of the uniqueness of individuals there is a "remarkable sameness in the ways in which they disturb themselves 'emotionally' "[14] and that re-education is the basis of behavioral change. The

13. Albert Ellis and Russell Grieger, with contributors, *Handbook of Rational-Emotive Therapy* (New York: Springer Publishing, 1977), p. 4.
14. Ibid.

main clinical theories of rational-emotive therapy are these:

A person's disturbances can be understood in terms of an A-B-C pattern; a person can create and uncreate his own disturbances. For example, at point A one has an activating experience or event such as getting fired from a job. At point C one has an emotional and/or behavioral consequence such as depression. Since C immediately followed A one incorrectly assumes that the loss of the job was the cause of his depression. Actually it was not A but B—a person's "belief" about A. That is, the person liked the job and did not want to lose it or search for another one. If, however, he exchanges that belief for the belief that the world does not end with the loss of that particular job and that another job will be available and may be even better, the depression can be avoided.

Irrational beliefs must be detected. We tend to distort reality by generalizing and overgeneralizing on the basis of limited data. For example, a person says, "I'll never find a good job again!"

Irrational beliefs must be the focus of debate, discrimination, and dispute. One debates the irrational belief by asking about the evidence that supports it. One discriminates by distinguishing between wants and needs, desires and demands, rational and irrational ideas. One defines terms more carefully.

The end result is a new "effect" or philosophy. For example, the conditions that occasioned the loss of the previous job may occur again in a new job. A new job may be gained and also lost. But that is a problem of living. On thinking things through one realizes that he can do differently in the future and perhaps in that way avoid losing another job. But in any case he can cope.

The Transactional-Analysis Approach

Transactional analysis (TA) was developed by Berne in the middle 1950s. It was informed by Sullivan's concepts of interpersonal transactions and has been expanded by numerous theorists, of whom Thomas A. Harris may be the best known. TA holds that the individual is motivated by stroke hunger (the need for attention and physical intimacy, such as an infant's need to be handled): recognition hunger (the need to be noticed and acknowledged, to engage in social interaction); structure hunger (the need to structure one's life, to have one's life pattern confirmed); leadership hunger (the need to help others structure their lives); and excitement hunger (the need to manage time and structure life in exciting ways).

From very early in life, individuals meet these needs in accordance with the way in which they view the world from the perspective of their particular "life position" ("I'm OK, you're OK"; "I'm OK, you're not OK", "I'm not OK, you're OK; "I'm not OK, you're not OK") and "life script" (the individual's attempt to plan his life to make it fit his life position). In significant measure, life position determines the script one will follow. Each person is born with the potential for positive growth and the adoption of the "I'm OK, you're OK" life position. To adopt another position is to develop maladaptive behavior. "Games" are a series of transactions which lead to certain consequences for the individual—perhaps guilt feelings or depression. People tend to justify their actions in the life script by the development of defensive feelings or "rackets."

Because the ultimate choice of a life script is the prerogative of the individual, TA clients specify what they want to achieve in the therapeutic relationship. If the therapist is in agreement he enters into a "contract" with the client. Therapy begins with a structured analysis of the client and others in terms of their "ego states": "Child" (the attitude and behavior patterns of a small child); "Parent" (values stemming from tradition and society), and "Adult" (correspondence with reality). This is followed by transactional analysis which involves a determination of objectives to be attained, the criteria for measuring them, and agreed-upon assignments designed to place responsibility for achieving objectives on the client.

The Reality-Therapy Approach

Stressing behavior change rather than insight and attitude change, William Glasser believes that the problem with which therapists must deal is failure at the interpersonal or social level of human functioning. He rejects the medical model, according to which psychological problems are thought of as illnesses. He does not emphasize the unconscious or case histories. According to Glasser, the common denominator among psychiatric patients is that they deny the reality of the world around them in their attempts to meet these needs. Successful therapy must help the patient give up his denial of the world, recognize reality, and fulfill his needs in that framework. Reality therapy utilizes a "psychiatric version of the three R's,"—reality, responsibility, and right and wrong.

Reality. Some people break the law; some deny the rules of society; some claim their neighbors are plotting against them; some are afraid of crowded places; some fear elevators and airplanes. Some people attempt to blot out irrational fears and behaviors by resorting to drink or drugs; others opt out by means of suicide. In therapy the patient must be taught to face reality.

Responsibility. Responsibility is the ability to fulfill one's needs in a way that does not deprive others of the ability to fulfill their needs. By nature we are endowed with certain needs but not with the ability to fulfill them. Learning how to fulfill them responsibly is a lifelong task. Of course there are many irresponsible persons who are not the concern of the therapist. Those who for one reason or another do come to the therapist for help should not be classified as neurotic, psychotic, or schizophrenic but rather as irresponsible. The former labels can be considered only descriptions of irresponsibility. Glasser advocates that his readers substitute the term *responsible* for "mental health" and the term *irresponsible* for "mental illness." People do not act irresponsibly because they are "ill"; they are "ill" because they act irresponsibly.

Right and wrong. Glasser says that the ethical issue cannot be ignored in therapy, even though it is not always possible to tell what is right and what is wrong. The need for self-worth is intimately related to the attempt to maintain a satisfactory standard of behavior. If Glasser is not always clear as to the exact source of the standard, it is clear that he believes that morals, and values, and ideas of right and wrong held by the larger society are of basic importance to the individual and to successful therapy.

The Integrity-Therapy Approach

Not a few social scientists have been openly critical of the tendency to shift responsibility for the problems of the individual to the larger society. Included are anthropologist Jules Henry, sociologist C. Wright Mills, and among psychiatrists, psychologists, and counselors (in addition to those already considered), Thomas Szasz, Richard Parlour, Perry London, and O. Hobart Mowrer. The last has provided some of the basic theorizing for integrity therapy, although he subsequently referred to his movement as "the new group therapy" or "integrity group therapy."[15] Mowrer was critical of both Scientism and Protestantism for destroying faith in man's free will and responsibility: the former by its determinism, the latter by its cheap grace.[16] Integrity therapy is based upon notions that will not seem at all foreign to those who are familiar with the New Testament. Some of the most basic include the following:

Everyone is capable of making decisions that affect the quality of his condition.

15. O. Hobart Mowrer, *The New Group Therapy* (New York: Van Nostrand Reinhold, 1964).

16. Ibid, pp. 128–30.

Everyone has a value system and conscience. Guilt results from violating one's values.

When wrongdoing and guilt are covered up or denied, imbalance and neuroses result.

The way to well-being is that of confession of past deeds before others, repudiation of "guilt-engendering behavior," and restitution for wrongdoing.

Finally, "expiatory efforts ... involve *service*, rather than gratuitous suffering."[17]

Some Taxonomies of Counseling-Therapy Approaches

The foregoing is by no means an exhaustive listing of therapeutic approaches. Sometimes approaches seem to be as numerous as counselors and therapists themselves. But if the brief outlines of the theories and techniques of these therapies are reasonably accurate and representative, then we have achieved our objective.

How, then, is it possible to more readily grasp what is happening in this relatively new discipline? It is with this very end in view that various taxonomies have been proposed. (Note that we are not concerned here with categories based on such things as the kind of problems treated or duration of counseling itself: categories such as crisis counseling, marriage counseling, grief counseling, or short-term counseling.)

The Analytic-Behavioral-Relational Taxonomy

One common way of characterizing secular therapies is to do so in terms of their emphases on analysis, behavior, or relationships respectively (see fig. 3).[18]

17. Ibid., p. 129.
18. This taxonomy was suggested by William T. Kirwan in a class in cross-cultural counseling at Trinity Evangelical Divinity School, 6 April 1981.

FIGURE 3   **The Analytic-Behavioral-Relational Taxonomy of Counseling Therapies**

	Examples	
Type	**Basic Theory**	**Exponents**
Analytic therapies	Psychoanalytic therapy	Sigmund Freud, Carl Jung
	Rational-emotive therapy (?)	Albert Ellis
Behavioral therapies	Behavior modification and therapy	Ivan P. Pavlov, Joseph Wolpe
	Contingent-reinforcement learning	B. F. Skinner
Relational therapies	Client-centered therapy	Carl R. Rogers
	Existential analysis	Rollo May

Analytic therapies. The emphasis here is upon thinking through the experience of the client; ascertaining the meaning of that experience; and proposing solutions on that basis. Examples include Freud with his focus on the unconscious and the effects of early (especially sex-oriented) experiences; Carl Jung with his emphasis upon gaining awareness and becoming more conscious of the forces and sources of energy operating through us; Aaron Beck's approach in which the client is disabused of illogical cognitive assumptions; and, perhaps, Ellis's rational-emotive therapy in which the client is talked out of "erroneous" and "irrational" ideas (although many would take issue with a taxonomy that classifies RET as analytic).

Behavioral therapies. In these therapies the primary emphasis is upon behavior modification. Behavior is thought of predominantly as internal and external responses to stimulation. The therapist attempts to modify unadaptive stimulus-response connections. Conditioning theory began with Ivan Sechenov and was advanced by Pavlov and, in this country, by John B. Watson. As Allen

Goldstein and Dianne L. Chambliss note, this influence in therapy evolved in two directions—the emotional-learning orientation of Pavlov and more recently of Wolpe; and the approach of Skinner with his emphasis upon observable behavior and change through contingent reinforcement.[19] Behavioral theories tend to be reductionistic, although important behavioral elements are present in most all theories.

Relational therapies. Here the qualities and involvement of the counselor as a person are considered paramount in the counseling situation. The quality of this relationship largely determines whether or not the client will be helped. Examples include Rogers's client-centered therapy, in which the attitude of the counselor and his willingness to involve himself with the client are primary; and May's existential approach, which encourages the urges for change and fulfillment that exist within the client's own being.

The Directive-Permissive-Interactional Taxonomy

Another common categorization of approaches is that employed by the Christian psychologist, Gary R. Collins.[20] Here the emphasis is upon the posture assumed by the therapist (see fig. 4).

Directive therapies. "In these approaches the counselor is viewed as an expert who diagnoses and analyzes the problem, sometimes labels or categorizes behavior, decides on solutions for the counselee's problem, and in various ways communicates these solutions to the counselee."[21] In this category Collins includes the behavior-modification therapies, the psychoanalytic therapies, and the rational-emotive therapy of Ellis.

19. Allen Goldstein and Dianne L. Chambliss, "Behavior Therapy," in *Current Psychotherapies*, ed. Raymond Corsini (Itasca, Ill.: F. E. Peacock Publishers, 1973), p. 207.

20. Gary R. Collins, *How to Be a People Helper* (Santa Ana, Calif.: Vision House, 1976), pp. 161–75.

21. Ibid., p. 165.

FIGURE 4 **The Directive-Permissive-Interactional Taxonomy of Counseling Therapies**

	Examples	
Type	Basic Theory	Exponents
Directive therapies	Psychoanalytic therapy	Sigmund Freud
	Rational-emotive therapy	Albert Ellis
Permissive therapies	Client-centered therapy	Carl R. Rogers (especially the early Rogers)
	Gestalt therapy	Frederick S. Perls
Interactional therapies	Reality therapy	William Glasser
	Interactional therapy	Harry Stack Sullivan

Permissive therapies. "The counselor here may see himself as an expert in dealing with personal problems, but his task is not to make diagnoses, prescribe solutions, or treat people. Instead, the counselor is a facilitator who stimulates people to solve their own problems and who creates a permissive environment where this problem can be solved and personal growth can occur."[22] Although the gestalt therapy of Perls and the experiential psychotherapy of Eugene T. Gendlin and other therapies might be included here, the therapy of the early Rogers is seen as the best-known example of this approach.

Interactional therapies. "This term describes counseling in which the counselor and counselee interact together more or less as equals."[23] Examples include the approaches of the Swiss physician Paul DuBois and the American Glasser, who has developed a reality therapy in which the counselor teams up with the counselee in order to encourage the latter to look at present reality and "work

22. Ibid., p. 166.
23. Ibid., p. 167.

out plans for the future which will help him feel loved, able to love, and more worthwhile as a human being.[24] Still another example is the interactional therapy of Sullivan.

We conclude that counseling in the Western world—especially secular counseling in the Western world—is characterized by a variety of assumptions as to the nature of man and his problems and the best way to ameliorate or resolve those problems. Even the foundational understanding provided in this chapter alerts us to the difficulties inherent in uncritical efforts to employ these approaches in the contexts of the non-Western world or in the context of the church, whether Western or non-Western.

24. Ibid.

5

Secular Approaches to Group Counseling and Therapy in the West

The very terms that are most intimately associated with psychotherapy and counseling reveal the individualized therapy that has characterized Western approaches from the beginning.[1] Recently, however, there has been an almost meteoric rise in the resort to group therapies, particularly in the United States. The phenomenon probably has been occasioned by various factors, among them the loss of permanence and security in nuclear and extended families and in stable work groups. As we have already noted, American society is a society in transition. It has been asserted that whenever a society is in transition—as is pre-revolutionary France, and contemporary America and Russia—small, face-to-face groups flourish.[2]

The growing trend toward the utilization of small ther-

1. Jurgen Ruesch and Gregory Bateson, *Communication: The Social Matrix of Psychiatry* (New York: Norton, 1951). p. 89.
2. Jerome D. Frank, *Persuasion and Healing: A Comparative Study of Psychotherapy*, rev. ed. (Baltimore: Johns Hopkins Press, 1973), p. 265.

apy groups in our society is apparent in the writings of the theorists whose approaches have already been summarized. Albert Ellis refers to rational-emotive group therapy and says that currently a good deal of therapy—especially sex therapy—is done in small groups.[3] Early on, Carl R. Rogers noted the importance of groups in helping relationships.[4] He has referred to these group activities as "the most significant social invention of the century."[5] (Given the Rogerian method, which often entails seemingly endless hours of counselor-counselee dialogue over an extended period of time, it is understandable that group therapy has come to play over an ever-increasing role in his approach.) William Glasser stresses the role of various groups in his report of the treatment of delinquent adolescent girls in Ventura, California.[6] O. Hobart Mowrer believes that, where therapy is protracted and individualized too much, an ominous kind of relationship and transference can readily occur in the relationship between counselor and counselee. He writes,

> I believe there is rarely any need for a therapist and patient to have more than two or three private interviews, which should then lead into intimate conversations with an expanding circle of other 'growing persons' and relatively rapid introduction into a 'therapeutic community' which will encourage and support the individual while he or she restructures and improves the quality of his relationship with 'significant others' and society in general.[7]

3. Albert Ellis and Russel Grieger, with contributors, *Handbook of Rational-Emotive Therapy* (New York: Springer Publishing, 1977), p. 208.

4. Carl R. Rogers, *On Becoming a Person: A Therapist's View of Psychotherapy* (Boston: Houghton Mifflin, 1961), p. 40.

5. Carl R. Rogers, "Interpersonal Relationships: Year 2000," *Journal of Applied Behavioral Science* 4 (July/August/September 1968): 268.

6. William Glasser, *Reality Therapy* (New York: Harper and Row, 1965), pp. 68–70.

7. O. Hobart Mowrer, *The New Group Therapy* (New York: Van Nostrand Reinhold, 1964), p. 162.

One recognized writer in the field concludes, "It is likely that more people have been and are being helped by peer self-help psychotherapy groups than have been and are being helped by all types of professionally trained psychotherapists combined, with far less theorizing, analyzing, and for much less money."[8]

Studies by Gordon L. Paul[9] and Adolph O. DiLoretto[10] show that significantly better results can be obtained from small-group therapy as compared with such therapies as insight-oriented psychotherapy, client-centered therapy, and rational-emotive therapy.[11] The success of Alcoholics Anonymous has prompted the founding of a great variety of organizations, each utilizing some of the principles pioneered by Alcoholics Anonymous, that deal with problems such as obesity, drug addiction, psychosis and neurosis, and compulsive gambling.

Initial Understandings Concerning Group Counseling and Therapy

The Origins of Group Counseling

The claim is often made that group counseling began with J. H. Pratt, who inaugurated classes for his tuberculosis patients in 1905. John W. Drakeford and others point

8. Nathan Hurvitz, "Peer Self-Help Psychotherapy Groups and Their Implications for Psychotherapy," in *Integrity Groups: The Loss and Recovery of Community*, ed. O. Hobart Mowrer et al. (Urbana: Integrity Groups, 1974), p. 153, quoted in John W. Drakeford, "Integrity Therapy," in *Helping People Grow: Practical Approaches to Christian Counseling*, ed. Gary R. Collins (Santa Ana, Calif.: Vision House, 1980), p. 248.

9. Gordon L. Paul, *Insight versus Desensitization in Psychotherapy: An Experiment in Anxiety Reduction* (Stanford: Stanford University Press, 1966), along with follow-up studies.

10. Adolph O. DiLoretto, *Comparative Psychotherapy: An Experimental Analysis*, Modern Applications of Psychology series (Chicago: Aldine-Atherton, 1971).

11. Raymond Corsini, ed., *Current Psychotherapies*, 1st ed. (Itasca, Ill.: F. E. Peacock Publishers, 1973), p. 238.

out, however, that group therapy has a much longer history than that. John Wesley's Methodist movement in the eighteenth century was characterized by highly organized and viable groupings including the society, the class meeting, the band, the select society, and the penitent band. "There was association at the society level, examinations and discussion of behavior at the class meeting level, and the use of self-disclosure at the band level."[12] Wesley himself was looking back to the first-century church and attempting to recover its dynamic and reconstruct its lifestyle in eighteenth-century England.

A Definition of Group Counseling

Of course, perspectives on group counseling and therapy have changed dramatically since the eighteenth century, and even since the early years of the twentieth. Among other things, the nomenclature that refers to this kind of counseling has come to be quite diverse: group therapy, milieu therapy, family therapy, systems therapy, group counseling, community counseling, folk counseling, consultant-management groups, transactional-analysis groups, sensitivity training, and so forth. Each of these designations has its distinct meaning. Perhaps the following definition of group counseling will serve to characterize the majority of counseling groups, although certainly not all of them:

> Group counseling is a dynamic interpersonal process focusing on the conscious thought and behavior and involving the therapy functions of permissiveness, orientation to reality, catharsis, and mutual trust, caring, understanding, acceptance, and support. The therapy functions are created and nurtured in a small group to the sharing of personal concerns with one's peers and the counselor(s). The group counselees are basically normal individuals with various

12. Drakeford, "Integrity Therapy," in *Helping People Grow*, p. 243.

concerns which are not debilitating to the extent requiring extensive personality change. The group counselees may utilize the group interaction to increase understanding and acceptance of values and goals and to learn and/or unlearn certain attitudes and behaviors.[13]

Some Important Distinctions

To further aid our basic understanding of the group counseling process it will be helpful to consider five types of distinctions. First, it is important to distinguish between therapeutic or problem-solving groupings that already inhere in any society and those groupings that are formed in order to meet these needs. Societies all around the world have face-to-face groups such as nuclear and extended families or clans and subclans that deal with members' problems as a matter of course. At the same time, most societies also allow for voluntary groupings composed of people who come together in order to solve problems, effect certain kinds of change, and achieve specified goals. These groups need not be made up of strangers, as Jerome D. Frank indicates.[14] The participants may be strangers or acquaintances. What distinguishes them is the reason for their being constituted as a group. In fact, the commonality that binds them together may, for a short or long period of time, eclipse even those bonds of kinship that characterize most stable groups. The therapeutic group, for example, may become a kind of surrogate family.

Second, groups may be differentiated on the basis of their constituents. From this perspective there are three basic types of groups:

Groups in which there is a plurality of counselors or advisers and a single client;

Groups in which there is a single counselor or adviser and a plurality of clients;

13. Quoted in James C. Hansen, Richard W. Warner, and Elsie M. Smith, *Group Counseling: Therapy and Process* (Chicago: Rand, 1976), p. 7.
14. Frank, *Persuasion and Healing*, p. 269.

Lay groups (in which professionals have no *immediate* involvement as professionals).

Third, we can distinguish between two types of objectives entertained by both inbuilt and voluntary groups. The locus of concern of some groups is the well-being of members of the group. Increasingly, multiple families learn how to operate as family systems within the larger system. H. Peter Laquer, one of the pioneers in this approach, calls it system therapy.[15] Growth groups of various kinds constitute another instance of this kind of concern for group members. In another type of grouping people come together in order to focus on problems that confront the larger society, not just the group itself or its members. The energies of this kind of group are directed more toward "external" problem-solving than "internal" therapy. Although the dynamics are often the same, the techniques geared to achieving goals are usually much different in these two kinds of groups.

Fourth, we can distinguish between the kind of techniques that are utilized, especially in therapeutic groups. These techniques can be distinguished in various ways. Jerome Frank, Gerald Corey, and Marianne Schneider Corey make the same differentiations in regard to group therapy and counseling as they do in the case of the individual variety.[16] James C. Hansen, Richard W. Warner, and Elsie M. Smith place the various groups in quadrants on two continua: those concerned with insight as over against action, and those concerned with the rational as over against the affective.[17]

15. Noted by E. Mansell Pattison, "A Theoretical-Empirical Base for Social System Therapy," in *Current Perspectives in Cultural Psychiatry*, ed. Edward F. Foulks et al. (New York: Spectrum Publications, 1977), p. 218.

16. Frank, *Persuasion and Healing*, pp. 269ff; Gerald Corey and Marianne Schneider Corey, *Groups: Process and Practice* (Monterey, Calif.: Brooks-Cole, 1977), pp. 24–30.

17. Hansen, Warner, and Smith, *Group Counseling*, pp. 252–53.

Fifth, a distinction is often made between "counseling in the small" and community counseling or "counseling in the large." Community counseling "is the deliberate use of counseling knowledge and theory to enhance natural problem solving in the community or assist other persons who are deeply involved in human interaction. . . ."[18] Instances of this are numerous in our culture. Examples include seminars on investments or agricultural problems, career-development classes, foreign-student orientation, and so forth. Generally, however, group counseling in the West—whether small group or community—tends to focus on individuals and their problems. This is most evident in small-group counseling where the group is, in a very real sense, constituted for the benefit of the individual members. The roles of counselor and therapist and the techniques utilized are largely extensions of the particular view of the nature of man, the human problem, and its solution that appertain in the one-to-one approach.

Group Counseling in the United States: Types and Techniques

This brief introduction to group counseling concludes with a summary of the workings of some representative groups. They generally reflect the approaches to individual counseling and therapy discussed in chapter 4.

Psychoanalytic Groups

Analytic groups are more conventional in their methodology and dynamics than the newer groups and generally are not as popular. They usually consist of more or

18. Norman D. Sundberg, "Toward Research Evaluating Intercultural Counseling," in *Counseling across Cultures*, ed. Paul P. Pedersen, Walter J. Lonner, and Juris G. Draguns, 1st ed. (Honolulu: The University Press of Hawaii for the East-West Center, 1976), p. 142.

less heterogeneous groupings of eight to ten people who meet once a week in order to exchange information concerning their problems and interpretations of one another's actions and words. They utilize modified psychoanalytic techniques such as free-floating discussion, analysis of resistance to change, transference and countertransference, interpretation, and "working through." Leaders give direction, stimulate interaction, extend communication beyond areas of fixation, and provide interpretations.

T-Groups

T-groups were developed by a group of educators (Kurt Lewin is usually given the most prominence) in order to produce social change. Lewin's goal was to build up an academic and community task force that would both further small-group psychology and deal with social change. In short, small groups were trained for social action. Subsequently, the terms *T-group* and *sensitivity group* came to be used interchangeably because as more and more people became involved in T-groups the emphasis shifted to better understanding themselves and others.[19] In spite of some differences, T-groups and sensitivity groups share some basic techniques of group dynamics—interpersonal honesty, feedback, self-disclosure, unfreezing (liberating a member from his rigid belief system and from traditional ways of thinking of himself and behaving toward others), and observant participation. Leaders are to create an environment conducive to learning, provide a model for behavior, and open channels of communication.

Self-Theory and Gestalt Encounter Groups

The encounter-group movement is a large movement. In their book on group counseling, Hansen, Warner, and Smith discuss two models: the self-theory model of Rog-

---

19. Hansen, Warner, and Smith, *Group Counseling*, pp. 76–77.

ers and the gestalt model. They label Rogers' approach to counseling as self-theory rather than as nondirective or client-centered therapy because of Rogers' understanding of the central role that the individual's self-concept has on his behavior. Of great importance in self-theory encounter groups is the establishment of a psychological climate in which the fear of shame before the group is nullified by engaging in feedback and confrontation in an atmosphere of intimacy and mutual trust. Techniques include "milling around," concern with the past, communication of immediate interpersonal feeling, self-acceptance, the cracking of facades, and so forth. The role of the leader is that of group facilitator.

Gestalt encounter-group therapy is connected with Frederick S. Perls and also with the controversial Esalen Institute in California. The school is basically in agreement with Rogers and other encounter-group schools in believing that the "so-called normal person is essentially alienated and that people need to have a greater awareness of themselves—their body sensations, feelings, and thoughts."[20] But it differs from Rogers' model in that encounter usually takes place between one individual in the group and the group leader. Key concepts and techniques include assuming responsibility (substituting "I won't" for "I can't" or "I resent" for "I feel guilty"); explaining, in "here-and-now" terms, a problem that is bothering one (a technique called the hot seat); imagining that an aspect of one's psyche is embodied and is sitting in a chair, and then "discussing" a particular problem with that aspect of oneself (a technique called the empty chair); expressing resentment and appreciation; sharing hunches; and utilizing a "confrontation warm-up game" or role reversal. The leader designs technique schemes and takes a central role in the group process.

20. Ibid., p. 165.

Transactional Analysis in Groups

Basic to TA group counseling are the five hungers, the three ego states, and the life positions discussed in chapter 4. In order to help individuals to decontaminate their ego states, or to develop the capacity to use all the ego states as the situation warrants, or to discard an inappropriate life script and replace it with a positive script, people are encouraged to meet with TA groups. Spelling out specific goals, group members enter into contracts with the counselor. Groups operate with external boundaries that separate them from nongroup individuals and influences, and internal boundaries that separate the counselor from the members. Transations between members are considered to be minor transactions, and those between the counselor and one of the members are considered to be major transactions. In the early stages of the group process, the counselor's ability to listen, observe, and analyze is central. Subsequently he provides protection (e.g., helping group members to experience all their ego states); potency (e.g., the sweeping away of the client's parental injunctions); and operations (e.g., the use of specific techniques such as interrogation, confrontation, or illustration). TA gives more or less equal weight to insight and behavioral change. It emphasizes the diagnostic skills of the leader more than group dynamics.

Behavioral Counseling in Groups

Behavioral counselors look upon symptoms as though they were ailments and attempts to treat them directly. This approach is predicated upon the notion that we do not come into the world as innately good or bad but rather as neutral beings. Personality is formed as people react to stimuli, thus developing behavioral patterns. The basic structure of the personality of an individual, therefore, is his learned pattern of behavior. Appropriate and maladaptive behavioral patterns are differentiated by whether or not they are satisfying to the individual and others around him. Members of these groups are usually people who have the same or similar problems. Members are concerned with their own behavior: describing the problem; describing factors that stimulate and reinforce it; describing the kind of behavior that would be more desirable; learning from the counselor; and following directions for behavioral change. Like Rogers, Joseph Wolpe, a primary proponent of this approach, emphasizes the need for the counselor to be accepting and nonjudgmental. The counselor's method is didactic—inquiring, lecturing, directing. Techniques employed include group discussion, modeling, role playing, desensitization, and psychodrama. Behavior-modification techniques include strengthening strategies such as shaping (shaping new behaviors from existing behaviors), behavior contracts (an agreement between two or more individuals to behave in certain ways), and modeling; and weakening strategies such as extinction (eliminating reinforcement) and satiation (presenting reinforcement at such a high rate that it becomes adversative). This form of group counseling relies less upon interaction of the group members than do the other types. Individuals are being counseled, but in a group situation.

Group counseling and therapy of various types has become increasingly important in the Western world. As we have noted, Mowrer emphasizes that after two or three individual counseling sessions one should move quickly to the therapeutic group.[21] Numerous other specialists are in essential agreement. The implications of this trend should not be lost on Christian leaders, especially those involved in cross-cultural ministries.

---

21. Mowrer, *The New Group Therapy*, p. 162.

6

Approaches to Christian Counseling in the Western World

As a distinct discipline and profession, Christian counseling is, of course, a comparatively recent phenomenon. As was briefly mentioned in chapter 2, it began more than half a century ago when a limited number of pastors and physicians turned their attention to a cooperative ministry to the emotionally distressed. Credit is given specifically to Anton T. Boisen, a Congregational minister who himself had experienced a number of breakdowns and had been confined to state mental institutions on three different occasions. In the mid-1920s he took the lead in establishing a training program for seminarians at Worchester State Hospital in Massachusetts. From that small beginning—Boisen as chaplain, four students, and one training center—the Clinical Pastoral Education (CPE) movement developed as a distinct movement and pastoral and Christian counseling gradually came to occupy the prominent place it enjoys in Christian education and ministry today.

The Ideological Roots of Christian Counseling

Although it is not at all difficult to trace the historical roots of the Christian counseling movement, to discover and identify its ideological roots is a much more challenging task. On the one hand, there can be no question that the movement draws much of its vitality and many of its ideas from related secular disciplines. On the other hand, the question remains as to the legitimacy of depending upon those roots when they so often fail to tap basic truth.

The Roots of the
Clinical Pastoral Education Movement

Gary R. Collins credits the CPE movement with some signal contributions in the field of pastoral counseling. He notes its contributions in

> providing standards for the training of pastoral counselors; convincing hospital personnel of the importance of involving pastors in treatment of the physically and mentally ill; investigating ways in which theology and the psychological sciences can be related; showing the importance of training in counseling for seminarians; demonstrating that the personal and spiritual development of the seminarian is at least as important as his or her intellectual training for the ministry.[1]

At the same time Collins faults the movement by noting three problems CPE poses for conservative Christians: it tends to consider personal experience rather than Scripture as foundational; it tends to borrow uncritically from humanistic secular psychology; and its proponents show limited tolerance for conservative theological positions.[2]

1. Gary R. Collins, ed., *Helping People Grow: Practical Approaches to Christian Counseling* (Santa Ana, Calif.: Vision House, 1980), p. 12.
2. Ibid., pp. 13–15.

One need only mention the names of some leading proponents and practitioners within this movement—Boisen,
Seward Hiltner, Leslie D. Weatherhead, Richard C. Cabot,
Russell L. Dicks, William E. Hulme, Wayne E. Oates, Carrol A. Wise, John S. Bonnell, and Norman Vincent Peal—
to recognize the validity of Collins's appraisal. Although
these and others add religious and spiritual dimensions to
counseling, their writings often betray a bewildering array
of beliefs regarding both the nature of God and Christian
truth. One quotation hardly constitutes proof for such a
statement, but the following paragraph from Boisen illustrates the point:

> The significance of the doctrine of the Cross as represented
> in Christian teaching at its best lies in its requirement of
> honest and thoroughgoing commitment to the heroic way
> of life. It lies also in the concept of God which it reflects—
> a suffering God, a God of love. In the teaching of Jesus all
> of the Law and the Prophets was summed up in the prin-
> ciple of love. His death, then, was the crowning act in a
> life of service to his fellows; it placed the seal of sincerity
> upon his life and teaching and freed men from the bondage
> to a God of fear.[3]

That the God of love is also the God of judgment; that
the cross is the place of expiation and redemption—these
and other biblical truths are eclipsed by interpretations
that are more palatable to modern man.

The Ideological Roots
of Conservative Evangelical Counseling

Evangelicals exhibit far less uniformity in their appreciation and appropriation of secular counseling and therapy approaches than do their more liberal counterparts.
All evangelicals agree that biblical revelation is the foun-

3. Anton T. Boisen, *Religion in Crisis and Custom: A Sociological and
Psychological Study* (New York: Harper and Brothers, 1943), pp. 206–7.

dation of truth concerning man and his problems; however, they vary greatly in their responses to secular or, at least, sub-Christian proposals.

A majority of evangelicals would agree with Augustine that all truth is God's truth, but they differ in their assessment as to the degree of truth non-Christian experts possess. Consequently, they differ on the advisability and even the possibility of integrating non-Christian approaches into Christian systems of counseling and therapy. Jay E. Adams, for example, distinguishes three general approaches to counseling (see fig. 5), but writes, "At bottom, the Christian believes that there are only *two* approaches: the Christian; the non-Christian. The first two approaches in the chart are mere sub-divisions of the latter. The basic antithesis of the Christian position to all others is demarked by the division in the chart."[4] Accordingly, Adams believes that non-Christian systems contain but dim reflections of truth and he holds out little hope for a successful integration of these materials into truly Christian systems.

Although most evangelical counselors would admit that integration is not always successfully achieved, they nevertheless rely quite extensively on the findings and insights of non-Christian scholars and therapists. Paul Tournier even speaks of Sigmund Freud as "in many respects an ally of Christianity."[5] Why? Because Freud believed that his patients' illnesses were due to inner conflicts occasioned by a battle against a contrary force. Tournier reads the details of 260 clinical cases in Freud's *Psychopathology of Everyday Life* and finds that all can be classified in one or another of the four categories of sins dealt with in the Sermon on the Mount. He says that "Freud confirms Christian teaching, since he shows that

4. Jay E. Adams, *The Christian Counselor's Manual* (Phillipsburg, N.J.: Presbyterian and Reformed, 1973), p. 72.
5. Paul Tournier, *The Healing of Persons,* trans. Edwin Hudson (New York: Harper and Row, 1965), p. 230.

FIGURE 5   **Jay E. Adams's Classification of Counseling Presuppositions and Approaches***

	General Approach	Specific Type	Man's Problem	Solution	
1	Expert Knowledge	Freudian	Poor Socialization	Resocialization by expert	I non-Christian approaches
		Skinnerian	Environmental Conditioning	Reconditioning by expert	
2	Common Knowledge	Rogerian	Failure to live up to potential	Resources in self	
		Integrity Groups	Bad behavior toward others	Resources in self and group	
3	Divine Knowledge	Christian	Sin against God	Spirit's Resources in Word	II Christian approach

*From *The Christian Counselor's Manual* by Jay E. Adams. Copyright 1973 by Jay E. Adams. Used by permission.

all psychological conflicts suffered by men stem from violation of Christ's commands."[6] Psychoanalysis lends insight into "the workings of the human heart since it shows us that we lie every day even though we do not utter a word."[7] Tournier applauds Freud for the honesty demonstrated in recognizing in himself "the sins which he denounced in others."[8] And he thinks that Freud has made a signal contribution in revealing the part played in our lives by sexual impurity.[9]

Adams, on the other hand, says that "Freud thought little of religion in general and less of Christianity in par-

6. Ibid.
7. Ibid.
8. Ibid, p. 231.
9. Ibid.

ticular. . . ."[10] He specifically calls Freud an enemy, not a friend.[11] Thus, Adams finds no time for searching out distorted reflections of biblical truth in the writings of Freud.

It would be difficult to find a more graphic illustration of the variant attitudes evangelical counselors entertain vis-à-vis non-Christian theorists and theories. The contrast may serve to teach us that profound insights are obtainable from unlikely sources. It may also serve to teach us that while we must be charitable to all, we should not make them say more than they would affirm.

Nevertheless, all evangelicals do agree that Christian counseling—truly Christian counseling—takes the Bible and such teachings as the divine origin and postfall sinful nature of man, the righteousness and redeeming love of God, the reality of satanic forces, the truth of the gospel, and the ministry of the Holy Spirit with utmost seriousness. Most agree, at least in theory, with Augustine's dictum that the amount of knowledge derivable from "pagan" sources is small as compared with that derivable from the Scriptures. And although they recognize that men can become psychologically and mentally ill, they are basically committed to a moral, as over against a medical, model of counseling therapy. All of this will be more apparent as we proceed.

From these fundamental commitments on the part of evangelicals we cannot infer that any counseling approach is legitimate if propounded by an evangelical, or that approaches avowedly based on Scripture are without cultural biases and blind spots. But they do mean that we can proceed with a confidence that the closer we come to the revealed truth of the Bible the more appreciative we will be of one another, and the more effective we will be in helping ministries at home and abroad.

10. Jay E. Adams, *Competent to Counsel* (Phillipsburg, N.J.: Presbyterian and Reformed, 1970), p. 15.
11. Ibid.

Some Representative Evangelical Counseling Approaches

For the sake of comparison, and to discover the difference that a commitment to Christ and the Bible makes in counseling, we turn next to brief overviews of several well-known and representative evangelical approaches to counseling. If, as has been asserted, there are at least one hundred Christian approaches to counseling and most of them can be termed evangelical, the difficulty of choosing representative approaches becomes immediately apparent.[12] Because the differences between Adams and Tournier have already been noted, and because their approaches are so pervasive on the evangelical scene, one probably does not err in selecting them. That we elect to deal with the approach of Howard J. Clinebell, Jr., takes note of his influence on the training programs of contemporary pastors.

The Nouthetic Approach of Adams

Adams finds an integration of secular counseling psychology or psychiatry and biblical counseling to be impossible because psychotherapists have attempted to solve man's basic problems in ways that ignore God and his solutions as found in the Bible. When Adam was created he was given authority by God to rule over the earth. As a result of Adam's sin man lost that dominion and he has never regained it. "The problem in counseling is that, contrary to God's mandate, clients have allowed the environment to control them."[13] No solution is possible until man recognizes that he is responsible for his own condition, until he repents and trusts Christ. Christ not only paid the penalty for sin, but also frees man from its power. Change is possible—change that enables persons to live in accordance with God's will as revealed in the Bible.

12. Collins, *Helping People Grow*, p. 317.
13. Adams, *Competent to Counsel*, p. 15.

Nouthetic counseling is therefore concerned with change, as are other counseling approaches. In Adams's words, the purpose is "to effect personality and behavioral change."[14] Change must occur at the deepest level. To help a non-Christian, evangelism is absolutely essential. Minimal help may be given to a person with problems in order to clear the way for presentation of the gospel and inculcate hope, but this is not counseling—it is precounseling. True counseling is designed to lead to regeneration—the prerequisite for change at a deep level—and from regeneration on to Christian living under the rule of Christ. "Pleasing Him [Christ]—not relief from the problem—must be uppermost. Every counselee is called upon to 'seek first God's empire and His righteousness.' "[15]

Adams transliterates the Greek word *noutheteo* in describing his approach because no English word conveys the full meaning of the Greek. New Testament translators have variously rendered *noutheteo*: "teach," "admonish," "warn," "put sense into," and "counsel."[16] Nouthetic counseling proceeds on the basis of a four-step biblical process for change outlined in 2 Timothy 3:16: the Christian counselee is to be instructed, brought to conviction, corrected, and trained in righteousness. Nouthetic methods are not to be borrowed from other systems but "must always grow out of and be designed to effect those ends that are set forth by God's Word."[17]

Adams' methods tend to be confrontational and authoritarian rather than dialogical and include emphasizing the counselee's personal responsibility before God and with his neighbor; analyzing problems in scriptural rather than medical or psychological terms; working within the framework of the church; and planning, prescribing, and expecting change following every session.

14. Ibid., p. 45.
15. Jay E. Adams, "Nouthetic Counseling," in *Helping People Grow*, p. 159.
16. Adams, *Competent to Counsel*, p. 44.
17. Adams, "Nouthetic Counseling," in *Helping People Grow*, p. 160.

The Interactional Counseling of Tournier

Next we will look at the approach of Tournier, the Swiss doctor and counselor. Tournier takes God and the Bible, and sin and redemption with utmost seriousness. Two chapters in an early work of his, *The Healing of Persons,* illustrate this.[18] In a chapter entitled "The Laws of Life" Tournier insists that because God created life we must learn the laws of life from his book, the Bible. The Bible contains rules for the physical, spiritual, moral, and social life of mankind. Tournier amply illustrates the importance of obeying these laws. In the next chapter, entitled "Inspiration," however, he emphasizes that the Bible is more than a collection of divine laws which ought to be obeyed. "The Gospel is not a call to effort, but to faith."[19] It is legalism that calls for more effort, passes judgment on others, and counts on the will. But the power of sin is too great to be broken by man's will. Therefore, God has provided for man's transformation by faith in Jesus Christ.

Tournier does integrate scientific knowledge but he finds it incomplete and nowhere more so than when it comes to man's basic need and the fulfillment of that need. He agrees with N. J. Mathieu, who writes of the "feeling of guilt and sin" as a "superior form of knowledge."[20] Man's ultimate need is for soul-healing, which can come only by contact with Jesus Christ. It is the Christian counselor's privilege to help men make that contact.

Thus, Tournier's "technique" is to build a relationship between himself and the client which will prove to be a "healing one." The Christian counselor is neither the expert who has all the answers nor simply a catalyst who helps provide an environment in which the client can solve his own problems. The counseling relationship is one where "acceptance, support, mutual sharing, honest

18. See Tournier, *The Healing of Persons.*
19. Ibid., p. 209.
20. Ibid., p. 229.

confession of sins and personal weaknesses, prayer, passive listening, and directive giving of advice may all be a part. . . ."[21]

The Growth Counseling of Clinebell

One of the psychologist-counselors who has been most influential in pastoral counseling at the seminary level is the early Clinebell. In his widely read text, *Basic Types of Pastoral Counseling*,[22] he defined pastoral counseling as "the utilization, by the minister, of a one-to-one or small-group relationship to help people handle their problems of living more adequately and grow toward fulfilling their potentialities. This is achieved by helping them reduce the inner blocks which prevent them from relating in need-satisfying ways."[23] At the time he wrote *Basic Types of Pastoral Counseling*, Clinebell called his approach "relationship-centered counseling."[24] Subsequently he has opted for the term *growth counseling*.[25]

Clinebell borrows from those outside the church without apology. Among "new thrusts" which he finds most relevant are "*role-relationship marriage counseling, family group therapy* (John E. Bell and Virginia M. Satir), *transactional analysis* (Eric Berne), *crisis intervention theory* (Gerald Caplan), *reality therapy* (William Glasser), *existential psychotherapy* (Rollo May, Viktor Frankl, J. F. Bugental), and the broad thrust of *ego psychology*."[26] Abraham H. Maslow's thought also provides some of the basic insights of growth counseling, but to Maslow's motiva-

21. Collins, *Helping People Grow*, p. 173.
22. Howard J. Clinebell, Jr., *Basic Types of Pastoral Counseling: New Resources for Ministries to the Troubled* (Nashville: Abingdon, 1966).
23. Ibid., p. 20.
24. Ibid., p. 23.
25. Howard J. Clinebell, Jr., *Growth Counseling: Hope-Centered Methods for Actualizing Human Wholeness* (Nashville: Abingdon, 1979); see also Howard J. Clinebell, Jr., "Growth Counseling," in *Helping People Grow*, p. 84.
26. Clinebell, *Basic Types of Pastoral Counseling*, p. 22.

tional pyramid of human needs, Clinebell adds a sixth and
overriding dimension: spiritual need.

Clinebell builds on biblical teachings such as the *imago
Dei*, pain and struggle, the "new being," growth, love,
shalom, and the church as a caring community. Some of
his key concepts are potentializing (full use of a person's
potential), hope (essential for creative change), intention-
ality (purposefully discovering and developing one's options), and blocked potentializing (another term for individual and collective human sin). Clinebell sees creative
change as having three interdependent dimensions: personal, relational, and institutional. His growth counseling
has two goals: the liberation of the counselee's full potential at every stage of life; and, to help accomplish this, the
creation of a "person-enhancing society."

Clinebell puts forward a formula that concisely expresses the basic principle of growth counseling:[27]

$$Growth = Caring + Confrontation$$

OR

$$Growth = Love + Honesty$$

This means that to the extent that a person experiences
concern and love in a relationship and is willing to hon-
estly confront reality (with its destructive and constructive elements) growth can occur.

Three Ways of Relating Counseling Theories to Scripture

The fundamental distinctives of counseling theories that
can be classified as Christian grow out of a commitment
to Christ as Lord and Savior, dependence upon the Holy
Spirit as Enabler and Guide, and a resort to the Bible as

27. Clinebell, "Growth Counseling," *Helping People Grow*, p. 84.

God's Word and the source book of truth about God and man. This being the case, Christian psychologists and counselors inevitably utilize Bible passages and teachings in their helping and healing ministries. Beyond this, however, many of them seek to demonstrate the biblical basis of their particular theory and a few of them employ Scripture (especially the New Testament) as a frame of reference for various Christian counseling theories. These latter endeavors are attempted in a variety of ways and with varying degrees of success. Let us examine three such attempts.

Some theorists attempt to build counseling theory on words in the Bible that have connotations which fall within the general orbit of counseling as understood and practiced today. These terms include *noutheteo* (confront, warn, admonish), *parakaleo* (exhort, comfort, encourage), *paramutheomai* (to speak to someone by way of admonition or to calm; therefore, to encourage or console), *makrothumeo* (to be of a "long" spirit; therefore, to persevere, to be patient in bearing the offenses of others), *antechomai* (to hold someone firmly; to give heed to; to aid and care for another), and *sumbouleuo* (to give counsel or advice). As a case in point, Adams selects the word *noutheteo* as providing the key concept for his counseling theory.

Obviously, the Bible supports the kind of activities that are undertaken in contemporary Christian counseling. That being the case, it is entirely legitimate to relate what is being done to that enjoined by Scripture by means of a careful study of the words which were employed by the writers of the Bible. Such a study can serve to guide all of us—and Christian counselors especially—in a full range of people-helping endeavors and approaches.

On the other hand, there are potential dangers. In the first place, this way of relating Scripture and contemporary theory may give the false impression that counseling in the more specialized meaning common today (i.e., curing when a pathology is present or, at least, counseling as provided by a trained specialist) was an aspect of the experience of Israel or the early church. Actually, as David E. Carlson rightly points out, the word *counseling* is never used in the Bible and when the term *counsel* appears its meaning is quite ordinary.

> When the word 'counsel' is used, it is limited to giving or taking advice. In the Old Testament, the words commonly translated 'counsel' mean to deliberate, resolve, advise, guide, plan, consult. (See Prov. 11:14; 15:22; 2 Chron. 25:16; Isaiah 1:26; Exodus 18:19.) In the New Testament, the word 'counselor' is used three times (*boulutees*—Mark 15:43; Luke 23:50; *sumboulos* Rom. 11:34) and is descriptive of a person's employment as an advisor.[28]

In the second place, this way of relating Scripture and contemporary theory may result in reading too much into a single word or group of words and thereby reinforcing an imbalanced theory. All of us are familiar with the dangers of prooftexting. An endless stream of strange and false doctrines has been supported by pointing to this or that Bible verse. Is it not true that supporting or explaining a particular counseling theory on the basis of finding a specific word in the Bible could issue in similar misunderstandings?

Other theorists relate their counseling theory to the model provided by the Lord Jesus. In the Gospels we see Jesus carrying out a multifarious ministry: preaching, teaching, confronting, calling for repentance, listening, forgiving, mediating, serving, nurturing, washing feet, and so forth. All of these activities are instructive both as to the attitude that should be taken by the Christian counselor and as to one or another aspect of counseling itself. Although he has not confined his theory to an analysis of

---

28. David E. Carlson, "Relationship Counseling," in *Helping People Grow*, pp. 26⅔7.

Jesus' ministry (as we shall see), Carlson has focused on that ministry in a way that is most helpful and challenging.

In relating counseling theory and practice to the gospel portrayal of Jesus and his work on earth, then, we can hardly err and stand to be instructed in a most positive way. Nevertheless, there is a fundamental weakness in this approach. When the full range of Christ's ministry to his contemporaries is taken into consideration, the model provided by Jesus becomes so encompassing as to make "biblical counseling" (on that model) almost indistinguishable from Christian ministry per se. In other words, as related to counseling in the modern sense, the model provided by the Lord Jesus says too much and too little to us.

Still other theorists relate counseling to what I have elected to call Christ's person gifts and their roles in the church and world. An example of this approach is the work of James Lyn Elder, who (following Hiltner) thinks of counseling as a kind of extension of the "communicative perspective" (teaching and preaching) of the pastoral ministry. "Counseling aims squarely at helping the individual to whose head and heart teaching and preaching have made their appeal to make the fullest and most complete 'digestive' response to those appeals."[29]

When Carlson proceeds to tie aspects of Christ's ministry to the roles of prophet, priest, and pastor he is doing something very similar. In his thinking, when Christ preached, confronted his listeners, and called for repentance he was ministering in a prophetic way. When Christ listened, forgave, mediated, and called for confession he was acting in a priestly way. When Christ served, washed feet, and otherwise cared for the needs of people he was acting in a pastoral way.

29. James Lyn Elder, "Pastoral Counseling and the Communication of the Gospel," in *An Introduction to Pastoral Counseling*, ed. Wayne E. Oates (Nashville: Broadman, 1959), p. 205.

There are pitfalls in the attempt to relate counseling theory to the person-gift roles of the New Testament. One pitfall is the tendency to misconstrue or stereotype these roles. For example, preaching as we know it may not have been a major task of the New Testament pastor (or pastor-teacher) at all.[30] In that case Elder's "communicative perspective" may need some modification. Another pitfall is to be discovered in the tendency to be selective. Thus, in the light of the New Testament list of person gifts, Carlson's treatment requires amplification.

In spite of the pitfalls, an approach that relates counseling theory to the roles of the person gifts Christ has bequeathed to his church has great potential. (This is not to argue against other approaches for, as we have seen, they are instructive and in any case are not necessarily mutually exclusive.) I would like to demonstrate that potential by briefly considering Collins' helpful taxonomy of alternative counseling theories[31] and then by adding some dimensions to the person-gift paradigm which seem to me to be both biblically required and practically compelling.

An Integrative Taxonomy of Counseling Theories

Building on the directive-interactional-permissive taxonomy of secular counseling theories and the roles of person gifts in the New Testament, Collins thinks of alternative Christian counseling approaches as being prophetic-confrontational, pastoral-conversational, or priestly-confessional (see fig. 6). In his thinking, Adams' nouthetic

30. See Craig A. Evans, " 'Preacher' and 'Preaching': Some Lexical Observations," *Journal of the Evangelical Theological Society* 24 (December 1981): 315–22. Evans says that "the common practice today of a clergyman preaching a sermon to a passive audience seems to have its origin in tradition (and/or experience) rather than in a scriptural pattern."

31. Gary R. Collins, *How to Be a People Helper* (Santa Ana, Calif.: Vision House, 1976), pp. 164–75.

counseling is prophetic-confrontational, and the CPE movement tends toward the priestly-confessional approach (perhaps more in its earlier years than currently). Collins himself favors interactional counseling but believes that there are times when either the more directive or the more permissive approaches may be warranted. He points to Clinebell as an example of one who demonstrates an appreciation for the permissive approach of Rogers and the CPE movement, but who believes that Christians must go beyond it.[32]

Although Collins' taxonomy does not avoid the pitfalls we have associated with the utilization of the person-gift paradigm, he has provided us with a framework that brings a certain clarity and integration to a comparative study that is often confusing and even frustrating. This can be seen by combining his analysis with the framework included in chapter 4 (see fig. 7). Added to this positive gain is that Collins relates the counseling approach to be used with the counseling context which, one assumes, would include such things as the nature of the presenting prob-

FIGURE 6 **Gary R. Collins's Taxonomies of Secular and Christian Counseling Approaches***

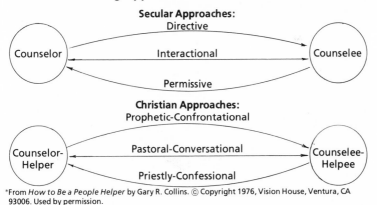

*From *How to Be a People Helper* by Gary R. Collins. © Copyright 1976, Vision House, Ventura, CA 93006. Used by permission.

32. Ibid., pp. 167, 174.

lem, the case history of the counselee, and the personality and preference of both counselor and counselee(s).

Relating Counseling Theory to the Person-Gift Roles of the New Testament

Our discussion has brought us to what I consider to be one of the most productive ways of relating counseling theory to the Scriptures. Certainly much is to be gained from examining the Old and New Testament lexicons as they relate to counseling-like activities if the weaknesses of this approach can be overcome. Many insights can undoubtedly be gained from a study of the ministry of our Lord Jesus (and, likely, from the ministries of various of the apostles) if we avoid the weaknesses of this approach. Still other ways of relating counseling theory and practice to Scripture which have not been explored here may also add to our understanding. However, it would seem that the greatest gain could well come from relating counseling theory to person gifts and their roles as enumerated and

FIGURE 7   **A Taxonomy of Christian Counseling Approaches**

| | **Examples** | |
Type	Basic Theory	Exponents
Prophetic-Confrontational (Directive)	Nouthetic counseling	Jay E. Adams
	"Spirituotherapy" (with caveats)	Charles Solomon
Pastoral-Conversational (Interactional)	Interactional (dialogical) counseling	Paul Tournier
	Discipleship ("helper-helpee") counseling (with caveats)	Gary R. Collins
Priestly-Confessional (Permissive)	Relationship-centered counseling	Seward Hiltner
	Growth counseling (with caveats)	Howard J. Clinebell, Jr.

described in the New Testament, especially in First Corinthians 12 and 14 and Ephesians 4. (In so doing I am
purposely including only those specifically termed
gifts, with one exception. Laypersons are included because
of the emphasis on priests in the taxonomies included
previously.)

To do justice to this task would require much more
time and space than are available within the scope of this
work. The attempt to describe it here is admittedly only
tentative and suggestive, and will include a summary
pointing to some of the advantages of this approach.

New Testament Person-Gifts and
Their Corresponding Roles

According to the apostle Paul, the risen Christ has given
special gifts to the church and its membership so that his
work might be accomplished in the church and in the
world. Some of his gifts—such as healing, helps, admin-
istrations, and the like—can be thought of as "gifts to
persons." Although some of these may entail the ability
to counsel (in the broad meaning of that term), we will
not concern ourselves with them here. Our concern is
with the person gifts and their specialized ministries.

The apostles (missionaries). It is not necessary to repeat
here what has already been said about the apostles in
chapter 2. It is necessary only to recall that in addition to
the Twelve and Paul the New Testament recognizes another group of men as "representatives [lit., apostles] of
the churches" (2 Cor. 8:23; Phil. 2:25, margin). We still
have apostles ("sent ones" or missionaries) of this latter
type whose role it is to cross geographical and cultural
boundaries in order to plant the church of Christ in new
areas and among new peoples. The cross-cultural aspects
of counseling theory are of special importance to them.

The prophets. A biblical case can also be made for con-
cluding that, as in the case of the apostles, there are two
types of prophets with their attendant roles in the New

Testament: the "foretelling prophets" (Acts 21:10–11) and the "forthtelling prophets" (2 Cor. 14:3). Many commentators take the position that with the completion of the prophetic Word of God in the Bible the foretelling prophets went into eclipse in the church. However that may be, it is evident that the forthtelling prophets continue to play an important role, although they often minister as speakers at Bible conferences or special conferences concerning prophecy or deeper life, and, therefore, are somewhat "incognito" from a theological point of view. According to a relevant passage (1 Cor. 14:3), their role is to edify, exhort, and console God's people. They must be prepared to employ differing approaches in dealing with God's people, whether in public speech or private conversation. It is apparent that, although those forthtelling prophets may indeed discover that the so-called confrontational, nouthetic, and "prophetic" approaches will be utilitarian in their ministry, flexibility in using these approaches will best suit the variety inherent in their role.

The evangelists. As the word denotes, the evangelist is the bearer of the good news concerning Christ and salvation. Evangelists are given in order that the gospel might be presented clearly and convincingly to individuals and the larger community (Acts 8:5, 12, 26–31; 21:8). The work of the evangelist, then, entails more than preaching the message of Christ to large audiences. It also entails the more personalized and private evangelistic presentations that we have come to associate with the ministries of "trained counselors" who counsel those who respond to public invitations to accept Christ and of "personal workers" who seldom preach but often witness in person-to-person evangelistic endeavors. It goes without saying that when the role of the evangelist is not restricted to the public preaching of the gospel but is also viewed in the way just described, a mastery of applicable counseling principles can only enhance the evangelist's ministry.

The pastor-teachers. If we subscribe to the Granville

Sharp rule,[33] the pastor-teacher (or shepherd-teacher) constitutes a single category of person gifts. And if we take Paul's charge to Timothy (the pastor-teacher of the church at Ephesus) as indicative of the divinely appointed role of this type of person gift, that role involves a variety of responsibilities in relation to the "flock of God": preaching the Word; being prepared in season and out of season; correcting, rebuking, and encouraging with great patience and careful instruction (2 Tim. 4:2).

Pastoral counseling, then, is more than an extension of the preaching-teaching ministry in the local church. It is an aspect of a ministry that is much more holistic and is related to the larger welfare, particularly the spiritual welfare, of the entire congregation. Furthermore, we can assume that since this ministry tends to be localized in space and extended in time, the pastor-teacher will know well the customs and needs of the people among whom he labors. (All of this helps us to understand why counseling education was introduced and has been identified and maintained as pastoral counseling in our theological schools.)

The lay priests. Finally, we note that in the New Testament economy, the church has no special priesthood as such. Christ is the High Priest through whom all believers have direct access to God the Father (Heb. 6:20). All saints or believers constitute a "holy priesthood" and as such minister in ways that build up the body of Christ (1 Peter 2:5; Eph. 4:11–16): teaching, admonishing, showing mercy, and "saving" (Col. 3:16; Jude 23). As it has been broadly defined, counseling is not the exclusive prerogative of the

33. According to the Granville Sharpe rule, "if a string of articular substantives is linked by the conjunctive *kai* and one of the substantives appears without an article immediately following another articular substantive separated only by the conjunctive, the two substantives may be regarded as describing the same entity. The rule is questioned, however, when the substantives are in the plural number." See Evans, " 'Preacher' and 'Preaching,' " p. 321n.

special person gifts. It is the privilege and responsibility of all believers. The only limitations are those of willingness and ability. Here, then, we find an important place in the body of believers for both highly trained professional counselors (psychologists and psychiatrists) on the one hand and for minimally trained people helpers on the other.

In all of this we should keep in mind that the foregoing categories are not set in concrete. Timothy, for example, began his Christian "career" as a layperson; was launched into full-time ministry as an apostle (missionary; Acts 16:1–3); became pastor-teacher in the church at Ephesus (2 Tim. 1:3); and as such was urged to do the work of an evangelist (2 Tim. 4:5). Thus we learn that one and the same person can change roles as a result of divine direction and, while primarily functioning as one type of person gift, may be expected to perform a task that is associated primarily with the work of another type.

Advantages of Utilizing the Person-Gift Approach

I believe that it is advantageous to relate counseling theory to the roles of persons gifts as we have enumerated and briefly described them. In the first place, this approach forces us to think theologically as well as functionally. By first coming to grips with the larger purposes and plans of God as revealed in sacred Scripture and then inquiring as to the ways in which the varied ministries of God's people contribute to those purposes, we as theorists become less likely to read our own predilections and preferences into the biblical text.

In the second place, this approach extends the possibility of drawing upon the store of counseling knowledge to the benefit of the entire membership of the body of Christ and to its leadership in particular. By taking this approach we are in a better position to see how specialists in psychology and counseling can assist in preparing missionaries for their pioneering task in other cultures. We are in

a better position to see how forthtelling prophets can enhance their ministries to individuals and small groups. We
are in a better position to see how evangelists can be aided
in the more private and personal application of the gospel
that should complement its public proclamation.

In the third place, our attention is drawn to the range
of ministries enjoined upon each of the several person gifts
and we are encouraged to become more eclectic in our
appreciation of often competing counseling theories and
in our appropriation of their best insights. With Augustine
we are encouraged to recognize all truth as God's truth
and put it to kingdom service. And with a growing number of contemporaries in the field we are encouraged to
recognize that various counseling theories and approaches
may be as much complementary as they are competing
and therefore usable in Christian ministry.

A person-gift approach to Christian counseling, then,
might be diagrammed as it is in figure 8. That figure is
meant to convey two basic ideas. First, the various person
gifts can draw upon such counseling theories as may suit
their respective ministries and particular situations. (The
taxonomy of counseling theories is not to be thought of
as being all-inclusive. In fact, the discussion in this chapter may be interpreted to indicate that it may need rethinking and enlargement.) Second, the order in which the
person gifts are listed may parallel the probable magnitude

FIGURE 8 **The Person-Gift Approach of Relating Counseling
Theories to the Bible**

Biblical Person Gifts	Available Counseling Theories	Magnitude of Culture Distance Between Counselor and Counselee
Apostle (Missionary) Prophet Evangelist Pastor-Teacher Believer-Priest	Confrontational/nouthetic Conversational/interactional Confessional/relational	Greater Smaller

of culture distance between the respective person gift and his counselee(s). (Culture distance has to do with the degree of difference that exists between the cultures of the counselor and the counselee.) Obviously, that difference is greater in the case of missionaries who counsel people in foreign cultures than it is in the case of local believers who help their neighbors. It is arguable that the same difference would hold true—although to a lesser degree—in comparing the ministries of prophets and evangelists with that of local pastor-teachers.

Christian counseling, broadly considered, owes a singular debt to secular psychology and counseling theory. Christian theorists differ as to whether or not, or the extent to which, integration is possible. However, even Adams owes a great debt to his mentor, O. Hobart Mowrer, of the University of Illinois. The great majority of Christian theorists do attempt an integration, although with varying degrees of success.

Evangelical psychologists and counselors are characterized by definite distinctives, among them a commitment to an authoritative Bible. Even within the evangelical ranks, however, there is a somewhat bewildering variety of proposals as to what constitutes biblical counseling.

One defensible and fruitful way of viewing Christian counseling is to link it with the roles of Christ's person gifts to the church. When this is done all of the counseling-related ministries of the Bible—and any of the secular approaches and techniques that are not in conflict with Scripture—can be related to the special tasks of the various person gifts. Accordingly, and of primary importance to our present concern, cross-cultural or missionary counseling will be seen as presenting its own unique obstacles and opportunities for study and practice.

7

Counseling Approaches in the Non-Western World

One can say that men and women everywhere in the world are beset with problems—intellectual problems, physical problems, emotional problems, spiritual problems. But to say that is simply to utter a truism or even a tautology. After all, problems are inherent in humanness. Of course, peoples of non-Western cultures have their problems and difficulties, many of them similar to our own. But very likely they will characterize and categorize those problems differently. And they will go about solving them in culturally appropriate ways.

Consider, for example, the Malays. Specialists have studied indigenous understandings of mental problems and therapeutic approaches in that culture. They find that common difficulties include such things as brain strain from too much studying; being charmed; excessive religious preoccupation; possession by spirits (*hantu* or *gin*); the loss of one's spirit (*semangat*); mental stress; and incorrect behavior. Any or all of these may be attributed to supernatural causes. The spirits may occasion disorders such as brain impairment or poor blood condition which, in turn, lead to mental illness.[1] Obviously, the kind of helpers and the nature of the help which Malays will likely seek depends in large measure upon the way they perceive the problem at hand.

We will proceed by looking at some culturally defined problem areas in the non-Western world, some typical types of helpers and advisers, and common approaches taken to resolve these problems. Then we will examine in more detail some typical therapeutic and counseling approaches, focusing on Japan. Finally, we will note the attention being given to culture-oriented counseling among Christians.

Indigenous Etiological Orientations

As an indication of the differences in ways of viewing causative factors of human problems around the world, one need only refer to a classic study which plots primitive theories of disease causation. A generation ago, Forrest E. Clements plotted these theories by means of an extensive survey of ethnographic literature. Ultimately, he focused on five types of causes most frequently cited among non-Western peoples: soul loss, breach of taboo, disease sorcery, object intrusion, and spirit intrusion.[2] A more recent case study of the indigenous people of Saint Lawrence Island, Alaska, illustrates the various "causes" that can be subsumed under these five types.[3]

1. David Kinzie, Jin-inn Teoh, and Eng-seong Tan, "Native Healers in Malaysia," in *Culture-Bound Syndromes, Ethnopsychiatry, and Alternate Therapies,* ed. William P. Lebra, Mental Health Research in Asia and the Pacific series, vol. 4 (Honolulu: The University Press of Hawaii for the East-West Center, 1976), pp. 130–46.
2. Forrest E. Clements, "Primitive Concepts of Disease," *University of California Publications in American Archaeology and Ethnology* 32 (1932): 185–252, quoted in Jane Murphy, "Psychotherapeutic Aspects of Shamanism on St. Lawrence Island, Alaska," in *Magic, Faith, and Healing: Studies in Primitive Psychiatry Today,* ed. Ari Kiev (New York: Free Press, 1964), p. 61.
3. See Murphy, "Psychotherapeutic Aspects of Shamanism," in *Magic, Faith, and Healing,* pp. 61–69.

Soul Loss. Saint Lawrence Island Eskimo informants explained the local belief that when a person sleeps or sneezes or is frightened, especially at night, his soul wanders away from his body. At these times the soul may be captured by evil spirits that abound in the universe. Until the soul is found and returned to the body the person remains ill.

Breach of Taboo. Such acts as incest, sexual perversion, and masturbation are widely considered to be taboo among Saint Lawrence Islanders. To break such taboos is to invite disease and perhaps insanity. In fact, the consequences may be visited not only upon the offender but also upon the family, the community, and even progeny to the seventh generation. Taboo-breaking is therefore a community concern. Thus, offenses of this kind that involve other people and are more or less public, such as sexual perversion or violation of the hunting code (e.g., killing a whale first sighted by someone else), are of greatest import.

Disease Sorcery. A clear distinction is made between the sorcerer who utilizes black magic and the shaman who employs "healing magic." Traditionally, Saint Lawrence Island Eskimos have believed that a sorcerer (or witch) has the power to effect all kinds of illnesses. This evil power is exercised through a variety of formulas, prayers, rituals, and mechanisms. For example, the sorcerer might persuade someone to secure some hair or a nail paring or a piece of clothing of his intended victim. By boiling these items in an animal skull he can bewitch the victim. Only by employing the aid of a shaman who is able to identify the sorcerer, discover the kind of black magic that has been used, and resort to the right kind of countermagic can the effects be nullified.

Object Intrusion. Still another source of disease is the intrusion of some foreign object into the body of the victim. These objects may be anything from "small stones" to "sticks" to "worm-like things." To extract them, shamans suck the appropriate part of the anatomy, hold seances, and perform "operations" in dimly lighted rooms, after which the offending object is sometimes "eaten" by the shaman or passed around to those present as evidence of its extraction.

Spirit Intrusion. Finally, Saint Lawrence Islanders have long believed that a foreign spirit can invade a person's body. In many primitive cultures this belief has two aspects. First, in some cultures (including Eskimo cultures), it is thought that the spirit must be identified before exorcism can be employed. More common and well developed in Saint Lawrence culture, however, is a second aspect of this belief in spirit intrusion. It is that the ghost of a recently deceased relative might hover about and cause the sickness of a living relative, especially when the living relative may be linked with the death by having broken a taboo. The ghost of the deceased is especially powerful during the period of mourning. Subsequently its power gradually wanes. One way of counteracting this sort of spirit intrusion is to name a newborn child after the deceased. This is tantamount to reincarnation and means that the deceased is once again a member of the human community.

Although this summary focuses primarily on one culture and world view, it reflects a much wider incidence and significance. Christian workers will encounter similar beliefs and practices among primitive peoples around the world—and their vestiges among many peoples with more developed cultures.

Types of Helpers, Healers, and Advisers in the Non-Western World

In the society of the Saint Lawrence Island Eskimos, the resort to shamans was almost universal. In the wider context of cultures and problems with which cross-cultural workers must concern themselves, help may be forthcoming through a wide variety of agents. Wise men, tribal elders, clan heads, religious leaders, family heads, governmental authorities, entrepreneurs, innovators—numerous types of leaders and agents of change are involved in resolving human ills and charting the future course of societies and their members.

"Nonspecialist" Helpers

Problem-solving activities and roles tend to be less specialized and discrete in the non-Western world than they are in the Western world. In his informative study, *A History of the Cure of Souls*, J. T. McNeill notes that the separation of healing functions from their religious and philosophical roots and their conversion into scientific activities are comparatively recent Western developments.[4] (He notes also that theological and other disputations in Western churches have obscured the fact that the churches' fundamental task is the "curing of souls.") Individuals and families in difficulty are less likely to seek out a "professional counselor" (as Westerners use that designation). In many if not most cultures, it is unlikely that such an individual could be found. The idea that formal education rather than broad experience qualifies one to be a counselor seems to be largely a Western notion. But even where professionals might be available, to seek one out may entail a degree of shame. In a personal conversation Mrs. Saphir Athyal of the Union Biblical Seminary in India informed the author that, for the present at least, most Indians feel that to resort to a professional counselor is tantamount to an admission that one is "sick in the head."

"Lay persons," especially heads of families and extended families, play a much larger role in helping and guiding in non-Western cultures than in Western culture.

---

4. J. T. McNeill, *A History of the Cure of Souls* (New York: Harper and Row, 1965), quoted in Julian Wohl, "Intercultural Psychotherapy: Issues, Questions, and Reflections," in *Counseling across Cultures*, ed. Paul P. Pederson, et al., rev. ed. (Honolulu: The University Press of Hawaii for the East-West Center, 1981), pp. 140–41.

Patriarchs, matriarchs, grandparents, and parents all are concerned that younger members will fit into the family and larger society in a positive and productive manner. With that end in view, the family is organized vertically and hierarchically rather than horizontally and in an egalitarian fashion. Decisions are usually made by the group rather than by the individual. In the Philippines, for example, even the civil code says that grandparents shall be consulted by all members of the family on all important questions.

One would be correct in inferring from the foregoing that group counseling and decision-making play a much larger role in non-Western cultures than has usually been the case in Western cultures and especially the United States. The recent interest in group support systems in the United States has long been reflected in non-Western societies.

"Specialist" Helpers

All societies have specialists who have the socially sanctioned role of healers. Because of the religious orientation of these healers, McNeill refers to them as a "spiritual elite."[5] Because they "stand between" persons and powers, P. Meadows refers to them as a "mediatorial elite."[6] Because these specialists constitute the non-Western counterparts to Christian psychiatrists, counselors, and pastors in the West, we will concentrate on them and their techniques in the remainder of this chapter.

Anthropologists distinguish two polar types of spiritual "helper leaders"—shamans and priests. They often work side by side in a complementary relationship. At other times they are in competition. Shamans characteristically are charismatic leaders who claim to have been in contact with the supernatural. By virtue of that contact they have the power to perform supernatural feats. They can also

5. McNeill, *A History of the Cure of Souls*, p. 330.
6. P. Meadows, "The Cure of Souls and the Winds of Change," *Psychoanalytic Review* 55, no. 3 (1968): 497.

deliver messages from the gods and ancestors in prophet-like fashion. The priest derives his authority from institutionalized religion rather than from his own charisma or personal contact with supernatural beings. He learns and passes on traditional beliefs and rituals. He speaks to the gods and spirits on behalf of the people and represents and leads them in appropriate rituals and rites.

In and between these two polar types are to be found healers and helpers such as the *bomoh* in Malaysia, the *babylan* in the Philippines, the *dang-ki* in Taiwan, and many others. When Western physicians are also present, the local people are often presented with quite an array of specialists to whom they might resort when confronted with psychological and other problems.

Nancy E. Waxler notes, for example, that Sinhalese villagers in Ceylon (Sri Lanka) currently recognize at least seven different types of agents to whom they might resort.[7] First, there is the Western doctor who is probably British and who uses drugs and shock therapy but seldom psychotherapy. Second, there is the ayurvedic physician or *vederala*, whose approach has an Indian orientation. He will likely explain mental illness as an imbalance caused by such factors as extreme climate, poor diet, and inappropriate lifestyle, and will prescribe an irritant to be put in the nostrils, an herbal concoction to be ingested, an oil to be rubbed on the head, or a regimen of baths. Third, an astrologer may be consulted in order to discover the bad influence of the planets, how long the bad influence will last, and what to do by way of treatment. Fourth, the soothsayer (*sastarakaraya*) makes diagnoses and prognoses by peering into a flame, globe, or bottle of oil. Fifth, an exorcist or *kattadiya* (often a fellow villager who practices this profession along with another job) may be consulted if it is felt that the patient is possessed by demons

---

7. Nancy E. Waxler, "Social Change and Psychiatric Illness in Ceylon: Traditional and Modern Concepts of Disease and Treatment," in *Culture-Bound Syndromes*, pp. 224–25.

or ghosts. Sixth, the *kapurala* (a priest in the Hindu tradition) is also available. If the problem is not serious, a family will promise to present gifts to the temple to assure the kapurala's prayers. If the problem is more serious, ritual threats may be made to the gods and the patient may be recipient of a symbolic beating by the priest. Seventh, if the suffering is explained in terms of sinful behavior in the present life or bad karma in a past life, a Buddhist priest may be given alms and asked to carry out ritual readings of holy verses or otherwise ward off demons and attain the security of the patient or his family. In lieu of engaging the services of a Buddhist priest, the family may ask one of its members or a neighbor to chant the appropriate verses.

Waxler offers this explanation:

> The range of theories of causation—some supernatural, some physical, and some social—is apparent in the range of treatment agents. Treatments are designed to deal, for example, with demon possession, too much bile in the system, and bad living. However, it would be a mistake to think that each treatment agent deals with only one type of causation; in practice there is considerable overlap. For example, the ayurvedic physician whose patients we studied prescribes both herbal concoctions and charmed coconuts, and attributes illness to both humoral imbalance and witchcraft. The fact that treatment agents do not adhere strictly to one ideological theory, when attempting to cure, hints that families of patients, as well, may not necessarily link, in a logical way, their beliefs about the cause of the illness with the treatments they select. Nevertheless, the culture does provide a wide variety of beliefs about the cause of mental illness as well as a wide range of possible treatments.[8]

This description and analysis forcefully alerts us to the fact that the Christian worker who ministers interculturally must be prepared for a wide variety of perceptions

8. Ibid., p. 225.

about his or her role and function. In the initial stages of any relationship at least, that role and function will in a significant sense be prescribed by the receptor society. On the positive side, this realization may jolt the Christian worker out of some mistaken preconceptions of Western culture and force him into a more biblical world view where the spirit world is more immediate and powerful. On the negative side, he may well be frustrated in his attempt to overcome local expectations as to his role and purpose.

One can anticipate the development of various surrogate support systems, although this depends upon the complexity of a society. Japan is a case in point. As we shall see, in spite of the continuation and resilience of traditional helper roles and institutions, modern Japan has numerous "helping" individuals and groups that are reminiscent of counterparts in the Western nations. The field of medicine has been expanded to include psychiatry. Moreover, a medical doctor not trained in psychology and psychiatry may nevertheless organize a group of sufferers (of diabetes, for example) in which members will benefit by his direction and by mutual helpfulness. Corporations normally organize their employees in such a way that specialists can aid them in everything from planning vacations to finding a mate. The so-called new religions provide guidance for every sphere of their members' lives. Christian churches seldom are so large that pastors cannot be involved with the day-to-day affairs of members. In all of this helping organization and activity one can discern the authority and caring patterns of the traditional family on the one hand, and a response to the stresses and strains of a highly technological society on the other.

Counseling and Therapeutic Approaches in the Non-Western World

Various scholars have attempted comparisons of Western and non-Western approaches to counseling and therapy. Not surprisingly, they come to somewhat different conclusions.

E. Fuller Torrey believes that psychiatrists and folk therapists perform basically the same functions in their respective cultures and that both get similar results in about the same ways. He says that the essence of psychotherapy is communication, which depends not only upon a shared language but also upon a shared world view. For Torrey there are four components of all psychotherapy: a world view that is common to healer and sufferer; the personal qualities of the therapist, which allow for a close personal relationship between therapist and sufferer; an expectation on the part of the patient that he will be helped; and therapeutic techniques. He insists that techniques, whether they be physical (drugs or shock treatment), psychosocial (confession, suggestion, hypnosis, psychoanalytic techniques, or conditioning), or group and milieu therapies, are essentially the same all around the world. He does concede, however, that a number of techniques are used in the non-Western world which are not used much in the West; that the same technique may be used, although for different reasons; and that the goals of therapy vary with the culture.[9]

Most researchers are less radical than Torrey in emphasizing cross-cultural commonalities. After making a thorough study of a schizophrenic girl and her treatment by a shaman in the Philippines, George M. Guthrie and David L. Szanton take exception. They note that three of Torrey's four components were operative in the case but that there was little that distinguished the shaman's personality when it came to genuineness, empathy, or warmth.[10]

Again, in his examination of the literature on psychotherapeutic procedures used around the world, Raymond

9. E. Fuller Torrey, *The Mind Game: Witch Doctors and Psychiatrists* (New York: Emerson Hall, 1972).

10. George M. Guthrie and David L. Szanton, "Folk Diagnosis and Treatment of Schizophrenia: Bargaining with the Spirits in the Philippines," in *Culture-Bound Syndromes*, pp. 161–62.

Prince examines the widespread use of indigenous mechanisms such as sleep, social isolation, and altered states of consciousness (dreams, mystic states, dissociation states) in psychotherapy.[11] However, as he moves in his considerations from America to Africa to Asia it is apparent that he believes that the ways in which these mechanisms are introduced and employed constitute major differences between cultures.

Finally, Wen-Shing Tseng of the department of neuropsychiatry in the School of Medicine at the National Taiwan University Hospital in Taipei emphasizes both commonalities and differences. He says that at first glance, the practices of folk therapy in Taiwan and of modern psychotherapy may seem to be very different and even unrelated. However, he feels that if psychotherapy is defined in very broad terms there are certain common elements. First, there is a healer and a sufferer and a process of psychological interaction between them. Second, the healer always interprets the cause of the problems for the client, whether it be interference by supernatural powers, incompatibility with nature's principles, the physical predisposition of the client, or intrapsychic conflicts. Third, the healer always prescribes something that the client should do in order to cope with his problems: perform a magic ceremony, change his environment, reorient relations with others, or change his value system about himself and the world.[12] At the same time, Tseng offers advice that underscores cultural differences.

> It is very important to study further how people handle their problems in ways which are provided for and channeled by their culture. From this point of view, the study of folk psychotherapy will certainly help us learn more about how the problems of life have been traditionally per-

11. Raymond Prince, "Variations in Psychotherapeutic Procedures," in *Handbook of Cross-Cultural Psychology: Perspectives*, gen. ed. Harry C. Triandis, 6 vols. (Boston: Allyn and Bacon, 1980–83), vol. 6, ed. Harry C. Triandis and Juris G. Draguns (1980), pp. 291–349.

12. Wen-Shing Tseng, "Folk Psychotherapy in Taiwan," in *Culture-Bound Syndromes*, p. 174.

ceived and interpreted by the local people and what coping strategies have been specified by the culture. Thus, we can learn how to modify modern psychotherapy in culture-relevant ways, so that treatment will be more effective.[13]

It seems justifiable to conclude that universal characteristics in cross-cultural counseling and therapy tend to be rather general in nature. When one considers specifics, one must be prepared for a wide variety of understandings and approaches. For example, in the study of the Saint Lawrence Islanders, we discover that the shaman employs a wide variety of culture-related "cures" (depending on the particular case). In case of soul loss, he often sends his "spirit familiar" to search for the lost soul and return it to the patient. In the case of taboo-breaking, he often prescribes public confession and expiation. And, as we have seen, in the cases of object intrusion and spirit intrusion he may resort to an "operation" or prescribe giving the name of the deceased to a newborn child.

Undoubtedly some of the more bizarre aspects of therapeutic advice and techniques in traditional Saint Lawrence society have undergone change or are gradually disappearing as an effect of increased intercultural contact. However, all cross-cultural counselors—and particularly missionaries working in cultures very diverse from their own—should be prepared to encounter important differences. These differences will not always be as apparent as some of those that have been described. They may be very subtle. But they will be no less significant for their subtlety. And to illustrate this we next study one of the most developed nations in the non-Western world—Japan.

Some Approaches to Counseling Therapy in Contemporary Japan

In spite of the tight-knit family structure and communal orientation that are so pervasive in Japanese soci-

13. Ibid., p. 165.

ety, statistics and experience make it clear that the pressures associated with coping and competing in modern Japan have occasioned an unusually high incidence of stress and frustration, psychological and spiritual disorientation, nervous breakdowns, and even suicides. Although its population is about half that of the United States, Japan has twice as many psychiatric patients in its hospitals.[14] There are various reasons for this besides the obvious one. Because the Japanese attach a stigma to emotional and mental disorders, those who need help are less reluctant to undergo treatment in a hospital than in their communities. Also, National Health Insurance offers little assistance to those who are not hospitalized. Nevertheless, because of the high incidence of psychological breakdowns, the persistence of cultural ways and values, and the familiarity with Western ways of approaching these problems, Japan provides us with some case studies that prove to be especially instructive in the present context.

Naikan Therapy

Naikan therapy is a form of guided introspection directed toward producing change in attitude and personality. Developed in the 1940s by Inobu Yoshimoto, it is closely related in philosophy and world view to the Jodo-Shin sect of Buddhism, one of Japan's most popular Buddhist groups. The therapy is based on the premise that people are basically selfish and guilty, yet are all the while favored with unmeasured benevolence from others. By focusing on all the kindness he has received and his own reactions toward those who bestowed it, the patient comes to grips with his own guilt and selfishness. He is then encouraged to adopt new patterns of behavior toward oth-

14. Joe Yamamoto, "An Asian View of the Future of Cultural Psychiatry," in *Current Perspectives in Cultural Psychiatry*, ed. Edward F. Foulks et al. (New York: Spectrum Publications, 1977), pp. 210–11.

ers. (Note that the emphasis on guilt seems to be somewhat out of keeping with the "shame orientation" that generally characterizes Japan. See chapter 9.)

The actual therapy consists of seven consecutive days of concentrated reflection from 5:30 A.M. to 9:00 P.M. each day. The patient, who voluntarily begins therapy, sits in a quiet, isolated corner, alone and free from distractions. He is guided and supervised by the Naikan counselor for about five minutes every one and one-half hours. The counselor makes certain that the patient is following the prescribed course of reflection and is thinking concerning the assigned topics. The patient is expected to examine himself along these lines: to recollect and examine memories of the care and benevolence received from a particular person (usually beginning with a parent) at a particular time in life; to recollect and examine memories of his response to his benefactor; and to recollect and examine the troubles and worries he has caused that benefactor. This cycle of self-examination is repeated again and again for different relationships and at different depths throughout the period of therapy.

The role of the counselor in Naikan therapy is to direct the counselee toward meaningful self-examination. He instructs the counselee in the procedure and lays down and enforces the ground rules by directives and persuasion. The brief interactions every hour and a half are designed to ensure that the patient has followed the cycle of introspection; to keep him from making excuses or rationalizations or from becoming aggressive toward others; and to lead him to vigorous and severe self-examination. The counselor is more concerned with procedure than with the content of the interactions or with the counselor-patient relationship. Direct contact with the patient is authoritarian, intensive, and highly directive. The therapy does not rely on empathy between counselor and patient. The counselor's goal is not to understand the patient, but to direct the patient into understanding himself.

Because the Naikan environment is both physically and emotionally difficult, some obstacles must be overcome. Many patients do not find it easy to concentrate, while others react negatively to the physical isolation and confinement. It usually takes two or three days to adjust to the new situation. Resistance to reviewing the past and accepting personal guilt (shame?) is often in evidence. But as the process goes on, introspection becomes more and more meaningful. Insights into personal faults and the love for others emerge abruptly or gradually, leading the patient to self-criticism and repentance.

The most common outcome of successful Naikan therapy is the improvement of the patient's interpersonal relationships as he rekindles gratitude for others, increases in sympathetic and empathetic regard for others, and realizes his own personal responsibility for his social roles. His personal identity is further established and security, confidence, and self-disclosure are achieved. Yet these feelings and resolves sometimes fade after therapy is concluded and the patient returns to the old environment.[15]

Morita Therapy

Morita therapy was developed in the early 1920s by Shoma Morita, a Japanese psychiatrist and professor. Morita decided to study psychotherapy as a graduate student after overcoming some serious problems of his own. He worked for almost twenty years with a variety of European methods, learning by trial and error and gradually incorporating more and more traditional Japanese insights and methods into his practice. Morita therapy evolved as he sifted through the various methodologies, as the nature of neurotic disturbance became better understood, and as he rediscovered the therapeutic value of traditional and indigenous ideas in psychotherapy.

15. Abstracted from Takao Murase, "Naikan Therapy," in *Culture-Bound Syndromes*, pp. 259–69.

Morita focused on a form of neurosis called *shinkeish-itsu* (nervousness or nervous temperament), a state characterized by chronic or constitutional neurosthenia, obsessive-ruminative states, and anxiety neurosis. According to Morita, this condition arises from the "hypochondriacal temperament" whereby a person feels that normal physiological or mental functionings are due to some serious disease or weakness. This hypochondriacal tendency reveals itself in hypersensitivity, excessive introspection, constant worry about bodily and mental conditions, perfectionism and idealism, and recurring worries and anxieties. Morita believed that these neuroses are merely negative extremes of a normal, universal human function. However, in some persons this function has become imbalanced and isolated from the whole united functioning of the person. The normal drive, existing to a greater or lesser degree in everyone, is the "desire to live." This desire to live is expressed negatively as the hypochondriacal tendency. Shinkeishitsu patients are out of balance because they interpret *normal* mental and bodily conditions as being abnormal or harmful, and then seek to exercise personal control over those conditions. This in turn produces anxiety and aggravates conditions all the more.

As Morita tried many different therapeutic methods in developing a "mature therapy" for shinkeishitsu, he developed several ideas that he incorporated in his treatment plan. They include the following:

The favorable influence of complete physical rest on the patient's mental state.

The value of occupational therapy, due to the shinkeishitsu patient's strong desire to live and craving for activity.

The use of a "life-normalization" method by which intellectual and manual activity is imposed on the patient according to a regulated timetable, yet without strict rules and detailed regulations.

The detrimental influence of trying to use methods of rational persuasion to help the patient understand and deal with his problem. These Morita held to be anxiety-producing. It is better simply to allow the patient's thinking to run its course.

The primary aim is transformation of experience rather than a verbal and logical explanation of the patient's psychological mechanism and experience. This is accomplished by guiding the patient to personal insight through positive experiences by the use of diaries, group meetings, and outpatient treatment.

The "mature therapy" that Morita eventually developed consists of four phases, usually beginning in a hospital setting but continuing as outpatient therapy. The first phase consists of complete bed rest, during which time the patient is separated from unnecessary paraphernalia and from his regular way of life. During this time of rest the patient is able to reflect on his condition, but more importantly, he becomes desirous of stimulation and activity. He already possesses a strong desire to live, and during rest this is built up in order that it might be channeled into constructive activities during the next three phases of therapy. These three phases are not really distinct, but consist of light work and activity which gradually become more and more complicated and constructive. The patient is given few specific instructions for this activity, but is pointed in a general direction and told to look for work himself. Throughout the therapy the patient is expected to keep a diary, which is given to the therapist every morning so the therapist can monitor his patient's progress. The therapist's counsel is usually communicated to the patient only through informal encounters during work therapy or at larger group meetings. The work and the diary are designed to give the patient positive and constructive outlets for his desire to live, instead of allowing it to be expressed aberrantly in hypochondria. Gradually he learns that he can live constructively in existing conditions. In Buddhist terms we might refer to this as right mindfulness.

In more specific terms the aims of Morita therapy can be enumerated:

> to make the patient realize that his symptoms are normal and tolerable, and that it is his interpretation of them that is abnormal or pathological;
>
> to destroy the patient's hypochondriacal tendency so that the desire to live, which is the active force behind the neurosis, can be utilized in a proper and constructive way;
>
> to free the patient from the attempt to get rid of, or change, perfectly normal mental or physical conditions;
>
> to help the patient accept conditions as they are.[16]

Rissho Kosei-kai Hoza

The Rissho Kosei-kai is a popular lay-oriented Buddhist sect in Japan that employs the *hoza* or group-counseling method as a major feature of its overall program.[17] The hoza group consists of approximately ten to fifteen people and includes a group leader who directs the counseling process. Sitting on the floor in a tight circle, members of the group engage in interchange and dialogue focused on the needs and problems of individuals in the group. It is, in a sense, individual counseling in a group setting, with the leader discussing a problem with one particular individual as the other members of the group offer their sym-

16. Abstracted from Kyoichi Kondo, "The Origin of Morita Therapy," in *Culture-Bound Syndromes*, pp. 250–58.

17. For more information about Rissho Kosei-kai hoza, refer to Kenneth J. Dale, *Circle of Harmony: A Case Study in Popular Japanese Buddhism with Implications for Christian Mission* (Pasadena, Calif.: William Carey Library; Tokyo: Seibunsha, 1975).

pathy, encouragement, and advice. (Note the similarity to some of the group-therapy approaches and Christian people-helping discussed previously.)

Leaders follow a basically uniform process in handling personal problems, whether physical, spiritual, economic, or interrelational. Because the ideology of Rissho Kosei-kai is based on fundamental Buddhism, the goal of the hoza leader is to determine the spiritual or moral cause of the person's suffering and teach him how to transform his wickedness into proper personal discipline or good deeds that will merit family and society approval and transform his suffering into peace.[18] Hoza sessions are held at the Rissho Kosei-kai headquarters in Tokyo on a daily basis and involve thousands of participants in scores of groups. The leaders are all laymen who have no training in counseling techniques or principles as we know them in the West. The focus of the groups is not primarily on personality change as such, but on the solution of personal problems through a religious change of heart.[19]

Before we proceed to an examination of the dynamics of hoza group counseling, let us study two typical exchanges in actual hoza sessions. The first case concerns Mrs. B, whose relationship with her husband is causing serious concern. (L is the group leader and other members are designated by appropriate letters of the alphabet.)

> Mrs. B: I have so many problems at home. My husband and I don't get along well. He doesn't treat me with consideration at all. I also have trouble with the lady who lives below us. She is complaining all the time, and criticizing me. Why are people so hard to get along with anyway? Why can't I have a good husband and good neighbors like other people have?
>
> L: (To the group) How do you folks think Mrs. B

18. *Rissho Kosei-kai* (Tokyo: Kosei Publishing, 1966), pp. 8ff.
19. Dale, *Circle of Harmony*, p. 76.

looks? Does she look like a happy person or a gloomy person?

Mrs. C: To be quite frank, Mrs. B has a rather sour look on her face.

Mrs. B: That's no help to hear that! My husband always tells me I look sad, but he wishes I had a smiling face. But how can I look happy when he's so mean to me!

L: But you see, your husband has simply been mirroring your attitude toward him. If you don't treat him smilingly and tenderly, you can't expect him to treat you with consideration either.

Mrs. D: Yes, that is right! The process has to start with you. Don't blame your husband for the trouble; look to yourself first.

Mrs. B: Maybe you're right. I haven't treated my husband very well.

L: Now you're coming to see the truth of the Law, Mrs. B. Change your mind right now, and repent of this critical attitude you've had toward others. Begin to be a brighter person yourself from now on!

Mrs. B: (In tears) I see now that I haven't been a good wife or neighbor. I'll try to do better from now on.

L: This is a great day in your life, Mrs. B! This has been a wonderful experience for you and for all of us here in this *hoza* today! You've understood for the first time that to change a bad situation to a good one, you have to start with yourself.[20]

The second case concerns another Mrs. B who is experiencing a somewhat different problem with her husband!

Mrs. B: My two children both have aches and pains in their legs. And the other day one of them got a very bad nosebleed. What is wrong with them?

---

20. Ibid., pp. 87–88.

L: The cause of this condition is lustful thinking. Trouble in the legs always points to a problem of sexual lustfulness. You probably have a problem with this, don't you?

Mrs. B: (With embarrassment) Yes, I do. I am a person of very strong passions, but my husband is even more that way. We've had so much trouble between us. (She tells the story of her marriage.) But today my husband is at a Rissho Kosei-kai retreat seeking spiritual help.

L: Oh, how obvious the nature of your trouble is! A wife should be the first one to apologize and repent, but here we have the opposite happening. Your husband has gone to the spiritual retreat before you have. He is the first to repent. But his religious exercises won't do him any good if you don't humble yourself before him right away. Go meet him today when they return from the retreat, and immediately apologize to him and do everything you can for him from now on.

Mrs. B: (Weeping) Oh yes, I will surely do that! I see now where I have been wrong.

(Everyone joined in telling Mrs. B that she must be more meek, and that today offers an especially crucial opportunity for their marital life to take a turn for the better, and that the Buddha has prepared the way for a new life in their family.)[21]

Analyzing the hoza, Kenneth J. Dale notes the profound differences between this approach and group-counseling approaches in the West, which he characterizes as follows: all group members have a common problem; the counselor functions from within the group as a resource person; a permissive atmosphere allows for free expression; and interaction and mutual help among members are expected.[22]

21. Ibid., p. 88.
22. Ibid., p. 89.

Dale analyzes the effectiveness of the hoza in relation to five factors—environment, rapport, acceptance, expression, and insight.

Environment[23] includes "the various physical and situational factors which together constitute the atmosphere in which *hoza* takes place,"[24] and assumes that such factors significantly effect the therapeutic efficacy of the group. Positive environmental aspects include the size of the group, which is usually kept to small-group size and is divided when it becomes too large; the close, yet comfortable, seating arrangement; and the piling of personal items such as purses and bags within the center of the circle. The group size, although it fluctuates greatly during the course of a session, allows for some intimacy and close "inter-cooperation." The seating arrangement also fosters intimacy, makes discussion easier, and enhances an atmosphere of harmony, unity, and warm mutuality. The pile of belongings frees the individual from concern over his or her own possessions, while creating a homey, earthy feel in the otherwise empty floor space. Negative environmental factors include the constant rumble of noise from neighboring groups, the children wandering about freely in the hoza hall, and official business constantly being conducted over a loudspeaker and by interrupting clerks. These negative factors, however, are of less concern than would be the case in the United States.

Rapport[25] is "the affective interaction or relationship between counselor and counselee, or among the members of a counseling group."[26] Concerned involvement and interaction seem to be the norm among members of most hoza groups. Several members of the group usually participate helpfully in solving the problems of others by relating similar experiences or by giving sympathy, support,

23. Ibid., pp. 77–79.
24. Ibid., p. 77.
25. Ibid., pp. 79–81.
26. Ibid., p. 79.

and advice. At the same time the constantly fluctuating membership of a particular group, both from day to day and even in a single session, keeps the members from getting to know one another intimately. Most people would know only two or three other members in their hoza on any given day.

Acceptance[27] "is closely related to rapport, but it touches a deeper level of mutual respect and support as well as the level of interpersonal warmth.[28] Again the hoza has both positive and negative aspects. There is no outright rejection of anyone who attends hoza; everyone is warmly welcomed and made to feel at home. Anyone can speak whenever he wishes. Often the sessions are characterized by laughter and a sense of warmth and fellowship between participants. The atmosphere can be very supportive to those with problems. But, on the other hand, the groups can lack cohesiveness, with little eye contact or overt signs of warmth or affection. To some extent this is dependent upon the hoza leaders, many of whom offer stereotyped answers without listening carefully or taking time and effort to understand the problem being expressed.

Expression[29] is usually considered to be of vital importance in determining the therapeutic value of any kind of counseling. Here, again, Dale finds positive and negative aspects in hoza. In many cases the group leader encourages uninhibited expression, which leads to the group member genuinely pouring out the details of his or her situation in a cathartic unburdening of emotional problems. The hoza at its best does offer a therapeutic experience because it gives participants the opportunity to freely unburden themselves of their emotional weights through verbal expression. But there are also many cases where free expression is clearly inhibited by an overly aggressive or

27. Ibid., pp. 81–82.
28. Ibid., p. 81.
29. Ibid., pp. 83–86.

insensitive leader. These negative situations may involve domination of the conversation by an overly authoritative leader, a blatant disregard for the feelings of the participants involved, premature advice-giving which quenches further expression, or insensitivity to the real concerns of the counselee. The leader may be quick to give a predetermined answer as a panacea for any situation, in which case true expression by the concerned individual at a deep level is not necessary.

Insight[30] is defined by Dale as "a new and deeper perception of one's self and one's situation, which enables the individual to work toward the solution of his problem."[31] This factor is very difficult to evaluate because it is not easily recognized or measured by external observation, especially in Japanese culture where "what lies behind the polite and proper expressions of gratitude for help received is very difficult to assess."[32] But there are on occasion obvious cases of genuine insight as revealed by the deep-level response of the participants.

Christian Counseling in the Non-Western World

As we would expect, pastoral and other types of Christian counseling have been exported from the schools and churches of the West to those of the non-Western world. Perhaps sometime in the future we will have a more complete inventory of the counseling programs, approaches, and personnel of the non-Western world. What we do know is that where Western models are employed significant modifications are usually required.

After spending a year as clinical director of the Churches' Counseling Service in Singapore, Charles A. Raher indicated that the "Rogers-with-a-dash-of-Freud" approach

30. Ibid., pp. 86–88.
31. Ibid., pp. 86–87.
32. Ibid., p. 87.

simply did not work because of too little experience in "caring" in that society, insufficient motivation on the part of counselees, and the influence of the authoritarian orientation of Asian societies. Interestingly enough, he thinks that another American model—that of Howard J. Clinebell, Jr.—is more useful in Singapore.[33]

A seminary professor in Thailand notes the cultural overhang in Thai theological training that results from a variety of factors. First, the Thai have a very different concept of human nature and community. Second, the traditional way of facing problems in Thai society is to withdraw and find an "inner core of peace." Third, the Buddhist priest is not related to people in the way that pastors are related to their congregations in the West. Because of these and other factors he finds it difficult to sustain the kind of pastoral education that makes a significant place for counseling.[34]

Even in Australia—geographically Asian but culturally Western in large measure—difficulties growing out of the philosophy of "keeping a stiff upper lip" and other cultural factors have resulted in a shortage of "pastoral theologians."[35]

Somewhat more encouraging is a report from Philemon Y. W. Choi, founder and director of the Breakthrough Counseling Centre in Hong Kong. The center was founded in 1975 and since that time has expanded until, in 1981, it had three administrators, six professional counselors, fifty volunteers in paraprofessional training, and preventive as well as therapeutic counseling programs. According to Choi, most of the clients are between eighteen and thirty years old.

33. Graeme M. Griffin, "Pastoral Theology and Pastoral Care Overseas," in *The New Shape of Pastoral Theology: Essays in Honor of Seward Hiltner,* ed. William B. Oglesby, Jr. (Nashville: Abingdon, 1969), p. 56.

34. Ibid.

35. Ibid., pp. 56–57.

The majority of counseling problems involve interpersonal relationships. Other problems involve studies, vacations, Christian faith, and psychological disturbances. A typical case is an eighteen-year-old student who becomes more and more alienated from his family and friends. Struggling with loneliness and depression, he seeks emotional support and meaning in life. He has to learn social skills to rebuild relationships. He needs to rediscover purpose in life. In treatment we helped him solve his immediate problems while at the same time we guided him to rebuild his relationships with God and with other human beings.[36]

Most missionaries with experience in Asia will identify immediately with Choi's statement and with his description of a typical client. They have been dealing with this type of young person and with these kinds of problems for years. What is different is the counseling center itself, the training of counselors, and the more exclusive focus on various kinds of counseling. It is also of interest to note that Choi feels that as counseling gains greater acceptance in Hong Kong society the range of ages and problems handled will expand significantly.[37]

A somewhat similar but theologically and ecclesiastically broader counseling center has been set up in Nairobi, Kenya. The Amani Counselling Center is sponsored by the Amani Counselling Society, whose membership is open to all who are interested. The day-to-day operation is supervised by an executive committee; policy is formed by an advising committee made up of prominent people; and counseling is supervised by committee composed of counselors and medical people. Voluntary contributions and fees (adjusted according to income) support the Center.

In answer to the question *What is counseling?* Amani materials reply, "Counselling is an opportunity to talk

---

36. "Counseling Centre in Hong Kong," *Asian Theological News* 7 (January-March 1981): 18.
37. Ibid.

over your special need in depth with another person trained to understand and help. Counselling can help you find new ways to handle your problem, can provide encouragement, support and fresh ideas in a confidential atmosphere."[38]

The center also sponsors seminars. Those offered in 1983 included seminars on alcoholism, marital and sexual problems, traditional healing, family planning, and mental illness.[39]

Across the African continent in Nigeria a Christian organization called Bethani Fellowship Resources is also sponsoring a significant counseling program.[40] This organization projects an extensive program, which includes such ministries as writers' workshops, library services, the development of talents and spiritual gifts in Christians, and much more. But at the heart of the program is an extensive ministry of care and counseling, including growth groups, counseling concerning "personal and interpersonal issues," vocational guidance, marriage and family counseling, child counseling, stress management and relaxation therapy, and psychotherapy.

Undoubtedly a significant although inadequate number of counseling endeavors exist within Christian communions in the non-Western world. As counselors gain experience and as their materials gain a place in international literature, all of us will be increasingly benefited.

Much more research remains to be done with regard to Christian counseling programs and approaches in the non-Western world. In the process it will not be to the credit of Christian scholars and practitioners if they are less sensitive to considerations of culture than are their secular counterparts. By the same token, care must be exercised

38. From a brochure published by the Amani Counselling Centre.
39. From an announcement distributed by the Amani Counselling Centre.
40. Letter from Joe S. Udoukpong, Bethani Fellowship Resources, to Timothy M. Warner, 29 July 1983.

lest Western patterns and approaches be uncritically exported to the non-Western world and lest the ministries of churches be preempted rather than complemented by auxiliary organizations.

PART 3

A Theory of Christian Cross-Cultural Counseling

8

"Like All Other Men"
The Search for Human Universals

The Christian counselor must be prepared to examine his theoretical understandings before he proceeds to diagnose the problems of counselees and aid in their resolution. Only when he is faithful to God and his Word in this twofold task can his counseling be termed *Christian*. Being a Christian in and of itself does not mean that the counselor's theory and practice are Christian. Then, to the extent that the Christian counselor actually directs counselees to the right solutions to their problems and points the way to meaningful change, his counseling may also be termed *effective*.

Of course, the foregoing holds true for Christian cross-cultural counselors as well. By now it should be apparent, however, that it is significantly more difficult for the cross-cultural counselor to counsel Christianly and effectively. In addition to evaluating the theories and approaches germane to his own cultural background and training, he also has the burden of evaluating counseling approaches indigenous to the counselee's culture. Moreover, when work-

145

ing with counselees who are culturally different, he must attempt to analyze their problems and propose solutions with reference to their cultural understandings and values. To be both Christian and effective in the face of such a challenge would seem to be an accomplishment of the order of scaling Mount Everest. From a human point of view we cringe before the difficulties and hazards involved. And yet multiplied thousands of us continually attempt to effectively counsel across cultures. Why? Because it is implicit in the worldwide task of the church. If we would be obedient to the Great Commission we have no other choice than to undertake this task. But we do have a choice as to how we will prepare for it.

Assuming that many will want to take advantage of the resources God has placed at our disposal in order to be better equipped to counsel cross-culturally ("To whom much is given, much will be required"), how might we proceed? Where shall we begin? Providentially, the sciences, in addition to the Scriptures, have provided us with some clues to the answers to these questions.

Attend to the words of Norman D. Sundberg:

At the heart of research on intercultural counseling is the problem of similarities and differences. One fact is that human beings around the world share many similarities, such as the ability to interbreed, the presence of physical environments, and the common experiences of birth, early helplessness, growing up, and growing old. Another fact is that human beings share many things with their groups of identification, though not with all mankind—knowledge of specific places, ways of socializing the young, language, and expectations about authority. Finally, each human being is unique, having one-of-a-kind fingerprints, a special history, and a particular life style.

The counselor meeting a client for the first time encounters all three aspects in one person—the universal, the group-specific, and the unique. The counselor also has these tripartite characteristics. Furthermore, the counseling pair also meets in a context, an interaction in a social and physical setting, which has a history and relation with similar contexts.[1]

Clyde K. Kluckhohn and Henry A. Murray anticipated Sundberg's conclusion when they wrote:

Every man is in certain respects
a. like all other men
b. like some other men
c. like no other man[2]

Effectiveness in Christian cross-cultural counseling and helping, as in all cross-cultural counseling, depends upon the ability to correctly identify and interpret universal, group-specific, and idiosyncratic factors which both counselors and counselees bring to the counseling situation. On the one hand, there might be a tendency on the part of culturally uninitiated counselors to conclude with Robert Burns that "a man's a man for all of that" and proceed on the assumption that people are the same wherever one meets them. On the other hand, once the counselor becomes immersed in a new culture or in cultural studies, he is apt to conclude that people are so different as to make effective intercultural counseling all but impossible. Both extremes are to be avoided. By considering, in this and the next two chapters, the ways in which a counselee is like all other men in the world, like some other men who share his cultural background, and unlike any other man who has ever existed (because of the particular configuration of his own experience), the counselor-helper will be better prepared to make the kind of analyses that

1. Norman D. Sundberg, "Research and Research Hypotheses about Effectiveness in Intercultural Counseling," in *Counseling across Cultures,* ed. Paul P. Pedersen et al., rev. ed. (Honolulu: The University Press of Hawaii for the East-West Center, 1981), p. 140.
2. Ibid.

will lead to *effective* interaction. By doing this in accordance with the precepts of God's Word and in dependence upon the person of the Holy Spirit he will be in a position to make the kind of proposals that will lead to *Christian* change.

Perspectives about Universals

If no man were like any other man in any respect, counseling would be impossible. If any particular man were not like all other men in certain respects, counseling would be implausible. It is the similarity between men that makes identification, understanding, and empathy possible. When Paul and Barnabas found it necessary to dissuade the Lystrans from sacrificing to them they said, "We too are only men, human like you" (Acts 14:15). When Paul wanted to impress the Athenians with the fact that all men everywhere are accountable to one God he emphasized that "from one man [God] made every nation of man, that they should inhabit the whole earth" (Acts 17:26).

Of course, superficial similarities characterizing men and women of all times and places are readily discoverable. But the authors of the Bible and perceptive communicators of every kind find it essential to look beneath the surface for a kind of psychic or spiritual unity which transcends biological and other obvious categories. It is precisely these deeper similarities or universals which are at one and the same time so manifestly essential and so seemingly elusive. Universals there must be, including universals of this deeper variety, but exactly where are they discoverable and how are they to be described? The answers to such questions vary, depending upon how one proceeds with the inquiry.

Among the social sciences, psychology and anthropology are as intimately related to our present concerns as are any of the others. Both have man as their main subject area, although their foci are somewhat different. Anthropologists have tended to focus upon man and culture while neglecting the individual. Psychologists have tended to focus on individuals to the neglect of cultural considerations. Victor Barnouw notes that although the influence of psychoanalytic theory on research about culture and personality has been valuable and stimulating, it has brought many problems for the anthropologist who seldom has had clinical experience and is not prepared to evaluate various conflicting psychoanalytic schools of thought.[3] Psychologists, on the other hand, seldom study culture in depth and bicultural psychologists are in short supply. So they are not often in a position to fully appreciate the import of cultural studies.

Felix M. Keesing points to the tension that has been evident as researchers in these fields have ventured into one another's territory.[4] In *Totem and Taboo* (1913), for example, Sigmund Freud attempted to show that basic elements of religion originated through a supposed 'parasital' (father-killing) act, in which sons, jealous of their father, killed him, and then in their repentence developed beliefs and restraints surviving most clearly among savages. . . ."[5] Keesing says that Freud's thesis has been a major target of anthropological scorn.[6] He cites anthropologist Bronislaw Malinowski, who compared individual cultures to snowflakes and insisted that they must be examined on their own terms and without assuming that they exhibit many universals. Malinowski wrote a book entitled *The Father in Primitive Psychology* (1927)[7] in which he

3. Victor Barnouw, *Culture and Personality* (Homewood, Ill.: Dorsey, 1963), pp. 164–68.

4. Felix M. Keesing, *Cultural Anthropology: The Science of Custom* (New York: Holt, Rinehart, and Winston, 1958), pp. 170–78.

5. Ibid., pp. 170–71.

6. Ibid., p. 171.

7. Bronislaw Malinowski, *The Father in Primitive Psychology* (1927; New York: Norton, 1966).

took relish in showing that, in a matrilineal organized society such as the Trobriands, the supposedly universal infantile tendency of a son to develop an 'Oedipus complex' (father hostility) did not exist in the classic Freudian manner, for a boy received his major social training on the male side not from his biological male parent but from the brothers of his mother.[8]

As we shall see in the next chapter, contemporary studies indicate that the conclusions of Malinowski (and Margaret Mead and others who tended toward cultural determinism) were overdrawn or even misguided, but Keesing is probably correct in noting that with the anthropological interest in childrearing, interdisciplinary criticism tended to be replaced with collaboration. In one important study, anthropologist Kluckhohn and psychoanalyst Murray collaborated on research and concluded that every man is like all other men in that there are certain background phenomena such as common factors in biological endowment, environmental influences, and culture and society which can be taken for granted in the development of human personality.[9]

Kluckhohn's and Murray's conclusion tended to confirm the studies of George P. Murdock and his colleagues at Yale, and also anticipated the similar and more contemporary findings of Walter J. Lonner and others.

Murdock began a work in 1936 at the Institute of Human Relations at Yale University which was later combined with other materials and elaborated into the well-known Human Relations Area Files with their ethnographic source material on more than three hundred cultural units throughout the world. Murdock looked at how certain common functional behaviors (such as those connected with birth, aging, and dying) can be classified and

8. Keesing, *Cultural Anthropology*, p. 171.
9. Clyde K. Kluckhohn and Henry A. Murray, eds., *Personality in Nature, Society, and Culture* (New York: Knopf, 1948).

organized.[10] He listed seventy-three such universals initially, although currently eighty-eight categories are used.

Recently Lonner has contributed a review of the quest for psychological universals defined as psychological principles or laws which are valid in all cultures. He examines the quest for universals, not only in anthropology and psychology, but also in biology and linguistics.[11] Some of Lonner's conclusions are seemingly pessimistic about the search if researchers take a behavioristic approach which insists that psychology is a science with fixed laws that are universally applicable in the same way that the laws of hard science are. On the other hand, he says, "there is ample evidence that striking similarities, if not an avalanche of universals in human behavior, far outweigh substantive differences. For that matter culture(s) may be viewed as an opague veneer covering an essential universality of 'psychic and somatic unity'. . . ."[12]

Lonner's assertion is not without justification. That there is a basic psychological similarity among all people is now widely recognized among social scientists. Illustrations of a change in this direction are not hard to come by. For example, Lucien Levy-Bruhl (among others who were influenced by Emilé Durkheim and espoused the notion of the "group mind" of "primitives") believed that primitives were characterized by a "prelogical" way of thinking which he contrasted with the "logical" thinking of civilized man. His view has been discredited and it is now generally agreed that although there are cultural differences resulting from variations in preunderstandings,

10. See George P. Murdock, "The Common Denominator in Cultures," in *The Science of Man in the World Crisis,* ed. Ralph Linton (1945; New York: Octagon, 1980); also George P. Murdock et al., *Outline of Cultural Materials,* 4th rev. (New York: Taplinger, 1961).

11. Walter J. Lonner, "The Search for Psychological Universals," in *Handbook of Cross-Cultural Psychology: Perspectives,* gen. ed. Harry C. Triandis, 6 vols. (Boston: Allyn and Bacon, 1980–83), vol. 1, ed. Harry C. Triandis and William W. Lambert (1980), p. 143–204.

12. Ibid., p. 147.

priorities, and categories, reasoning processes are fundamentally the same the world over.

Again, the excesses of the Sapir-Whorf hypothesis (which says that language, rather than reporting a world view and reflecting a natural logic, is actually the means whereby we acquire our world view and logic) have been modified by the findings of linguists like Noam Chomsky and Robert Longacre. These men have shown that the language universals that underlie the surface structures of particular languages are of greater importance than those surface differences.

A review of perspectives suggested by the anthropological data indicates that although there are significant similarities among cultures at all levels, the most universal of human variables seem to exist at the individual level, with somewhat more variability at the interpersonal level and still more variability at the institutional level.[13] Individual variables are grounded in physiological and psychological functions and include

1. biological needs
2. perception (depth perception, intersensory integration, and object constancy)
3. language
4. cognition (the ability to generalize, form concepts and abstractions, and reason logically)
5. sex typing
6. achievement
7. values and morality (Recent data indicate "significant agreement in the value domain.")[14]
8. psychopathology (Where disorders are organically based there is less variability. However, broad categories must be used.)

13. Robert L. Munroe and Ruth H. Munroe, "Perspectives Suggested by the Anthropological Data," in *Handbook of Cross-Cultural Psychology*, vol. 1, pp. 253–319.
14. Ibid., p. 214.

In some early important research on psychotic disorders in various cultures and among different ethnic groups in the United States, Marvin K. Opler concluded that because of basic psychophysical characteristics which make for normality and abnormality in individuals, universal patterns of mental disease do exist. Nevertheless, both the behavior related to, and the treatment of, such disorders tend to be highly reflective of cultural characteristics.[15] Subsequent studies tend to bear out Opler's conclusion and suggest that although there are significant similarities in this area, psychopathologists should use manuals such as the *Diagnostic and Statistical Manual of Mental Disorders* with great caution, especially when working cross-culturally.

Studies in the behavioral sciences, then, point in the direction of a significant "psychic unity" among men in addition to the biological unity which has provided the basis for such a great part of social-science theory. We can sum up the trends in social-science thinking with respect to human universals as follows:

All men share certain *biological* commonalities such as body characteristics (e.g., sex); bodily needs (e.g., for food and drink, elimination and rest); body development (e.g., growth and puberty); and body limitations (e.g., aging, the tendency to sickness, and the inevitability of death). These biological similarities cut across all differences of geography, culture, and even race—and greatly outweigh them in importance.

All men share *psychological* commonalities such as the ability to think through their problems and learn from experience; the ability to communicate by the use of verbal and nonverbal symbols; the need for love, belongingness, security, and meaning; the potential for loving or hating others; and limitations resulting in anxiety, fear,

15. Marvin K. Opler, *Culture, Psychiatry, and Human Values: The Method and Values of a Social Psychiatry* (Springfield, Ill.: Charles C. Thomas, 1956).

and illness. These psychological similarities are receiving more and more attention among social scientists and are supported by an increasing amount of data.

All men share *sociocultural* commonalities related to the need for caring for biological, psychological, and (in the vast majority of societies) spiritual requirements on a community basis. As a matter of fact, in providing for such needs, sociocultural demands for customs and laws are engendered. In spite of some justifiable criticisms, the cross-cultural utility of Murdock's categories (age-grading, division of labor, religious rituals, and so forth) demonstrates the importance and pervasiveness of these sociocultural commonalities.

Lonner's conclusion becomes of special interest to us at this point. He insists that philosophy bears on the quest for psychological universals as much as science does. This is an important insight and should serve as a cure for the myopia that plagues most theorists and practitioners. Philosophy (especially as informed by theology) has *more* to tell us about human universals than any other discipline. It also has much to tell us about the preunderstandings of researchers and about their inability to reach a consensus. This is not to denigrate the behavioral sciences but simply to underscore their limitations. It is no surprise that behavioral scientists, especially in a post-Christian Western world, seldom if ever mention the spiritual commonalities of mankind. Their tools do not lend themselves to measuring the things of the spirit. Moreover, the philosophy prevailing among behavioral scientists blinds them to these commonalities.

Universals and World Views

Like truth-seekers of whatever discipline or profession, psychologists, psychiatrists, and counselors are faced with an epistemological question. And like all others, they find themselves divided into camps which are determined by their respective world views—whether religious or naturalistic.[16]

their respective world views—whether religious or naturalistic.[16]

Robert Redfield defines "world view": "If there is an emphasized meaning in the phrase 'world view,' I think it is in the suggestion it carries of the structure of things as man is aware of them. It is in the way we see ourselves in relation to all else."[17]

With that latter sentence in mind we might enlarge the phrase *world view* to "man and world view" or "life and world view." One's world view is chosen largely on the basis of faith. Despite all their pretensions about accepting only that which can be verified by experience and reason (the scientific method), even naturalists must go beyond experience and reason to reach the conclusion that all that is a result of natural law. It is on this "faith premise" that they propose to accept the authority of experience and reason only.

For their part, proponents of one or another of the various religious man and world views usually rely on the authority of some kind of revelation, although reason may also play an important role. Hinduism, for example, has produced a voluminous philosophical corpus in which reason plays a major epistemological role. The only written authority to which *all* Hindus would appeal, however, is the Vedas—the product of early *rishis* or sages who experienced divine truth. And investigation will reveal that even the Vedas are not the ultimate authority because they can be attributed to the enlightenment of each individual alone. An infinitesimally small number of Hindus have had this "ultimate enlightenment experience" (by comparison with the total number of Hindus); thus a

16. For the definition, categorization, and description of basic world views, refer to David J. Hesselgrave, *Communicating Christ Cross-Culturally: An Introduction to Missionary Communication* (Grand Rapids: Zondervan, 1978), pt. 3, pp. 121–94.

17. Robert Redfield, *The Primitive World and Its Transformations* (Ithaca, N.Y.: Cornell University Press, 1957), pp. 85–86.

vast amount of faith must be exercised if one is to accept the possibility of attaining such an experience and the notion that it will be self-authenticating once it is achieved.

Orthodox Christianity, on the other hand, accepts as completely authoritative the revelation of God in Christ and the Bible. This too is a matter of faith. Experience and reason have their place in defending the authority of the Living Word and the written Word. But although they lend great support to faith they are not the ultimate ground of that faith. Otherwise divine revelation would no longer be the ultimate authority.

Our present purpose is neither apologetic nor polemic, although we must insist upon the important role that "faith" plays in naturalistic as well as religious world views. Rather, our concern is to place Christian ethnopsychology and cross-cultural counseling in the context of competing views on the nature of man and the world as integral parts of opposing world views. And it is the nature of a world view (or man and world view) to provide or inform those universals that will govern the way in which both counselors and counselees approach the counseling situation. *The universals may be true to reality or they may be ill-conceived and false, but so long as they are believed to be true they will be of paramount importance.*

Western Psychology and the Naturalistic View of Man and the World

C. S. Lewis has described the naturalistic (he calls it the "materialist") world view in the following fashion:

> People who take that view think that matter and space just happen to exist, and always have existed, no one knows why; and that the matter, behaving in certain fixed ways, has just happened, by a sort of fluke, to produce creatures like ourselves who are able to think. By one chance in a thousand something hit our sun and made it produce

planets; and by another thousandth chance the chemicals necessary for life, and the right temperature, arose on one of these planets, and so some of the matter on this earth came alive; and then, by a very long series of chances, the living creatures developed into things like us.[18]

The discipline of psychology in general has betrayed a reliance on this view of the world and man. The development of this naturalistic (secularistic, materialistic, humanistic) psychology in the West is often described in terms of certain forces or forceful trends. A brief overview of these psychological trends follows.

First-force psychoanalysis. Freud was indebted to thinkers such as the evolutionist Charles Darwin, the neurologist Jean Martin Charcot, sexologist Havelock Ellis, and his collaborator (in the writing of *Studies in Hysteria* and in developing psychoanalysis) Josef Breuer—debts he did not always see fit to acknowledge.[19] Nevertheless, Freud's name is almost synonymous with psychoanalysis. He has exerted a seminal influence since the turn of the century and his approach was dominant in American psychology during the period from the First World War through the Second World War. As we have seen, Freud placed a great emphasis on social influences in the early years of life (nurture), but with his antireligious bias Freud assumed that man is basically a biologically determined being. In a way Freud was very pessimistic about human nature generally. He believed that by nature most men are "lazy and unintelligent" with "no love for instinctual renunciation," and are of such a make-up that "arguments are no avail against their passions."[20] There were opti-

18. C. S. Lewis, *The Case for Christianity* (1948; New York: Macmillan, 1962), pp. 18–19.
19. Jean Strouse, "Freud without Myths," *Newsweek,* 29 October 1979, pp. 97–98; a review of Frank J. Sulloway's *Freud, Biologist of the Mind: Beyond the Psychoanalytic Legend* (New York: Basic, 1979).
20. Sigmund Freud, *The Future of an Illusion,* trans. W. D. Robsen-Scott (1927; New York: Liveright, 1953), p. 87.

mistic aspects of his approach, however, because he put many psychological problems in the category of sickness for which people are not responsible and which could be "cured" by psychoanalysis. Also, he entertained hope that intelligent men of science would chart a path into the future.

Freud's younger colleague, Carl Jung, took exception to some of Freud's ideas, including his biological determinism. Jung felt that there is a spiritual side to man's being and that it is a vital component of his psychological makeup. Jungian theory constitutes a smaller stream in psychoanalysis.

Second-force behaviorism. During the decades of the 1950s and 1960s, behavioristic psychology became more or less dominant in America. During those decades the classical conditioning theory of Ivan P. Pavlov and Joseph Wolpe was complemented (and countered!) by the instrumental-conditioning theory of B. F. Skinner. Unhappy with the "unscientific" approach (especially with its emphasis on the inner working of the mind), behaviorists generally were critical of psychoanalysis and insisted upon strict scientific observation. But on one point they agreed with Freud—man is a biological entity, nothing more and nothing less. Like Freud they left no room for either the existence of God or the spiritual aspect of human personality. Man was viewed as a collocation of stimulus-response mechanisms. The behavior of men, like that of animals, is determined by factors of heredity and environment. Skinner's *Beyond Freedom and Dignity* carried the ideas of Darwin and Freud to their logical conclusion.[21] Man is a machine—a human machine, but a machine nonetheless. With no room for a choice, there is no room for freedom and no room for dignity. The only questions that remain are "Who will control human behavior?" and "To what end?" (Having said this, one must hasten to add that there are Christian behaviorists who, while subscrib-

21. B. F. Skinner, *Beyond Freedom and Dignity* (Toronto: Bantam, 1972).

ing to conditioning approaches, obviously are at odds with Skinner and the vast majority of behaviorists when it comes to the nature of man.)

Third-force humanism. The 1950s saw the birth in America of a psychology that challenged and ultimately eclipsed Freudian and Skinnerian models of personality and behavior. Perhaps the most important impetus to its emergence as a dominant approach was provided by Abraham H. Maslow's *Motivation and Personality* (1954).[22] Maslow insisted that although man shares certain similarities with animals, he is also very different. Unlike animals, he has a conscience and values; he experiences love, beauty, loyalty, and guilt; and he has a capacity for art, music, and philosophy. Maslow's motivational pyramid became well-known. His hierarchy of human needs ascended from those that are physiological (e.g., food and shelter) to those that are concerned with safety (e.g., order and stability) to those that are social (e.g., love and belonging), and, finally, to those connected with growth or self-actualization (e.g., meaningfulness and self-sufficiency). Maslow held that when one category of needs is cared for the next category comes to the fore. He believed that when one reaches the apex and becomes self-actualized he becomes fulfilled as a person.

Maslow reopened the door, not only to freedom and dignity, but also to some kind of spirituality and transcendence, although his world view cannot be categorized as religious. To his voice were joined those of Rollo May, Carl R. Rogers, and others. In the late 1960s and in the 1970s the emphasis on growth, self-actualization, and self-realization spawned numerous growth, sensitivity, and encounter groups in the United States. Paul C. Vitz denominates this movement the "cult of self-worship."[23]

Humanistic psychology usually is optimistic about man

22. Abraham H. Maslow, *Motivation and Personality*, 2d ed. (New York: Harper and Row, 1970).

23. Paul C. Vitz, *Psychology as Religion: The Cult of Self-Worship* (Grand Rapids: Eerdmans, 1977).

and his world. Evil does not really exist. To be human is to be autonomous and good. Man's choices are good, man's potential is practically unlimited, and all change is for the better. As Vitz comments, humanistic psychology involves "no duties, denials, inhibitions, restraints—only rights, privileges and opportunities for change."[24] That there are serious problems with this view of man and the world must be apparent to all, even to humanistic psychologists and counselors. But in the face of biological determinism on the one hand and political totalitarianism on the other, the elixir of humanism has been, for many, too heady a potion to refuse.

"Fourth-force" transpersonalism. Before considering distinctly religious man and world views we should note that some former naturalists and humanists in the psychological disciplines have once again turned to a spiritual path. The reference is not to a Christian conversion, although that too has occurred in some instances. Rather, the reference is to a more mystical transpersonalism.

Transpersonal psychology, sometimes called fourth-force psychology (perhaps prematurely for it is yet to be determined how much of a force it will be), embraces the emphases of humanism but pursues the transcendence of which Maslow speaks. Listen to the testimony of Gerald G. Jampolsky:

> In 1975, the outside world saw me as a successful psychiatrist who appeared to have everything he wanted. But my inner world was chaotic, empty, unhappy and hypocritical. My twenty-year marriage had recently ended in a painful divorce. I had become a heavy drinker and had developed chronic, disabling back pain as a means of handling guilt.
>
> It was at this time that I came across some writings entitled *A Course in Miracles.* The *Course* could be described as a form of spiritual psychotherapy that is self-taught. I was perhaps more surprised than anyone when I

24. Ibid., p. 38.

became involved in a thought system that uses words like *God* and *Love*. I had thought that I would be the last person to be interested in such writings. I had been extremely judgmental toward people who pursued a spiritual pathway; I saw them as fearful and I believed they were not using their intellect properly.

When I first began studying the *Course*, I had an experience that was surprising but was also very comforting. I heard an inner voice, or possibly it would be more accurate to say an impression of a voice, which said to me, 'Physician, heal thyself; this is your way home.'

I found the *Course* essential in my struggle for personal transformation. It helped me recognize that I really did have a choice of experiencing peace or conflict, and that this choice is always between accepting truth or illusion. The underlying truth for all of us is that the essence of our being is Love.[25]

Jampolsky goes on to explain that there are only two emotions, love and fear. Love is the "natural inheritance" of mankind. Fear is manufactured in our minds. By practicing forgiveness and seeing ourselves and all mankind as guiltless and blameless we can let go of fear. All that will remain is love.

The Eastern—and particularly the Indian—orientation of Jampolsky's thought is made apparent by the ease with which "love" becomes "Love" and "self" becomes "Self." He concludes, "Let us recognize that we are united as one Self and illuminate the world with the light of Love that shines through us. Let us awaken to the knowledge that the essence of our being is Love, and, as such, we are the light of the world."[26]

This represents little more (and probably a great deal less) than the world view and anthropology of the East. But it finds numerous expressions in the West in the

25. Gerald G. Jampolsky, *Love Is Letting Go of Fear* (Toronto: Bantam, 1981), pp. 1–2.
26. Ibid., p. 131.

teachings of Esalen, Arica, Rajneesh, and Transcendental Meditation; and in such therapies as past lives, inner healing, and guided fantasy. As Frances Adeney has put it, "Stretching toward full human potential becomes a search for the God within, a oneness with the universe, a knowledge of the transcendent power in oneself."[27]

Psychology and Religious Views of the Nature of Man and the World

According to some scholars, Cicero derived the word *religion* from *relegere*, which means "to consider." According to others, Lactantius derived it from *religare*, which means "to tie, link, or bind." The latter explanation is more widely accepted. And most world views can be said to be religious in this sense: they are concerned with linking (or "relinking") man and the Divine.

The tribal view of man and the world. No single description has been universally accepted, but there is a religious world view variously categorized as tribal, animistic, or primitive which is held by great segments of mankind. Stephen C. Neill believes it to be the effective world view of as much as 40 percent of the world's population.[28] In this view the world is characterized by a unity in which boundaries between deities, spirits, men, animals, and even natural phenomena are more or less obscure and shifting. Man himself has a soul which is distinct from his body and which may take leave of the body during such states as dreaming, fainting, trance, and death. While alive, man struggles to attain the favor of deities and departed ancestors and to ward off the malevolent power of the world of spirits and nature which surround him. After death the body disintegrates and the soul

27. Frances Adeney, "The Flowering of the Human Potential Movement," *S.C.P. Journal* 5 (Winter 1981–82): 15–16.

28. Stephen C. Neill, *Christian Faith and Other Faiths: The Christian Dialogue with Other Religions*, 2d ed. (London and New York: Oxford University Press, 1970), p. 125.

joins the spirit world. Properly remembered and supplied by the living, the soul moves into another state of existence in the spirit world or is reborn on earth in a new body.

The Indian (Hindu-Buddhistic) view of man and the world. In the Indian view (confining ourselves first to that which is more characteristically Hindu), the world as one experiences or perceives it is *maya* or illusion. That which is "really Real," the Brahman, is behind it and "issuing forth" in it. One might say that Brahman *"in*volved" into the world and that the world will *"re*volve" back to Brahman. Such a view is termed monistic.

And what about man? Man, in addition to a body, has a *jiva* or soul and an *atman* or spirit. The *jiva,* like the Greek *psuche,* is the animating part of man. Upon death it migrates to the upper or lower regions and is reincarnated into another body—that of a god, human, animal, or even plant in accordance with one's karma (the consequences of one's actions). But both body and soul are parts of maya. That which is "really Real" is the atman or spirit—the expression of the Brahman within the individual. Man's greatest problem is *avidya* or ignorance of his true state and "true self." Works, wisdom, or devotion constitute the principal way to *moksha* (enlightenment, liberation, union with the Brahman), which frees one from the chain of rebirths.

Buddhism shares the same Indian heritage, but has replaced the idea of the Brahman with that of Nirvana, a state of bliss beyond all separateness, striving, and desire. It has also replaced the idea of atman with that of *anatman* or "no soul" (no self). According to Buddhist teaching, man consists of a material body and four immaterial components (*skandhas*): feeling or sensation, perception, volition, and consciousness. That which is called the self or the soul is actually the ever-changing interplay of these five components. In Hinduism there is a jiva that transmigrates. In Buddhism there is neither atman nor jiva to transmigrate. Only one's karma survives—much as the flame of an almost spent candle may be the means of lighting another candle.

The Chinese (Confucian-Taoist) view of man and the world. Chinese religious thought represents a confluence of various streams—tribalism or animism, classical emperor worship, Confucianism, Taoism, and Buddhism. In more recent times Christianity and dialectical materialism have made an impact. At the core, traditional Chinese thinking has been dualistic. A high God exists but in day-to-day living ordinary people are more concerned with multitudinous spirits: *shen* (good spirits) and *kwei* (evil spirits). Related to this spiritual dualism is a scientific dualism, the idea that the phenomenal world is the result of interaction between the Yin (negativity, earth, darkness, femininity, death) and Yang (positivity, heaven, light, masculinity, life). The interaction of these opposing but essential principles is in accordance with the Tao (road, path, way, law, or truth).

Both Confucius and Lao-tze (the "founder" of Taoism) accepted this basic world view. They also agreed that man is born good; that he should give God, the spirits, and the ancestors their due; that man and nature have a common origin; that both man and nature should follow a similar course in accordance with the same principle of the Tao. They differed in their emphases, however. Confucius emphasized man in society and said that man will be kept good if he is taught the wisdom of the past. Lao-tze emphasized man in nature and said that man will remain good if he retires to a natural environment to learn and practice the Tao. Neither put a great emphasis on developing what we might call a philosophy of the supernatural. But the teachings of both developed into religions in China. And, as far as Chinese thinking and practice are concerned, the ethicism of Confucius and the naturism of Lao-tze were augmented by Buddhism. The result has been a certain complexity and confusion with reference to life after death and the spirit world.

The monotheistic view of man and the world in Judaism, Christianity, and Islam. Judaism, Christianity, and Islam share some significant commonalities as to world view and their understanding of man, in spite of profound differences among them. Because of this commonality and the fact that its basic characteristics are generally understood, and because the Christian view of man will be dealt with in some detail, this view will not be elaborated here. Two important points should be made before proceeding, however.

First, Judaism and Christianity have been greatly influenced in their view of man by Western naturalism, especially since the Enlightenment. As a result, many prevailing approaches to, and understandings of, the dilemmas of man and the world dimly reflect the teachings of the Old and New Testament Scriptures.

Second, although Islam gives credence to both Testaments and to Jews and Christians as being "people of the Book," Muslims believe that both the Old and New Testament Scriptures have been corrupted and that Allah's final revelation is to be found in the Koran. The Koran teaches that man is created as a finite, weak being by Allah; that in spite of Allah's favor man has miserably failed; that man is completely and abjectly subject to the will of Allah; that he must mend his ways and obey the Five Pillars; and that his deeds will be weighed in a final judgment and, accordingly, he will be assigned to heaven or hell. The Koran is never more insistent than it is in teaching that God is by nature sovereign and that man is by nature subject. "Allah leaves in error whom He will and guides whom He pleases."[29] Although Islam, like Judaism and Christianity, teaches that man is created by an

---

29. *The Koran,* trans. N. J. Dawood, rev. ed., Classics series (Baltimore: Penguin, 1964), sura 14, p. 98.

all-wise and all-powerful Creator, Islam exhibits a remarkable fatalism concerning man, his problems, and his
future which is quite different from the Judeo-Christian
outlook.

A Biblical View of Man and the World

It is, of course, manifestly impossible to detail a full-
blown biblical man and world view here. But it is unthinkable to proceed without attempting to set forth such
a view in bold outline, concentrating on those aspects that
are of special importance in the present context.

God, his world, and man. Any view of God, the world,
and man that can properly be termed biblical must be
theocentric, not anthropocentric. In other words, God
triune—Father, Son, and Holy Spirit—must be at the very
center. He was before all things. All things, whether ani-
mate or inanimate, animal or human, angelic or demonic,
were created by him and for him. And he is above all
things. All are held together by him. All is, or will be,
subservient to him. To acknowledge him as Creator, Redeemer, and Judge of all things is the beginning of wisdom
and true knowledge. To live for him as present Lord and
coming King is the essence of peace and healing. All that
culminates in God's greater glory contributes to man's—
and the whole world's—greater good.

Man—created in God's image and likeness. According
to the Genesis account, man was created in the "image"
and "likeness" of the Creator (Gen. 1:26, 27). The Hebrew
words are *tselem* and *demuth*. The Septuagint translates
them *eikon* and *homoiosis*. The difference between these
words is largely in their breadth, *demuth* and *homoiosis*
being broader and more inclusive. To make a more precise
distinction and draw implications from it would be risky.
In context it seems clear that God's image and likeness
were evident in the first man—as a spiritual, moral, intelligent, volitional individual. It was in these respects
that he was distinguished from the beasts around him.

Consequently, self, the world, and God were objects of his knowledge; fellowship with God (and, subsequently, other human beings) was desirable; dominion over earthly creation was decreed; a choice between good and evil was possible (apart from a bias to evil); and human existence had an eternal dimension.

In a manuscript about the *imago Dei*, R. Ward Wilson emphasizes the character of God as revealed in the Old Testament, reflected perfectly in Christ and in the New Testament, and reflected imperfectly in men everywhere.[30] Proceeding in this fashion, Ward finds evidence of the imago in "transcultural dispositions" to such values as truth, steadfast love, mercy, graciousness, slowness to anger, forgiveness, and preserving love. Of course, men in all cultures do not *practice* these traits with a high degree of regularity, but all men value cultural expressions of them in ways that, although distorted, reflect their common origin in the Creator who exhibits them in their fullness.

Man—a material and nonmaterial being. The Genesis account clearly indicates that there were two aspects of man's being—the material and the nonmaterial. His body was fashioned from the dust of the ground. Then God breathed the breath of life into his nostrils and he became a living soul (Gen. 2:7). The Hebrew for "soul" is *nephesh* and the Greek is *psuche.* Both of these words must be understood in context because they can refer to soul, to biological life, or simply to breath. In Genesis 2 it is unlikely that the term signifies anything more than "life-breath." The passage indicates that humans are characterized by both a material body and the immaterial principle of life.[31] Those aspects of his immaterial nature which

30. R. Ward Wilson, "God's Image in Mankind: The Essence of Human Nature," mimeographed manuscript, n.d.

31. Carl F. Keil and Franz Delitzsch, *Biblical Commentary on the Old Testament*, 10 vols., trans. James Martin (Grand Rapids: Eerdmans, 1968), vol. 1, *The Pentateuch*, p. 78.

differentiated man from the beasts are to be inferred from the special emphasis given to his creation and from other references to his nature and activities. His body, although earthly, was a special creation of God. And his life-breath was not an infusion of a pervasive "world life," but of a special "inspiration" from God. Again, the name *Adam* (from Hebrew words meaning "ruddy," "to show blood [in the face]," or "human being") was reminiscent of the earthly side of his being. But the fact that God named him and charged him with the responsibility of naming other creatures sets him apart and indicates that he was something more than both earth and beast. He was created to live under the rule of God and to commune with God and other human beings, and he was created to rule over the rest of earthly creation.

Although it is true that the material body of man has become a vehicle of evil, man's body was included in that which was pronounced "good" by God at the time of creation. The Bible does not teach that the body is the tomb of the soul, nor does it teach a merely "soulish" redemption. Material and nonmaterial components unite to form one personality—and both share in ultimate salvation.

Man—aspects of his nonmateriality. With reference to the nonmaterial side of human nature, James O. Buswell, Jr., writes,

> The biblical languages have a rich variety of words referring to the nonmaterial being of man. It is generally characteristic of these words, as of the corresponding words in English, that they are derived from physical terms, but in their psychological usage they have lost the physical meaning almost entirely. It is also characteristic that the nonmaterial being of man is designated by different words corresponding to the function or relationship implied in the context. Just as the same individual may be referred to as husband, father, brother, uncle, etc., so the nonmaterial substantive entity, which is the man, may be referred to as heart, mind, will, spirit, soul, affections (bowels), etc. These several nouns are not synonymous, anymore [sic]

than uncle and father are synonymous, but they may all designate the same substantive entity, the same nonmaterial human being.

Moreover, it is a characteristic of biblical languages as it is of English that any functional aspect of man may be spoken of as the man himself and also as something which he possesses. Thus we may say, "I *have* a self, a soul, a spirit, a mind, a will," or we may say, "I *am* a self, a soul, a spirit, a heart, a mind, a will."[32]

In line with this understanding Buswell proceeds with a brief explanation of biblical terms that should be of special importance in psychology.[33] With certain modifications, his general outline and explanations are followed in figure 9.

As the brief summary in figure 9 indicates, there is a good deal of ambiguity and overlap when we speak about aspects or entities of the nonmaterial part of man. It may not be profitable to insist in every case upon precise definitions. But it is evident that man is a choosing, thinking, acting, feeling being of more than temporal significance.

Man—a fallen creature. When God surveyed his creation and pronounced it "good," man was included (Gen. 1:31). All was in harmony and balance. Man's instincts, drives, aspirations, and motivations were "good." His relationships with creation and Creator were "good" and he was in a "good" environment. Distrust and rebellion were stirred up by "that old serpent, the devil." Man disobeyed, and in so doing poisoned his relationship with God, creation, other human beings, and himself. He became involved in the cosmic struggle between good and evil, God and Satan. He became a fallen creature, a sinner, possessed of a sinful nature.

Before their disobedience it is recorded that Adam and

32. James O. Buswell, Jr., *A Systematic Theology of the Christian Religion,* 2 vols. (Grand Rapids: Zondervan, 1962), vol. 1, p. 238.
33. Ibid., pp. 238–41.

FIGURE 9   **Biblical Terms Defining
the Nonmaterial Part of Man**

English	Hebrew	Greek
Soul—the essence, substance, or animating principle of man; the actuating cause of life. (The word is used especially in circumstances where relationship to the body or earthly connections are in view.)	*Nephesh*—physical breath, biological life, soul	*Psuchē*—as in Hebrew
Spirit—the Latin root originally signified physical breath; now the word refers to a personal being in circumstances in which reference to earthly connections and ordinary human functions are absent	*Ruach*—physical breath, wind, or spirit	*Pneuma*—as in Hebrew
Heart—the seat of man's emotions, especially pity and sympathy	*Lebhabh* or *lebh*—man's conative function of choice and determination; also his cognitive nature	*Kardia*—as in Hebrew
Mind—the seat of cognition; the reflective part of man	Almost always a translation of some word elsewhere translated "heart," "soul," or "spirit"	*Nous*—cognition; man as a thinker *Dianoia* and *ennoia*—the inwardness of a mental attitude *Phronema* and *phronesis*—the diaphragm or midriff (lit.); by extension, man as a deep, reflective thinker
Will—desire; purpose; choice; the power to control, dispose or determine; the conative aspect of man as a creature who puts forth effort and makes choices	*Ratson*—good will, favor, acceptance; what one pleases; will, self-will	*Boule*—counsel; decision; motives *Thelema*—desire(s); will

Affection(s)—a feel-ing or emotion; attachment, concern for others; a better translation of the Hebrew and Greek words than "bowels" (KJV)	Rachamin—man as an emotional and affec-tionate being, espe-cially in sympathetic regard and love for others	Splangchna—as in Hebrew

Eve were naked but were not ashamed (Gen. 2:25; the Hebrew word *bosh* means "to be ashamed" or "to feel shame"). After they disobeyed, they lost their innocence. When the Lord God came to the garden, they hid them-selves because they were naked and afraid (Gen. 3:8–11). When Paul comments on what happened to mankind as a whole (not just the original pair) he says that God gave them unto sinful desires so that they degraded their own bodies (Rom. 1:24); to "shameful lusts" (Rom. 1:26); and to a "depraved mind, to do what ought not to be done" (Rom. 1:28). Buswell translates the phrase (Greek, *me ka-thekonta*) in the twenty-eighth verse as "shameful" and notes that Paul is using a non-Christian Greek philosoph-ical term—"evidence that both pagan and Christian eth-ical thought have observed in human conduct those evi-dences that man is not what he ought to be."[34]

But beyond that which is descriptive is that which is ascriptive. Man was and is guilty of disobeying the divine command. Although that awareness did not break in upon man's consciousness until later, and sometimes does not seem to break in upon his consciousness at all, the fact remains that Adam and his progeny are guilty sinners and worthy of the sentence of death which God has pro-nounced upon all such (Rom. 6:23).

34. Ibid., p. 260.

Man—his struggle and potential. The bad news about man must be understood as a precondition of understanding the good news that Christ died for man's sin in order to redeem his life from destruction and to reconcile him to God (Col. 1:19–20). It is in the restoration of this relationship that man realizes his highest potential for sanctification and service. Before reconciliation and regeneration through Christ the struggle within man is between the elements of God's image and likeness which survive in, among other things, his conscience. He struggles against Satan and his evil forces. But, as Martin Luther said so well, "Did we in our own strength confide, our striving would be losing; Were not the right Man on our side, the Man of God's own choosing." Even after man comes into right relationship with God through Christ, the struggle continues. In fact, the struggle is intensified. Satan and his evil host—always arrayed against God and therefore opposed to the best interests of man—still stalk their human prey (1 Peter 5:8; Eph. 6:12). The present world system, so hospitable to the values and lifestyle of the once-born man, tempts the man who is twice-born (1 John 2: 15–17).

But now the struggle takes on a new and positive dimension. No longer does fallen human nature fight totally unaided and largely unsuccessfully to keep the law of God that is written in man's conscience and in God's Book. Now the "old self" or "old man" (*ho palaios anthropos;* Rom. 6:6; Eph. 4:22) coexists with a "new self" or "new man" (*ho kainos anthropos;* Eph. 4:24) "created in righteousness and holiness of the truth" (Eph. 4:24, NASB). More, in the economy of God the old self has already been doomed through the death and resurrection of Christ (Rom. 6:6). And still more, the Third Person of the Trinity, the Holy Spirit, indwells the believer and makes it possible for him to glorify God in both his body and spirit (1 Cor. 6:19–20).

Two distinctions which prove to be extremely important to cross-cultural Christian workers must now be made. Perhaps they can be made most clearly in reference to different groupings of people in the Bible.

First, the indelible distinction between the children of God and the children of the devil, between the converted and the unconverted, between the believer and the unbeliever must always be kept in mind. Paul speaks pointedly to this difference when he says that as long as men are slaves of sin they are "free from the control of righteousness" (Rom. 6:20), but that those who have "obeyed the . . . teaching" have "been set free from sin and have become slaves to righteousness" (Rom. 6:17, 18). If my readers will not misunderstand, there is a profound sense in which the one great duty of unbelievers is to obey the gospel and become God's children. Until then they are spiritually dead. A great part of God's Word does not even apply directly to them because much of it is addressed to God's family. The importance of this is seen, for example, in relation to forgiveness. An unbeliever possessed by bitterness and the desire to get even hurts himself even as he hurts others. Only when he forgives another can he himself be helped. But there is a completely new dimension to *Christian* forgiveness. When Paul urges Christians to forgive each other he adds, "just as in Christ God forgave you" (Eph. 4:32). To urge the unbeliever to forgive because "to forgive [is] divine," or to exhort the Christian to forgive because in so doing he will be healed, is to blur a fundamental distinction at great peril. Both suasions may be true but in the former case the unbeliever must also understand that "without faith it is impossible to please God" (Heb. 11:6). And in the latter case the Christian must know that obedience is the Christian's first duty.

Second, the distinction between the children of Israel in the Old Testament and the members of the body of Christ in the New Testament serves to illustrate the difference between a culturally-focused and a transculturally-focused religion. From the time of Abraham and throughout the Old Testament era God was dealing primarily with one people in one geographical and sociocultural setting. Many of his laws and promises relating to diet, worship, and rituals reflected that orientation. In the New Testament the distinction between Jew and Gentile is broken down. The gospel is to go everywhere and such things as temple worship and dietary laws are not to stand in the way (John 4:21; Acts 10:15). At the same time, all of the Decalogue, with the exception of the command about keeping the Sabbath, is repeated in the New Testament. The universal requirements of Scripture must be distinguished from the culture-specific requirements. Here too the cross-cultural worker must exercise care lest he impose the culture-specific requirements or cultural adaptations of scriptural universals upon members of the body of Christ in other cultures.

Man—his destiny. Finally, it should be recalled that man has an eternal destiny. His life on earth, however pleasurable or insufferable, is but a brief span in comparison with eternity. "You are a mist that appears for a little while and then vanishes" (James 4:14b). Death is certain. And so is judgment (Heb. 9:27). Believing men and women are destined to eternal life with God. Unbelievers are destined to eternal separation from him. As Lewis put it, every one of us will become either an immortal horror or an everlasting splendor.[35] All problems and all solutions, all choices and all decisions, and all successes and all failures must finally be viewed not just in the light of time, but also in the light of eternity.

Such, in skeletal form, is the biblical view of the world and, especially, man. From a Christian point of view, this is the "raw material" of mankind. Wherever we see human beings, whenever we encounter solitary persons, this

35. C. S. Lewis, *The Weight of Glory and Other Addresses* (New York: Macmillan, 1949), p. 15.

is the stuff out of which they are made and the basis of understanding both their potential and their predicaments. Whether psychologists, anthropologists, sociologists, and others representing the various sciences recognize spiritual universals or not, they are absolutely basic to adequate understanding of man and to any final resolution of his problems.

Human Universals and Counseling Theory

Christian cross-cultural counselors have the responsibility to examine competing views of man and the world (particularly those of their own culture and the host culture of their counselees) in the light of Scripture. Only through this process will they be enabled to share world views (not in E. Fuller Torrey's "believe sense," but in the sense of true understanding) and communicate Christ. Second, they have the responsibility to evaluate the various Western theories of psychology and counseling so they avoid that which is erroneous and enhance only that which is true. Third, the theories and approaches of the non-Western world need to be reviewed for purposes of comparison and contrast. This sounds like a formidable task—and it is. But to some extent it is undertaken by every cross-cultural counselor out of sheer necessity. The only issue, then, has to do with the degree of understanding and consequent effectiveness. This analytic task is diagrammed in figure 10.

FIGURE 10   **Universals and Cross-Cultural Counseling Theory (1)**

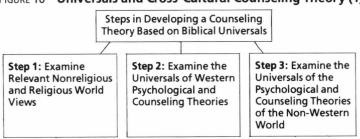

Step 1: Examine relevant nonreligious and religious world views. Explicitly or implicitly, world views inevitably dictate certain human and other universals that are absolutely fundamental to cross-cultural counseling. To compare and contrast world views, therefore, becomes a necessary first step toward developing a viable and effective theory. To aid in this process we propose certain questions and reflections.

Question: Which of the basic world views and understandings of man that have been briefly described are most pervasive in the cultures of the counselor and counselee?

Reflection: Obviously, a thorough knowledge of all the major world views is essential for the expert in cross-cultural counseling theory. But a theoretical understanding of at least two world views other than their own must be grasped by all cross-cultural counselors. Take, for example, the Christian counselor, trained in a Western secular university, who works with Vietnamese refugees in the United States or elsewhere. Our counselor friend must have an understanding of at least three very different views of what humankind and the world really are—the Christian (biblical), the naturalistic (Western secular), and the Hindu-Buddhistic (Vietnamese version). Without a thoroughgoing and biblical theology, his secular training may influence him to offer counseling that is deficient or even heretical from a Christian point of view. Without an understanding of Vietnamese Buddhism, his counseling may be ineffective from a practical point of view.

Questions: On what fundamental points do the world views in question agree with and complement one another? At what points do they clash? What are the counseling implications of these similarities and differences?

Reflection: In nearly every cross-cultural counseling situation there are plusses and minuses that accrue to the world view involved. The Christian counselor must be alive to them! To counsel adherents of animistic or folk religions without taking into consideration their struggle with evil spirits is lamentable. On the positive side of such a struggle is a belief in the reality of the spirit world. On the negative side is the misunderstanding of its true make-up. To counsel Hindus without reference to karma is inexcusable. On the positive side of such a faith is the notion that reality is spiritual and that a man reaps what he sows. On the negative side is the insistence that karma is irreversible and that one can be helped only by future good deeds. To counsel Buddhists without an understanding of teaching about no self is incongruous. On the positive side is a certain "selflessness." On the negative side is a feeling that, as far as the individual is concerned, "selflessness" has no remedy other than acceptance of things "as they are." To counsel Muslims without taking into account the frailty of humanity in the face of Allah's sovereignty is unthinkable. On the positive side is the implicit notion that man is created. On the negative side is a profound fatalism that pervades Islamic societies. (For a summary of these concepts, refer to figure 11.)

FIGURE 11 **Universals and Cross-Cultural Counseling Theory (2)**

Steps in Developing a Counseling Theory Based on Biblical Universals

Step 1: Examine Relevant Nonreligious and Religious World Views

Nonreligious World Views: Secularistic, Naturalistic, Materialistic, Humanistic

Religious World Views: Tribal, Hindu-Buddhistic, Confucian-Taoist, Monotheistic

Step 2: Examine the universals of Western psychological and counseling theories. Inasmuch as there are disagreements between behavioral scientists as to the identity and nature of universals we can afford to be tentative and cautious. Honest scientists themselves are cautious. Jurgen Ruesch and Gregory Bateson candidly write,

> It goes without saying that any scientific theory is manmade; the scientists who formulate it live in a given country at a given time, and are subject to the influence of their contemporaries. Any scientific theory therefore reflects in some way the culture in which it was created. The system of cues and clues which the given culture provides to enable people to understand each other is necessarily used by the theorist in forming and stating his theory: and therefore the theory can only be fully understood after this system of cues has been studied.
>
> Moreover, the culture enters again into the formation of psychiatric theory because the goals of psychiatry are culturally determined; the concepts and evaluation of health and disease which determine the operations (and therefore the viewpoints) of psychiatrists differ from culture to culture.[36]

Accordingly, Christian counselors do well to ask some very serious questions.

Questions: To what degree do the universals of the Western behavioral scientists (especially psychologists) reflect and reinforce biblical universals? To what degree are they inimical to them?

Reflection: Although we speak humbly, as Christians we can speak confidently when we say that to the degree that the conclusions of behavioral scientists represent real science and not pseudoscience they will tend to reflect biblical universals. When, for example, scientists conclude that biologically and psychologically all men are essentially the same, they reinforce (perhaps unwittingly)

36. Jurgen Ruesch and Gregory Bateson, *Communication: The Social Matrix of Psychiatry* (New York: Norton, 1951), p. 79.

that "from one man [God] made every nation of men" (Acts 17:26). When they conclude that reasoning processes are essentially the same, that language structure exhibits great similarities at the deeper levels, and that men universally search for "some kind of symbolic eternity" and also exhibit "the essential self-interest of the human individual" we can readily agree with them in the light of "*imago Dei* anthropology."

On the other hand, the inability of most psychologists and psychiatrists to take the Bible seriously (to say nothing of their inability to accept it) alerts us to the need for care in subscribing to their conclusions. Paul Tournier may well applaud Freud's assertion that people do not suffer inner conflicts because they are ill (have a primary deficiency) but are ill because they have inner conflicts.[37] We can affirm that position on theological grounds, but it is enlightening that Freud held it. However, David Bakan puts Freudianism in proper perspective when he informs us that Freud saw himself as a modern-day messiah leading men away from the moral bondage imposed by the Hebrew people and the Mosaic law. According to Freud, many of man's social problems and all of his psychic disorders grow out of the internalization of the law into the superego or conscience. Guilt itself is evil. It is *the* problem of the neurotic. Its removal is good. Moreover, "if God is the guilt-producing image, then the Devil is the counterforce." In a very real sense Freud aligned himself with the devil, says Bakan.[38]

By the same token, Jung wrote that in all his years of practice he had not found anyone over thirty-five years of age whose basic problem was not that of achieving a religious outlook on life. However, Jung insisted that no concept of God, no moral law, and no religion has ever

37. Paul Tournier, *The Healing of Persons,* trans. Edwin Hudson (New York: Harper and Row, 1965), p. 230.

38. David Bakan, "Sigmund Freud and the Jewish Mystical Tradition," *The Christian Scholar* 44 (Fall 1961): 206–22; see also O. Hobart Mowrer, *The New Group Therapy* (New York: Van Nostrand Reinhold, 1964), p. 37.

fallen down from heaven upon mankind, but that man creates these out of himself. And he concluded that primitive religion is better suited to primitive man than is Christianity.[39]

Questions: To what degree do Western theorists and practitioners of counseling reflect and reinforce biblical universals? To what degree are they inimical to them?

Reflection: It goes without saying that counseling theory and practice will tend to follow the lead of the basic behavioral sciences. And it perhaps should be said that much secular theory is poorly integrated into some approaches to Christian counseling. Here again, our theory needs to reflect biblical universals and reject that which is unbiblical or sub-biblical.

We must, for example, take care lest we become too ready to follow the lead of secularists in branding certain unfamiliar (to our culture) notions as being "prescientific" or superstitious. The naturalistic bias of Julian Wohl, for instance, easily infects the Christian counselor as well. Wohl provides a report of one of his experiences in Rangoon.[40] A student at the University of Rangoon was referred to him for help. The student explained that he was very nervous and had great abdominal distress. He went on to explain that this was due to a demonic spiritual power which he had offended. In reporting the incident, Wohl, who is a clinical psychologist, expresses surprise that a university student of anthropology would entertain such a "prescientific" notion. He says that he was even more surprised when the student went on to explain that he knew that the belief in demons was a belief of primitive people and that since he was one of this class of people he, of course, held to this belief. Wohl admits that it was fortunate for both himself and the student that he was not called upon to continue therapy! By virtue of his academic

39. See David Duffie, *Psychology and the Christian Religion* (Nashville: Southern Publishing Association, 1968), pp. 20–21.

40. Julian Wohl, "International Psychotherapy: Issues, Questions, and Reflections," in *Counseling across Cultures*, p. 133.

background and professional training even the Christian counselor may be tempted to react in a somewhat similar way.

In specific counseling theories and approaches (whether directive, permissive, or interactional), the naturalistic bias of Western psychology is widely reflected.

The directive rational-emotive therapy of Albert Ellis claims to be completely nonjudgmental: "The core of rational-emotive therapy consists of teaching the client that no one is to be blamed, condemned or moralistically punished for any of his deeds, even when he is indubitably wrong and immoral—because he is a fallible human and can be accepted as such even when he makes serious blunders and commits crimes."[41] Ellis and those who follow him actually prescribe behaviors for their clients that are designed to eliminate shame: wearing a shirt or blouse with vulgarities printed on it or propositioning a person of the opposite sex.

The permissive client-centered therapy of Rogers is a very different but also takes issue with the "Protestant Christian tradition" that says that man is basically sinful and that his sinful nature can be negated only by something approaching a miracle. Rogers believes that the "innermost core of man's nature, the deepest layers of his personality, the base of his 'animal nature,' is positive in nature—is basically socialized, forward moving, rational and realistic."[42] Rogers's client-centered therapy is permissive and nondirective. Whatever problem the client might have, it is not sin. Therefore guilt is unwarranted and shame is unneedful. And whatever the solution might be, it is within the client. Therefore, God is not needed either.

The interactional reality therapy of William Glasser represents an about-face at this point. Glasser is emphatic

41. Albert Ellis and Russell Grieger, with contributors, *Handbook of Rational-Emotive Therapy* (New York: Springer Publishing, 1977), p. 222.

42. Carl R. Rogers, *On Becoming a Person: A Therapist's View of Psychotherapy* (Boston: Houghton Mifflin, 1961), p. 91.

in pointing out to clients that they are "ill" because they have acted irresponsibly and that the ethical issue of right and wrong must be faced in therapy. Closely akin to Glasser's approach is O. Hobart Mowrer's integrity therapy, which is even more explicit. In Mowrer's view man's problem is that he does not live up to his own moral convictions. Men sin and deceive and then make an inchoate attempt to deal with guilt "by means of disguised confession and self-punishment, but without clear recognition of what it is they are punishing themselves for."[43] The problem is not so much disease as "dis-ease":

> There is, I submit, something decidedly "corrective" about such diseases, or at least potentially so. If the "hysteric" has sinned and deceived, he has also the decency (ultimately) to punish himself, in attempted atonement. However, we make this process exceedingly difficult for him. We try in our "therapeutic" ardor, first of all to assure him that he has not *sinned* [author's emphasis]; and then we set about preventing him, insofar as possible, from suffering redemptively.[44]

This is the irony of much contemporary theory. Instead of assuring the neurotic that he has not sinned and preventing him from suffering redemptively, the therapist should help him recognize the source of the "neurotic suffering," confess it, make restitution, and serve humanity.

There is an ideological Grand Canyon between Ellis and Rogers on the one side and Glasser and Mowrer on the other. But if our counseling is to be Christian, it must incorporate the biblical view of man's problems and their resolution with but limited reference to the fractured reflection of it in even Mowrer's theory. And what is Mowrer's theory? Mowrer says that for the first four hundred years or so of the Christian era both personal confession of sin and prescribed penance were largely public. During

43. Mowrer, *The New Group Therapy*, p. 129.
44. Ibid., p. 142.

the fifth century the church began to seal confession to make both confession and penance more or less private. By about the year 1200 the seal had become absolute and universal—as a matter of course penitents confessed their sins privately and confessors were enjoined not to betray the confidences of the confessional. Mowrer conjectures that the Protestant Reformation was a result of the consequent loss of integrity and vitality. He further believes that in one respect the Protestant cure was worse than the disease. Instead of destroying the seal of confession and once again placing confession and restitution in a more or less social or public context, confession was made even more private. Both the one human intermediary (Mary) and the church were disregarded—the sinner could go directly to God in prayer. Today, more than four and a half centuries later, we realize that although this approach corrected the abuses of indulgences, *"it has also left us with no fully satisfactory means of dealing with personal guilt."*[45] Mowrer disclaims any interest in theological disputations about what might be required for salvation of immortal souls. But he is vitally concerned about what happens to men's souls in the present world. And he thinks that the result of this privatizing of personal guilt and its remedy has been nothing short of disastrous.[46]

The universals of Western behavioral sciences and counseling theories, then, must also be evaluated in the light of Scripture. Inner conflict (Freud), spirituality (Jung), human responsibility (Mowrer), self-actualization and "peak experiences" (Maslow) all reflect something of the universal human condition. But to determine the degree to which this may be so, or to determine the truth or falsity of these asserted universals, requires attention to divine revelation (see fig. 12).

Step 3: Examine non-Western psychological and counseling theories. Of course, cross-cultural theory would be

---

45. Ibid., p. 19.
46. Ibid., pp. 18–19.

FIGURE 12   **Universals and Cross-Cultural Counseling Theory (3)**

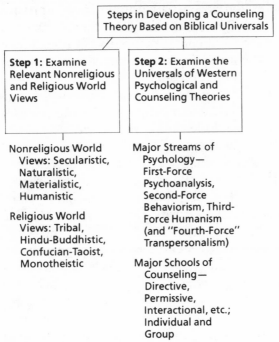

incomplete without an examination of the universals of alternative world views as they are reflected in the psychologies and helping approaches of the non-Western world, and particularly those discoverable in the counselee's culture.

Question: Does an examination of the counseling and helping approaches of other cultures allow us to conclude that "counseling universals" exist?

Reflection: The available literature does make reference to transcultural counseling but the designation seems to be a misnomer.[47] So far specialists have not really settled

47. See, for example, Gary R. Walz and Libby Benjamin, eds., *Transcultural Counseling: Needs, Programs, and Techniques,* New Vistas in Counseling series, vol. 7 (New York: Human Sciences, 1978). Interestingly enough, the great majority of references in this book are to subcultures within the United States.

on counseling universals. Torrey's "four universals of psychotherapy" are widely referred to in the secular literature. They are a world view that is shared by therapist and client; a close personal relationship between them; an expectation of being helped on the part of the sufferer or patient; and specific techniques.[48] In spite of general appreciation for Torrey's work and conclusions, however, certain misgivings have been voiced. Wohl, for example, notes that Torrey says nothing about transference, a fundamental notion in much of Western counseling and psychotherapy.[49] Wohl agrees with Torrey when he writes approvingly that "at least one, universal, fundamental feature of psychotherapy is an emotionally special interpersonal relationship created and managed to foster personal change in the client."[50] But the force of this is somewhat blunted when he goes on to say that cultures vary in their understanding of what constitutes a good interpersonal relationship.[51] From a biblical point of view we see a reflection here of such values as hope and love for one's neighbor. However, the counseling universals suggested by experts like Torrey and Wohl share at least two weaknesses. First, they are very general. Second, they should be amended in such a way as to make room for spiritual categories, the power of the Word, and the ministry of the Holy Spirit.

Question: What can be learned by inquiring into the theories of the non-Western world where it would seem that psychology and counseling are not as well-developed as in the West and where the Christian view of man and the world is even more dimly reflected?

48. E. Fuller Torrey, *The Mind Game: Witch Doctors and Psychiatrists* (New York: Emerson Hall, 1972); see also Wohl, "International Psychotherapy," in *Counseling across Cultures*, p. 145.

49. Wohl, "International Psychotherapy," in *Counseling across Cultures*, p. 194.

50. Ibid., p. 146.

51. Ibid.

Reflection: We should not conclude that the non-Western world lags far behind our Western world in probing the mysteries of the human psyche or in helping approaches. The non-Western world may not be as advanced in terms of clinical and statistical studies, but when it comes to other types of analysis, relevant Indian and Chinese literature, for example, is anything but naive. Indeed, the difference between East and West is more a function of difference in world view than a difference in insightfulness.

In any case, what can and must be learned from the non-Western world in the outworking of universals are the ways in which people are viewed, their problems are diagnosed, and changes are effected in non-Western cultures. Common sense tells us that we can learn much from Morita, Naikan, and Rissho Kosei-kai hoza psychology and counseling if our aim as Christians is to help Japanese. In Morita therapy neurotic conditions are not interpreted as deviations from normalcy but as misinterpretations of normal reactions. In Naikan therapy the patient is required to face up to his unfulfilled obligations, "repent," and make restitution. In Rissho Kosei-kai therapy the believing group is important in helping the inquiring individual. In each of these cases we can see distinct similarities to one or another Western approach. But we err greatly if we do not understand that, whatever debt there may be to the West, the primary orientation of all three is to a Buddhist view of man and the world, according to which the individual self is ephemeral, karma is universal, and God as we know him is inconsequential.

Questions: Is it advisable to attempt to match one or another Western counseling theory with another culture and employ that approach? Or should we, as some have suggested, find out how counselors and helpers in another culture operate and fit into their scheme of things?

Reflection: There is little warrant for uncritically choosing one ready-made style or approach to people helping and counseling and proceeding on that basis. Both secular and Christian experts—and intercultural and intracultural specialists—agree on that point.

Writing from a Christian and intracultural perspective, David E. Carlson surveys the field of Christian counseling and concludes there is no one school of thought that can claim exclusive rights to being Christian or biblical; there is no list of principles upon which all Christian counselors agree; and there is no agreed-upon focus of change in the various approaches.[52]

Writing from an intercultural secular perspective, Derald W. Sue writes, "It is my contention that cross-cultural helping cannot be approached through any one theory of counseling."[53] He then proceeds to give three reasons for this observation. First, ideas about the nature of man and human personality are highly culture-bound. Second, most available theories are based upon the erroneous notion that their techniques and strategies are applicable to all populations, situations, and problems. Third, theorists of counseling disagree among themselves as to what constitutes a desirable outcome in counseling. (For a summary of the principles that have been discussed in this section, see figure 13.)

The Importance of World View: An Illustration

A classic illustration of the impact of world views on counseling and curing is provided by missionary and anthropologist Paul G. Hiebert.[54] Hiebert says that he was teaching school in Shimshabad one day when Yellayya, an elder from the church in Muchintala, appeared. Tired from

52. David E. Carlson, "Relationship Counseling," in *Helping People Grow: Practical Approaches to Christian Counseling*, ed. Gary R. Collins (Santa Ana, Calif.: Vision House, 1980), pp. 32–33.

53. Derald W. Sue, *Counseling the Culturally Different* (New York: Wiley, 1981), p. 52.

54. Paul G. Hiebert, "The Flaw of the Excluded Middle," *Missiology: An International Review* 10 (January 1982): 35–47.

FIGURE 13   **Universals and Cross-Cultural Counseling Theory (4)**

Steps in Developing a Counseling Theory Based on Biblical Universals		
Step 1: Examine Relevant Nonreligious and Religious World Views	**Step 2:** Examine the Universals of Western Psychological and Counseling Theories	**Step 3:** Examine the Universals of the Psychological and Counseling Theories of the Non-Western World
Nonreligious World Views: Secularistic, Naturalistic, Materialistic, Humanistic	Major Streams of Psychology— First-Force Psychoanalysis, Second-Force Behaviorism, Third-Force Humanism (and "Fourth-Force" Transpersonalism)	The Universals of Psychotherapies in the Counselee's Culture
Religious World Views: Tribal, Hindu-Buddhistic, Confucian-Taoist, Monotheistic	Major Schools of Counseling— Directive, Permissive, Interactional, etc.; Individual and Group	The Universals Reflected in Counseling and Helping Theories and Practice in the Counselee's Culture

the walk of many miles and obviously distraught, Yellayya explained that an outbreak of smallpox had taken a number of children in his village. Doctors trained in Western medicine were unsuccessful in their attempt to bring the epidemic to an end. Village elders had called in a diviner who told them that the goddess of smallpox, Maisamma, was angry with the people of the village. A sacrifice of a water buffalo would be required.

Everyone in the village was asked to contribute to the cost of the water buffalo. When Christians refused, the village elders put pressure on them, saying that unless all contributed something, however small, the goddess would not be appeased, and therefore Christians would not be allowed water from the wells and merchants would not be allowed to sell food to them. Some Christians wanted to contribute a *paisa* (penny) but Yellayya would not let them.

Now a Christian girl had contracted smallpox. Yellayya wanted Hiebert to pray with him for the child's healing. Like all true Christian missionaries, Hiebert believed that God could heal in answer to prayer. But as he interacted with Yellayya he was uneasy in this particular set of circumstances. Hiebert explains his uneasiness in terms of the interface between his Western background, local expectations, and biblical teaching.

The Western world view and the "excluded middle." Hiebert explains that all people have a kind of folk science to explain ordinary, immediate experiences of the natural world (the lower or first level)—how boats should be sailed and crops grown. Above this level are beings (spirits, demons, ancestors) and forces (mana, planetary influences, magical and sorcerous powers) which cannot be explained directly but are real and exist on earth (the middle or second level). Beyond this immediate world (at the higher or third level) are transcendent worlds (heavens and hells), persons (gods), and forces (karma, kismet).

Two analogies are used to help people comprehend this larger world. Some see it as an organism in which everything is alive. Many tribalists even attribute life, personalities, and wills to such things as plants, earth, rocks, and water. All of these relate to each other much as humans do. Good and evil, ethics and morality are involved. Others view the world as one vast machine in which everything, perhaps even humans, operate in accordance with impersonal laws and forces. Good and evil have little or no importance. Ultimately the world is amoral and deterministic.

Most non-Western cultures give attention to all three levels of the larger world, but they tend to give special attention to the middle level where beings such as local gods, spirits, demons, and departed ancestors are present and where forces such as those related to mana, fetishes, and the planets must be taken into account. In the West, belief in this middle level began to erode in the seventeenth and eighteenth centuries, resulting in the "secularization of science and the mystification of religion." Science dealt with sense experience and experimentation and gradually expanded the area of its "scientific" explanation. Religion was left with visions, dreams, feelings, and exceptions to the natural order. The middle level was gradually squeezed out as religion became more and more "other worldly" and as science explained more and more of "this world." Ultimately the Western world view became two-tiered, for the middle level has been excluded (see Hiebert's diagram, figure 14).

The applications for counseling. Hiebert points to his Western orientation and the excluded middle as the reason for his uneasiness in dealing with Yellayya and the problems of the Christians in Muchintala. The village elders accepted the counsel of the diviner, that is, a sacrifice to the goddess of smallpox would effectively stay the epidemic. Hiebert had certain scientific understandings that militated against notions that smallpox epidemics could be ameliorated by sacrificing a water buffalo. He also believed that God is sovereign and could heal the diseased Christian child. To pray and expect God to heal the Chris-

FIGURE 14   **A Western Two-Tiered View of Reality***

| Religion | faith
miracles
other-worldly problems
sacred |

(Excluded Middle)

| Science | sight and experience
natural order
this-worldly problems
secular |

*From "The Flaw of the Excluded Middle" by Paul G. Hiebert, in *Missiology: An International Review* 10 (January 1982): 43. Used by permission.

tian child was in effect an attempt to demonstrate that Christians could pray and their God would protect his own and do deeds as great or greater than those of the goddess of smallpox. But, not knowing God's will in the matter, he was uneasy about Yellayya's request.

As it turned out, church elder and missionary joined in prayer. Still the child died. Hiebert felt defeated. But Yellayya was triumphant. Hiebert concludes the account with Yellayya's explanation and a moral.

> "The village would have acknowledged the power of our God had he healed the child," Yellayya said, "but they knew in the end she would have to die. When they saw in the funeral our hope of resurrection and reunion in heaven, they saw an even greater victory, over death itself, and they have begun to ask about the Christian way."
>
> In a new way I began to realize that true answers to prayer are those that bring the greatest glory to God, not those that satisfy my immediate desires. It is all too easy to make Christianity a new magic in which we as gods can make God do our bidding.[55]

In terms of cross-cultural counseling, there is more here than Hiebert makes explicit. Notice some of the problems and lessons other than the awakened realization of the excluded middle and the true nature of Christian prayer.

The problem of the "power encounter." We can accept Yellayya's explanation that hope of a future resurrection is in some ways a greater miracle than present healing. But this is not the import of most missiological literature on power encounter. Most such writings advocate meeting paganism on its own ground and expecting the true God to demonstrate a power greater than that of local gods, devils, magic, and charms in the manner he did when Boniface chopped down the sacred Oak of Thor. In all likelihood Yellayya could have been rather easily per-

---

55. Ibid., p. 47.

suaded in this direction. Moreover, certain cross-cultural missionaries with a somewhat different set of universals ("It is always God's will to heal in answer to the prayer of faith") would have counseled him in this direction.

It is, then, important to recognize the view according to which the right sacrifice (or prayer, or ritual) will result in a (nearby) god or spirit doing as petitioners ask. How we as Christians counsel the Yellayyas of the world to respond to such a challenge, however, will not be simply or primarily a matter of strategy but also a matter of theology. That God is able we all agree. That Christ and the apostles performed miracles we also agree. That Christ applied otherwise unnecessary clay to the blind man's eyes when he healed him and in so doing met the expectations of people not unaccustomed to similar methods used by their magicians—on this too we can probably agree. But when it comes to the status of evidential miracles today (the significance of anointing the sufferer "with oil in the name of the Lord" [James 5:14], or the meaning of "the prayer of faith [that] will make the sick person well" [James 5:15]), we differ. And in every counseling situation—but particularly in cross-cultural counseling—those differences are crucial.

The "sacred-secular" distinction. In some ways this distinction may be more important than the organismic-mechanistic one. The tendency on the part of many "organismic animists" to deal with the whole world as congeries of various kinds of forces[56] has certain similarities to the mechanistic paradigm. And the inability of "mechanistic Westerners" to consistently live as though the world is nothing more than a machine seems to push them in the direction of the organismic analogy at times.

Be that as it may, an all-important aspect of the tension between Western and other views is that Westerners do

---

56. See Janheinz Jahn, *Muntu: An Outline of the New African Culture*, trans. Marjorie Greve (New York: Grove, 1961).

not see *natural* laws as *sacred* laws, whereas the inhabitants of Muchintala, for example, do not recognize any "laws" as *natural*. As the case turns out, both Yellayya and missionary rejoice—one in the hope of the resurrection and the opportunity for witness and the other in a new understanding of world views and the nature of prayer (it is nonmanipulative). But what about the future? Is it not likely that there will be another smallpox epidemic? How, then, should Yellayya be counseled "in the small" and Muchintala villagers "in the large"? This would seem to be crucial. Yellayya and (through him?) the villagers need to understand that

- a true and loving God has provided a medicine (vaccine) that prevents smallpox outbreaks;

- beyond the power he has placed in medicine (vaccine), God can redeem lost people and heal his children when they look to him in prayer and when he is glorified thereby;

- Maisamma (the goddess of smallpox) is an idol but behind her is Satan who is a real and diabolical person, and who has limited power to do that which promotes his purpose to thwart the plan of God;

- mankind is indeed surrounded by good and evil beings who are subject to and carry out the purposes of God or Satan.

If we can agree upon these points, we can probably also agree that right at the heart of this cross-cultural counseling opportunity is the challenge to truly believe and effectively communicate that *all of life is sacred*.

In the case before us *both* the indigenous and Western man and world views require important correctives. All things are sacred even though some are inanimate. All laws are sacred even though some are "natural." Counseling can be effective only when the transcendent God and his angels (and, for that matter, Satan and his demons) and God's word and prayer are as near as our neighbors; when God's name and word are constantly on our lips; and when prayers of praise and petition are as "natural" as breathing.

The demand for authority. It is also important to note that the elders in Muchintala went to a diviner who could provide *the* answer to their problem. As Hiebert explains (and as we shall see in the next chapter), various "helper specialists" were available to them. But although specialists differed in the types of help they provided, all could be expected to provide authoritative answers and effective solutions. Otherwise they need not be paid. In the village view, helper specialists can be expected to *help*—universally.

It was not by accident or on a whim that church elder Yellayya walked many miles to seek out the help of his missionary friend. Nor is it without significance that Christ's representatives have God's Word, the Bible. We do not imply by this that there are easy answers—only that there are authoritative ones.

In contrast with the continuous search of the unbeliever, the Christian "search" for universals is to a significant degree a completed one. Not that some of us by virtue of special holiness, extraordinary wisdom, or prodigious effort have discovered that which has eluded lesser men. It is truer to say that, unworthy though we may be, we "have been found of God." And in being found of him we have discovered ourselves to be just what he has revealed us to be in his Word—body, soul, and spirit his creation, but fallen and therefore defaced and defeated in our sin.

We can agree with many of the conclusions of the naturalists and humanists in the West because all men do share characteristics and needs that grow out of their common humanity. We can also agree with the exponents of non-Christian religious systems when they resist the notion that man is composed solely of material stuff and that he knows and feels nothing except that which accrues to a large amount of protoplasm and minute charges of electricity. Man does indeed have a spiritual nature. But he is neither God, nor a god, nor in the process of becoming God. He is the creature of God—endowed by his Creator with the capacity to know and glorify God, estranged from God and his fellow creatures because of his rebellion, and informed by his conscience and God's revelation as to his need to arise and return to a loving Father whom he has forsaken but who has never forsaken him. The biblical model for people-helping is more of a moral model than it is a medical model, although the latter is certainly not ignored.

9

"Like Some Other Men"
An Inquiry into Cultural Differences

"Every man is in certain respects like some other men"—some, but not all. Why? Clyde K. Kluckhohn's answer can be summed up in one word: *culture.* Man's cultures are very diverse and the divergencies among cultures make for significant differences among men. In fact, Walter Goldschmidt asserts—in spite of the controversies among behavioral scientists concerning human universals—that "people are more alike than culture."[1]

This diversity has consequences for cross-cultural counseling. One study reveals that, whereas 30 percent of Anglo clients in the United States terminate counseling after only one contact, 50 percent of Asian American, black, Chicano, and native American clients do the same.[2]

1. Walter Goldschmidt, *Comparative Functionalism: An Essay in Anthropological Theory* (Berkeley: University of California Press, 1966), p. 134, quoted in Charles H. Kraft, *Christianity in Culture: A Study in Dynamic Biblical Theologizing in Cross-Cultural Perspective* (Maryknoll, N.Y.: Orbis, 1979), p. 202.
2. Derald W. Sue, *Counseling the Culturally Different* (New York: Wiley, 1981), pp. 27–28.

Another study reveals certain negative views on counseling to be representative of members of minority groups in North American culture: counseling is a waste of time; counselors do not accept, respect, and understand cultural differences; counselors are arrogant and contemptuous; and counselors do not know how to deal with their own hang-ups.[3]

Ronald M. Wintrob says that "we are least anxious and probably most effective as psychotherapists when we treat people whose world view corresponds with our own."[4] At the same time, he notes that the outsider is sometimes called upon to help members of a different social group, class, or subculture, primarily because he *is* an outsider.[5]

Julian Wohl writes that the experts are now saying that "at least one, universal, fundamental feature of psychotherapy is an emotionally special interpersonal relationship that is created and managed in such a way that personal change is fostered in the client."[6] Then he goes on to say that "despite this universality, it is possible, and even probable, that the constituent elements of the 'good human relationship' are different in one culture than they are in another."[7]

Norman D. Sundberg concludes,

A person who would teach or counsel in another country would do well to find out as much as he or she can about the living situations of the prospective clients and how they handle personal problems. It might be that the best thing the visitor could do would be to help clarify these

3. Ibid., pp. 3–4.

4. Ronald M. Wintrob and Youngsook Kim Harvey, "The Self-Awareness Factor in Intercultural Psychology: Some Personal Reflections," in *Counseling across Cultures*, ed. Paul P. Pedersen et al., rev. ed. (Honolulu: The University Press of Hawaii for the East-West Center, 1981), p. 123.

5. Ibid., p. 124.

6. Julian Wohl, "Intercultural Psychotherapy: Issues, Questions, and Reflections," in *Counseling across Cultures*, p. 146.

7. Ibid.

processes and work with the community to enhance and supplement them appropriately, rather than to superimpose imported counseling concepts and practices.[8]

If in the past Christian workers have rushed in where knowledgeable secularists feared to tread, these comments may be sufficient to cause us to stop, look at the cultural diversities, and listen to the indigenes of a respondent culture before offering too much cross-cultural counsel and advice.

Understanding Culture

People are usually born with a wide range of potentiality afforded by their biological, mental, and spiritual capabilities. Various factors impinge upon that potential, however. Cultural factors constitute one important kind of limitation.

What Is Culture?

Literally scores of definitions of the term *culture* have been offered although there is a general consensus as to what it means. Kluckhohn sums up the consensus rather nicely when he says, "Culture is a way of thinking, feeling, believing. It is the group's knowledge stored up for future use."[9] Or, as he writes in another context, "Culture is a great storehouse of ready-made solutions to problems which human animals are wont to encounter."[10] In essence, then, culture provides answers to the great questions having to do with that which members of a group think, feel, and do.

8. Norman D. Sundberg, "Research and Research Hypotheses about Effectiveness in Intercultural Counseling," in *Counseling across Cultures*, p. 332.

9. Quoted in Louis Luzbetak, *The Church and Cultures* (Techny, Ill.: Divine Word Publications, 1963), pp. 60–61.

10. Clyde K. Kluckhohn and Henry A. Murray, eds., *Personality in Nature, Society, and Culture* (New York: Knopf, 1948), p. 54.

The Components of Culture

Within a culture exist units such as institutions, complexes, traits, and items. *Items* have little significance in and of themselves, but become important as a part of a *trait*—that is, a "minimal constituent of a way of life which is functionally organized and regarded as having an independent existence."[11] A group of interrelated traits having a common immediate function constitutes a *complex*. And interrelated complexes which answer to a basic human need are called *institutions*. What is important is not so much the nomenclature as the linkage. Every part of culture is linked to larger groupings and these in turn are connected to still larger groupings. Moreover, as parts of larger and more complicated groupings, "pieces" of culture help meet basic human needs. Cultures, then, are not simply the sum total of isolated bits and pieces but are intricately interrelated and functional wholes. To touch one part is to touch, in some sense, all the rest.

The Workings of Culture

In order to describe the linkages and inner workings of culture, Ralph Linton, Ralph L. Beals, Harry Hoijer, and other anthropologists distinguish form, meaning, use, and function. *Form* is that which makes a culture part observable (for example, the costuming of a choir or the mode of baptism). *Meaning* is the sum of connotations and values attached to a form (for example, the elements in the Lord's Supper have one meaning to Roman Catholics, another to Protestants). *Use* has to do with the purpose for which a cultural form is employed. For example, incense plays an important role in the worship of some non-Christian religions and in some branches of Christianity as well. *Function* in this context has to do with the place a cultural form has in the larger culture. For

11. Luzbetak, *The Church and Cultures*, p. 136. See Luzbetak's discussion of the components of culture, pp. 135–38.

example, the offering in a church is used to carry on the ministry of that church, but in the context of the larger society functions to limit taxes (in our society) and ameliorate societal conditions. Function is so important that an increasing number of anthropologists concentrate on studying it (this approach is called functionalism).

Culture and Personality

We will give special consideration to personality in the next chapter, but it is important here to note that culture is reflected in the individual personality.

> All people are born helpless—without language, culture, or the ability to survive alone in the external, impersonal world. Yet within a surprisingly short period of time, the same person can be molded into an American, Dutchman, Chinese, or member of one of a thousand other societies. One of the important discoveries of the social sciences has been the crucial importance of childhood years in the formation of human personality. [12]

This molding process is called socialization or enculturation. I prefer to use the term *socialization* to refer to the process of assuming full membership in a social group and the term *enculturation* to refer to training in culture. Following Margaret Mead, however, most anthropologists use the older term *socialization* with reference to this molding process common to all people everywhere, and the newer word *enculturation* to refer to this process as it occurs within a particular culture. Thus, "human socialization," but "Zulu [or Eskimo, or Iroquois] enculturation." For a generation or more certain anthropologists have been concerned with the degree to which culture shapes personality as over against the degree to which personality is biologically based.

12. Paul G. Hiebert, *Cultural Anthropology* (Philadelphia: Lippincott, 1976), p. 434.

Among American anthropologists, one of the best known so-called cultural determinists of the first part of this century was Franz Boas of Columbia University. Reacting against biological determinists who believed that behavior is molded by heredity, Boas and his followers authored impressive studies which purported to demonstrate the cruciality of the cultural factor in personality formation.

Some of the most influential (and probably the most popular) of these studies were carried out by Mead. In a study of sixty-eight girls in Samoa, Mead concluded that in contrast to American child-rearing practices, the sexual expression of Samoan adolescents is not repressed.[13] As a result there is very little conflict and turmoil and no guilt among them. In a study of three tribes in New Guinea—the Mundugumor, the Arapesh, and the Tchambuli—she set out to discover the ways in which cultures mold the so-called masculine and feminine personality traits.[14] She found both sexes to be aggressive and fierce among the Mundugumor but mild among the Arapesh. However, among the Tchambuli the women are aggressive; the men are concerned with women, art, and hairdos. Mead concluded that culture exerts a major influence in differences often thought to be standard sexual differences. As we shall see, however, some of Mead's conclusions have been called into question.

Cultural Ethos

Because cultures are viewed as integrated social "organisms," it has become commonplace for anthropologists to attempt to characterize them according to unifying psychological principles which are at their centers. Words with somewhat varying nuances have been used, but all represent attempts to describe these principles: ethos, pat-

13. Margaret Mead, *Coming of Age in Samoa* (New York: Morrow, 1928).
14. Margaret Mead, *Sex and Temperament in Three Primitive Societies* (New York: Morrow, 1935).

tern, configuration, mentality, world view, *Weltan-schauung, Geist,* or mainspring. Among the first to attempt a serious and extensive study of this kind was another protégée of Boas, Ruth Benedict. Concerning the importance of her work, Geoffrey Gorer has written, "I should choose 1895, the year of the publication of Freud and Breuer's *Studien Uber Hysterie,* as the year in which the scientific study of individual psychology was born, and 1934, the year of the publication of Ruth Benedict's *Patterns of Culture,* as the birth year of the scientific study of national character."[15]

In *Patterns of Culture* Benedict proposed that each society exhibits a major organizing principle derived from certain aspects of basic human temperament.[16] She variously called this organizing principle "ethos," "pattern," or "mainspring." Drawing upon the work of Boas, the Nietzschean distinction between Dionysian and Apollonian ways of arriving at the values of existence, and her own studies, she differentiated between the ethos of various tribal groups, especially the Indians of the southwestern and northwestern United States. Benedict found that the Northwest Coast Kwakiutl and most other North American Indian groups manifested a Dionysian ethos. They valued violent experiences whereby human beings could transcend usual sensory routines. Whether by motionless concentration, arduous torture, or frenzied ritual, they sought to break through the bounds of the five senses to supernatural illumination and power. The Zuni ethos she found to be very different. Staying within the known map of law, the Zuni did not "meddle with disruptive psychological states." They were orderly, unemotional, and stoic. They attempted to solve problems rationally. She termed this ethos Apollonian. (She located certain

15. Geoffrey Gorer, "The Concept of National Character," in *Personality in Nature, Society, and Culture,* p. 247, quoted in Victor Barnouw, *Culture and Personality* (Homewood, Ill.: Dorsey, 1963), p. 39.

16. Ruth Benedict, *Patterns of Culture* (New York: Penguin, 1934).

other Indians in a middle ground between the two extremes.)

With reference to psychiatry, Benedict concluded that normality and abnormality must be defined within cultural contexts. A "normal" Zuni would be "abnormal" among the Kwakiutl, and a "normal" Kwakiutl would be "abnormal" among the Zuni.

Shortly after the publication of *Patterns of Culture,* Mead characterized the traditional or "puritan" American character type as being guilt-oriented.[17] The child takes the values of the parent as his own and learns to act as if the parent were present even when the parent is absent. Failure to do so results in a retrospective discomfort which technically can be called guilt. Conformance is reinforced by the system of rewards and punishment. The picture is completed by a conception of deity which sees God as supporting the parent and primarily concerned with moral behavior. Mead believed that North America was experiencing a shift in moral emphasis from parental guidelines to "age-grade standards" in which the disciplinary force would shift from guilt to the shame of peer-group disapproval.

Once again Benedict contributed to the study of national character in *The Chrysanthemum and the Sword.*[18] Drawing upon Mead's analysis, she categorized Japanese culture as a shame culture in which ideal behavior is determined by an elaborate system of obligations to the larger society and its included groups. Conformance to the expectations of society brings approval. Failure to live up to those expectations results in disapproval and shame. By carefully cataloging and illustrating the various types of obligations and the attendant system of rewards and punishment, Benedict attempted to describe Japanese national

17. Margaret Mead, ed., *Cooperation and Competition among Primitive Peoples* (New York: McGraw-Hill, 1937), pp. 307, 343.

18. Ruth Benedict, *The Chrysanthemum and the Sword: Patterns of Japanese Culture* (Boston: Houghton Mifflin, 1946).

character and make otherwise enigmatic behavioral patterns more understandable to the West.

Controversy in Cultural Studies

Do not expect to find a consensus among anthropologists on questions such as the relative importance of biology and culture in personality development, the psychological classification of cultures, or even in the description of what takes place in the enculturation process of this or that particular culture. As John Leo reports,

> Robert Redfield's 1930 study of Tepoztlan, Mexico, found warm, laid-back peasants. Oscar Lewis studied the same people in 1951, finding a culture in which murder, gossip and stealing were rampant. Early reports on African bushmen labeled them the "harmless people"; later research revealed a distinct aggressiveness. Bronislaw Malinowski, in a famous 1923 study of the Trobriand Islanders, found that the area's young boys grew up without an Oedipus complex, a refutation of one of Freud's presumed universals. But last year anthropologist Melford Spiro, using Malinowski's own data, said Malinowski's conclusions were unwarranted.[19]

Anthropologists also have frequently pointed to some of the inadequacies of Mead's ethnographic field work even while showing appreciation for her contributions to our understanding of human behavior. Recently, however, the controversy over her research on Samoa has reached a peak, fueled by a stinging critical work from Derek Freeman. He contends that she based her conclusions on a small sampling; that she imposed her (and Boas's) commitment to cultural (as over against biological) determinism on the evidence; and that in any case Samoans are both competitive and characterized by a cult of virginity,

19. John Leo, "Bursting the South Sea Bubble: An Anthropologist Attacks Margaret Mead's Research in Samoa," *Time,* 14 February 1983, p. 70.

features which make for very different persons than those painted by Mead as being sexually free and without neuroses and guilt feelings.[20]

But Freeman himself is now the subject of numerous and pointed criticisms, many of which seem to be well-founded. Concerning the Samoans, Bradd Shore says, "Why people would believe Samoans could be as wimpy as Margaret Mead says they are, or as violent as Derek Freeman says they are, I just don't understand."[21] Concerning Freeman's contention that Boas sent Mead to Samoa to prove his extreme ideas about cultural determinism, anthropologist-reviewers agree that this is a misrepresentation of the relationship between Boas and Mead and also a distortion of Boas's position. In reacting against the notion that group behavior is genetically determined, Boas did not adopt an extreme form of cultural determinism. As Marvin Harris says, "The major task to which Boas and his students devoted themselves was not to prove that there is no human nature, but to prove that there is only *one* human nature that allows for an enormous amount of mutually encoded variation."[22]

The controversy is an ongoing one. Writing in the *Royal Anthropological Institute News,* Paula Brown Glick indicates that although she anticipates a number of discussions on the relationship of biology and culture to human behavior in the future, "No final judgement on the work of Margaret Mead is to be expected."[23]

Guilt or Shame?

Numerous dialogues and debates about the distinction between guilt and shame have occurred during the last

20. Derek Freeman, *Margaret Mead and Samoa: The Making and Unmaking of an Anthropological Myth* (Cambridge, Mass.: Harvard University Press, 1983).

21. Leo, "Bursting the South Sea Bubble," p. 69.

22. Quoted in Paula Brown Glick, "The Attack on and Defense of Margaret Mead," *Royal Anthropological Institute News* 58 (October 1983): 14.

23. Ibid.

thirty to thirty-five years. One such discussion took place in connection with the Symposium on Transcultural Psychiatry (February 1965) supported by the Ciba Foundation and attended by more than twenty leading educators in these fields. One interchange on guilt and shame which took place at that symposium serves well to characterize typical lines of agreement and disagreement.

In a paper entitled "Phenomenology of Affective Disorder in Chinese and Other Cultures," P. M. Yap noted that although the problem of the development of the superego is central to the cross-cultural problem of depression, this area of study is in chaos. He insisted, however, that it had become increasingly clear that "the opposition of 'shame' to 'guilt' is intellectualistic, arbitrary, and without empirical justification."[24] He held that it is more helpful to distinguish between unconscious guilt feelings on the one hand, and conscious guilt feelings and conscious moral shame feelings "generated by the anticipation of discovery of wrong conduct by others" on the other.[25] He discounted the notion that guilt feelings are confined to any particular religious system, such as Protestantism with its doctrines of sin and atonement. And he agreed with G. A. De Vos that among the Japanese, guilt feelings based on a sense of failure to fulfill moral obligations to ancestors and the emperor showed a development analogous to that inherent in Max Weber's Protestant ethic. In the West, Christianity heightens the sense of guilt and also reduces it; in the Orient, a system of obligations and rites of ancestor worship or reverence serve the same function. In the Orient, however, "the absence of teachings on original sin and the supernatural basis of conscience has also made possible among the elite a rationalistic acceptance of moral values, with conscious acknowledgement of wrong and

24. P. M. Yap, "Phenomenology of Affective Disorder in Chinese and Other Cultures," in *Transcultural Psychiatry,* p. 100.
25. Ibid.

the need for further self-cultivation after the example of the Confucian 'Superior Man.' "[26]

The ensuing discussion was somewhat confusing at times, but overall it was rather enlightening on the points with which we are concerned.[27]

Tsung-Yi Lin disagreed with Yap. He said that when the definitions of sin and guilt are widened so that failure to fulfill obligations to ancestors and parents are included, guilt complexes are apparent among Chinese depressives. Nevertheless, the kind of complexes associated with the doctrine of original sin and seen in Christian communities is rare among Chinese unless one is talking about educated Christian Chinese.

Vera Rubin agreed with Yap's ideas on guilt and shame, but at the same time recalled her own findings in a comparative study of Negroes and East Indians in Trinidad. In that study Negro Christians and East Indian Hindus reported different reactions in guilt situations. The former reacted with feelings of guilt when doing something "which they thought involved guilt" irrespective of whether this had been done in public or private. The latter reported feelings of guilt primarily if they had been seen committing the "guilty" act. "There was a difference between internal feelings of guilt and what might be called shame."

Mead noted that discussions of the guilt-shame dichotomy are often truncated because the question of pride is disregarded in personality development. She cited Erik Erikson's theory that a sense of sin develops very early and is followed by a period of shame and pride associated with the development of autonomous feeling, which in turn is followed by guilt at a still later stage. This reinforces the notion that guilt is associated with certain kinds

26. Ibid., pp. 102–3.
27. The various responses are to be found in Yap, "Phenomenology of Affective Disorder," in *Transcultural Psychiatry*, pp. 102–3.

of character formation and religious ideas. According to Mead, this approach makes a coherent picture possible.

Further Developments in the Study of Personality and Culture

In focusing on the nature-nurture and guilt-shame debates and some major contributors to those debates, we have by-passed the contributions of numerous other scholars in this area. A listing of these individuals would include Abram Kardiner, A. I. Hallowell, Melford Spiro, J. W. M. Whiting, Irvin L. Child, and Francis L. K. Hsu, among others.

Kardiner attempted to describe the basic personality of an entire people by demonstrating congruence between a psychoanalytic interpretation of personality and the major features of a culture. On the one hand, for example, life histories and the results of certain psychological testing might be studied. On the other hand, such things as the mode of subsistence, child-rearing, and the salient features of folklore and religion might be scrutinized. By a comparison of outcomes Kardiner purported to describe the basic personality of the particular culture under study.

Hallowell and Spiro exhibited interests similar to those of Kardiner but also exhibited a greater facility in making psychological (Hallowell) and psychoanalytic (Spiro) analyses.

Whiting and Child brought a new approach to these studies by developing the hologeistic method.[28] Instead of studying behavior directly, they depended on ethnographic field studies (especially those reported in the Human Relation Area Files) for their analyses. Largely abandoning the attempt to make specific interpretations of the relationship between personality and culture, they con-

28. For a complete treatment of this method see J. W. M. Whiting and Irvin L. Child, *Child Training and Personality: A Cross-Cultural Study* (New Haven: Yale University Press, 1953).

centrated on the relationship between personality processes and certain aspects of culture. They attempted to
show, for example, how the socioeconomic system of a
society influenced child-rearing which, in turn, helped
shape personality features which, finally, manifested
themselves in customs and forms of art and religion.
Freudian hypotheses played an increasing role in his
thinking as Whiting developed his approach over the years.

More recently, Hsu has taken exception to the individualistic orientation of these approaches nourished, as they
quite often have been, by Sigmund Freud's focus on intrapsychic functions. He also has taken exception to the
method of another prominent theorist, Erikson, who gives
a much larger place to interpersonal factors but who still
operates on an "individual-centered model of man," according to Hsu. Hsu himself proposes a "sociocentric"
model expressed in a "psychosociogram of man." Representing a refinement and an elaboration of Hsu's earlier
distinction between repression culture and suppression
culture, this model describes man in terms of eight con-
centric layers of elements. These elements start with the
Freudian unconscious and preconscious and are overlaid
with two levels of the conscious and four levels of society
and culture. Hsu believes that Western politicians, preach-
ers, clinicians, and even university researchers are so wed-
ded to the notion that both the roots of human problems
and the source of human achievements are to be found in
individuals that they are blind to the crucial importance
of society and culture in both explaining the human personality and proposing solutions to human problems.[29]

We have only touched on some of the highlights in the
study of personality and culture, but perhaps this has been
sufficient to demonstrate how perspectives have changed

29. Francis L. K. Hsu, *Rugged Individualism Reconsidered: Essays in Psychological Anthropology* (Knoxville: The University of Tennessee Press, 1983),
pp. 199–202.

and diversified up until the present. In this development one can discern shifts from a study of the relationship between personality and culture in general to a study of that relationship in particular societies; from attempts to discover basic personality to a consideration of modal personality; from a treatment of personality and culture as being distinct entities to a study of personality as an instrument to better understand socioculture processes; and other shifts as well. In all, perhaps researchers have become somewhat more humble even as they have become more knowledgeable. Gustav Jahoda, to whom I am indebted for some of the foregoing insights, addresses himself to the inadequacies (as well as the strengths) of the approaches of people like Mead, Kardiner, and Whiting and then concludes that "there are extensive and important areas of behaviour about which academic personality theory has little if anything to say."[30] He reinforces this conclusion by citing first-hand experiences, one of which is included here because of its pertinence.

> The first occasion when these shortcomings were brought home to me was when I was teaching in a university in West Africa and came across the problems connected with envy. During examination periods, a number of students, including some of the most gifted ones, succumbed to a syndrome that was sufficiently common to have acquired the local label of "brain fag." It was characterized by extreme tiredness and inability to concentrate, severe headaches, and other similar symptoms. On inquiry it emerged that the most of the sufferers (or victims, as they felt themselves to be) attributed their troubles to the *envy* of less fortunate kinsfolk who did not have the same chances of getting on in the world and therefore employed supernatural means to spoil the possible success of the person in question.

30. Gustav Jahoda, *Psychology and Anthropology: A Psychological Perspective* (New York: Academic Press, 1982), p. 96.

Naturally I tried to find out more about envy, and the anthropological literature revealed that it is extremely widespread across the world and is often an important factor affecting behaviour. . . .

. . . .

When I turned to psychology books in order to learn more about envy, I drew a blank—by and large, it is simply ignored, and the only serious discussions were to be found in psychoanalytic writings such as those of Melanie Klein (1957). There has been hardly any change in this regard during the more than two decades that have elapsed since then.[31]

Typologies of Cultures

It will be apparent from the previous discussion that the attempt to identify the ethos or national character of a given culture is also fraught with a certain amount of danger inasmuch as the description of a culture in psychological terms is much like the description of basic or, if one prefers, modal personality. Nevertheless, various scholars have attempted this and with no little benefit to our understanding. The differentiation of Gemeinschaft/Gesellschaft, cultures (Ferdinand Tonnies), repression/suppression cultures (Hsu), traditional-directed, inner-directed, and other-directed cultures (David Riesman), or collectivistic-dependency/individualistic-independency cultures (Susumu Akahoshi) are some of the better known characterizations of culture, as well as those of Mead and Benedict. Perhaps the theme theory of Morris E. Opler should also be mentioned. Believing that a single, all-pervading principle is too simple to adequately describe the "heart" and "soul" of a culture, Opler developed the idea that cultures have not one but several interrelated themes that supply unity and direction. Rather than searching out one principle, then, the anthropologist is obliged to dis-

31. Ibid., pp. 96–97.

cover a set of underlying and consistent values, premises, and goals which, when taken together, will more completely characterize any given culture.[32]

With special reference to cross-cultural counseling, Derald W. Sue distinguishes between two psychological orientations of cultures—the locus of control (personal control) and the locus of responsibility.[33] These may be "internal to the person" or "external and in the system." This results in four types of cultural orientations to life: internal control-internal responsibility (IC-IR), external control-internal responsibility (EC-IR), external control-external responsibility (EC-ER), and internal control-external responsibility (IC-ER). The dominant white middle-class culture of the United States exemplifies the IC-IR type and emphasizes uniqueness, independence, and self-reliance. Counselors tend to be of the opinion that clients have responsibility for their behavior and by self-effort can improve themselves and the conditions in which they live—an appropriate assumption for the white middle-class counselees who make up the bulk of their clients. Such subcultures as those of the blacks and native Americans in the United States can be classified as EC-ER. If counselors are to help them, blacks and native Americans need to be aided in developing new coping strategies, in experiencing some kind of success, and in establishing their identity.

Some recent missionary literature has emphasized three types of culture—Western guilt culture, animistic fear culture, and tribal shame culture.[34] This elaboration of the guilt-shame dichotomy is of some significance, although the categories exhibit a considerable amount of overlap. Animism and tribalism often go hand in hand.

32. Morris E. Opler, "Themes as Dynamic Forces in Culture," *American Journal of Sociology* 51 (September 1945): 198–206.

33. Sue, *Counseling the Culturally Different*, pp. 80–90.

34. See, for example, Hans Kasdorf, *Christian Conversion in Context* (Scottdale, Penn.: Herald, 1980), p. 113.

Fear is in evidence in both guilt and shame cultures. In guilt cultures there is the fear of the consequences of disobeying the laws of God, society, or one's own conscience. In shame cultures there is the fear of being found out. But it does seem that in many animistic societies the overriding concern is the fear of retribution by the spirits and of the results of black magic. In some instances animists have died if they know that a hex has been put on them. Whether or not this fear of supernatural powers and spirits is unique enough to warrant a special category in our typology of cultures is a matter that will not be debated here. We can be sure, however, that the emphasis is not an unwarranted one.

These various approaches to describing cultures have much to commend them. If it is possible to characterize a culture by identifying some themes or premises without at the same time misrepresenting that culture, we will find it easier to proceed with counseling within that cultural context. On the other hand, because cultures are complex, the likelihood of a certain amount of arbitrariness in selecting a very few premises to the exclusion of others cannot be discounted.

For present purposes I prefer a typology which represents an integration of some of the typologies already mentioned. It is apparent, after all, that most of the insights and ideas of the scholars mentioned are not mutually inclusive.

My typology, then, distinguishes between collectivistic-dependency cultures, which may have either an ancestor orientation or a peer-group orientation, and individualistic-independency cultures, which may have either a subjectivity or objectivity orientation (see fig. 15).

To make the significance of these cultural differences more explicit, let us take the case of a white, middle-class Christian counselor who falls in the individualistic-independency/objectivity-oriented (II-OO) category typical of United States culture in past years. He places great value

FIGURE 15   Collectivistic-Dependency Cultures and Individualistic-Independency Cultures*

| | Collectivistic-Dependency Cultures | | Individualistic-Independency Cultures | |
	Ancestor Orientation	Peer-Group Orientation	Subjectivity Orientation	Objectivity Orientation
Values	**Traditional:** "It has always been done this way."	**Popular:** "Everyone is doing it."	**Intuitional:** "Follow the gleam."	**Lawful:** "It is written...." "The evidence shows...."
Avoidance Goal	Shame of dishonoring the ancestors	Shame of disappointing the peer group	Guilt of disregarding the "vision"	Guilt of disobeying the "laws"
Attainment Goals	Acquiescence to the will of the ancestors leads to harmony.	Conformance to the expectations of peers leads to acceptance.	Attention to inner self leads to identity.	Obedience to requirements leads to reconciliation.
Models	"Great men" of the tribe or clan	"Good guys" of the gang or club	Gurus and "tycoons"	Lawmakers and prophets

	China	Modern United States	India	United States in the past
Media	Myths and legends	Interviews and opinion polls	Arts, poetry, reports of "visions" or success	Lawbooks, sermons, and scientific treatises
Decision Type	Group decision expected rather than individual	Group decision or individual decision expected to reflect group expectations	Individual decisions expected	Individual decisions expected
Decision Timing	Time is required for either group or individual.	Time may be required to ascertain "group mind."	Time may be required. Decisions should be immediate when the way becomes known.	The time for decision is now. The way is known. Any decision is better than none.
Decision Strength	Group decision is binding; individual decision tends to be risky and tentative.	Group decision binding, but both group and individual decisions subject to change with mood or fashion	Group decision regarded with some suspicion; individual decision binding but subject to change with new "light"	Group decision regarded with some suspicion; individual decision expected to be followed through
Example	China	Modern United States	India	United States in the past

*Taken from Communicating Christ Cross-Culturally, by David J. Hesselgrave. Copyright © 1978 by David J. Hesselgrave. Used by permission of Zondervan Publishing House.

on the laws of God and the rules of evidence. He believes that by breaking the laws of God and man, individuals are largely responsible for their own problems. He assumes that guilt attends wrongdoing. He expects counselees to accept applicable evidence, admit guilt when the evidence indicates culpability, and make appropriate decisions—individually and immediately.

Important elements in this orientation are not only cultural but also supracultural in that the United States culture of past years relied more upon the Christian heritage than it does today. Nevertheless, lack of bicultural sensitivities and appreciation for the distinctives (often, desirable distinctives) of other cultures, or the lack of understanding of changes that have occurred within his own culture, will tend to blind our counselor friend to the implications of fundamentally different cultural orientations.

When the counselee is a more or less "pure" representative of a dominant culture orientation, many of these implications become rather obvious. For example, a modicum of study and experience will enable the American counselor to understand that a collectivistic-dependency/ancestor-oriented (CD-AO) traditional Chinese counselee places great value on the ways of the ancestors; appeals to tradition; loses face when he brings the extended family into disrepute; resorts to his primary group when making important decisions; tends to delay decisions as long as possible; and favors decisions that are tentative. Our II-OO American counselor will probably find that the CD-AO Chinese counselee responds favorably to a counseling approach that is directive (structural and emphasizing advice and suggestions) but, by the same token, will find it difficult to follow through with decisions that do not take Chinese values, group process, and time orientations into account.

When the counselee is marginal to "his" culture, or belongs to a minority subculture, or is a member of a culture in transition, the implications of our typology are less obvious although no less important. Take, for example, a Chinese young person who, with a number of members of his extended family from Taiwan, has taken up residence in Los Angeles. Within a short time this youthful immigrant may well find that he is sometimes Chinese and sometimes American, always a member of the Chinese-American subculture, and in some sense a part of an emerging generation in a society in transition. In this case our II-OO counselor will be required to take both the CD-AO orientation of the traditional Chinese and the CD-PO orientation of American youth culture into account in the counseling situation. In addition, he must be able to understand the psychology of, and empathize with the feelings of, a member of a minority culture in the United States.

Culture and "Problem Syndromes"

Numerous medical studies indicate that the incidence of certain diseases varies greatly from one society to another, depending on diet, lifestyle, physical environment, and other factors. By the same token, we can expect that the incidence of mental disorders, nervous conditions, personality problems, social conflicts, and the like will vary from culture to culture. More than that, these problems will be attended by culturally determined diagnoses and solutions. The chapter about non-Western methods of counseling pointed in this direction.

To explore this matter a bit further we will first examine some current discussions on culture and mental and psychological disorders and then turn to other types of problems of particular importance to Christian workers.

Cultural Conceptions and Mental/Psychological Disorders

To ascertain the impact of cultural studies on psychology and psychiatry, one has only to review approaches to the diagnosis and treatment of mental disorders. Traditionally, in the West, mental disorders have been put in the general category of disease or illness and have been diagnosed and treated accordingly. This clinical approach has been attended by a clinical universalism which says that major psychoses are found universally. John Marshall Townsend quotes three prominent psychiatrists (each with cross-cultural experience) who support this view. E. B. Forster, with experience in Ghana, writes,

> Psychiatric syndromes or reactions, by and large, are similar in all races throughout the world. The mental reactions seen in our African patients can be diagnosed according to Western textbook standards. The basic illness and reaction types are the same. Environmental, constitutional and tribal cultural background merely modify the symptom constellation. Basically, the disorders of thinking, feeling, willing and knowing are the same.[35]

E. L. Margetts, author of numerous pieces on cultural anthropology and psychiatry, agrees:

> The more I listen to the discussion of transcultural psychiatry, the more I am coming to believe that perhaps there is no such thing . . . [we have not] learned a great deal about it since the time of Kraepelin. As far as I am concerned, psychiatry is the same all around the world: the signs and symptoms of mental diseases are the same, the diagnoses are the same and there is probably just as much possession syndrome in England as there is in equatorial Africa.[36]

And in an amusing account, Alexander Leighton reports on his interview with a native healer in Nigeria:

35. Quoted in John Marshall Townsend, *Cultural Conceptions and Mental Illness: A Comparison of Germany and America* (Chicago: University of Chicago Press, 1978), p. 66.
36. Ibid., pp. 66–67.

On one occasion a healer said to me, through an interpreter: "This man came here three months ago full of delusions and hallucinations; now he is free of them." I said,
"What do these words 'hallucination' and 'delusion' mean?
I don't understand." I asked this question thinking, of
course, of the problems of cultural relativity in a culture
where practices such as witchcraft, which in the West
would be considered delusional, are accepted. The native
healer scratched his head and looked a bit puzzled at this
question and then he said: "Well, when this man came
here he was standing right where you see him now and
thought he was in Abeokuta" (which is about thirty miles
away), "he thought I was his uncle and he thought God
was speaking to him from the clouds. Now I don't know
what you call that in the United States, but here we consider that these are hallucinations and delusions!"[37]

Nevertheless, clinical universalism and the clinical approach which considers mental disorders as disease have
come under attack on two counts, both based on cultural
factors. The first criticism is made by Thomas Szasz and
others who argue strenuously against the clinical approach on the ground that psychiatrists seldom proceed
as medical scientists. Rather they operate as reinforcers of
middle-class society's values and beliefs. He compares
"contemporary psychiatry to the Inquisition which labeled deviant people 'heretics' and 'witches' in order to
dispose of them."[38]

The second criticism is made by numerous theorists
who believe that the principles propounded by Benedict
(and others) half a century ago still have great relevance
today. With her they believe that mental disorders vary
with the stresses imposed by culture, and that culture
determines what is normal and abnormal. "She did not
deny the possibility of universal criteria for normality-

37. Ibid., p. 66.
38. Ibid., p. 106.

abnormality, but she felt that, with adequate cross-cultural research . . . this universal definition of abnormality would probably be quite unlike our 'culturally conditioned, highly elaborate' psychoses, schizophrenia and manic depression."[39] This culturally relativistic approach has variously been called the sociological model, cultural determinism, and the social-role approach.

Townsend himself takes a somewhat mediating position in this dispute. He agrees that certain mental conditions which resemble our categories (such as "affective psychoses" and "schizophrenia") are likely to be identified and thought to be abnormal in any culture. However, he presents irrefutable evidence that diagnoses differ considerably, depending on the diagnostician, and that diagnostic labels are sometimes arbitrary and are, in part, a cultural product. Townsend believes that the dichotomy between viewing problems as illness or as imposed by social roles is misleading and false. He ends his study in a helpful and yet tentative way: "Finally, we need more research on the causes and cures of mental disorders. A proper research strategy would include a multiplicity of parameters: genetic, psychological, developmental, and cultural. The present study suggests that only by thus recognizing the complexity of human behaviors can we finally begin to solve the problems of mental disorders."[40]

Note the emphasis on culture. Research indicates that it is well-taken. Cultural divergencies result in differences in the understanding, incidence, symptomology, and treatment of mental disorders. To see how this is so we will focus on the affective disorder (or, "mood disorder") called depression ("major depressive episode"). For a detailed description of this disorder, consult the *Diagnostic and Statistical Manual of Mental Disorders.*[41]

39. Ibid., p. xiii.
40. Ibid., p. 117.
41. American Psychiatric Association, *Diagnostic and Statistical Manual of Mental Disorders*, 3d ed. (Washington, D.C.: American Psychiatric Association, 1980), pp. 210–24.

The essential feature [of this disorder] is either a dysphoric mood, usually depression, or loss of interest or pleasure in all or almost all activities and pastimes. This disturbance is prominent, relatively persistent, and associated with other symptoms of the depressive syndrome. These symptoms include appetite disturbance, change in weight, sleep disturbance, psychomotor agitation or retardation, decreased energy, feelings of worthlessness or guilt, difficulty concentrating or thinking, and thoughts of death or suicide or suicidal attempts.[42]

It is the opinion of many authorities that depression is one of the most common and pervasive maladies afflicting mankind. One expert estimates that as many as eight million people suffer from it annually (half of them in the United States!), although it is hard to see how anyone could objectively establish this or any specific figure.[43]

Let us consider briefly how depression is related to culture.

Understandings and conceptions of depression. One study of French Canadians revealed that "only 5 per cent of the sample labeled a case involving 'sadness, insomnia, fatigue, and loss of interest' as depressed." They thought of depression as something akin to "nervous breakdown."[44] Similarly, a comparison of Japanese nationals, Japanese Americans, and Caucasian Americans suggested "that depression has a different connotative meaning for each of the groups."[45]

Incidence of depression. Differences of understanding and approaches to assessment lead researchers to admit that we know very little about cultural differences in rates

42. Ibid., p. 210.

43. Walter C. Johnson, "Depression: Biochemical Abnormality or Spiritual Backsliding?" *Journal of the American Scientific Affiliation* 32 (March 1980): 18.

44. Anthony J. Marsella, "Depressive Experience and Disorder across Cultures," in *Handbook of Cross-Cultural Psychology: Perspectives,* gen. ed. Harry C. Triandis, 6 vols. (Boston: Allyn and Bacon, 1980–83), vol. 6, ed. Harry C. Triandis and Juris G. Draguns (1981), p. 241.

45. Ibid., p. 242.

of depression.[46] One researcher indicates that extended family structures in non-Western cultures may minimize frustrations in early life and lessen the incidence of depression.[47] Another suggests that reports of subjective mood distress are absent in cultures that are less individualistic and possess a metaphorical language structure and an imagistic or pictorial way of experiencing reality.[48]

Symptoms of depression. Though research on the incidence of depression in other cultures does not always result in a consensus, there is general agreement that where it does occur it assumes forms that vary from Western patterns. For example, one study indicated that "guilt feelings, depressive affect, and suicidal ruminations are generally absent" in sub-Saharan Africa.[49] Again, a study of depressed patients in Indonesia revealed a loss of vitality and sleep disturbances, but feelings of sadness, a sense of inadequacy, and guilt feelings were generally absent.[50]

Treatment of depression. Treatment varies with both cause and culture. It is estimated that about ninety-five percent of those suffering from depression in America could find relief by treatment with antidepressant drugs and/or electric convulsive therapy.[51] Contrast this knowledge and potential with the fact that there are hundreds of cultures and subcultures around the world where such therapies are completely unknown.

After reviewing the relevant research, Anthony J. Marsella reaches the following conclusions (among others):

> No universal conception of depression is readily apparent. In cultures where variants of depressive disorders (in the Western sense) are found, perhaps another la-

---

46. Ibid., p. 249.
47. Ibid., p. 270.
48. Ibid., p. 273.
49. Ibid., p. 250.
50. Ibid., p. 253.
51. Johnson, "Depression," pp. 18–26.

bel should be used because of the different meanings and experiences involved.

Allowing for methodological limitations in the determination of distribution rates, depression does seem to be less common in non-Western cultures than it is in the West.

Depression in less Westernized societies often does not exhibit psychological components such as guilt, self-depreciation, and suicidal tendencies. The key to this difference may be the lack of emphasis on the labeling of psychological experience in some cultures.[52]

Problem Syndromes and the Christian Counselor

We can expect that cultures will tend to exhibit a high or low incidence of certain difficulties (in addition to organic and mental/psychological problems) which will be of special concern to Christian workers. By anticipating the problem syndromes that will characterize a given host culture, Christian counselors can prepare themselves in advance.

Experience in the United States alerts us to the importance of problem syndromes to the Christian worker. Rapid change has forced Christian ministers to deal with the breakdown of the family, divorce, sexual questions, alcoholism, drug use, and similar problems to a degree unparalleled in previous generations. It is not to the credit of the church that for the most part her leadership did not predict the magnitude of these problems and minister accordingly. In fact, the preaching, teaching, and counseling ministries of many local churches even today do not do credit to their cultural and spiritual awareness. But the plethora of books on these subjects, and the prevalence of tragedies forced upon often unprepared church leadership, testify to our plight.

---

52. Marsella, "Depressive Experience," in *Handbook of Cross-Cultural Psychology*, vol. 6, pp. 274–76.

Alerted, then, by cultural studies, American social change, and missionary experiences, cross-cultural personnel do well to study carefully the problem syndromes of the culture in which they will represent Christ. Workers in sub-Saharan Africa can anticipate case after case relating to bride-price, polygamy, and witchcraft. Workers in Muslim areas will encounter problems occasioned by the concept of *ummat* (society, brotherhood) and the extremely severe penalties imposed on family members who convert to another religion. Workers in Brazil will be challenged by spiritism. Workers in Melanesia will have to deal with cargo-cult values. Workers in Taiwan will be challenged by the concept of ancestor loyalty and the implications of filial piety.

It will not be enough to catalogue frequently faced problems in a given receptor culture, however. The cross-cultural worker must be able to analyze problems correctly. Consider, for example, the institution of marriage. Of the varying problems relating to it none is more pervasive than that of plural wives. This problem takes various forms: simultaneous polygamy in sub-Saharan Africa, serial polygamy (divorce and remarriage) in the United States, and a wife plus mistress(es) in Latin America and Asia. The form differs from culture to culture. Even more importantly, the meaning and function vary. Polygamy in Africa usually functions in such a way as to provide esteem, a pool of labor for home and garden, and progeny to carry on the family name. Serial polygamy in the United States functions to give some legitimacy to otherwise unacceptable marriage arrangements. It also functions negatively to disrupt child-rearing and domestic life. In Latin America and Asia the arrangement of having a wife plus mistress(es) functions as an additional sexual outlet for males and to maintain some (usually) single women. (Arranged marriages—especially in Asia—may be an important contributing factor.) Form, meaning, and function differ in each case, so the nature of the problem changes from culture to culture. In one case, the culture encourages polygamy. In another case, the culture increasingly makes allowance for it. In yet another case, the culture largely ignores the problem. The Christian counselor must also recognize that some aspects of this problem (including, for example, all questions having to do with polygamy and church order) are occasioned by the entrance of Christianity itself.

Each culture, then, presents its own problem syndromes. The cross-cultural Christian counselor will encounter surprises. But he or she need not be surprised too often. Certain problems will occur with monotonous regularity. Many of these can be anticipated, studied beforehand, and matched with Christian options.

Learning from the Peace Corps

Several hours spent in reading objective evaluations of the Peace Corps will cause the experienced Christian cross-cultural worker to alternately laugh and cry. He will see multiplied secular reflections of the cross-cultural missionary movement—the vision of helping the Third World; the dedicated, hard-driving staff in Washington; the "ten-countries-in-twenty-days" visits by members of the home staff; the desire for immediate and tangible results; culture-pressed volunteers; and failure and success.

The Peace Corps Act (PL 87–293) was enacted on September 22, 1961. The United States Congress stipulated three broad objectives in that act: to help the countries inviting volunteers to meet their needs for trained manpower; to promote abroad a better understanding of Americans and American society; and to promote in the American people a broader understanding of other peoples.[53]

These objectives were broad enough to allow for all

53. David Hapgood and Meridan Bennett, *Agents of Change: A Close Look at the Peace Corps* (Boston: Little, Brown, 1968), p. 8.

sorts of altruistic innovation. Finally the way had been made clear for Americans who wanted to actually do something about the great needs of the world.

> From the moment of its creation the Peace Corps was one of the finest flowers of the post-Roosevelt liberal era; intelligent, rational in its refusal to be bamboozled by arbitrary rules, highly literate, dependent upon verbal expression. It contained some of the intellectual hubris which other observers have described as a characteristic of the New Frontiersman. Civil informality was also around in quantity; first names without undue familiarity was the tone. Church membership and athletic prowess were valued, if only as secondary virtues; there were practically no dingy, Bible-clutching fundamentalists around, and very few people who didn't look fairly bursting with good health.[54]

Although the Peace Corps Act did not make any mention of directed change, "the idea of doing something positive and concrete to effect change and to solve problems in the Third World is an implicit assumption of almost everything the Peace Corps has done."[55]

Although he was inclined to appreciate the work of the Peace Corps, five years after its inauguration psychologist Robert B. Textor edited a book that realistically pointed to many difficulties.[56] With reference to the Philippines, for example, his book pointed out that "gung-ho" administrators urged volunteers to plunge quickly into community affairs; to be perfectly frank in discussions with Filipinos; and to work for results that could be seen, touched, and quantified. By virtue of their upbringing in American culture most volunteers were ready to comply. But sooner or later they discovered that the patient, grad-

---

54. Ibid., p. 12.
55. Ibid., p. 24.
56. Robert B. Textor, ed., *Cultural Frontiers of the Peace Corps* (Cambridge, Mass.: The M. I. T. Press, 1966).

ual approach is much more suited to the Philippines; that the Filipinos' recurrent complaint about Americans is that they are "brutally frank"; and that built-in obstacles to change resulted in more frustration on their part than in change among Filipinos. Two years later David Hapgood and Meridan Bennett wrote, "Whatever history's final comment on the Peace Corps, we venture to guess that its spice is most likely to be tasted in the Volunteer's own society."[57] Time proved this prophecy to be largely true. Although we do not deprecate the value of a change in our own traditional attitudes with regard to other peoples, we would all agree that that is not the only—or even the primary—objective of either the Peace Corps or the Christian missionary movement.

The Bible and Culture

Of the many questions that might be legitimately asked at this point, three stand out as being inescapable: What is the Christian view of culture? How can we separate that which is cultural from that which is supracultural? How are biblical requirements to be related to cultural expectations? Let us look at these in order.

A Christian View of Culture

Christian cross-cultural workers, in contrast to theoreticians of whatever variety, find it impossible to think about the relationship between Christ and culture without working out the implications of their conclusions, because they touch culture every time they speak and wherever they work. They must have a biblical view of culture as well as a biblical view of man and the world, recognizing that every culture has elements of divine order and satanic rebellion—potential for the revelation of God's truth and for its concealment.

57. Hapgood and Bennett, *Agents of Change*, p. 239.

At creation God gave man a cultural mandate which entailed rulership over man's environment (Gen. 1:28). The fall, however, left its mark on creation, creature, and culture (Gen. 3:14–19), interrupting God's provision for, and fellowship with, his creatures. Man's hope for restoration rested on the promise of the "seed of a woman" who would bruise the Serpent's head. Because mankind as a whole failed as miserably as Adam and Eve, God pronounced judgment on man, beast, and land by sending a flood (Gen. 6:6–7). After the flood Noah and his family received promises and a social mandate that was to apply to them and to subsequent generations (Gen. 8:21–9:17).

The significance of these first chapters in Genesis is that they form the basis of a theology of culture that is amplified throughout all of Scripture. Man's relationship with God precedes and prescribes all other relationships. True religion is prior to culture, not simply a part of it. The fall did not result in the eradication of the *imago Dei* in man but it did impose a false authority over him and it did mar man's person *and his productions.* Only under Christ can man be redeemed and his culture renewed.

John Calvin's view of culture reinforces this brief overview of relevant biblical teaching in important ways.[58] Calvin held that after the fall man became "ethically alienated and morally depraved, but ... retained his religious nature and his *sensus deitatis* (God-consciousness)."[59] He was not thereby excused from carrying out the cultural mandate, however, any more than his transgression of the law resulted in its abolition. He is still required to replenish the earth, although in jeopardy. Culture remains but loses its unifying principle—love for God. Man repeatedly falls in love with some aspect of the cosmos and worships the creature rather than

58. Refer to Henry R. Van Til, *The Calvinistic Concept of Culture* (Grand Rapids: Baker, 1959). See especially chapter 5, "The Calvinistic Conception of Sin and Its Effects on Culture."
59. Ibid., p. 57.

the Creator. Human culture is essential but it will always be determined by the fall until we become citizens of the "city of God."

The gospel mandate (Matt. 28:18–20) requires that Christians teach men everywhere to observe all that Christ has commanded. In doing so they necessarily touch culture, for all culture needs transformation in motivation if not in content. Although God had ordained culture, he has not been "allowed" to order culture in our world. Therefore, as Calvin says, believers must work to make culture Christian or at least conducive to Christian living. Or, as J. H. Bavinck puts it, Christianity must take possession of heathen forms of life and make them new: "Christ takes the life of a people in his hands, he renews and re-establishes the distorted and deteriorated; he fills each thing, each word, and each practice with a new meaning and gives it new direction."[60]

The missionary who responds to the gospel mandate is directly and indirectly involved in this process. It is impossible for him to stay above the culture line and deal only with matters of the soul. The missionary cannot *communicate* without concerning himself with culture because communication is inextricable from culture. And the missionary cannot communicate *Christ* without concerning himself with culture because Christianity is cultural in application, although supracultural in origin and truth.

Separating the Cultural and the Supracultural

At first blush, it would seem to be a rather simple procedure to distinguish between that which is cultural and that which is supracultural. It seems necessary only to decide what our culture says and what God has said in his Word, the Bible. It will come as no surprise to anyone

---

60. J. H. Bavinck, *An Introduction to the Science of Missions,* trans. David Hugh Freeman (Grand Rapids: Baker, 1969), p. 179.

familiar with missiological studies, however, when we say that this seemingly simple task is really so complex as to constitute one of the greatest contemporary challenges to effective and biblical Christian mission. This complexity has two aspects. First, we have a tendency to "canonize" the dictates of our own culture. Second, there is difficulty in disentangling the cultural and the supracultural elements in Scripture itself.

Every culture has the tendency to divinize its own norms and ways. This is true in Western cultures also, even though in America, for example, we do not ordinarily think of all Americans as the "people of God" and all national goals as the "way of the gods." A good example would be our rugged individualism, which has sometimes been termed ragged individualism. Nothing seems quite so sacred in our culture as the freedom and rights of the individual. The larger society is in danger of reaching an impasse in its attempt to protect itself from the lawless, largely because even convicted criminals can create delays or even elude justice by claiming their "rights." The notion of forfeiting one's individual "rights" for the larger good is almost totally foreign to our culture. It is a very easy and common thing to think of this American form of individualism as supracultural and export it along with our Christian communication and counseling, with disastrous results.

Distinguishing the cultural and supracultural principles and requirements of Scripture is an even more difficult task. Examples are the greeting with a holy kiss, footwashing, and the head covering on women in prayer—all of which were enjoined on the early church. Although some small groups within the Christian community consider it essential to follow these first-century forms, the majority have recognized them as cultural ways of expressing fellowship, servanthood, and reverence. But on what basis do we legitimately conclude that these are not universals and that they are not enjoined upon all men?

How do we determine that people today are to observe their true meaning and functions (love, humility, and reverence), but with forms that are contemporary and culturally appropriate? How do we interpret the Scripture rightly, differentiating the cultural and the supracultural on the basis of principle rather than preference?

With a debt to widely accepted understandings of proper interpretation, Grant R. Osborne suggests three general principles and five specific principles to guide the interpreter of the Scripture in this task.

General Principles
1. Didactic passages should be used to interpret historical passages.
2. The original setting and meaning of the command must be understood before its significance can be determined.
3. Individual statements must be placed within the broader context of Scripture.

Specific Principles:
1. Try to determine the underlying theological principle.
2. Discern whether the writer depends on traditional teaching or provides a solution to a specific problem.
3. When the teaching transcends the cultural biases of the author and readers, it is likely to be normative.
4. If the command is wholly applicable to a cultural situation, it is not timeless in itself.
5. Commands which by nature are moral or theological will be closely related to the divine will.[61]

We should not conclude that by applying these principles, the true significance of every Bible passage will be easily discerned. But these principles constitute a compass

61. Grant R. Osborne, "Contextualization: A Hermeneutical Approach," paper delivered at the Third Consultation on Theology and Mission held at Trinity Evangelical Divinity School, Deerfield, Ill., 18–20 March 1982.

and keep us from striking out in directions dictated by cultural and personal biases. For example, by applying general principles 2 and 3, and specific principles 1, 2, 4, and 5, we can see that the command which requires women to cover their heads while praying or prophesying (1 Cor. 11:2–15) is very likely cultural, whereas the injunction that women do not assume authority over men (1 Tim. 2:11–14) is supracultural and universal. The importance of this distinction is evident when we realize that although neither command would represent a problem in an Islamic culture, both of them are out of synchronization with North American culture.

Relating the Bible to Cultural Expectations

In cross-cultural counseling the Christian worker will invariably face the demanding task of responding to cultural expectations on the one side and divine requirements on the other. It is important that both be kept in view in order that cultural values, goals, and ways be affirmed or amended as God's Word requires. For example, in many traditional societies the ancestors occupy a very important place in the daily life of indigenes. Their pictures are in evidence; their sayings and exploits are recalled; their spirits receive offerings; their influence is felt; and their deaths are commemorated. In such societies attitudes and activities relating to elders and ancestors may pose a significant problem for Christians and those contemplating conversion to Christ. The response to these problems taken by many missionaries is that all of these practices constitute ancestor worship. Consequently they anathematize or ignore them. The response of some indigenous Christian leadership is that such practices are simply a cultural form of ancestor veneration which answers to the biblical injunction to honor one's parents. They sanctify and reinforce them.

Neither response will do. The best way is to look at the problem closely, analyze it in terms of local forms and functions, explain its worthy and unworthy elements, and deal with it forthrightly and sensitively.

Culture-Sensitive Christian Counseling

It is one thing to be informed concerning the various ways in which culture can impact upon counseling. It is quite another thing to incorporate that information into a biblically sound and culturally sensitive counseling theory and practice.

Unfortunately, many Christian workers do not formulate a culture-sensitive approach to counseling prior to embarking upon cross-cultural ministry. Suddenly they are put in a position of having to face one difficult problem after another. Their only recourse is to fall back upon solutions suggested by Christian experience in their own culture. One of two things is apt to happen from that point. Either they will resign themselves to "doing the best they can" on the basis of their own cultural experience, or they will gradually develop a more culturally sensitive approach *on the basis of trial and error.*

One hopes that a third possibility will appeal to more and more cross-cultural Christian workers. It is to stop (wherever one might be in the course of study or ministry) and begin to decide upon an approach on the basis of available knowledge as well as personal experience. This process can—and probably will—occupy one's attention throughout the entire course of one's ministry in any given area. But it may be facilitated here by pointing out the direction that it might take—namely, the analysis of problems in the light of an understanding of the culture and a biblical theology of culture; the determination of one's role as an agent of change; and the development of a culture-sensitive, Christian counseling approach (see fig. 16).

FIGURE 16   **Counseling and Culture (1)**

Steps in the Development of a Christian, Culture-Sensitive Counseling Theory and Practice		
Step 1: Analyze Problems in the Light of the Host Culture and the Bible	**Step 2:** Determine One's Role as an Agent of Change	**Step 3:** Develop a Culture-Sensitive Counseling Approach

Step 1: Analyze Problems in the Light of the Host Culture and the Bible

Question: What is the difference between this proposal and the problem of distinguishing between cultural and supracultural principles?

Reflections: Here we are dealing not with the question of culture in general, but with problems posed by the particular culture or subculture in which we are called to serve Christ. Donald A. McGavran focuses on this difference in a helpful way when he says that our clash is not with *culture* but with *cultures* and, in the final analysis, not even so much with cultures but with components of culture. He goes on to say that three categories of components must be distinguished:

1. Components that Christianity welcomes: for example, the Naga way of welcoming guests; the Satnami custom of helping bereaved by immediately gathering to help dig a grave.
2. Components that Christianity changes or improves: for example, the traditional Naga practice of housing boys together during formal education in the ways of the tribe; a similar practice is the introduction of boys' dormitories in Christian schools.
3. Components unacceptable to Christianity which must be abolished or abandoned: for example, the

Naga practice of head hunting or the Chinese custom of making offerings to the spirits.[62]

Although it is relatively easy to devise these categories, all experienced cross-cultural workers will know that there is no small amount of disagreement between Christians as to the categorization of many components and the proper ways in which to encourage, reform, or abolish them. (Examples are caste segregation at meals as it relates to the Lord's Supper or bowing before ancestral tablets in China as an act of respect now that it has largely become an act of worship.) Of course, where people have already been won to Christ and the church already exists, answers to these problems will have been forthcoming in the community of faith which ultimately must make these decisions. This makes the expatriate counselor's task easier in the event he agrees with positions already taken by Christians in the host culture, but more difficult if on the basis of Scripture he cannot concur with them.

Question: Does the concept of cultural relativism provide answers to these questions?

Reflection: Every culture has its own "map of the world," values, and customs. These must be studied as integrative wholes in order to understand a culture and work in it effectively. But this does not mean that cultures must be accepted in the whole or in any given part. In the sense that the meaning and function of a given cultural form can be understood only in relation to the larger culture of which it is a part we are relativists. But we oppose cultural relativism when that is taken to mean that one way of looking at the universe "is as good as another" or that "head hunting is wrong for us but acceptable in Naga culture." All cultures must be judged by the universals we have considered previously—by that which is objectively true and divinely required.

62. Donald A. McGavran, *The Clash Between Christianity and Cultures* (Washington, D.C.: Canon, 1974), pp. 38–43.

Question: How does the culture type relate to this analysis?

Reflection: If one follows the taxonomy of world views and cultures suggested in this and the preceding chapter, one would, for example, classify traditional Chinese culture as having a Confucianist-Taoist world view, and as a collectivistic-dependency culture with an ancestor orientation. Problems related to ancestor worship (or veneration) in *a traditional Chinese setting* must be analyzed with reference to these particular categories and the biblical injunctions having to do with parents and forebears. Only in the light of this kind of analysis can the true nature of problems and the relevant biblical solution be discovered.

Questions: What is the dominant decision type in the host culture? What problems and potentials does this decision type suggest?

Reflection: The emphasis on multi-individual or group conversion in contemporary missiology is not misplaced. Nor is the emphasis on consensus decision-making. Although there are numerous cultures in which individual decisions and decision-making by debate and vote are the norm, this is not so in the majority of cultures around the world.

The foregoing is only a sampling of relevant questions, but from a counseling perspective they are some of the most important. (Refer to figure 17 for a summary of the principles discussed in this section.)

Step 2: Determine One's Role as an Agent of Change

Whether one is an evangelist, developer, teacher, counselor, or all of these, there is an advantage to thinking of oneself as an agent of change. In so doing the cross-cultural worker is partially lifted out of the familiar role defined by his own culture and is forced to think in terms of his place in the new cultural situation.

Figure 17   **Counseling and Culture (2)**

Steps in the Development of a Christian,
Culture-Sensitive Counseling Theory and Practice

Step 1: Analyze Problems in the Light of the Host Culture and the Bible

Components that Christ approves, improves, and reproves

The culture type of the host culture

The changes that are in order

The decision-making process that is appropriate

Questions: Is it possible to identify the various people who fulfill the role of counselor in the host culture? How do they compare with the role a counselor takes in one's own culture? What are some of the implications of this?

Reflection: As we have seen, perhaps a majority of cultures around the world do not have professional counselors in the Western mold. But all societies do have counselors, religious and secular. It may be that the Christian counselor can ally himself with these in some way. This would certainly be the case where native Christian pastors are present. On the other hand, when tribal elders or witch doctors occupy this role, caution is in order.

Question: For the cross-cultural worker, what role has the greatest potential for fostering Christian change in the host culture?

Reflection: An objective answer to this question may entail some self-effacing decisions. Specialists insist that in many cross-cultural situations the cross-cultural worker—regardless of his credentials—accomplishes the most when he takes a low profile and functions as a facilitator of change by offering for local consideration ideas and solutions that otherwise may not be forthcoming.

Question: With whom can I ally myself in my counseling ministry?

Reflection: There may be a place for "Lone Ranger" counselors, but it likely is not in an alien culture. In the nature of the case, the Christian counselor is not likely to become fully acculturated. His ministry may well be a temporary one. And in any case, he is part of the body of Christ. It is important that he be allied with nationals in order to compensate for his own weaknesses and to enhance their strengths. (For a summary of these principles, see figure 18.)

Step 3: Develop a Culture-Sensitive Counseling Approach

We have already started to evaluate Western and non-Western counseling approaches. By identifying the specific counseling approaches utilized in the host culture (or even

FIGURE 18   **Counseling and Culture (3)**

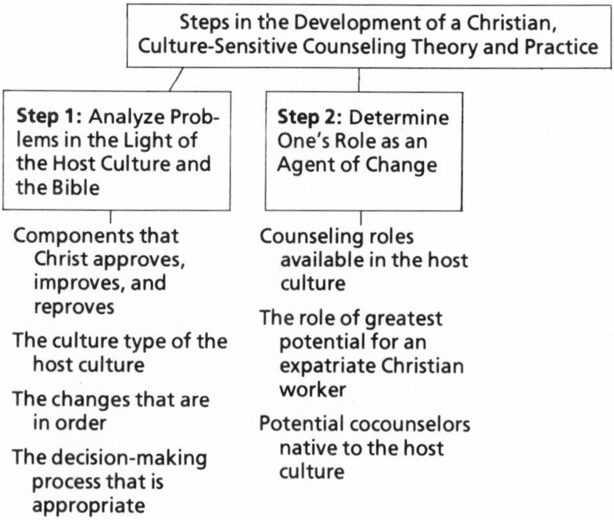

present by virtue of transfer innovation) we further this task. Attempting, then, to be faithful to Christ *and* culture, we shall continue to develop a counseling strategy by asking and answering additional questions.

Questions: What constitutes a minimum facility in the language of the receptor culture for effective counseling? What about nonverbal forms of communication? Can I understand and be understood?

Reflection: Obviously, communication is essential to counseling, whether it be intracultural or intercultural. In the latter case, however, the difficulties are greatly compounded. Because comparatively few nationals can be expected to have enough facility in the foreign counselor's language to make correct interpretation possible, and because communicating through an interpreter is inadequate at best, the counselor should plan to study language and communication in the respondent culture. "Counseling and psychotherapy may be viewed legitimately as a process of interpersonal interaction and communication. For effective counseling to occur, the counselor and client must be able to appropriately and *accurately send* and *receive* both *verbal* and *nonverbal* messages."[63]

Sue explains the importance of nonverbal communication in counseling blacks in North America.

In Black culture, it is often assumed that being in the same room or in close proximity to another person is enough to indicate attentiveness. Going through the motions of looking at the person and nodding your head is not necessary. White middle class people when speaking to others, look away (eye avoidance) approximately fifty percent of the time. However, when Whites listen, they make contact with the speaker over eighty percent of the time. This is in marked contrast to Black Americans who when speaking make greater eye contact and when listening make infrequent eye contact. The fact that Blacks also have a

63. Sue, *Counseling the Culturally Different*, p. 27.

shorter conversing distance and greater body activity when speaking may lead many teachers, counselors, and mental health professionals to make unconscious interpretations.[64]

Question: If we say that a good relationship is important to effective counseling (although this is open to debate), what constitutes a good relationship in the host culture?

Reflection: As we have seen, Carl R. Rogers describes a good relationship in terms of genuineness, empathy, positive regard, and unconditionality of regard. F. E. Fiedler characterizes the ideal relationship in a way reminiscent of communication and counseling theory: the therapist is able to participate completely in the patient's communications; the therapist's comments are always right in line with what the patient is trying to convey; the therapist is well able to understand the patient's feelings; the therapist really tries to understand the patient's feelings; and the therapist always follows the patient's line of thought.[65]

These constituents unquestionably have a certain cross-cultural validity. That is not all that needs to be said, however. Relationships break down in every culture. So we must still ask how a good relationship is defined *in the host culture.* For example, increasingly in our society the counselor is expected to take a nonauthoritarian, nondirective, supportive role in which he relates to the counselee on a more or less egalitarian basis. Presumably this kind of relationship enhances mutual trust and respect. However, in numerous societies the counselor is expected to give authoritative answers and direct advice. Not to do so is interpreted as weakness, indecisiveness, and perhaps even lack of concern. Jay E. Adams's nouthetic counseling approach would seem appropriate in such a culture. At the same time, decisions to change must be those of the counselee(s), not those of the counselor.

64. Ibid., p. 42.
65. F. E. Fiedler, "The Concept of an Ideal Therapeutic Relationship," *Journal of Consulting Psychology* 14 (June 1950): 239–45.

Also, in American society it is common to attempt to get to the core of a problem by encouraging counselees to communicate their true feelings. In a shame society, however, to do this prematurely or in the wrong way (and often to do it all) entails a loss of face, which is precisely what the counselee seeks most to avoid.

Questions: How can one be true to Scripture and relevant to the ethos of a host culture which is uninformed by Christian teaching? To what extent can one appeal to the ethical agendas of a pagan culture?

Reflection: Here we find ourselves touching the very heart of culture-sensitive counseling. Answers are not easy to come by. And yet all who minister cross-culturally in the name of Christ answer such questions implicitly or explicitly, validly or invalidly.

Cultures are spiritually ambivalent. In some respects they mirror the imago Dei which the Creator has placed in every man. But they also reflect the fall which mars man and all that he touches. Whatever the nature of the particular problem—biological, psychological, intellectual—it has a spiritual dimension. This is not to say that every human problem is hamartigenic in its immediate origin. In response to the question concerning the man blind from birth ("Who sinned, this man or his parents, that he was born blind?" [John 9:2]), Jesus replied, "Neither this man nor his parents sinned, . . . but this happened so that the work of God might be displayed in his life" (John 9:3).

Still, in another sense, all human maladies are occasioned by sin. Something akin to this is recognized even by some unbelieving psychologists and anthropologists. O. Hobart Mowrer has called neurosis "a medical euphemism for a state of sin"![66] He writes, "My own personal and professional experience and that of a small but grow-

66. O. Hobart Mowrer, *The New Group Therapy* (New York: Van Nostrand Reinhold, 1964), p. 6.

ing number of other psychologists, psychiatrists and social workers shows that the so-called psychoneuroses and functional psychoses can be understood only (sola!) in terms of palpable misconduct which has neither been confessed nor expiated."[67] The anthropologist Alfred L. Kroeber writes,

> Of late years, with conscious effort to define the ethos of cultures, a whole array of observers have made a similar finding on culture after culture. They encounter plenty of shame, but little or no sense of sin. Other people's opinions, their remarks, their ridicule or laughter, are what the average man, in most cultures, is sensitive to, is what deters him. This has been remarked equally with non-literate tribes and for literate nationalities. The Chinese are guided by "face-saving"; the Japanese lack the sense of "contrast of real and ideal" and "do not grapple with the problem of evil."
>
> But the findings about the importance of shame as a social force are a bit too consistent. They leave little explicit sin sense to any culture but our own Occidental one; and within that largely to its Protestant portion, in fact, outstandingly its Calvinistically influenced sector. It is true that sin and guilt, sin and trespass, sin and evil were rather imperfectly distinguished in Europe until the Reformation. It seems to have been this religious movement that internalized guilt and shame into sin, and reared conscience on a great pedestal.[68]

To return to our questions, we respond, first, that to faithfully communicate the Word of God in the ethos of a host culture is to be relevant. Jew and Gentile alike are "under sin" (Rom. 3:9). The Holy Spirit was given to "convict the world of guilt in regard to sin and righteousness and judgment" (John 16:8). The only antidote to guilt is

---

67. Ibid., p. 20.
68. Alfred L. Kroeber, *Anthropology*, rev. ed. (New York: Harcourt, Brace, 1948), p. 612.

forgiveness provided by God in Christ. Shame, *even before God*, is but a part of it. And the shame of shame cultures is seldom that. It is usually inimical to repentence because a person is preoccupied with the approval or disapproval of other men and therefore crowds out consideration of the requirements of God.

Second, the notion that missionaries should direct their counseling to items high on the ethical agendas of their respondents—guilt in "guilt culture," shame in "shame culture," fear in "fear culture"—is not without merit. Nor is the idea that conversion experiences have corresponding psychological overtones—for example, conversion freeing man from existential guilt in one culture, self-defeating anxiety in another culture, and haunting fear in still another. To begin the communication or counseling process with people where *they* are instead of where *we* are is psychologically and biblically defensible. That some of the most recognizable freedoms that accrue to conversion are in the areas of the most obvious bondage is not surprising. However, to suggest that guilt before the true and holy God, shame before departed ancestors and present contemporaries, and fear before spirits and ghosts are somehow equal and interchangeable as motivations for conversion is to err. Sin and guilt, atonement and forgiveness—these are not culturally derived accidents which are seized upon by God. They are supracultural and spiritual realities insisted upon by him. Wise counselors will listen to what the Spirit says, and be instruments of what *he* does.

Ultimately, however, no malady can be cured, no wrong righted, and no problem solved until payment is made. In a discussion of "the goodness of guilt," John W. Drakeford writes,

> The word guilt has a significant root. Originally it was the payment of a fine for an offense. It comes from the Anglo-Saxon word "gylt," meaning "to pay." At a conference on

integrity therapy, a rabbi pointed out that in Yiddish the word "gelt" means "money." Of guilt, Tournier says: "It is inscribed on the human heart; everything must be paid for." McKenzie asserts: "Guilt must be paid for."[69]

Christian counselors are not concerned with short-term solutions only or primarily. Whether sin and guilt are important as causative factors in any particular human predicament or not, they are decisive in terms of larger and longer relationships with both man and God. Only those who recognize their guilt will value the payment made on the cross; only those who value the cross will embrace the Savior; and only those who embrace the Savior will find the ultimate healing.

Questions: To what extent should counseling ministries in the host culture be directed to individuals? To what extent should they be directed to groups? What are the possibilities for community-wide counseling?

Reflection: Counseling can be directed to the community, a small group, or an individual. In North America, one-on-one counseling has been predominant. In fact, one gets the distinct impression that much group therapy (Rogerian, for example) has evolved as much out of frustration with seemingly interminable sessions with individuals as out of an appreciation for the therapeutic potential of groups themselves. In much of the non-Western world we do well to rethink the usual American pattern. In not a few cases larger communities can be counseled in ways that will promote community health, development, and well-being. Smaller groupings—particularly the church and its included groups—provide the matrices for significant caring, counseling, and curing.

Western approaches to group counseling will require modification, however. Egalitarianism in which social sta-

69. John W. Drakeford, *Integrity Therapy: A New Direction in Psychotherapy* (Nashville: Broadman, 1967), p. 36.

tus is disregarded; abrupt interaction of a rather intimate sort (types of acceptable intimacy vary!) with persons previously unknown; the tendency to multiply such groups only on the basis of need—these and other characteristics of Western group counseling may have little place in the cross-cultural situation. When it is in accord with local cultural preferences, however, group counseling has decided advantages in most non-Western societies for a number of reasons:

It fits in with the group orientation of most non-Western societies.

It enables the cross-cultural Christian worker to influence a larger number of individuals for Christ.

It is best calculated to meet the needs of those (individuals or small subgroups) who in many cases suffer a measure of estrangement and even persecution in the larger culture.

It encourages an ongoing ministry of mutual helping within the churches.

It enhances the development of local leadership.

Refer to figure 19 for a summary of the principles discussed in this section.

The Importance of Culture: An Illustration

For an illustration of the importance of cultural analysis to cross-cultural Christian counseling we turn to a classic case study, one that will be familiar to many who have read *I Loved a Girl* by Walter Trobisch.[70]

70. Walter Trobisch, *I Loved a Girl: Young Africans Speak* (New York: Harper and Row, 1965).

FIGURE 19 **Counseling and Culture (4)**

Steps in the Development of a Christian, Culture-Sensitive Counseling Theory and Practice		
Step 1: Analyze Problems in the Light of the Host Culture and the Bible	**Step 2:** Determine One's Role as an Agent of Change	**Step 3:** Develop a Culture-Sensitive Counseling Approach
Components that Christ approves, improves, and reproves	Counseling roles available in the host culture	Facility in the language of the receptor culture
The culture type of the host culture	The role of greatest potential for an expatriate Christian worker	Ingredients of a good relationship
The changes that are in order	Potential cocounselors native to the host culture	Relevancy to ethos, values, and ethical agendas
The decision-making process that is appropriate		Individual versus group counseling

François and Cecile: Love and Marriage in Africa

The two principals in the case reside in Cameroon. François is a twenty-one-year-old African Christian. He has been disciplined by the church for commiting the sin of fornication, a part of the discipline being the forfeiture of his teaching post at a Christian school. However, François has repented and has made a new dedication to Christ. (Trobisch advocated swift reinstatement for François, a decision with which Pastor Amos, a national, disagreed.) He has also fallen in love with Cecile, a Christian student who returns his affection. With the help of a friend of Cecile, François finds a job.

François and Cecile want to be married but run afoul of an all-pervasive custom in Africa, that of bride-price (bride wealth). Cecile's father demands four hundred dollars as down payment with much more to be paid when the marriage is consummated. Pastor Amos agrees to visit Cecile's father in the company of François and his half-brother, Jacques. (Pastor Amos is a distant relative of the

father. Although he was involved in the decision to discipline François, Pastor Amos is nevertheless friendly to
him.) The visit is unfruitful. With three sons and only one
daughter, Cecile's parents need money. The bride-price
remains high—seemingly much too high for the orphaned
François to pay.

An already complicated situation is further complicated
when an older and well-to-do unbelieving national by the
name of Monsieur Henri also is attracted to Cecile. He
has a wife in the bush, but needs an educated wife to
entertain his government guests. (Neither the disparity in
age nor the polygamous arrangement is unusual in African
culture.)[71] Monsieur Henri ingratiates himself with Cecile's parents by giving them expensive gifts and substan-
tiates his intention to marry Cecile by paying them a significant amount of money. Fearful that Cecile will be
forced into an unwanted and unscriptural marriage, the
couple run away and consummate their relationship physically, without regard to government, society, or even the
church. During their flight, however, Cecile catches a cold
which results in pneumonia. With pangs of conscience
they return. In grave condition she is taken to her home
village. François goes to the Trobisches, with whom he
and Cecile had been in correspondence throughout their
ordeal. Missionary Trobisch accompanies François to Cecile's village and spends a week at her bedside. Cecile's
illness seems to meet with concern on the part of her
father. She recovers, and all involved are left to reflect
upon what has happened and to begin a new chapter in
their lives.

Custom and Culture

The problem(s) faced by François and Cecile can be
understood only in the context of their culture. Bride-price

71. For a helpful study of marriage and familism in African and other
cultures, consult Stuart A. Queen and Robert W. Habenstein, *The Family in
Various Cultures*, 4th ed. (New York: Lippincott, 1974).

might be considered (by one outside the culture) as a cultural item that stems from greed and needs to be abolished forthwith. François and Cecile love each other. They should disregard the custom and marry as soon as practicable.

But bride-price in African societies can be thought of as a cultural trait that is linked very directly to the institution of marriage. Along with procedures for arranging marriage, provisions for divorce, and certain other customs, it fulfills some very important functions. This becomes more apparent when one observes the cultural forms that attend it—the meeting between the prospective bride's father and representatives of the prospective groom; the discussions concerning the amount of bride-price; the traditional payment in goats or cattle; the wedding ritual itself; the "testing" of the bride; the provision for her return if she proves unsuitable; and so on.

Marriage traditionally has a different meaning to the African than it does to the Westerner. It is not a commitment between two individuals on the basis of love. It is rather an agreement between two families or clans, to a significant degree on the basis of economic values. "Good" marriages function to decrease the workload of other wives, nourish the family, and produce wealth. They also result in offspring who perpetuate the traditions of the ancestors and secure the future of parents in both present and future lives. Bride-price functions to compensate the bride's family for the loss of labor and helps to make the marriage more permanent by making it the concern of all interested parties.

Traditionalists in Africa and Asia take a very different view of love and marriage than does the Westerner. As one man from India expressed it to a European, "You marry the girl you love, we love the woman that we have married." Or, as another Indian expressed it, "We put cold soup on the fire, and it becomes slowly warm. You put hot soup into a cold place, and it becomes slowly cold."[72]

The foregoing is not written to exonerate the African culture at this point, but rather to help us understand it. There can be no doubt that bride-price has its attendant evils, especially now that money often replaces cattle. But counselors can best help people like François and Cecile when they advise on the basis of understanding bride-price in situ. In fact, able counselors will place the dilemma faced by François and Cecile in the larger framework of a more or less typical CD-AO cultural orientation. When they do, the larger picture will become much clearer.

Implications for Counseling

The preceding summary includes but a few of the most salient features of the case before us. Given the complexities of African marriage customs and the complications that attend the incursion of Western industry, ideas, and ideals, it is not surprising that Jean Banyolak of Cameroon writes, "Africa needs marriage counselors."[73] But we must ask, "What kind of marriage counselors?" Among cross-cultural counselors of the passing generation few have been more perceptive than the Trobisches. Yet in respect to the case of François and Cecile even Trobisch writes, "Suddenly I realized how much I had failed. I had not tried hard enough and not asked for Divine guidance."[74]

Trobisch's primary misgiving seems to have been with his reliance on counseling by letter and in his failure to see Cecile and to visit her father personally when the problem of bride-price first surfaced.[75] But, although we are not prepared to pass judgment from this distance in

72. Trobisch, *I Loved a Girl*, p. 193.
73. Walter Trobisch, *My Wife Made Me a Polygamist*, rev. ed. (Downers Grove, Ill.: Inter-Varsity, 1971), pp. 38–40.
74. Trobisch, *I Loved a Girl*, p. 105.
75. Ibid.

time and space, we might tentatively ask various questions about still other aspects of the case.

First, what is the significance of the fact that Trobisch sought speedy reinstatement for François after his confession of fornication, and of Pastor Amos's response that this could not be done in view of the impact of this sin on the community? True, there may have been mitigating factors such as the widespread African belief that manhood is proved sexually and that to refrain from sex may result in illness. But one must also give consideration to the great premium placed upon a young woman's virginity and the fact that nonvirginity is just cause for returning a bride to her parents and demanding repayment of the bride-price. Again, in a shame culture, the shame that François brought upon the Christian community was very real. Discipline had to be evaluated in the light of that reality. Did François really feel both his guilt before God and the communal consequences of his act? In his letters to the Corinthians, the apostle Paul indicates that there is a time for excluding an offending brother and a time for receiving him back into fellowship. What would have been the right timing in François's case?

Second, what is to be said concerning Trobisch's opposition to bride-price and his wholehearted support for love marriages? After talking to Cecile's father, Pastor Amos concluded that the only viable option was to be patient, industrious, and raise the necessary money. And African churches have been known to assist with bride-price rather than disregard it. True, the system has many abuses, especially since the introduction of monetary payment. True, biblical teaching indicates that the oneness of marriage involves a certain separation from family (Gen. 2:24). True, François and Cecile came to the point where they saw no alternative to turning their backs on the community, culture, and even the church. But arranged marriages and bride-price (*mohar*) were part and parcel of early Hebrew culture, and the New Testament does not speak against these practices in the way it speaks against polygamy. Both arranged marriages and bride-price as practiced in much of Asia and Africa and love marriages and gift-giving as practiced in much of the Western world have their strengths and weaknesses, their uses and abuses. Did their solution indicate that François and Cecile fully understood the *Christian* alternative to the ways of both Africa and the West? Could not the Christian cross-cultural counselor be the catalyst for a better solution than either the clan-controlled system of Africa or the highly individualized system of much of the West? With so much at stake, would group counseling be better than individual counseling in this and similar cases?

Third, what should we conclude in respect to Trobisch's belated feeling that he should have visited Cecile's father personally? Obviously, if he had done so after Pastor Amos's visit, his own view would have reflected negatively on his African colleague. It may have been appropriate for Trobisch to accompany Pastor Amos, Jacques, and François on their official visit. Do Trobisch's misgivings at this point arise from desperation and frustration? Or do they arise from a rethinking of a wider range of cultural factors bearing upon the case?

In asking these questions we cast no aspersion whatsoever on the Trobisches. We ask them so that contemporary Christian counselors may benefit from the missionary experiences of the past. Perhaps we should add that when we have assigned to experienced missionaries the task of reevaluating their personal involvement in a memorable case of cross-cultural counseling, all have responded that on the basis of further reflection they would proceed differently if history could be relived. This has not been so just because hindsight is better than foresight. It has been so because employment of new concepts and understanding results in counseling approaches that are more sensitive to both culture and Scripture.

To the extent that people share a culture they will evidence commonalities with each other and differences from others. From a Christian point of view we are cultural relativists in the sense that we recognize that persons in every culture have distinctive ways of thinking, feeling, and behaving. A knowledge of culture in general—what it is, of what it consists, and how it functions—is essential for the Christian who ministers cross-culturally. Equally important is a knowledge of the particular host culture.

We are not cultural relativists, however, if that term is taken to mean that there is no higher standard of what we should believe, feel, and do than those standards provided by the various cultures. We believe that God has revealed his will with regard to faith and practice in the Bible. Cultural information, therefore, must be scrutinized in the light of theological reflection. When these two streams of knowledge are properly integrated, the development of a biblically sound and culturally sensitive counseling approach becomes possible.

10

"Like No Other Man"
Understanding Uniqueness

Ultimately, analysis comes down to a consideration of uniqueness—the idiosyncrasies of particular human beings and their beliefs, feelings, and behavior.

It is remarkable that out of the billions of persons who have inhabited planet Earth no two of them have ever been exactly alike. Each individual has a unique appearance; possesses a certain configuration of strengths and weaknesses; has a personal history shared with no one else; has his own "privatized" world view; and even speaks his own language (called an idiolect). Therefore, although every person shares certain characteristics with all mankind and still other characteristics with those of his own culture, he also has certain traits that are shared with no one else. Each person is "one of a kind."

Social scientists have various ways of making these distinctions. The terms *personality* and *character* draw attention to them. We have already used these terms in our discussion of cultures. Now that we have come to consider individual uniqueness it would be well to note some of the special meanings assigned to them.

253

Psychologists Henry Clay Lindgren and Leonard W. Fisk, Jr., relate personality to the ways in which an individual adjusts to his environment; the ways in which he learns to adjust; and the attitudes, values, and traits which result from this process.[1] John J. Honigmann, an anthropologist, defines personality much more simply as the "actions, thoughts, and feelings characteristic of an individual."[2] These definitions are helpful to a point, but they fail to bring the difference between shared and idiosyncratic characteristics into sharp focus.

In the 1930s, Cora DuBois and Abram Kardiner collaborated on a seminar at Columbia University in which the anthropological insights of the former and the psychoanalytic expertise of the latter were brought together. Later Ralph Linton and Kardiner continued the same seminar for some five years. The research and interaction of these specialists (reinforced by other studies) yielded ideas that are especially valuable to us in this context. Their special interest was in commonalities of personality configurations shared by members of certain societies. Emphasizing childhood experience, Kardiner called this basic personality structure. Linton emphasized that although certain cultural elements are, in essence, required of all individuals in a society, others are options. In the building of personality over a period of time the individual builds both a basic personality core (which is shared) and a status personality (which grows out of his various roles in the society). DuBois preferred the term *modal personality* to describe the shared characteristics. This term became more widely used than either "basic personality structure" or "basic personality." Margaret Mead's studies on culture structure contributed to the use of the word *character* (e.g., national character) to describe group characteristics.

1. Henry Clay Lindgren and Leonard W. Fisk, Jr., *Psychology of Personal Development*, 3d ed. (New York: Wiley, 1976), p. 33.

2. John J. Honigmann, *Culture and Personality* (New York: Harper and Row, 1954), p. 28.

It is quite common among social scientists to use the word *character* in reference to modal group characteristics (without ethical or moral nuances) and the word *personality* in reference to individuals with their unique components. But uniformity is not to be expected. The words are sometimes used interchangeably.[3]

Determinants of Personality

Differing schools of thought give priority to one or another type of determinants of personality. Lindgren and Fisk discuss physiological, situational, and social determinants.[4] We will follow their approach, although it should be emphasized that the differences grow out of priorities among the various kinds of determinants. The determinant types are not mutually exclusive. On the contrary, factors of all three kinds usually, if not always, contribute to personality development.

Physiological Determinants of Personality

Well known to students of psychology and anthropology of the previous generation is the work of Ernst Kretschmer and his successor, W. H. Sheldon. Kretschmer studied 260 psychotic patients and concluded that there is a relationship between body type and personality. He believed that lean people tend to be more sociable and realistic, although moody and changeable.[5] Sheldon went on to identify three body types and the characteristic personality associated with each: endomorphs (plump; fond of food, insecure, apprehensive, amiable); mesomorphs (muscular; informal, adventurous, high thresholds of pain);

3. Felix M. Keesing, *Cultural Anthropology: The Science of Custom* (New York: Holt, Rinehart, and Winston, 1958), pp. 170–71.
4. Lindgren and Fisk, *Psychology of Personal Development*, pp. 195–216.
5. Ernst Kretschmer, *Physique and Character*, trans. W. J. H. Sprott (New York: Harcourt, Brace, 1925).

and ectomorphs (delicate; not amiable, not adventurous, low threshold of pain).[6]

Subsequent studies have called these conclusions into serious question. But there is a consensus that physique does influence personality characteristics. Short people may become aggressive in order to compensate for lack of height. In our society, leaders tend to be taller and heavier than average.

About the time that Kretschmer did his studies, Louis Berman reported findings to the effect that glandular variations (particularly in the endocrines) constituted the key to personality differences.[7] He associated pituitary, adrenal, thyroid, thymocentric, and variations with certain personality characteristics. For example, when the thyroid gland does not function properly, lethargy and sluggishness may result.

Biological studies in general and genetic studies in particular have come a long way since the days of Berman. As we shall see when we consider personality disorders, it is now clear that genetic and biological make-up play important roles as determinants of personality. Recent research has explained the effects of the prospective mother's diet, drug intake, and even emotional state on the fetus and its pre- and postnatal development. Arthur Janov argues that the personality of the newborn—and whether the child will grow up to be aggressive, passive, addictive, or compulsive—may well be decided during the nine months of pregnancy.[8] The extent to which this is true is open to debate. But extreme positions taken by Janov and

6. W. H. Sheldon, with the collaboration of S. S. Stevens and W. B. Tucker, *The Varieties of Human Physique: An Introduction to Constitutional Psychology* (1940; New York: Coward-McCann, 1983).

7. Louis Berman, *The Glands Regulating Personality*, rev. ed. (New York: Macmillan, 1928).

8. Arthur Janov, *Imprints: The Lifelong Effects of the Birth Experience* (New York: Coward-McCann, 1983).

numerous other theorists must not be allowed to obscure the importance of determinants of this type.

Situational Determinants of Personality

Two kinds of situational environments—natural and manmade—also have much to do with personality development and human behavior. It is common knowledge that persons in colder climates tend to be energetic, whereas constant, oppressive heat occasions lethargy and apathy. There is some evidence that members of groups which subsist by hunting and fishing tend to be independent personalities, whereas those who subsist by farming tend to develop a more cooperative personality type. And the open spaces of plains and mountains exert a much different influence on people than does the congested, polluted environment of the modern asphalt jungle.

Sociological Determinants of Personality

Many of the most significant influences in personality development stem from interaction with other human beings. There are many facets of this interaction and each is important.

According to one school of thought, personality is more or less fixed very early in life—likely by the age of five or six—and is determined by such factors as nursing, weaning, toilet training, and sexual experiences. Influenced by Ruth Benedict, Mead, and John Dollard, the British anthropologist Geoffrey Gorer studied the national character of the Lepcha of Sikkim and the Japanese. Gorer, influenced also by Sigmund Freud, located the determinants of national character in childhood experiences. He believed that the Japanese preoccupation with ritual, tidiness, and order results from severe methods in toilet training.[9]

9. Refer to Douglas G. Haring, ed., *Personal Character and Cultural Milieu: A Collection of Readings* (Syracuse: Syracuse University Press, 1949), pp. 273–90.

Studies by those who attempted to read too much into early experiences evoked criticism. One early criticism was that different personality traits were sometimes attributed to an identical experience. For example, restraints were said to produce passivity in some cultures, but were said to have produced aggressiveness in another. Yet, research does suggest that postnatal handling, bonding, and other experiences have lasting effects. An indication of this is provided by one study of American children which indicates that, as contrasted with second-born children, first-born children are "more likely to be reported as being quick-tempered, emotionally intense, easily upset by defeat, inclined to 'alibi,' and able to articulate clearly while speaking."[10] Other studies indicate that, when compared with later-borns, first-borns in North America tend to be

more likely to conform to parental standards

more creative and less authoritarian

more timid with respect to dangerous activities

more likely to join social organizations

more popular

more achievement-oriented

more likely to attend college[11]

Of course, high on the agenda of those who discuss sociological determinants of personality is culture itself. It seems obvious that cultural influence on individual personality development is a logical corollary of the identification of national character. As a matter of fact, not only cultural influence on a national or tribal scale, but also subcultural influence has been found to be significant in

10. Lindgren and Fisk, *Psychology of Personal Development*, p. 208.
11. Ibid., pp. 208–9.

personality development. A Connecticut study, for example, revealed that Irish Catholic parents expected less independence on the part of their children than did Protestants or Jews, and Italian Catholics expected still less.[12]

The Development of Personality

It is more common to speak of a newborn's temperament than it is to speak of his or her personality. Ordinarily personality is thought of as something that develops and matures.

It is manifestly impossible to deal with the numerous and complex theories of personality development here, but it is interesting to note in passing that this is another area of inquiry where psychology and anthropology have converged in recent years. For example, two psychologists who were strongly influenced by anthropologists, Erik Erikson and Erich Fromm, proposed that personality develops through various stages. Erikson spoke of eight stages through which a person passes in developing a mature personality:

First year:	A person develops a sense of trust or mistrust of the world
Second year:	A person develops a sense of control over self and environment or a sense of inadequacy
Third to fifth years:	A person develops an initiative and purpose or becomes jealous and unimaginative
Fifth to eleventh years:	A person develops an appreciation for work or feelings of inferiority

12. Ibid., p. 206.

> Adolescence: A person develops a sense of
> identity
>
> Adulthood: A person develops
> relationships
> A person develops in
> productivity
> A person develops self-
> integrity[13]

Erikson, then, put a special emphasis on early development, as can be seen in his eight-stage schema.

Fromm (and Michael Maccoby) emphasized four stages during which one learns, first, to accept; second, to take; third, to conserve; and fourth, to be creative and productive.[14] One of the major concerns of Fromm had to do with the cultural influences in personality development. Both stages of development and ideal personality types vary from culture to culture. Some societies produce what Fromm called "culturally patterned defects"—behaviors that are socially approved but emotionally debilitating.

Personality Differences

Of necessity I have already alluded to ways in which personality has been categorized. As we would expect, these categories reflect not only differences among kinds of personality per se, but also differences among those doing the categorizing. All of the categorizers evidence their own interests and backgrounds—whether psychological, anthropological, or communicational. A sampling of typologies will illustrate this.

13. Erik Erikson, *Childhood and Society*, 2d ed. (New York: Norton, 1963).

14. Erich Fromm and Michael Maccoby, *Social Character in a Mexican Village: A Sociopsychoanalytic Study* (Englewood Cliffs, N.J.: Prentice-Hall, 1970).

Hippocrates' Four Temperaments

One of the oldest classifications of personality traits is that of Hippocrates, the Greek philosopher and physician who lived some four centuries before Christ. Hippocrates thought that the human body contained four basic kinds of liquids and that different temperaments resulted from the predominance of one or another of these liquids (see fig. 20). Hippocrates was in error as to the cause of these temperaments. Psychologists today generally take a dim view of his typology. Nevertheless, Hippocrates' differentiation and descriptions have persisted through the centuries and are quite popular today.

Jung's Two Modes of Relating

More widely recognized is Carl Jung's distinction between two possible modes of relating to one's environment: extroversion and introversion.[15] On the basis of his work popular psychology has differentiated between two types of individuals. The extrovert is oriented toward the people, objects, and events of the outer world. The introvert is oriented toward the inner world of his own mental states, thoughts, and feelings. At an even more popular level the extrovert is thought of as being outgoing and at ease with others, whereas the introvert is thought of as

FIGURE 20 **Hippocrates' Four Temperaments**

Predominant Body Liquid	Temperament Type	Chief Characteristics
Blood	Sanguine	Warm, lively, ardent, hopeful
Yellow bile	Choleric	Active, hot-tempered, easily irritated
Black bile	Melancholy	Gloomy, irascible, dejected
Phlegm	Phlegmatic	Calm, sluggish, apathetic

15. Carl Jung, *Psychological Types*, trans. H. Goodwin Baynes (London: Routledge and Kegan Paul, 1923).

being withdrawn, shy, and somewhat maladjusted to the real world. Jung himself did not consider one mode to be healthy and the other unhealthy, nor did he think of persons as being given to just one or the other mode of orientation, although he recognized that one mode may be predominant.

Linton's Status Personality

As we have already mentioned, Linton (like Fromm, Maccoby, Erikson, and Jung) stressed the development of personality over the course of a lifetime. Applying the emphasis on status and role, he said that no single individual embodies the whole tradition of his culture. Rather he learns and reflects characteristics appropriate to the particular set of statuses he occupies and the roles he plays. Such factors as sex, sibling order, age, class, occupation, and specialization are important determinants of these. Some statuses are fixed by his culture and therefore are ascribed. Others depend on the individual's free choice and effort and are, therefore, achieved. Thus, in addition to the basic personality core, individuals evidence status-personality traits growing out of their societal statuses and roles.[16]

A large body of literature focuses on this distinction. Individuals are described as rebels, conformists, or marginals, depending on whether they live up to expectations associated with their ascribed status. They are entrepreneurs, achievers, or nonachievers, depending upon how well they exploit possibilities for achieved status. Moreover, a differentiation is often made between what might be called one's public personality and his private or real personality. Paul Tournier (with a debt to Jung) refers to this when he uses the term *personage* to describe the social, outer mask a person wears when playing out his role;

16. Ralph Linton, *The Study of Man: An Introduction* (New York: Appleton-Century, 1936).

the word *person* refers to the thoughts, feelings, and actions of the individual. In writing *Games People Play*[17] and in developing Transactional Analysis, Eric Berne seems to express similar concepts.

It goes without saying that these differentiations are important to the cross-cultural counselor. Care must be exercised lest we make the mistake of imposing our cultural expectations on individuals of another culture. For example, it is a mistake to expect individuals in societies where little room is left for individual initiative to measure up to the expectations of our achievement-status and role-oriented society. But, allowing for cultural differences, it is important to know whether a respondent is characteristically rebellious, conformist, or marginal as viewed by society and by himself. And if we would really advise and help someone it is important to know whether we are communicating, as Tournier would say, "person-to-person" or "personage-to-personage." It is possible, after all, for both helper and helpee to retain their masks and never communicate as persons. It is with an eye to the possibility of meaningful person-to-person communication that Jacob Loewen encourages self-exposure on the part of cross-cultural Christian workers.[18] When foreigners are enabled to see us as humanly the same (i.e., subject to the same failures, temptations, and weaknesses; and dependent on the same grace of God) although culturally different, the way is opened to a helping relationship.

Rogers's and Shoemaker's Adopter Categories

Everett M. Rogers and Floyd F. Shoemaker have differentiated personality types on the basis of how open individuals are to new ways of thinking and doing things.

17. Eric Berne, *Games People Play: The Psychology of Human Relationships* (New York: Grove, 1964).

18. Jacob A. Loewen, "Self-Exposure: Bridge to Fellowship," *Practical Anthropology* 12 (March-April 1965): 49–62.

They believe that on this basis human populations can be divided into five broad categories.[19]

Innovators or "highly adoptive" people constitute about 2–3 percent of most cultures. These people are eager to try new ideas. By the same token they are seldom opinion leaders because they tend to "run ahead" of their peers. Moreover (to think in Christian terms), although they may be the first to convert to Christ, they may also be the first to convert *from* Christ to yet another new faith or revert to their old ways when the newness of the Christian faith wears off.

Early adopters constitute 13–15 percent of a population. They readily see the value of certain new ideas but are also concerned with the integration of these ideas into the local culture. Many opinion leaders come from this group. In missionary terms, they have great potential for church leadership.

The **early majority** constitutes 20–35 percent of the population. These people adopt new ideas earlier than most but do so only after considerable deliberation. Acceptance by members of this group is important to legitimizing and stabilizing change.

The **late majority** comprises about 30–35 percent of the population and is characterized by an unwillingness to accept the new idea until some social pressure toward acceptance has built up.

Finally, the **bromidic** category constitutes about 12–15 percent of most cultures. These people are traditionalists and suspicious of agents of change, innovators, and change in general.

Obviously we have considered but a few of the numerous ways in which human personality types can be classified. In doing so it has become apparent that these and similar classifications have some utility. When Tim

19. Everett M. Rogers and Floyd F. Shoemaker, *Communication of Innovation* (New York: The Free Press, 1971), pp. 183ff.

LaHaye uses Hippocrates' categories as the basis for a discussion of the strengths and weaknesses of Christians and the spiritual means God has provided for overcoming the latter, he is able to communicate in a way that arrests the attention of the average Christian.[20] When D. P. Kelley relates Rogers's and Shoemaker's typology to successful missionizing, he arouses an awareness of the fact that people respond to the gospel differently, not just on the basis of their attitude toward the gospel itself, but also on the basis of their "inbuilt" disposition to accept or reject new ideas generally.[21]

Nevertheless, great care in the use of such categorizations is in order. In the first place, it is all too easy to overlook cautions that the categorizers and popularizers themselves suggest. Few categories of human personality are air tight. The same person may, for example, exhibit phlegmatic traits at one time and sanguine traits at another. This suggests, in the second place, a caution against putting a person in a category and thereafter dealing with him as "that kind of a personality." In the third place, cultural variations make for differences in the incidence and expressions of personality difference. It is highly questionable, for example, that the percentage of innovators and early adopters would be the same in the United States and Taiwan. Americans value that which is new for its newness. Traditional Chinese and tribal people tend to value that which has proved useful over the long haul. Finally, categories other than those provided by Scripture can be misleading. There is a temptation for Christians in our culture to identify extroversion with spirituality. Apart from the intrusion of Western values, the tendency among Indian Christians would be to identify introversion with

20. Tim LaHaye, *The Spirit-Controlled Temperament* (Wheaton: Tyndale, 1966).

21. D. P. Kelley, *Destroying the Barriers: Receptor Oriented Communication of the Gospel* (Vernon, B. C.: Laurel Publications, 1982), pp. 171–73.

spirituality. In any case, the use of secularists' categories to communicate biblical truth raises serious questions.

Personality Disorders

Because psychiatry and psychology are highly developed in our culture, prominent professionals have collaborated in recent years in order to produce manuals designed for students and practitioners of psychiatry, psychology, social work, nursing, and other mental-health-related professions. Experts from around the world have collaborated on the systems found in the *Diagnostic and Statistical Manual of Mental Disorders*, the third edition of which is now the standard in the field.[22] It is popularly known as DSM-III. Because this reference tends to be exhaustive (more than two hundred specific disorders are included) and uses the language of the specialist (phobias listed include arachibutyrophobia—the fear of peanut butter sticking to the roof of the mouth!) it will be of somewhat limited value to most Christian workers. However, a simplified version of DSM-III, which is of more value to nonspecialists, is also available.[23] It rearranges the twenty classifications of disorders presented in the larger manual into eighteen "classes or groups of conditions." These classifications generally flow from disorders that arise among the very young, to disorders displaying an organic element, to major psychotic disorders, and on to personality and developmental disorders:

    1. Disorders usually first evident in infancy, childhood, or adolescence

22. American Psychiatric Association, *Diagnostic and Statistical Manual of Mental Disorders*, 3d ed. (Washington, D.C.: American Psychiatric Association, 1980).
23. Robert L. Spitzer et al., *DSM-III Case Book: A Learning Companion to "The Diagnostic and Statistical Manual of Mental Disorders"* (New York: American Psychiatric Association, 1981).

2. Substance use disorders
3. Organic mental disorders
4. Schizophrenic mental disorders
5. Psychotic disorders not elsewhere classified
6. Paranoid disorders
7. Affective disorders
8. Anxiety disorders
9. Dissociative disorders
10. Somotoform disorders
11. Facitious disorders
12. Psychosexual disorders
13. Disorders of impulse control not elsewhere classified
14. Adjustment disorders
15. Psychological factors affecting physical condition
16. Conditions not attributable to a mental disorder (e.g., child abuse, borderline intellectual functioning)
17. Personality disorders
18. Specific developmental disorders (e.g., infantile autism and mental retardation, which are occasionally found in adults as well as children)

Finally, multiaxial classification (five axes are provided) makes possible the systematic evaluation of an individual's condition in terms of several variables. Using a multiaxial system of diagnosis reduces the likelihood that clinicians will overlook important factors. Suppose, for example, that a person is suffering from diabetes, anxiety disorder, and personality disorder. An internist and a psychologist would diagnose all these conditions. The anxiety disorder would be noted on axis 1, the personality disorder on axis 2, and the diabetes on axis 3.

Training in the proper use of DSM-III and the DSM-III training guide is, of course, provided to qualified students in Christian schools and seminars around the country. For Christian counselors who lack such qualifications, an acquaintance with the basic classification systems and evaluative approach suggested in the training guide should prove helpful.

Difficulties in Psychiatric Diagnosis

As widely used and helpful as the DSM-III has proved to be, we should not suppose that experts in the field have now achieved a high degree of uniformity in their diagnoses. As this is being written, in a case pending before the Supreme Court of New York State, a woman charged with murder has been diagnosed by various psychiatrists and psychologists as having a "histrionic personality disorder," a "major depressive reaction," a "psychotic depression," an "adjustment reaction of adult life" and as "faking mental illness." One psychiatrist notes that she has been "called everything in the diagnostic nomenclature." The newspaper reporter writes that a hearing in the case "emerged as a battle between psychiatrists and psychologists."[24]

It would seem quite obvious that if the diagnosis and classification of mental disorders present problems within the North American context, these problems will be compounded in cross-cultural contexts. And research indicates that this is so. Such factors as different perceptions of "normal" and "abnormal" behavior and the evaluative judgments of professionals in mental health combine to occasion significant difficulties in attempts to develop classifications that are valid cross-culturally.

Nonetheless, since the middle of the 1950s the psychiatric profession has been moving in this direction. Psychiatrist Gary L. Almy believes that ultimately Freud may be looked upon as a detour in the history of psychiatry. In evolving classifications, psychiatrists have reverted to Emil Kraepelin's interest in the diagnostic approach but now possess the biotechnical knowledge essential to a

24. Raymond A. Wittek, "Woman Charged in Murder Was Given Weekend Passes," *Staten Island Advance,* 19 March 1983, sec. A, p. 5.

more proper diagnosis and, especially, more effective treatment.[25]

Almy says psychiatrists generally accept research that indicates, for example, that 10 percent of the people in *any given culture* will have treatable depression. Cardinal symptoms of depression will include early morning awakening; loss of 15 percent of body weight within thirty days for no physiological reason; and mood disorder that lasts four weeks or more. Other important symptoms will be hopelessness and motor change. Electroshock will result in 95 percent alleviation, and antidepressant drugs will result in 72 percent alleviation. From scientific and clinical points of view, these statistics, symptoms, and treatments are unaffected by culture.[26]

Almy would likely agree with Frank Engelsmann when he says that the meaning of depression varies with psychological, social, and cultural circumstances; that depressive affect must be distinguished from depressive illness (called melancholia by Hippocrates and manic-depressive insanity by Kraepelin); that episodes of depressive affect are common to human life; and that depression is not an imitary but a heterogenous syndrome.[27] But he insists that the evidence shows that there is a type of depression which overtakes people in all cultures and for no reason other than their genetic makeup. Therefore the cross-cultural counselor who is not qualified to prescribe drug therapy, for example, can help by dealing with the mental, emotional, and spiritual aspects of any given case. In doing so, he should guard against an error similar to that made by secular counselors who regularly overlook the spiritual origins of depression. Namely, he should be aware of biological causes and should not inadvisedly as-

25. Gary L. Almy, in a lecture delivered at Trinity Evangelical Divinity School—School of World Mission and Evangelism, 28 December 1982.
26. Ibid.
27. Frank Engelsmann, "Cultural Depression," in *Culture and Psychopathology*, ed. Ihsan al-Issa (Baltimore: University Park, 1982), p. 251.

sume (or allow the counselee to assume) that sin must be at the root of the problem.

Psychological Testing

By the time most Western (especially American) missionaries reach their respective mission fields they will have taken various tests designed to measure their educational achievements, personality characteristics, suitability for cross-cultural service, and so forth. In effect, some of these tests are designed to prediagnose personality disorders. In very recent years considerable attention has been given to studying the validity of these tests when used in cultures other than the culture of their origin and to the possibility of developing personality tests that are not culturally biased.

Probably one of the most well-known and widely used personality tests, and therefore a good example, is the Minnesota Multiphasic Personality Inventory (MMPI). It is based on the idea that people who have tendencies to maladaptive behavior and personality dysfunction tend to respond to certain questions in similar ways. Various criticisms have been leveled against the MMPI. In spite of its limitations, however, the test has continued to yield significant results in our culture.

Sid H. Irvine and William K. Carroll draw attention to two studies, both of which were designed to evaluate the MMPI as an instrument for prediagnosing schizophrenia among blacks and whites in the United States. Both studies came to the same conclusion: "The MMPI interacts differently with different ethnic groups when educational levels are not held constant. . . ."[28]

---

28. Sid H. Irvine and William K. Carroll, "Testing and Assessment across Cultures: Issues in Methodology and History," in *Handbook of Cross-Cultural Psychology: Perspectives*, gen. ed. Harry C. Triandis, 6 vols. (Boston: Allyn and Bacon, 1980–83), vol. 2, ed. Harry C. Triandis and Juris G. Draguns (1980), p. 227.

After surveying the results of numerous studies that focus upon the validity of using the MMPI cross-culturally, Walter J. Lonner concludes that in some ways it can be considered usable, at least on an exploratory basis.[29] First, some commonality of dysfunction across cultures is "likely to be found if not already evident."[30] Second, the MMPI has been used so widely that a great "mountain of data" is available. Third, as a result of the diffusion of patterns of complaints and systems of diagnosis across cultural lines, both symptoms and diagnoses may become increasingly universalistic. At the same time the MMPI may be inappropriate for cross-cultural use because "it started with a Western system of psychiatric classification, its original normative groups came primarily from small groups of University of Minnesota hospital patients . . . , and it is essentially atheoretical or criterion-oriented."[31]

In view of the fact that Hans J. Eysenck has a low opinion of the reliability of psychiatric diagnoses in general, one need not be at all surprised that his recent appraisal of the cross-cultural validity of the MMPI and other tests based upon the psychiatric model is discouraging to those who search for a culturally unbiased test. Eysenck and S. B. G. Eysenck hold out more hope for their "dimensions of personality model" (extroversion-introversion; neuroticism-stability; psychoticism-superego control), inasmuch as these dimensions seem to them to be much the same in various nations and cultures. However, the major result of their findings—that mental abnormalities *within* cultures exhibit such great variation that comparative studies inevitably result in small and relatively unimpor-

29. Walter J. Lonner, "Psychological Tests in Intercultural Counseling," in *Counseling across Cultures*, ed. Paul P. Pedersen et al., rev. ed. (Honolulu: The University Press of Hawaii for the East-West Center, 1981), pp. 290–92.

30. Ibid., p. 291.

31. Ibid.

tant differences—can be interpreted as disconcerting or reassuring, depending on one's viewpoint.[32]

Psychological testing has been an important adjunct of counseling in the Western world. Used cross-culturally, however, it presents some unique problems which serve to reinforce a preference on the part of many for the interview, medical history, and other means of inquiry into the counselee's state. Those who are expert and have special interest in psychological testing will continue to use improved versions of the MMPI and newer tests such as the Taylor-Johnson Temperament Analysis. How close they can come to devising a culturally unbiased test is still a matter of conjecture.[33]

Some Guidelines for Cross-Cultural Workers

It is helpful, then, for any Christian cross-cultural counselor to know something of the causes and symptoms of personality disorders. Guidelines certainly should be observed in applying whatever understanding the counselor might attain.

As we have noted previously, although the features symptomatic of personality disorders may be observed among people of various societies, local ways of understanding and dealing with them may be very divergent. These local understandings cannot be dismissed out of hand.

To go beyond one's expertise in either diagnosis or therapy is unethical. If possible, trained specialists should be consulted when the case dictates.

The spiritual dimension should have its proper place in the helping process. Spiritual factors should be neither overlooked nor assumed to be the sole or primary cause of personality disorders.

32. Hans J. Eysenck and S. B. G. Eysenck, "Culture and Personality Abnormalities," in *Culture and Psychopathology*, pp. 302–14.

33. Lonner, "Psychological Tests," in *Counseling across Cultures*, p. 298.

Personality Disorder and Demon Possession

One of the most crucial areas of cross-cultural ministry in some parts of the world is dealing with demon possession. Naturalists can be expected to discount the phenomenon and many Christians disregard it. But classical and contemporary studies, the rise of interest in the occult in the West, and the experiences of numerous missionaries and national leaders in churches around the world (to say nothing of the clear testimony of Scripture) combine to alert us to the reality and seriousness of demonic influence on many people around the world.[34]

In his classic study on the subject of demon possession, the missionary to China and strategist, John L. Nevius, countered evolutionary, pathological, and psychological theories antithetical to Christian understanding, and in the process provided us with three distinguishing marks and four stages of obsession and possession—information which is still valid for identifying and counseling such cases.[35]

Four Stages of Obsession and Possession

According to Nevius, spirit manifestations are as follows:

First Stage: Obsession; first approach; introductory and tentative efforts by the demon; difficult for the Christian worker to ascertain whether the problem is to be explained in terms of demonic activity or otherwise.

Second Stage: Transition or crisis; temporary; struggle

34. For example, refer to the citations to the writings of the early Fathers in John W. Montgomery, *Principalities and Powers: A New Look at the World of the Occult* (Minneapolis: Bethany Fellowship, 1973), p. 179, and the numerous writings of Kurt Koch.

35. John L. Nevius, *Demon Possession*, 8th ed. (Grand Rapids: Kregel, 1968). Nevius's book was first published in 1894 but it is interesting to note that in the preface of this eighth edition Merrill F. Unger says that he was helped immensely by this work when doing research for his *Biblical Demonology*, 6th ed. (Wheaton: Scripture Press Foundation, 1965).

for possession; subject sometimes resists successfully but generally yields involuntarily to the will of the demon.

Third Stage: Subjection and subserviency; "development" in possession; subject generally healthy and peaceful but experiences periodic paroxysms in passing from normal to abnormal state; may last for years.

Fourth Stage: Developed and voluntary subservience to the demon; subject becomes a medium, sorcerer, or witch (terminology differs with cultures).[36]

Nevius would have us understand that these distinctions are general and may change with the individual case. Also, stages may be bypassed in certain cases.

Distinguishing Marks of Demon Possession

Perhaps most important for the practitioner is the ability to distinguish between supernatural possession and natural pathologies. Nevius provides us with three differentiating marks which aid us in the task. (The first is perhaps most important inasmuch as most of the literature emphasizes it.)

First Mark: The appearance of a "new personality"; subject declares he is a demon; demon speaks of himself in the first person whereas the subject is generally spoken of in the third person; demon uses appropriate names or titles for himself and the subject; the new personality is manifested by appropriate actions and facial expressions.

Second Mark: The evidence of knowledge and intellect not possessed by the subject (e.g., the ability to speak in another language).

Third Mark: A complete change of moral character; the subject is debased and malicious; he gives evidence of aversion to the Christian religion, Christ, the Bible, and prayer.[37]

36. This summary is based on information from Nevius, *Demon Possession*, pp. 285–86.
37. Ibid., pp. 186–206.

Motivation and the Individual

For many years one of the most heated arguments among psychologists had to do with the degree to which instincts (innate tendencies) motivate human behavior. Implicit in the debate was the question of free will. Is individual behavior the result of free will or is it instinctually determined? Theorists came to the point where they explained almost any behavior by naming a corresponding instinct. In 1925, L. L. Bernard catalogued more than ten thousand instincts that were mentioned in relevant literature![38] Meanwhile, anthropological studies evidenced the fact that many of these "instincts" varied from one culture to another.[39]

Subsequently, many psychologists tended to search for a more unified theory of motivation. Need-drive theories were the result—needs having to do with the requirements of the human organism for survival and drives being the resultant state which motivates behaviors that result in fulfillment of the needs. (Freud had anticipated this approach by saying that all motivational forces stem from two basic drives—the loving or creative force [libido] and the destructive death force [thanatos].) Not a few theorists held to the view that needs for food, shelter, and the like constitute primary motivations and that secondary motivations (e.g., for interaction with others) grow out of these. Many psychologists, including Abraham H. Maslow, however, were not satisfied with the idea that all motivations are basically biological. Maslow's theory is that the needs can be hierarchically ranked from the elemental physiological needs to those that are more mature socially and psychologically (see fig. 21). Maslow believes

---

38. L. L. Bernard, *Instinct* (New York: Holt, 1925), noted in Lindgren and Fisk, *Psychology of Personal Development*, p. 59.

39. Lindgren and Fisk, *Psychology of Personal Development*, p. 61.

that as the basic needs are fulfilled, a person seeks to satisfy higher needs.[40]

Some researchers would say that Maslow has misread the evidence. Small infants seem to prefer complex visual figures to simple ones. Even hungry rats have been observed exploring a novel environment rather than accepting food. Some theorists conclude therefore, that curiosity and novel stimulation may be so important to brain development as to qualify as a biological need.[41] As a matter of fact, even such evidence seems quite puny in the face of the enormous potential that persons have for developing meaningful relationships and displaying creativity.

For their part, Christian theorists have given considerable attention to the foregoing developments in motivational research. Although they reject theories that reduce man to a biological organism and severely or entirely eliminate his power of choice, they nevertheless have given credance to such notions as the hierarchy of needs, self-actualization, and curiosity motivation. In addition, Christian cross-culturalists have elaborated relationships between "felt needs" and "real needs"; between felt needs and Christian communication; and between felt needs

FIGURE 21   **Abraham H. Maslow's Motivational Pyramid**

40. Abraham H. Maslow, *Motivation and Personality*, 2d ed. (New York: Harper and Row, 1970).

41. Lindgren and Fisk, *Psychology of Personal Development*, p. 61.

and conversion. Secular studies on motivation are helpful; however, they can be misleading because they usually omit a most fundamental aspect of human nature—the *imago Dei*.

The Individual and Decision-Making

Previously we have referred to cultural orientations to decision-making and the ways in which they affect culture-sensitive counseling approaches. Once we have taken into account such things as cultural preferences for group decisions and for delaying decisions, however, we must recognize that individuals are responsible as individuals. Each man and each woman is responsible for the way he or she responds to the truth concerning his or her condition. That fact leads us to a consideration of decision-making as it applies to individuals.

Decision-Making as a Process

It is common in our culture to think of decision-making as it relates to a *point* in time. In fact, there is usually a point at which a change in direction becomes reportable and visible and, if not irreversible, at least uncomfortable to reverse. However, we tend to downplay the *process* of decision-making and thereby fail to appreciate its cognitive and emotive accompaniments.

With that in mind I have proposed an approach which views decision-making as a five-stage process.[42] A brief explanation of each of the five stages will aid our understanding of what is involved.

Discovery. At this stage the individual becomes aware that a certain course of action or option of accepting a belief exists as a possibility *for him or her*.

Deliberation. At this stage the individual is weighing

42. David J. Hesselgrave, *Communicating Christ Cross-Culturally: An Introduction to Missionary Communication* (Grand Rapids: Zondervan, 1978), pp. 446–52.

the pros and cons of adopting the proposed belief or course of action.

Determination. The individual accepts or rejects the proposal. This stage is often thought of as the decision *point.*

Dissonance. At this stage the decision-maker experiences a state of unsettledness.[43] Has the right choice been made? Can he live with it?

Discipline. Unless the individual reverts to his previous position he arrives at a final stage in which he accepts the consequences of his choice and proceeds accordingly.

Decision-Making and the Extended Fishbein Model

More involved is the explanation of the process of decision and change proposed by Martin Fishbein and others.[44] Here an attempt is made to demonstrate the interrelationship between beliefs (the cognitive dimension), attitudes (the affective dimension), and intention (the behavioral dimension). Fishbein contends that change in attitude (a positive or negative attitude toward undertaking a proposed course of action) will usually lead to a corresponding behavior change, provided such influences as social pressure are taken into account. The Fishbein model is shown in figure 22.

Anyone familiar with current missiological literature will be aware of how significant these and similar concepts and ideas have become. We will have occasion to point to this significance somewhat later in our discussion. Of course, all of the foregoing helpful insights into human personality and personal behavior are true and utilitarian only to the degree that they conform to sacred

43. Refer to Leon Festinger, *A Theory of Cognitive Dissonance* (Evanston, Ill.: Row and Peterson, 1957).

44. See Martin Fishbein and Icek Ajzen, *Belief, Attitude, Intention, and Behavior: An Introduction to Theory and Research* (Reading, Mass.: Addison-Wesley, 1975); and James F. Engel, *Contemporary Christian Communication: Its Theory and Practice* (Nashville: Nelson, 1979), pp. 180–83.

FIGURE 22 **The Extended Fishbein Model of Decision-Making**

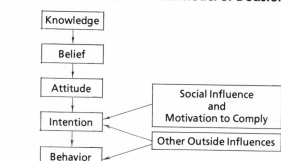

Scripture. With that in mind let us now turn our attention to what might be called a theology of the person.

A Theology of the Person

Every individual in the world bears at least four marks upon his person—that of God who created him, that of Satan who deluded him, that of Adam and the human parents who bore him, and that of the culture that nourished him. Every individual has tremendous potential for good or evil, for success or failure, for service or selfishness, for heaven or hell.

Interestingly enough, the English word *person* is derived from the Latin *persona*, which means a mask, personage, or part. The meaning is archaic now, but the term *person* originally referred to a character or part in a play. Today it refers to a particular human being or individual, or often to the real self. Behind our "masks" are real persons and behind the "play" is the real drama of life. How the drama turns out depends primarily upon God. But Satan and his demons influence the outcome. And so do you and I and persons everywhere.

The Struggle in Persons

Once more we must go back through the mists of time to that original pair, Adam and Eve. Formed of earth, in-

breathed by God, they and their environment were pronounced "good" (Gen. 1:31). Physiologically, sociologi-
cally, and situationally all was well. Moreover, they had
no limitations other than those imposed by their humanity and a minimum of divinely imposed prescriptions and
a proscription designed for their good and the good of
all creation. Enter the Tempter, and within the space of
one chapter (Gen. 3) all that was good had been stained
by the fall!

Historical theology records varied interpretations (some
of them strange to an extreme) of the temptation and the
fall of our first parents. But the historical record itself is
startlingly simple. Adam and Eve were tempted. They
obeyed the Tempter and disobeyed God. The Tempter was
judged. Adam and Eve were driven from the Garden. The
woman was sentenced to pain in childbearing and subjection to her husband. The man was sentenced to toil ("By
the sweat of your brow you will eat your food," Gen. 3:19).
Both were sentenced to death. But in all there was a promise—the seed of the woman would bruise the head of the
Tempter, although the Tempter would bruise the heel of
the Seed (Gen. 3:15).

The Bible—God's written revelation of his person and
will to mankind—contains all that is essential for
the construction of a Christian approach to a person's
problems.

First, God deals with fallen mankind as a whole, and
nations and persons in particular, just as he dealt with our
first parents—in law and in grace.

The primary Greek word for law, *nomos*, is related to
nemō, which means "to divide or distribute" and refers to
that which is assigned. "The word *ethos*, custom, was
retained for unwritten law, while *nomos* became the established word for law as decreed by a state and set up as
the standard for the administration of justice."[45] God's

45. W. E. Vine, *An Expository Dictionary of New Testament Words* (Westwood, N. J.: Revell, 1940), p. 313.

standard is his law, not culture's custom. And that law "reigned" from Moses until Christ (the "seed of the woman"). It had its various expressions, but Christ himself said that it could be summed up in two commands: to love God with heart, soul, and mind, and to love one's neighbor as oneself (Matt. 22:37–40). The problem of man under law is that no child of Adam and Eve has ever fulfilled even these two commands, as is made clear everywhere in Scripture and in human experience. No anthropology or psychology can long stand that does not recognize the truth of Paul's extended statements in the first three chapters of Romans. He writes that from creation "primal persons" not only did not love God, but also did not honor him as God or give thanks (Rom. 1:21); that "civilized persons" (among the Gentiles) not only failed to love God, but also were guilty of the very sins they condemned in the "uncivilized" (Rom. 2:1); and that privileged Jewish persons not only did not love God, but also broke the very law concerning which they proposed to instruct others (Rom. 2:17–21). Paul's conclusion is as clear as it is crushing:

> What shall we conclude then? Are we any better? Not at all! We have already made the charge that Jews and Gentiles alike are all under sin. As it is written:
> "There is no one righteous, not even one;
>   there is no one who understands,
>   no one who seeks God.
> All have turned away,
>   they have together become worthless;
> there is no one who does good,
>   not even one." [Rom. 3:9–12]

Since the promise concerning the "seed of the woman" has been fulfilled in Christ the divine Redeemer, a second ministry of the law assumes a special significance. The law not only condemns the lawbreaker. It also leads him to the Christ who is the personification of grace as well as truth. John wrote, "For the law was given through Moses; grace and truth come through Jesus Christ" (John 1:17). Paul writes that "as sin reigned in death, so also grace might reign through righteousness to bring eternal life through Jesus Christ our Lord" (Rom. 5:21). Set in contrast not only with law (John 1:17) but also with debt (Rom. 4:4, 16) and works (Rom. 11:6), the word *grace* (*charis*) is used with reference to both God and man. On the part of God it refers to "the friendly disposition from which the kindly act proceeds, graciousness, lovingkindness, goodwill generally."[46] On the part of the person who receives God's lovingkindness, *charis* refers to man's sense of gratitude or thankfulness (Rom. 16:7). The term *grace* has a wide application, but biblically it has special reference to the Triune God's redemptive mercy to sinful man— the Father's promise, the Son's procurement, and the Holy Spirit's presentment.

Second, arrayed against a person's highest interests are three formidable foes—the world, the flesh, and the devil.

The term *world* (*kosmos*) in this sense refers to the mass of humanity as being hostile to Christ and alienated from God (John 7:7), and to worldly affairs, the "aggregate of things earthly" which "seduce from God" and comprise an obstacle "to the cause of Christ" (Gal. 6:14).[47]

The word *flesh* (*sarx*) refers to "the earthly nature of man apart from divine influence" (2 Cor. 7:5).[48] The description applies to more than the body; the whole of a man, his entire nature, is included.

Finally, that "old serpent, called the Devil and Satan" (Rev. 12:9, KJV) still stalks his prey, "seeking whom he may devour" (1 Peter 5:8, KJV). He does not always assume so sinister a form, however. He is quite capable of transforming himself into an "angel of light" (2 Cor. 11:14; a

46. Ibid., p. 170.
47. Joseph H. Thayer, *Thayer's Greek-English Lexicon of the New Testament* (New York: American Book Co., 1889), p. 357.
48. Ibid., p. 571.

fact which helps account for the brilliance of psychologies that disregard the activities of both God and Satan!). Moreover, he commands a host of demons or angels who do his nefarious work in the world (Matt. 25:41).

In fact, the Bible writers record at least four ways in which demons or evil spirits act upon men in accordance with satanic direction and purposes: temptation by false spiritual suggestions; disease and illness induced by evil spirits; control resulting from voluntarily and habitually yielding to temptation; demon possession resulting in a new personality.[49]

Third, law and grace are not mutually exclusive. In law God remembers grace. In grace God does not forget the law. And whether law or grace is in the ascendency, God requires a response. In this connection it is interesting to note that in the Old Testament where it is so common for God to deal with communities of persons—tribes, nations, cities, families—in relation to the demands of his law, the individual is not thereby neglected or absolved of responsibility. Indeed, in that oft-quoted passage which sums up the teaching of Ecclesiastes (12:13–14), it is every man who is in view. So it could be read, "Fear (reverence) God, and keep His commandments for under obligation thereto is every man. For God will bring every deed into judgment with every secret thing, whether good or evil."[50] And, as for grace, we have already noted that on the human side it entails thankfulness or, one might say, grateful acceptance. That is why Paul writes,

> God is just: He will pay back trouble to those who trouble you and give relief to you who are troubled, and to us as well. This will happen when the Lord Jesus is revealed from heaven in blazing fire with his powerful angels. He

49. Nevius, *Demon Possession*, pp. 287–88.
50. Franz Delitzsch, *Commentary on the Song of Songs and Ecclesiastes*, trans. M. G. Easton (Grand Rapids: Eerdmans, n.d.), pp. 439–40.

will punish those who do not know God and do not obey
the gospel of our Lord Jesus. [2 Thess. 1:6–8]

Three Categories of Persons

However men (whether scientists or philosophers) may
categorize persons, God reveals categories determined in
accordance with human response to divine invitations and
requirements. We do well to ponder at least three categories with the certain knowledge that every person of
whatever culture will fall within one or another of them.

The first category is the natural (*psuchikos*) man (1 Cor.
2:14). The emphasis here is upon the lower part of a person's immaterial being—the soul. James (3:15) and Jude
(19) refer to this kind of person. Paul says that he is "in
Adam" (1 Cor. 15:22) and that the "things ... from the
Spirit of God" are foolishness to him. Unaided by the
Spirit, he is incapable of knowing them (1 Cor. 2:14–15).

The next category is the spiritual (*pneumatikos*) man
(1 Cor. 2:15). The emphasis here is upon the higher part
of a person's immaterial being—the spirit. More than self-
awareness and social awareness is involved. Instead of
being judged by men, the spiritual man himself—ener-
gized and aided by the Spirit of God—judges all things
(1 Cor. 2:15). He even has the responsibility and capability
of helping believers who are "overtaken in a fault" (Gal.
6:1, KJV).

The last category is the carnal (*sarkikos*) man (1 Cor.
3:3). The emphasis is upon the material part of man's
being—the flesh. Both the natural man and the spiritual
man have this aspect in their natures, of course. The difference is that in the spiritual man it is not allowed any
governing power. If it is allowed to govern him, the man
is not really spiritual because although he is a believer
and is capable of making spiritual judgment, he has not
progressed in Christ or has regressed spiritually.

Such is the framework in which the most fundamental
of spiritual distinctions must be made. To be sure, God is

no respecter of persons (Acts 10:34), but he has done all he could to bridge the gap between himself and his fallen creation. He demands a response. And persons are differentiated in time as well as eternity on the basis of what they will allow God to do for and in them.

Persons in Relationships

Created as sentient, social, and spiritual beings, persons are not isolates. They are fundamentally persons in relationship. At the heart of personal wholeness, therefore, are right relationships with God, other men, and the self. At the heart of personal problems are the deception of the human heart (Jer. 17:9), the onslaughts of Satan and his demons, and pressure from the world system which conspire to upset priorities, pervert affections, and prostitute personal potential. At the heart of Christian people-helping is the aiding of persons in thinking, feeling, and behaving in accordance with the teaching of God's Word concerning the human problem and the divine solution.

A person's relationship with God has first priority. When one stops to think about it, the command to love God carries with it the possibility of knowing and loving him—certainly the highest and noblest privilege a person possesses. "This means that no one can understand a human being unless he sees him in relation to God," says David G. Benner in summing up the conclusion of theologian G. C. Berkouwer.[51] But it means more than that. It means that no one can help a human person in any ultimate sense unless he sees that person in relation to God. This is not necessarily to agree with Jay E. Adams in placing evangelism as a first priority in every case when one is counseling an unbeliever. Prayer and pre-evangelism may take priority, as Tournier's approach would indicate. But it does mean that, like a wheel off center, the person who does not have God at the center of his life

51. David G. Benner, "Psychotherapies: Stalking Their Spiritual Side," *Christianity Today*, 11 December 1981, p. 33.

will experience a wrenching and, sooner or later, a
wretchedness.

A person's relationship with others has second priority.
This sounds strange in almost all cultures, but for different reasons. In what we have previously called collectivistic-dependency cultures it sounds strange because, although the gods and spirits may be deemed most
important, in practical day-to-day living relationships with
other people seem to have prior claim. In what we have
called individualistic-independency cultures it has a
strange ring because, although other people merit consideration, in a preponderance of theory and practice it is
freedom from others and faithfulness to self which take
priority.

In both cases, God's perspective is required. We are to
love others—with all that implies—as a corollary of loving God and a consequence of loving self. And notice that
the second commandment focuses especially upon the
others who are our neighbors and our brothers. Christ defines our neighbor as anyone we *encounter* who is in need
(Luke 10:36). John defines our brother as a fellow believer
whom we can *see* (1 John 4:20).

A person's relationship with the self has third priority.
Admittedly there is a certain ambiguity here because the
second commandment—"love your neighbor as yourself"—presumes both the fact and the quality of self-love.
Unlike Buddhism, Christianity does not teach that there
is no self—that is, no "I" that has separateness and permanence. Unlike Hinduism, Christianity does not teach
that the self is God—that is, that when we truly see the
atman within us we will recognize its oneness with the
Brahman or Absolute. What the Bible teaches is that every
human person is of inestimable value because God has
created man to be placed at the pinnacle of his creation
and to enjoy his presence forever. To value one's self in
this sense is wholesome and right. To love one's self in
any other sense is perverted and wrong.

And what shall we say about priorities? Let us say what Scripture says, namely, that "Christ's person" is to deny himself, take up his cross, and follow him (Luke 9:23). And that a man has no greater love than this: to lay down his life for his friends (John 15:13).

In conclusion, let it be said that all that God has said and all that he has done—and all that he commands his servants to say and do—is said and done with the highest good of every person in view. He desires for every person blessedness in the life that is now and in the life to come.

Individual Uniqueness and Counseling Analyses

Christian cross-cultural counselors often have opportunities to affect entire tribes, societies, and communities in very positive ways. But *in the final analysis* their responsibility is to help individual persons find healing and wholeness in Christ because *in the final analysis* every person stands alone before God. (Although it is true that the Old Testament has much to say about divine judgment on families, tribes, nations, and cities, an increased emphasis in the Bible is placed upon the judgment of individual persons.) It is not enough, then, to know human universals (the general characteristics of all men) and cultural particulars (the special characteristics of counselees' cultures). We must also enquire into personal uniqueness (the specific characteristics of counselees). Only by so doing is the counselor completely faithful to the provision and purpose of God, and to the problem and potential of persons.

In bold outline, then, we ask ourselves how we might proceed, step by step, in understanding culturally different persons (see fig. 23).

Step 1: Discover Important Factors in the Background of the Counselee

Although as Christians we do not accept the notion that a person is simply the sum total of previous experi-

288

FIGURE 23 **Counseling and the Individual (1)**

Steps in Understanding Individual Uniqueness and Making Counseling Analyses

Discover Important Factors in the Background of the Counselee

Determine the Personality Type and Status of the Counselee

Ascertain the Precise Nature of Presenting Problems

Understand the Needs, Motivations, and Values of the Counselee

Apply Knowledge of the Decision-Making Process

ences (that view accords better with naturalistic and Hindu-Buddhistic world views), we do have biblical warrant for believing that one's parentage, upbringing, and surroundings affect him in very significant ways. Therefore, to the degree practicable it will help to inquire into the counselee's background.

Questions: What is there in the biological and physical heritage of the counselee that would bear upon his problems? How do such things as parentage, diet, sex, physical make-up or physical impairment contribute to his problems?

Reflections: Genetic factors and past medical records are so important to the diagnosis and treatment of many illnesses that many hospitals in the United States require full-fledged medical doctors to record the personal history of new patients before they are admitted to the hospital. What is important to medicine is also important to counseling. This is so from both psychological and spiritual points of view. Unfortunately, it is not always practical or even possible to get a very complete record for many cross-cultural counselees, but any information is better than no information. Although it may not seem important, the fact that a counselee was born in the home of a priest or witch doctor; or that the counselee is female instead of the male child for which her parents earnestly besought the gods; or that the counselee's lameness is "due to a hex," these and myriads of similar factors are essential ingredients of understanding apart from which wise counsel is impossible.

Questions: What might be the effect of the environment(s) in which the counselees have lived? Must the natural environment (climate or terrain) be taken into consideration? What kind of houses or neighborhoods do the counselees live in? What are the means of livelihood?

Reflections: It is easy to misjudge persons when life situations are as different as they often are. Although we may not be able to fully empathize with the results of spending a lifetime in a debilitating climate, or the fear that may attend living in a house where a suicide occurred years ago, or the fatalism that often attends abject poverty, we can nevertheless appreciate something of the impact such factors have on people of other environments and experiences.

Questions: What can we learn by inquiring into the societal background of counselees? What was the religious faith of their parents? What about sibling order or rivalry? What about upbringing and education? Does the social, political, or religious environment loom large?

Reflections: Once again, counselors must make the attempt to project themselves into very different circumstances than those with which they are familiar. The eldest son in many tribal families carries an unusual responsibility for aged parents, younger siblings, and the family business. Twins in many African tribes may still bear a stigma; a generation ago they would have been left to die. Acceptance of a child or young person into a Christian school may be tantamount to assuring the family of future employment in certain countries of Asia. Numerous inbuilt sociological effects and expectations project themselves into the counseling situation and necessitate understanding persons in situ (see fig. 24).

Step 2: Determine the Personality Type and Status of the Counselee

We must recognize the danger of categorizing persons in terms of the types we have considered. Nevertheless, it might be worthwhile to attempt to make some analysis of the personal characteristics of the counselee. The five types of counselees mentioned in chapter 3 are still valid. But now we are prepared to press further. Of course, in so doing the counselor must be careful not to exceed the bounds of his expertise and, in any case, will hold his conclusions with an appropriate degree of tentativeness.

FIGURE 24   **Counseling and the Individual (2)**

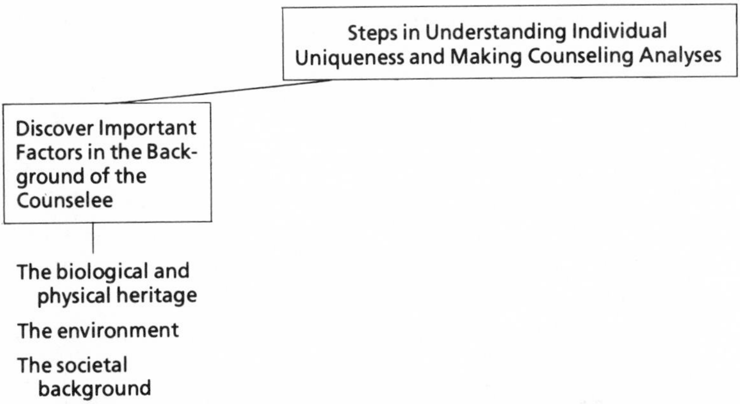

```
                        ┌─────────────────────────────────────┐
                        │   Steps in Understanding Individual   │
                        │ Uniqueness and Making Counseling Analyses │
                        └─────────────────────────────────────┘
 ┌──────────────────┐
 │ Discover Important│
 │ Factors in the Back-│
 │ ground of the     │
 │ Counselee         │
 └──────────────────┘
        │
   The biological and
      physical heritage
   The environment
   The societal
      background
```

Although the spiritual status of the counselee may be less ambiguous, the same caution is germane.

Questions: Can we obtain sufficient information to classify the counselee(s) in any given situation from an anthropological perspective? Would it not be helpful to determine such factors as societal status and orientation to change?

Reflections: From one perspective it makes little or no difference to God what a person might be in relation to others in his society. But it does make a difference to the person himself. Being aware of such concepts as public personality and social personality reminds us that the individual often sees himself through the eyes of others. "I am a failure"; "I have no will power"; "I am under a curse"—these and many other self-assessments may be more a mirror of the ideas of others than a reflection of actuality. The counselee may not be in a position to really distinguish between the two. But the counselor must attempt to do so.

Missiological materials have not really emphasized the foregoing. What has been emphasized is that when converts are marginal to a society the possibility that others will embrace the faith is lessened, or that when opinion leaders and/or early adopters become Christians the Christian cause is enhanced. Information of this sort is worth knowing, but must not be allowed to eclipse other psychological and spiritual realities.

Questions: In psychological terms, can we ascertain reliable reasons for determining the personality type, temperament, and character of the counselee(s) in a given counseling situation? If so, how are these characteristics judged by the culture? How should they be evaluated by a counselor?

Reflections: Understandably, counselors tend to be attracted to certain personalities and repelled by others. Western counselors in particular can be expected to appreciate the sanguine, extroverted, entrepreneuring, achievement-oriented individual in almost any culture. By the same token they may find it difficult to appreciate persons with other personality characteristics. And they may find it extremely difficult to read other cues to personality characteristics—cues which locals pick up without much difficulty. Factors such as these often combine to make the cross-cultural worker a rather poor judge of persons. The thing to remember is that we dare not trust our natural and cultural biases in making such an assessment. *Every* person is valuable in the sight of God, and, in any case, *he* can change persons.

Question: What about spiritual status?

Reflections: We do not want to imply that all problems can be readily resolved if only a person is in proper relationship to God. But most *Christian* counseling must be done with a recognition of the spiritual state of counselees. And, as a matter of fact, much if not most cross-cultural Christian counseling is undertaken on the basis that the counselor is willing and able to bring spiritual instruction and relief. Obviously change has three major points of reference—what counselees *are,* what they *should be,* and what we hope they *will be.* Therefore we begin by ascertaining where counselees are *now.* And, ordinarily, we counsel with them very differently, depending upon whether they are natural men and nothing more, or whether they are spiritual or carnal Christians (see fig. 25).

Step 3: Ascertain the Precise Nature of Presenting Problems

Counselees in many societies can be expected to communicate the nature of personal problems (insofar as they understand them) with much more embarrassment and much less directness than do counselees in our society. In cases of extreme psychological or spiritual disturbance, the subject may be in no position to understand or explain the nature of his problem. A great deal of patience and wisdom often will be required in order to ferret out the true nature of presenting problems, and until that is known solutions will be hard to come by!

In chapter 3 we said that there are four broad rubrics of problems that will be faced by cross-cultural Christian workers: problems relating to life and well-being; questions related to conversion; issues concerning Christian growth and lifestyle; and problems relating to divine guid-

FIGURE 25 **Counseling and the Individual (3)**

	Steps in Understanding Individual Uniqueness and Making Counseling Analyses
Discover Important Factors in the Background of the Counselee	Determine the Personality Type and Status of the Counselee
The biological and physical heritage	From an anthropological point of view
The environment	From a psychological point of view
The societal background	From a spiritual point of view

ance and Christian service. A complete catalogue of problems and answers falling within these broad categories would be overwhelming. But sensitive and patient probing may be required in order to identify the real problems of counselees.

Question: What special difficulties can be anticipated in ascertaining the precise nature of a counselee's problem in the cross-cultural situation?

Reflections: As in any other counseling situation, the one counseling cross-culturally must first be a good listener. A counselee may have an erroneous view of what his problem actually is. For example, one counselee may see his problem as bad luck, another as the breaking of a local taboo, and still another as the vindictiveness of a departed ancestor. The counselee may conceal the real problem by speaking of something seemingly unrelated. Or the counselee may be incapable of describing his problem in any meaningful way (as in the case of a Japanese girl who was probably a manic depressive but who could do little more than speak of her unhappiness). The problem must be identified if the solution is to be known.

Question: What is the value of knowing local perceptions of a presenting problem?

Reflections: Insofar as a counselee's problem is known by others in the society, the likelihood is that the "insiders" will have their own interpretations of the problem. These may or may not coincide with the counselee's understanding. The Japanese girl mentioned previously was hastily diagnosed by a Japanese psychiatrist as being "nervously exhausted" and was immediately given electroshock therapy. Local believers in many societies will be more intimately acquainted with the influence of evil spirits than will Christian workers from the West. But, depending upon the degree of their spiritual maturity, they may analyze a given case in accordance with the biblical understandings elucidated, or they may accept local and pagan explanations. In a hostile culture, any problem experienced by a new convert may be widely interpreted as related in some way to his conversion. Whether laymen or local experts are offering explanations, those interpretations become a part of the counselee's social reality and therefore should be on the counselor's agenda.

Question: To what degree can counselors trust their cross-cultural analyses?

Reflections: Over and over I have cautioned against going beyond one's expertise. All of us are fallible. There are times when the only proper thing to do is to refer the counselee to someone else, or to invite a local counselor into the situation. However, anyone having a rather thorough knowledge of people, culture, and especially the Bible is in a position to make some valid interpretations of a host of human problems. Carefully inquire into the circumstances; prayerfully ponder the effects; and humbly anticipate that the Holy Spirit will guide you in drawing conclusions (see fig. 26).

Step 4: Understand the Needs, Motivations, and Values of the Counselee

Questions concerning the motivations and values brought to the counseling situation by any single counselee are among the most difficult questions to answer.

FIGURE 26   **Counseling and the Individual (4)**

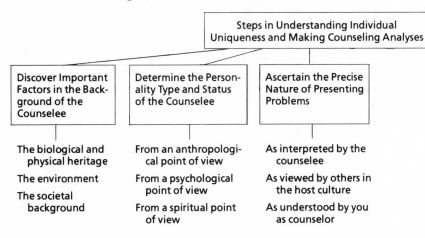

Steps in Understanding Individual Uniqueness and Making Counseling Analyses		
Discover Important Factors in the Background of the Counselee	Determine the Personality Type and Status of the Counselee	Ascertain the Precise Nature of Presenting Problems
The biological and physical heritage	From an anthropological point of view	As interpreted by the counselee
The environment	From a psychological point of view	As viewed by others in the host culture
The societal background	From a spiritual point of view	As understood by you as counselor

We may attempt to deduce them from general and cultural research. We may attempt to "divine" them on the basis of special insight. Neither approach is without validity. But one thinks of a bit of homespun wisdom reported to have been offered by Maslow when commenting on the relationship between research on human motivation and research on mice, rats, chimpanzees, and the like: "One advantage in enquiring into the motivation of human persons is that you can ask them!" Ask, and we may not get the right answer. A great deal of general and cultural knowledge and special insight may still be required. But in all likelihood if we ask we will at least have a starting point for conversation.

Questions: What is the relevance of the immediate and felt needs of the counselees? What basis do felt needs offer for conversation and interaction?

Reflections: Increasingly widespread in missionary literature is the notion that cross-cultural workers should first of all address themselves to the felt needs of respondents. In part, these needs are culturally determined. In part they depend upon the particular condition of the individual or group. Charles H. Kraft believes that Spirit-led missionaries will address their message to conscious and latent needs of people in such a way that people will subjectively recognize that God is meeting them at the point of need.[52] Louis Luzbetak emphasizes that "without deliberately omitting any aspect of Christ's mission and teaching, the missioner appreciating the principle of felt needs would seek a starting point in his instruction that would be most in accord with the existing felt needs."[53] Hans Kasdorf says that when individuals are converted to Christ their motivation will likely reflect cultural con-

52. Charles H. Kraft, *Christianity in Culture: A Study in Dynamic Biblical Theologizing in Cross-Cultural Perspective* (Maryknoll, N. Y.: Orbis, 1979), pp. 195–97.
53. Louis Luzbetak, *The Church and Cultures* (Techny, Ill.: Divine Word Publications, 1963), pp. 67–68.

cerns. Conversion will be motivated by a desire to be free from existential guilt in one culture, self-defeating anxiety in another culture, and haunting fear in still another. To address people in accordance with this understanding not only is legitimate, but also is encouraged.[54]

Questions: What needs can be agreed upon as having validity? On what basis?

Reflections: A good deal of objectivity is required at this point—objectivity on the part of the counselor as well as on the part of the counselee.

Think of the Western counselee and his value system. Self-interest has become so characteristic of motivational theories and approaches in the West that it has been confirmed, baptized, and incorporated into the church with little attention to its Christian credentials. Self-actualization, self-realization, self-love, self-assurance, fidelity to the self—these emphases recur constantly. It is only right that the Western counselor reevaluate this understanding in the light of Scripture. Then he will be in a much better position to cooperatively work with counselees (who have their own value systems and personal motivations) in a process of sorting things out and determining which needs, motivations, and values have validity and the kind of validity they possess.

Question: Can a mutually agreed upon priority of needs be established?

Reflections: There can be no question but that crosscultural Christian workers have given, and must continue to give, attention to the totality of human needs. Hundreds and thousands of hospitals, leprosariums, orphanages, and schools plus countless examples of aid administered to suffering individuals belie the notion that we evangelical Christians see people as "souls with ears." On the contrary, we emulate the Good Samaritan who pours oil into

---

54. Hans Kasdorf, *Christian Conversion in Context* (Scottdale, Penn.: Herald, 1980), p. 113.

the wounds of the beaten traveler and seeks to assure his recovery. Nevertheless, we believe that a man's earthly body will return to dust. And on biblical as well as secular grounds we question the idea that unless an individual's stomach is full he cannot respond to the gospel. While viewing people holistically and, insofar as possible, giving attention to all their needs, Christian counselors must place a priority on that which is spiritual and undying.

By the same token, there can be no question but that counselees of other cultural backgrounds continue to come to Christian workers with a wide variety of needs, wants, and desires. If we allow the word *rice* to symbolize all of these varied needs, the number of "rice Christians" in the world must be legion. And when one stops to think of it, many of these needs and wants are valid. Who can be condemned for wanting a healthier baby, a higher standard of living, an increased facility in the lingua franca of the business world, and so forth? And yet, unless an agreed upon priority can be established, there can be no question but that a good deal of frustration will result despite good intentions on the parts of both counselor and counselees (see fig. 27).

Step 5: Apply Knowledge
of the Decision-Making Process

As we have learned previously, cultures vary greatly in their approaches to decision-making. That understanding and additional knowledge of the individual decision-making process must be applied to particular counseling situations.

Question: How are the counselees expected to make decisions that answer to any given problem?

Reflections: In collectivistic-dependency cultures it is expected that some decisions will be made by consensus, although others will be expected of the individual. Decisions to convert, to be baptized, to follow the Lord into Christian service, and to be married will likely be of the

299

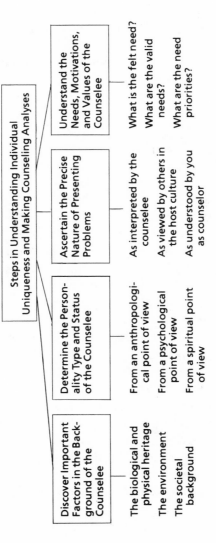

FIGURE 27   Counseling and the Individual (5)

Steps in Understanding Individual Uniqueness and Making Counseling Analyses

Discover Important Factors in the Background of the Counselee

The biological and physical heritage

The environment

The societal background

Determine the Personality Type and Status of the Counselee

From an anthropological point of view

From a psychological point of view

From a spiritual point of view

Ascertain the Precise Nature of Presenting Problems

As interpreted by the counselee

As viewed by others in the host culture

As understood by you as counselor

Understand the Needs, Motivations, and Values of the Counselee

What is the felt need?

What are the valid needs?

What are the need priorities?

former type. Decisions having to do with restitution, self-improvement, and personal habits may well fall within the latter category. It may be wise to involve the group in the decision process.) Even where the family or community can be expected to be antagonistic to an individual's decision, certain compensations are possible. For example, a son or daughter in a Confucianist family may be encouraged to report his or her decision to follow Christ in the following way:

> Father and Mother, I have good news. First I must confess that I have not always been the obedient and dutiful son (or daughter) that I should have been. I hope you will forgive me. All that is changed. You see, I have become a Christian. From now on I will follow Christ. And that means I will be a more loving and faithful son (or daughter). . . .

Question: Which counselees are responsible individuals as far as the host culture is concerned?

Reflections: Not all persons are deemed to be capable of certain types of decision-making in many if not most cultures. Even Western Christians should be able to understand that, because we argue over the age of accountability with little biblical data to support our varied conclusions. It is important to note that in many societies children are not thought to be capable of making life-changing decisions; the decisions of young people still supported by parents are not taken all that seriously (they will conform later); and the independent decisions of wives are frowned upon. Of course, Christian counselors do not have to *adopt* local understandings. But if they are to be effective they should learn how to *adapt* to them.

Question: How does our knowledge of the individual decision-making process apply to the counseling situation?

Reflections: Counselors can obtain many practical insights from various analyses of the decision-making process. By reflecting on the five-stage model in figure 28 (which includes such notions as dissonance and incorporation) they are alerted to crucial aspects of decision-making that are often neglected.

Again, by reflecting on the chart that James F. Engel (following Fishbein and others) has constructed, counselors are alerted to the potential difficulties inherent in short-circuiting the process by omitting one or another stage (see fig. 29). To be sensitive to this process is not to disregard the power of the Holy Spirit, but is rather to cooperate with him in bringing unbelievers to faith and believers to maturity in Christ.

We are now able to construct the complete diagram of an approach to analyzing individuals and their problems in the cross-cultural situation (see fig. 30).

Understanding Individual Uniqueness: A Guatemalan Case

For an illustration of the importance of being able to analyze counselees and their idiosyncracies, let us study

FIGURE 28*

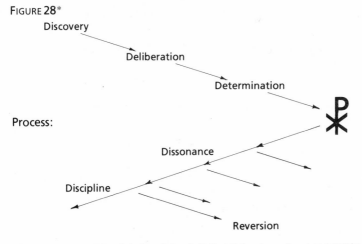

*Taken from *Communicating Christ Cross-Culturally*, by David J. Hesselgrave. Copyright © 1978 by David J. Hesselgrave. Used by permission of Zondervan Publishing House.

FIGURE 29 **The Complete Spiritual Decision Process***

God's Role	Communicator's Role		Man's Response
General Revelation		−8	Awareness of Supreme Being
Conviction	Proclamation	−7	Some Knowledge of Gospel
↓	↓	−6	Knowledge of Fundamentals of Gospel
↓	↓	−5	Grasp of Personal Implications of Gospel
↓	↓	−4	Positive Attitude Toward Act of Becoming a Christian
↓	Call for Decision	−3	Problem Recognition and Intention to Act
↓	↓	−2	Decision to Act
↓	↓	−1	Repentance and Faith in Christ
Regeneration			**New Creature**
Sanctification	Follow Up	+1	Post Decision Evaluation
↓	↓	+2	Incorporation Into Church
↓	Cultivation	+3	Conceptual and Behavioral Growth • Communion With God • Stewardship • Internal Reproduction • External Reproduction
↓	↓	•	
↓	↓	•	
↓	↓	•	
↓	↓	Eternity	

*From James F. Engel, *Contemporary Christian Communication: Its Theory and Practice*, p. 225. Copyright © 1979 by James F. Engel. Used by permission of Thomas Nelson Publishers.

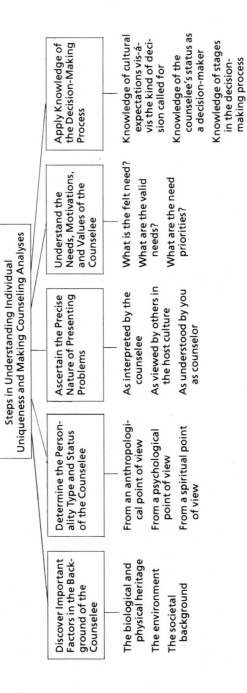

FIGURE 30 Counseling and the Individual (6)

the case of one Marcelino of Guatemala as reported by an American anthropologist, Benson Saler.[55] First we will look at the essentials of the case. Then we will reflect on Saler's analysis and proposal, and on appropriate responses from missiological and counseling perspectives.

The Case of Marcelino, the Converted Shaman

One of the earliest converts to Protestantism in Santiago El Palmar (in the Pacific Piedmont of Guatemala) was Marcelino. Marcelino had "served the saints" by holding offices in the lower rungs of the religious branch of the civil-religious hierarchy. It is doubtful, however, as to whether he would have ascended to the most prestigeful offices in the religious branch inasmuch as he was not wealthy. He was, however, a shaman, and according to what he told me, a highly successful one. But one day he overheard some men discussing him. It was the consensus of these men, from the snatches of their conversation that he was able to overhear, that he was a sorcerer. Marcelino was angered by this accusation. He reasoned that he could not be a sorcerer inasmuch as he had effected a number of cures in his role of shaman, and a shaman who indulges in sorcery is supposed to lose his power to cure. But he continued to brood over the accusation for it disturbed him deeply. He suffered a loss of appetite and general malaise. He concluded that he had enemies who were spreading lies about him, and he was preoccupied with trying to calculate who they might be.

Shortly thereafter, Marcelino encountered an emphatic North American Protestant missionary who informed him that the people of Palmar were worshipping "idols" (the saints). The missionary called upon Marcelino to set an example that would lead others to God, to become a Protestant.

Soon after this encounter with the missionary, Marce-

55. Benson Saler, "Religious Conversion and Self-Aggrandizement: A Guatemala Case," *Practical Anthropology* 12 (May-June 1965): 107–14.

lino began to experience vivid dreams. In these dreams, Marcelino learned that Santo Mundo, the earth essence which selects a man to be a shaman, was in reality a devil. In one dream, God placed a crown on Marcelino's head and told him that he must lead the ignorant people of Palmar to God, even if those same people were to persecute him for attempting to do so.

Following another meeting with the missionary, Marcelino became a Protestant. For several weeks after his conversion, he told me, he was "persecuted" by transforming witches. These evil beings, in the forms of birds, flew over his house, beating their wings and crying out in order to prevent him from sleeping. Inasmuch as the witches are believed to derive their power from a covenant with the devil and to delight in harassing the virtuous, Marcelino interpreted his "persecution" to be a corroboration from an infernal source of his own righteousness.

In addition, Marcelino was the recipient of open scorn and verbal abuse from other Indians. He asserted that several conspired to murder him by direct physical assault—sorcery would be of no avail against a person as close to God as himself. In several long interviews he detailed for me the events of what he called his "martyrdom." Interestingly enough—and I take this to be another example of his strong proclivities to self-affirmation—Marcelino never repudiated the cures he had made when a shaman and a Catholic. In response to my questions, he assured me that the cures were real enough but that he had accomplished them when he was "ignorant." If a sick person were to come to him today, Marcelino told me he would give him a Bible so that he might read, or have read to him the word of God.

In all of my sessions with Marcelino, he impressed me as being strongly convinced of his own uniqueness, spiritual superiority, and sacred mission. He was, moreover, greatly respected by his fellow Indian Protestants, indeed, they looked to him for leadership. And a North American missionary of my acquaintance spoke of him with admiration and affection. The opinions of Catholic Indians, however, were mixed and decidedly less favorable. Some of my Catholic informants professed to admire him for his resolution and courage; but such admiration, I think was colored by the fact that Marcelino was an old man, and the Indians traditionally show a certain deference to the aged. At the same time that they voiced compliments, however, they also intimated that they considered him to be excessively outspoken as to the value of his religion and his own moral and spiritual worth.[56]

An Anthropological/Psychological Analysis

Saler's explanation of Marcelino's behavior and its consequences falls quite easily into four parts: the psychology of self-identification; the sociocultural setting of Santiago El Palmar, Guatemala; an analysis of Marcelino's conversion as a form of self-aggrandizement; and a review of missiological implications.

Saler agrees with A. I. Hallowell that self-identification or self-expression is a general human trait (a human universal) and essential for social order. It is an expression of the drive to affirm the self. Within acceptable bounds it occasions no problems. If he exceeds those bounds the individual invites the accusation of self-aggrandizement. In some cases, then, conversion to a new religion may represent a "psychic economy" and a therapeutic act of self-aggrandizement.

At the time of the study Santiago El Palmar had 997 Indians and 113 Ladinos, the majority of the population being Catholic (actually, Christopagan). There are three primary ways to achieve status and prestige in that society: through the civil-religious hierarchy (time and money are required); through the role of calendar shaman (curer, diviner, imparter of moral advice); and through the practice of sorcery (a disapproved but available role). Sorcery, shamanism, and civil service—in that order—present opportunities for self-aggrandizement which goes beyond self-

56. Ibid., pp. 110–11.

experience. Recently Protestantism has presented another such opportunity in that Protestants disparage the saints and set themselves apart.

Saler believes that Marcelino's temperament was such that, had he not converted to Protestantism, he might have responded to social criticism by withdrawing into himself and turning to the dark rites of the sorcerer. Instead he turned to Protestantism. In so doing he gained the gratification that comes from being spiritually superior, persecuted by fellow Indians, and admired by missionaries and believers.

Saler thinks it ironic that Protestantism, which idealizes humility, can lead to a self-aggrandizement bordering on megalomania. On the other hand, in opening a door to affirmation of the self, Protestants have performed a psychologically and socially valuable service to citizens of Santiago El Palmar. In any case, the fact that only thirty-five souls have been converted would seem to indicate that the wrong kind of people (marginals) have been converted. Were missionaries to win individuals of greater prestige (i.e., religious-civil leaders), their task might be greatly facilitated. Saler concedes, however, that in keeping faith with their intention to reach any who appear sincere in their willingness to embrace the new faith, the missionaries may ultimately prove to be tactically as well as dogmatically correct. As converts are transformed not only spiritually but also socially and psychologically, villagers may eventually come to admire and imitate those converts.

Some Observations on Marcelino's Case

Saler has performed a helpful service in providing cross-cultural Christian workers with this study. It is especially helpful in the present context because Saler has attempted analyses for journals of both anthropology and psychology, thus addressing himself to issues concerning both society and personality.

As far as we are informed, none of the principals related to the case is asking for counseling or assistance of any kind. Our present purpose is best served, however, by addressing our response to all of them, including Saler himself.

Of Saler we might well inquire as to the man and world view that forms the basis of his analysis. In terms we have used here, Saler's otherwise helpful insights in the areas of cultural and personality factors suffer from a blind spot with respect to human universals. Saler's naturalism (insofar as this particular research is indicative of his world view) seemingly renders him incapable of dealing adequately with the spiritual dimensions of Santiago El Palmar culture in general, and Marcelino's conversion in particular. This partial blindness does not necessarily negate his conclusions, but it does place them in a different light.

As far as the missionaries and their strategies are concerned, we would counsel that they do not become defensive. Saler's analysis is pertinent and may be correct. Understandably, they do not want to withhold the message of Christ from anyone who sincerely listens and responds. But think a moment! Is it not true that members of civil-religious hierarchy might respond to the gospel if approached tactfully and given some time for decision? Is it not at least very possible that someone of Marcelino's temperament (his shamanic cures having been misunderstood and he himself accused of sorcery) would be a candidate for conversion from unworthy motives? And, finally, is it not likely that although the conversion of Marcelino would be very appealing to the missionary, it would actually impede others in the community from coming to Christ? (Review what has been said concerning innovators and change.)

To ask such questions is not to suggest that Saler's analysis is correct. But it is to suggest that it may be correct. Missionaries as well as anthropologists have blind spots.

The difference is that they tend to be blind to a different area of reality.

What shall we say concerning Marcelino himself? Simply that his is a very complex personality. Because he was converted by missionaries and occupies a place of leadership in the church, he should be carefully counseled—especially so after a careful reading of Saler's ideas. Marcelino may indeed be a true child of God. But even if that is so, such phenomena as his "persecution" by transforming witches and his "martyrdom" at the hands of other Indians clearly indicate his need for help—not because the devil is incapable of orchestrating persecution or because a conspiracy to murder him is impossible, but because of the ways in which he responds to the real or supposed happenings behind these explanations. Marcelino may be suffering from some sort of hysteria. At the very least, Marcelino needs spiritual help in becoming the kind of mature Christian leader who will attract others in Santiago El Palmar to Christ and his church.

We have overviewed individual uniqueness from several vantage points—anthropological, psychological, theological, and missiological. Then we have attempted to apply this information to the counseling of individuals in cross-cultural situations. We have gained helpful insights. But in the process we have been reminded once again of our dependence upon *the* Paraclete, *the* Helper, *the* Counselor par excellence.

PART 4

Counseling Individuals and Groups Cross-Culturally

11

Solving Problems and Producing Change

The world has gigantic problems. Societies present pressing problems. The churches have their share of problems. And no individual on planet Earth is a stranger to problems.

The world needs to change. Cultures must change. Churches require change. Individuals have to change.

In chapter 3 we outlined our interest in introducing change—change that comes about as people make the right choices in regard to beliefs, feelings, and actions. (These are often referred to as cognitive, affective, and behavioral changes, which is straightforward enough—although one must take care to interpret the term *behavioral* in context.)

In chapter 8 we emphasized that the status quo is, in significant measure, the result of sin. God's program is one of change—the regeneration and sanctification of the individual, the formation of a new "society" called the church, and the introduction of new heavens and a new earth of righteousness and peace.

In chapter 9 we noted that cultures both encourage and

313

discourage change, but not often in a balanced way. Our culture puts a high value on change; traditional China discouraged it. Similarly, some cultures support decision-making in general and individual decision-making in particular. Others discourage decision-making in general and support group decision-making when decisions must be made. Culture and attitudes concerning change are intimately related.

In chapter 10 we looked at the relationship between personality and change and also at the decision-making process as it applies to individuals.

In the remainder of this book we will focus on cross-cultural counseling *practice*—the art of solving problems and producing Christian change in peoples of other cultures. First we will inquire into aspects of change not previously discussed. Then in succeeding chapters we will attempt preliminary analyses of certain case vignettes drawn from various cultures—cases having to do with well-being, conversion, Christian growth and lifestyle, and Christian service.

Criticisms of "Exporting Change"

Although everyone who works or even travels cross-culturally has a part in producing change, criticism of cross-cultural Christian workers especially has been common. Perhaps most concerted are those criticisms voiced by anthropologists and directed at missionaries working with tribal peoples. Alexander A. Goldenweiser, for example, writes, "The imposition upon natives still half immersed in their own traditional attitudes, of a system of belief and worship which could establish no contacts with their behavior, interests or understanding, constitutes perhaps the most stupid act of racial pride and cultural snobberishness ever perpetrated by White civilization."[1]

1. Alexander A. Goldenweiser, *Anthropology: An Introduction to Primitive Culture* (New York: F. S. Crofts, 1937), p. 429.

Much more objective is the criticism of Colin M. Turn-bull—directed as it is against just about everyone who is in the business of exporting changes that have occurred in societies, either large-scale or small-scale, around the world.[2] He sees a heightening of the contemporary trend from moral coercion as practiced in small-scale societies to physical coercion and, finally, to violent compulsion. He sees a move from justice and democracy to law and order and on to order without law. He sees a shift from attention and concern for the rights of society to the rights of the individual and on to the demands of the system. "It seems inescapably true that we are moving toward a steady path of depersonalization and dehumanization; some might say from God through Man to System, others, who prefer to eschew the notion of God, may substitute the notion of Society, which in no way alters the picture or lessens the chill of creeping paralysis."[3]

Turnbull is no romanticist. He does not paint traditional African life in idyllic terms. He sees its dark side—not its darkest nights of fear and suffering, but its lingering shadows of disease and deprivation. To that extent he is no friend of all that traditional black Africa represents. But he is even less a friend of the monumental change imposed upon Africa overnight, not just by "fundamentalist missionaries" intent on saving souls, but also by well-meaning Christians who are obsessed with a desire to improve the lot of their fellows, and, indeed, by all advocates of Western technology. Concerning the former, he says,

> They tried to impose a set of beliefs that to them were functional and supported by faith, but to the Africans were nonfunctional and unsupported by faith. The result was often that the new beliefs were manipulated to be of use

2. Colin M. Turnbull, *Africa and Change* (New York: Knopf, 1973), pp. 363–81.
3. Ibid., p. 364.

to the new convert in his new context, and it was quickly found that this strange Christian belief in individual salvation suited the new cut-throat world admirably. The new religion then became a means of justifying the grossest immorality of all: unsociality. The converts were a part of society but no longer fulfilled any obligations toward it; they were no longer integrated and interconnected by that all-important web of human relationships. And they were no longer even bound together by a common faith because that was the first thing the missionaries sought to destroy, replacing it with mere belief. The only faith possible in this modern civilized world is faith in oneself, and that does not have much integrative force.[4]

Turnbull sees Western technology and secularism breaking down the African's world where the invisible and the spiritual combine with the physical to produce a single, total reality. He sees the introduction of a society devoid of spirit, of an individualism that is a prelude to ultimate dehumanization, of a monotonous daily routine with wage-earning activity as its only focus of interest, of the breakdown of family which is our basic model, if not the basis itself, of sociality.

Thus Turnbull inveighs against our notions of progress, comfort, material benefit, technological advance, political stability, and individualism, under whatever banner they may fly. More essential than all of them are affective and effective human relationships. Without such relationships humanity itself will be destroyed. Therefore all else is expendable.

If one can dismiss Goldenweiser's charges on the grounds of either a congenital myopia or a temporary dyspepsia, Turnbull's criticism must be taken seriously in view of his objectivity and evenhandedness. Evidently he would prefer no externally induced change whatsoever in preference to any change that disrupts the system of human relationships that already exists in tribal Africa. If one prizes horizontal human relationships over the ver-

4. Ibid., pp. 377–78.

tical relationship with God this, it seems, is at least consistent. If the change we ultimately advocate is one of humanization rather than redemption, it may well be that we serve this interest best when we leave hands off, or at least make sure that nothing is done except that which enhances existing social relationships.

But, of course, more must be said. Christians are under orders to make disciples of all nations. Their commission comes from none other than Christ their Lord. They can no more be expected to disregard that commission than naturalists can be expected to understand it. Large-scale societies, small-scale societies—it makes little difference. The vertical relationship with God through Christ which discipleship implies will inevitably bring some social dislocations (Matt. 10:36). Christ and cultures often clash. What one prescribes the other proscribes and vice versa.

At the same time, as Christian cross-culturalists we will have to admit to a recurring failure to distinguish between Christ and culture (our culture!). And we must also admit to our frequent failure to bring larger and smaller segments of society—nuclear and extended families, clans and subclans—into the family of God. To the extent that this is so we can only humbly confess our own shortsightedness to God and man, and resolve to be more sensitive to cultural and social realities even as we are more faithful to divine requirements.

For years it was my practice in the mission situation to counsel new converts in the following manner:

> Now that you have decided to follow Christ, you may encounter opposition within your family or among your friends. Be true to your own convictions. Be prepared to stand for Christ in spite of any opposition and persecution. Pray for strength to stand firm. Let us join together in that prayer and resolve.

It seemed that Scripture supported me in this approach. And, indeed, it did. Any informed Christian could cite injunctions and illustrations that encourage believers to stand true to Christ in the face of opposition. Even a person's own father or mother may be his "enemy" as concerns the faith (Matt. 10:36).

But a careful study of a locally flourishing religious sect and its approach to the identical problem alerted me to a better way. Subsequently I counseled in the following manner:

> Your new faith will perhaps be opposed by family members and friends. But when you tell them of your newfound faith in Christ also confess that you have not been the dutiful son (or daughter, or loving mother or father, or faithful friend) that you should have been. Tell them that with Christ's help you are going to be a better son (or daughter, or mother or father, or friend) in the future than you have in the past. Tell them that it is the true God through his son Jesus Christ who makes better family members, better friends, and better citizens. That you know Christ and have been transformed by him. That they should not expect perfection but they can expect improvement. And that you want nothing more than their very best in this world and their salvation in the world to come.

The difference may seem to be one of semantics. But it is far more than that. Psychologically and practically, these two approaches are oceans apart. And although this latter approach does little to quiet the protestations of either a Goldenweiser or a Turnbull, it does point in the direction of a major adjustment in cross-cultural preaching, teaching and, especially, counseling.

Types of Change

Our discussion of change needs to be informed by an awareness of some of the different directions that change might take. We will briefly discuss four types of change important to Christian cross-cultural personnel.

Counselor and Counselee Change

An important aspect of effecting change in the counselee is the counselor's willingness to change himself. "Few counselors ever ask what they can do to change themselves; few want to know what they can do to become better human beings in order to relate more effectively with other human beings who, through birth, are racially and ethnically different. The failure of counselors to ask these questions indicates why counseling minorities continues to be a problem in this country."[5] The desire on the part of the counselor to be changed in the counseling process as well as initiate and guide change in others is often called bilaterality. There needs to be a willingness on the part of both counselor and counselee to accept change. And, from a Christian point of view, the counselor at least must be a candidate for growth in grace. Something of this attitude must be behind Abraham Kuyper's terse statement: "I, as a man, must encounter the man in the heathen."[6] It must have been in Hendrik Kraemer's mind when he wrote that the person of the missionary constitutes the most promising point of contact with those of other faiths."[7] It must constitute the ground on which Jacob A. Loewen stands when he insists that self-exposure on the part of the cross-cultural worker is the key to identification with fellow Christians in other cultures.[8]

Autoplastic and Alloplastic Change

A French social psychologist, Alexandre Vexliard, first articulated this distinction in 1968. He called it the "autoplastic-alloplastic dilemma." The term *autoplastic* refers to adaptation to a given sociocultural setting and structure. The word *alloplastic* has reference to attempts

5. Clement E. Vontress, "Racial and Ethnic Barriers in Counseling," in *Counseling across Cultures*, ed. Paul P. Pedersen et al., rev. ed. (Honolulu: The University Press of Hawaii for the East-West Center, 1981), p. 105.

6. Quoted in J. H. Bavinck, *An Introduction to the Science of Missions*, trans. David Hugh Freeman (Grand Rapids: Baker, 1969), p. 243.

7. Hendrik Kraemer, *The Christian Message in a Non-Christian World*, 3d ed. (Grand Rapids: Kregel, 1956).

8. Jacob A. Loewen, "Self-Exposure: Bridge to Fellowship," *Practical Anthropology* 12 (March-April 1965): 49–62.

to change and shape that setting. In the counseling situation it is the difference between assisting the counselee to adapt to his society and culture as over against advising and helping to change the situation in which he lives.

At first this seems to be a rather innocent "dilemma." If we view it from the perspective of missions history, however, it is an immensely complex and, at times, bewildering one. John Eliot concluded that his Indian converts not only could not change the pagan situation in which they lived, but also could not live and grow as Christians within that environment. His "praying towns" were places where Christian Indians could come in order to establish a sociocultural environment more conducive to Christian life and growth. John L. Nevius, on the other hand, encouraged Korean converts to stay in close contact with their non-Christian families and friends—even at great cost—in order to win them to Christ and build the church.

In more contemporary missiology, an often heated controversy has occurred as to priorities in mission. Some give priority to changing the conditions under which men live as over against attempting to change the people themselves. Others are convinced that people must be changed before any other changes can be permanent. Various terms describe opposing views in the controversy: development versus evangelism, humanization versus redemption, liberation versus conversion, and the transformation of the person versus the transformation of culture. To delve into these discussions would take us far afield. Perhaps Donald A. McGavran does as well as anyone in putting the biblical position in contemporary terms when he speaks of "redemption and lift." By this he means that the general pattern of life in any culture is elevated as more and more people come to know Christ and live in accordance with his will.[9]

---

9. Donald A. McGavran, *Understanding Church Growth* (Grand Rapids: Eerdmans, 1970).

Emic and Etic Change

In studying the dynamics of cultural change, anthropologists have evolved two major models: change from the inside of a culture and change introduced from the outside. Changes emanating from within the culture and by virtue of its own concepts, values, and motives, are often described as emic. Those from outside the culture are described as etic. (Sometimes the difference is described in terms of aspects of change peculiar to a given culture and universal aspects of change brought to bear upon a culture.)[10]

Illustrations of the importance of this distinction to cross-cultural counselors are not hard to find. The medical work of Dr. Thomas A. Dooley and the missionary work of Bruce Olson are cases in point.

Dooley worked in Laos in the 1950s. Although Americans in the Economic Aid Mission poured millions of dollars into that country with comparatively negligible results, they roundly accused Dooley of practicing nineteenth-century medicine, for he had no X-ray machine, no elaborate equipment, and only the simplest of techniques. Dooley responded that his accusers were correct and that he did not mind practicing nineteenth-century medicine because when he departed indigenous personnel would practice eighteenth-century medicine and that would be progress since most of the villagers lived in the fifteenth century.[11]

Dooley not only trained midwives and nurses among the younger locals, but also involved those who were already midwives in surgical operations. He not only refused to hold the local shamans up to ridicule, but also showed an interest in their weird assortment of sticks, bamboo slivers, betel nuts, boiled leaves, pig grease, spider webs, and the like. He acknowledged the effectiveness of

10. See the introduction in *Counseling across Cultures.*
11. Thomas A. Dooley, *The Edge of Tomorrow* (New York: Farrar, Straus and Cudahy, 1958), p. 54.

some of these (such as spider webs for open wounds) and involved the shamans in his ministrations: "We would administer a shot of penicillin, Joe (the local witch doctor) would invoke the proper spirit. We would splint a fracture, then permit old Joe to tie the indispensable red, white and black strings around the splints. If we were paid two coconuts for fee, old Joe received one."[12] When Dooley counseled and when he cured he removed himself as far as possible from the prejudices of his own culture, and related to the Lao in accordance with his ever-expanding knowledge of their culture and of Southeast Asia.

Within a year after the publication of Dooley's book, *The Edge of Tomorrow,* William A. Smalley from his perspective as a missionary anthropologist and linguist raised some pertinent questions about medical missionary programs—their motivation, function, and practice. He asked whether a dying man is always better off in an antiseptic hospital where he is terribly frightened than he would be in an unantiseptic home where he is secure. He asked whether missionary doctors truly understand local medicine men. And he asked if it might not be true that in medicine, as in so much of our missionary work, we think too highly of our techniques. Finally, he concluded that Dooley in a short period had succeeded in making friends on a scale that few missionaries do. And he concluded that this may have been because the Lao sensed a freedom of content "which is one of the most cherished of all freedoms."[13]

Just the approach Smalley was advocating has been taken by Olson in his work among the Motilone Indians of Colombia and Venezuela.[14] The first foreigner to work among the Motilones, Olson wanted to help them in any

12. Ibid., p. 79.

13. William A. Smalley, "Some Questions about Missionary Medicine," *Practical Anthropology* 6 (November-December 1959): 90–95.

14. Bruce Olson, *For This Cross I'll Kill You* (Carol Stream, Ill.: Creation House, 1973).

way he could, but primarily he wanted them to know God through Christ. On several occasions when they became ill he offered them medicine.

"Leave it to the witch doctor," they replied. "She knows our customs and our ways."

Sometimes they became well. Sometimes they did not. But when pinkeye affected almost the entire tribe and the witch doctor's potions and incantations were unavailing, Olson saw his chance. He infected his own eyes and sought the help of the witch doctor. She had refused his treatment. Now he tried hers. It did not work. He persuaded her to put Terramycin in his eyes. She agreed. In three days, Olson was cured. Everyone else was still miserable.

After Olson had several sensitive meetings with the witch doctor she agreed to use the Terramycin along with her chants. The people were cured. Now a good friend of the missionary, she explained that so many sicknesses come to the Motilones because long ago they left God and followed a man by the name of Sacamaydodji. Ever since that time evil spirits have brought disease to the people to show their power.[15]

The way had been opened for the conversion of the Motilones! Cultural, social, and psychological barriers to change were gradually neutralized. Stimulants to change were tapped. The supracultural and universal truths of the Bible were joined with reflections of those truths within the culture and, at the same time, were correctives for their distortions.

Of course we cannot afford to be simplistic in our understanding of the approach of missionary Olson. He was working in a culture that was practically sealed off from the outside world. He had to resort to some unusual techniques in order to gain acceptance. It should also be noted that he joined forces with a shaman (not a sorcerer) whose role was confined to the more positive aspects of

15. Ibid., p. 148.

advising and curing. On the other hand, we should not write off Olson's approach too quickly on the basis of unusual circumstances. The principle that he employed has wide application.

From his point of view as a clinical, counseling, and community psychologist, Norman D. Sundberg says,

> One of the important tasks for future research is the study of 'folk counseling' and 'natural' systems of problem solving and influence for change in various cultures. . . . The person who would teach or counsel in another country would do well to find out as much as he or she can about the living situations of the prospective clients and how they handle personal problems. A visit could help clarify these processes, and the counselor could work with the community to enhance and supplement these processes appropriately, rather than to superimpose imported counseling concepts and practices.[16]

And from their viewpoint as Christian biculturalists, Dale W. Kietzman and Smalley suggest that we perform one of our greatest services to believers in other cultures not when we solve their problems for them, but when we become the catalysts for change by providing new ideas and ways of doing things—information *they* can employ in effecting change.[17]

First- and Second-Order Change

In their book on brief counseling, Paul Watzlawick, John H. Weakland, and Richard Fisch distinguish between first- and second-order change.[18] First-order change is

---

16. Norman D. Sundburg, "Research and Research Hypotheses about Effectiveness in Intercultural Counseling," in *Counseling across Cultures*, p. 332.

17. Dale W. Kietzman and William A. Smalley, "The Missionary's Role in Culture Change," in *Readings in Missionary Anthropology II*, ed. William A. Smalley, 2d rev. ed., Applied Cultural Anthropology series (Pasadena, Calif.: William Carey Library, 1978), pp. 524–30.

18. Paul Watzlawick, John H. Weakland, and Richard Fisch, *Change: Principles of Problem Formation and Problem Resolution* (New York: Norton, 1974).

change within a given system which does not itself change. For example, a person having a nightmare may do various things *in* his dream, but the fact that he is having a nightmare remains the same. Second-order change is change that entails a change of system or state. When the person having a nightmare wakes up, he is *out* of his dream entirely. Waking is not part of the dream but a different state altogether.[19]

From this perspective, the "solutions" to human problems often become *the* problem. For example, when the members of a quarreling family deny that anything is wrong and maintain a public façade of unity, the façade becomes a problem. When they deny the denial (i.e., that the façade is a cover-up), the problem becomes compounded and pathogenic.[20]

At the other extreme, utopian goals and solutions also become problems because of their unrealizability. Watzlawick, Weakland, and Fisch believe that, with the possible exceptions of the approaches Alfred Adler, Harry Stack Sullivan, and Karen Horney, the solutions offered by most schools of psychotherapy (e.g., individuation and self-actualization) are utopian.[21] These solutions seem humane but often become inhumane because they are so open-ended and unrealistic. For example, a client may submit to an endless number of sessions designed to achieve self-confidence and then say, "I am still lacking self-confidence but now I understand why I don't have it!"

Second-order change is not really concerned with causes, with the "why" of human behavior. Rather, it is concerned with the "what," with that which is the case here and now. It places presenting problems in a new frame of reference (called reframing) and deals with them in this new light.[22]

19. Ibid., p. 10.
20. Ibid., p. 43.
21. Ibid., p. 56.
22. Ibid., pp. 82–83.

Because we will make some use of the paradigm of change proposed by Watzlawick, Weakland, and Fisch, it is appropriate that we inquire whether Christian counselors are concerned with first- or second-order change, or both. The answer, however, must be put off until we have studied the paradigm itself.

Prerequisites to Counseling Concerning Change

As we have seen previously, E. Fuller Torrey analyzes counseling and curing approaches worldwide and concludes that four universals characterize all of them: a shared world view, a good relationship, the expectation of being helped, and specific techniques.[23] As a matter of fact, counseling approaches in the United States do reflect these "universals." Recall Carl R. Rogers's emphasis on the constituents of a good counselor-counselee relationship, for example. Both in theory and in practice considerable attention is given to such things as the nature of empathy and the principles of being a good listener. Similarly, the importance of positive expectations on the part of clients is also stressed. One reason for the widespread use of Valium for certain pathologies is that immediate relief is realized and the expectation of being helped is greatly enhanced.

At the same time, Torrey's conclusion has received no small criticism because, among other things, as practiced in the various cultures these "universals" become so diverse. For this and other reasons already suggested, cross-cultural counselors should be aware of these limitations. On the other hand, when interpreted in the light of that which has gone before in this book, Torrey's universals do constitute a practical prolegomenon to a paradigm of change for the Christian cross-cultural counselor. Let us see how this is so.

23. E. Fuller Torrey, *The Mind Game: Witch Doctors and Psychiatrists* (New York: Emerson Hall, 1972).

A Shared World View

We have discussed world views rather extensively in an earlier context. In effect, we have made a shared world view the touchstone of effective cross-cultural counseling. There is a sense in which the world view of a counselee either determines or reflects all of the various components of his culture. There is a sense, therefore, in which all that we have said about the necessity of developing a culture-sensitive counseling approach can be subsumed under the phrase *a shared world view*.

It must be made clear, however, that, for us, sharing does not imply adherence to. We need not espouse a world view as our own in order to communicate and even empathize with counselees with other world views. But we do need to have an understanding of their world view that goes beyond an academic knowledge. And we can be certain that if we do not know the difference between an intellectual knowledge and an empathetic understanding, they will know the difference. The ability to share world views in this sense is not just a prerequisite to talking about cross-cultural counseling theory; it is essential to effective practice.

A Good Relationship Between Counselor and Counselee

The adjective *good* may mean "close" in a Latin American culture if we assume that Eugene A. Nida is correct when he writes, "In Latin America a dominant theme is personal friendship, involving personal identification and often strong emotional attachment for leadership. Friendship is almost always an even more important factor than equity or justice."[24] But "good" may imply more of respect than closeness in some Oriental cultures. It is necessary, therefore, to define a good relationship in a culturally relevant way.

24. Eugene A. Nida, "Communication of the Gospel to Latin America," in *Readings in Missionary Anthropology II*, p. 632.

A good relationship also requires a biblical definition. Consider the qualities of a good relationship emphasized by Rogers, for example (congruence, empathy, positive regard, and unconditionality of regard). As defined by Rogers, these qualities take on biblical connotations. In fact, Rogers likens positive regard to *agape* love. We must be discerning, however. Although the counselor must not "play God," he must not hesitate to let "God be God." Certain propositions must be insisted upon, not because they are the counselor's opinion but because they are God's truth.

However, there is much in both counseling and missiological literature that makes it clear that such qualities as love, empathy, and mutual respect are desirable ingredients of the counseling relationship wherever one goes.

An Expectation of Being Helped

Jerome D. Frank writes, "The success of all methods and schools of psychotherapy depends in the first instance upon the patient's conviction that the therapist cares about him and is competent to help him."[25] People who have problems need to know that there is a way out (a solution) or a way through (a higher purpose). By the same token it is highly probable that counselors work with people because they believe that they can help them.

From a secular point of view this aspect of effective therapy and counseling implies a significant amount of faith in a human person, in fate, in a technique, or in a curative agent or placebo—or, indeed, in a combination of these. All of these are known to have failed, however. The Christian worker has a distinct advantage. He does not ignore the power of men, methods, or medicine. But there is another dimension to his faith, the vertical dimension. He brings the counselee and his problem to God.

25. Jerome D. Frank, *Persuasion and Healing: A Comparative Study of Psychotherapy* (Baltimore: John Hopkins Press, 1963), p. 165.

He also brings God to the counselee and his problem. He cannot do less. Sometimes he can do little more. But when God is present, hope cannot long remain a stranger.

Specific Techniques

Torrey contends that the techniques of psychotherapy familiar to us in the West are used around the world. Techniques, therefore, are not culturally unique in his view. A case can be made for his contention. For example, a study of 488 societies showed that practitioners in 90 percent of the societies used altered states of consciousness as a technique in psychotherapy.[26] More must be said, however. Noting the influence that culture has on the use and effectiveness of psychological and even drug treatments, Martin M. Katz very gingerly approaches the task of evaluating drug and other therapies across cultures. He says, for example, that "despite more than 25 years of research on the psychotropic drugs and several crossnational clinical trials, it is safe to state that a truly sound study of the efficacy of a drug treatment across diverse cultures has yet to be carried out."[27]

Similarly, although techniques of counseling are always and everywhere in evidence—even when not consciously described as such—there is a sense in which they need to be rediscovered and re-evaluated in each situation. Although appreciative of the contribution of Torrey, Arnold P. Goldstein comments that it is no longer valid to speak in global terms and ask such questions as, "Is counseling method A better than counseling method B?"

26. Raymond Prince, "Variations in Psychotherapeutic Procedures," in *Handbook of Cross-Cultural Counseling: Perspectives*, gen. ed. Harry C. Triandis (Boston: Allyn and Bacon, 1980–83), vol. 6, ed. Harry C. Triandis and Juris G. Draguns (1981), pp. 291–349.

27. Martin M. Katz, "Evaluating Drug and Other Therapies across Cultures," in *Cross-Cultural Counseling and Psychotherapy*, ed. Anthony J. Marsella and Paul P. Pedersen, General Psychology series (New York: Pergamon, 1981), p. 159.

Rather, methods and techniques must be related to outcomes which, in turn, are related to specific cultures, counselors, and clients.[28]

It is preferable to be somewhat more tentative than Torrey when drawing conclusions in this area. It is also preferable to expand his terminology so as to include the terms *approaches* and *methods*, insofar as these may be more inclusive than the word *techniques*. And, finally, cross-cultural counselors need to think in terms of not one but at least four determinants of the usefulness of any given approach or technique to cross-cultural counseling cases.

The first determinant is the validity (especially from a Christian point of view) of the technique itself. Most counselors can be expected to hail the virtues of the counseling approaches they themselves employ, and probably with some justification. But on Christian, if not other, grounds certain techniques used, for example, in rational-emotive therapy and client-centered therapies would be eliminated in any situation.

The second determinant is the qualifications and abilities of the counselor. One is ill-advised to experiment with therapeutic and counseling techniques in the use of which he is not thoroughly prepared. Free association, the compulsive use of transference and countertransference, and dream analysis would fall in this category in most cases. On the other hand, treatment contracts, reliving the past, expiatory service, systems therapy, and numerous other techniques can be mastered and utilized effectively even by nonprofessionals.

A third determinant is the preferences of the counselee culture. Irrespective of the validity of the techniques themselves, such techniques as nondirection, confronta-

---

28. Arnold P. Goldstein, "Evaluating Expectancy Effects in Cross-Cultural Counseling and Psychotherapy," in *Cross-Cultural Counseling and Psychotherapy,* p. 87.

tion, and self-affirmation have strong cultural overtones which require re-evaluation in each culture. Cultural incongruence does not rule them out, but it does render their use more tentative.

The final determinant is the requirements of the situation at hand. Persons and circumstances differ greatly within cultural and social settings. If we multiply the diversities of our own experiences by the diversity of human cultures we recognize again the notion of uniqueness. As we have seen in the previous chapter, the ongoing experiences of a person as well as his personality itself bear the marks of uniqueness. To some degree, techniques, methods, and approaches will be appropriate or inappropriate in relation to that uniqueness.

A Paradigm of Change

At their Brief Therapy Center, Watzlawick and his colleagues utilize a four-step procedure in dealing with human problems which they believe is as applicable to non-therapeutic contexts as it is to the clinic. The steps are

1. a clear definition of the problem in concrete terms;
2. an investigation of the solutions attempted so far;
3. a clear definition of the change to be achieved;
4. the formulation and implementation of a plan to produce this change.[29]

They profess to have seen the similarity between these steps and the Four Noble Truths of Buddhism—all life is suffering; the origin of suffering is desire; desire can be stopped; and it can be stopped by following the eightfold path—only after introducing the paradigm.

The first step indicates that if a problem is to be solved, it must be a real problem. In stating the problem in con-

29. Watzlawick, Weakland, and Fisch, *Change,* p. 110.

crete terms one runs the risk of discovering that it has no solution, but one also avoids "solutions" that are not solutions.

The second step shows what kind of change should *not* be attempted and where change must be applied.

The third step reveals reachable goals and avoids utopian solutions which become their own pathology.

The fourth step involves the use of paradox, the translation of tactics into the counselee's own language, and a form that utilizes the counselee's way of perceiving "reality."

The Use of the Four-Step Paradigm

The use of the four-step procedure can be illustrated by the case of a young couple requesting marriage therapy.[30]

The problem. The wife of a thirty-year-old successful husband can no longer tolerate his dependence upon his parents. Parental gifts and interventions have caused a rift in their marriage. The husband, however, does not want to hurt either his wife by continued dependence, or his parents by informing them that they are not being good parents. Husband and wife agree on this definition of the problem.

The solutions that have been tried. The couple have "done everything" from arguing with the parents over restaurant checks to giving them expensive gifts. The more they try to do, the more the parents do for them.

The goal. The couple agreed that they wanted the husband's parents to stop treating them like children, to let them make their own decisions and earn their own way. Specifically and concretely, they wanted the husband's father to acknowledge that his son is grown and on his own, and to do this voluntarily and without hurt.

The implementation. A plan was agreed upon whereby the parents could be "good parents" until "good parent-

30. Ibid., pp. 116–19.

ing" became intolerable. (Note the paradox.) When the parents came for their next quarterly visit, dirty laundry, unwashed dishes, and general disrepair awaited them. The most expensive restaurants were visited with no move on the part of the son to pay the astronomical bills. After days of labor and expense, the father drew his son aside and informed him that he had been pampered too much and that the time had come for the couple to assume their own responsibilities rather than depend on their parents!

Notice that this second-order change came about not by a change within the system (i.e., attempting to get the parents to stop their intervention in defiance of their ideas of "good parenting") but by reframing the problem and resolving it within the framework of a new "system" of "good parenting."

In similar fashion, the "cure" for fear of public speaking is not bringing insight into its nature and origin, as in traditional psychotherapy. In this case the "solution" becomes part of the problem. Rather, brief therapy is directed at the traditional "solution." The speaker is to announce his anxiety at the beginning of the speech and say that fear will likely overwhelm him. In this case, "the problem disappears as his problem solving behavior is abandoned. . . ."[31] Behavior is paramount.

The Four-Step Paradigm and Christian Cross-Cultural Counseling

What is the value of this four-step approach to the cross-cultural counselor? It is worthwhile noting that it is somewhat similar to the approach used by Gerhard Egan and others.[32] As proposed by Watzlawick the paradigm ob-

---

31. Ibid., p. 125.
32. Gerhard Egan, *The Skilled Helper: A Model for Systematic Helping and Interpersonal Relating* (Monterey, Calif.: Brooks-Cole, 1975). Egan proposes a three-step model: exploration, goal setting, and action.

viously presents some problems, the main one being that it does not recognize "causes" as they are traditionally understood. This approach may be innocuous and even helpful in the examples given. However, consider the case of a rebellious student. His problem is reframed in such a way that he eventually does his homework to spite the school principal who would like nothing better than to have the occasion to expel him.[33] In this case the basic problem of rebellion is not even touched. Only the symptoms are cared for.

The similarities of the paradigm of change and the Four Noble Truths of Buddhism have already been noted. However, one wonders if more should not be said. To be sure, Buddhism has emphasized the "what" rather than the "why"—life as it *is* rather than the *reasons* for it being as it is. But karma, the law of dependent originations, and the Noble Truths themselves speak to the "why" as well. Why is it that "life is suffering"? Because we desire it to be something other than what it really is. We desire permanence and "selfness." True, Buddhism (especially Zen) purports to induce "enlightenment" not by logic but by paradox and other nonlogical "devices." True, our usual "solutions" are a part of the problem. But Buddhism aims to point us to life and reality as they "really are." It deals with the massive portion of the iceberg beneath the surface, not just with the visible peak above it. The "changed system" puts us in the context of the "real cause" of our human problems and the "real solution" to them. "Reframing" is in terms of a different view of "reality"!

Now we are prepared to understand the value of the four-step approach. For, giving full attention to such things as man and world view, cultural commonalities, individual uniqueness, and even the counselor-counselee relationship, counselee expectations, and appropriate techniques, we find that, rightly understood, Watzlawick's four

33. Watzlawick, Weakland, and Fisch, *Change*, pp. 142–46.

steps can bring us to the heart of Christian change as well. In all likelihood, second-order change, reframing, and even paradox will be parts of it, although not necessarily as Watzlawick, Weakland, and Fisch explain them. Christian solutions, after all, do not emanate from either the counselor's culture or the counselee's culture. Ultimately they are not introduced etically or emically as these terms are usually explained. Although it is important that we view problems, solutions, and change from these perspectives, solutions to human problems must, in any ultimate sense, come from God himself. They are beyond our frail reasoning. Paradoxical? Yes. Recall Christ's words: "Whoever finds his life will lose it, and whoever loses his life for my sake will find it" (Matt. 10:39). Or consider Paul's words: "I have been crucified with Christ and I no longer live, but Christ lives in me" (Gal. 2:20). Reframing? Yes. Second-order change? Most assuredly. The ultimate solution involves a change of "system," a change that puts problems and solutions into a Christian context.

Applying Theory to Practice

One hopes the student or counselor is now better prepared to integrate and apply the principles and ideas with which we have been concerned in the earlier sections (parts 1–3) of this book. He or she has looked at the background of relevant disciplines; has reviewed some of the main theories of psychology and counseling; and has been introduced to a theory which takes into account human universals, cultural commonalities, and individual uniqueness.

But sound theory should culminate in successful practice (the concern of part 4 of this book). Sooner or later, in interacting with colleagues and counselees, the counselor will need to identify and analyze existential problems and promote cognitive, affective, and behavioral change. The counselor does this in the knowledge that, whether by Christ, culture, or conscience, certain changes are prescribed, others are proscribed, and still others are problematic. This is so whether the problem at hand has to do with ordinary life and well-being, conversion, spiritual growth, or Christian service. Case by case the counselor proceeds in this task of helping others, mindful that believers are to "do good to all people, especially to those who belong to the family of believers" (Gal. 6:10).

Before proceeding to specific case studies, then, let us attempt to diagram the overall methodology being commended to the Christian cross-cultural counselor (see fig. 31).

All that has been written in parts 1–3 in this book is indicative of the kind of basic understandings that the Christian counselor should bring to a cross-cultural counseling task. Of course, the material in those sections, although comprehensive in terms of the areas covered, is primarily suggestive in the sense that it points to an almost limitless reservoir of research and literature that continues to increase with every passing day.

When it comes to practice—to actually counseling the culturally different—the counselor must be able to select and apply relevant theory to specific cases. Part 4 is designed to aid the counselor in this task by proposing and illustrating ways of focusing accumulated understandings on specific cases, much as we might use a magnifying glass to concentrate the sun's rays upon a dry leaf in order to start a campfire (see fig. 31).

To see how this process works, imagine a situation where the world view (or man and world view) of the counselee is vastly different from the Christian world view of the counselor. Let us say that it is the traditional Chinese world view. In that case, an understanding of world view in general and these two world views in particular must be in focus before a world view can be shared and communication can be meaningful. This focus becomes even more concentrated when counselor and counselee reframe

337

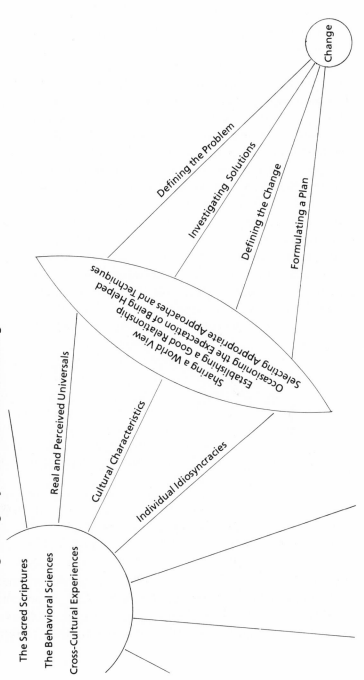

FIGURE 31 **Effecting Change by Cross-Cultural Counseling**

the problem in such a way that the difference between Christian and traditional Chinese solutions are clearly understood and the Christian solution is adopted (or rejected).

Note that when we arrive at the four-step paradigm of change we are proposing a specific counseling technique which has definite limitations. The counselee may be in no condition or position to actually think about his problem and its solution in this way. The counselee may be predisposed by experience or the work of the Holy Spirit to accept the conclusions of the counselor without questioning them. The training and preferences of the counselor may dictate that this approach be supplemented or replaced by other approaches. If so, and if the counselor is able to make such adjustments, we can be encouraged. It was with the intention of promoting this kind of flexibility that space was given to alternative approaches and techniques in an earlier chapter.

Finally, note also that the case vignettes that come at the end of each of the succeeding chapters are just that—vignettes. To supply more than the most basic information concerning these cases and ideas to aid in possible counseling analyses and approaches would be out of the question in the confines of the present work. The material is documented only when the information is already public. Most of the cases have been presented by doctor of missiology students in the School of World Mission and Evangelism at Trinity Evangelical Divinity School. Because living persons and actual situations are involved, identifications of people and places are intentionally vague. In most cases the counselors have reflected upon these cases and offered helpful evaluations of their involvement. When appropriate and helpful, their reflections are included. Of course, we agree that it is almost always true that "hindsight is better than foresight." But it is also true that hindsight of the right kind almost always improves foresight. And precisely that is our objective.

Change is in order—especially in the divine order. And cross-cultural Christian workers are agents of change—especially the kind of change that brings the culturally different into relationship with God. To further this kind of change, Christian workers themselves need to change. They need to grow in an understanding of what they are doing and how they are doing it. This is true in the areas of helping, advising, and counseling as well as other types of endeavor.

We have considered counseling theory. We now attempt to translate theory into practice. Although we do not deprecate what has been done by great and noble bearers of the Good News who preceded us, we recognize that we walk and work in a new day. We are candidates for change even as we are agents of it. We do not want counselees in other cultures to relate to us as they might have related to indulgent parents during their childhood. And as counselors we gladly forego the psychological "rewards" of playing the role of the "Great White Father" (or "Great White Mother")! We are sent to serve.

In the final analysis, *all* of us, whether counselors or counselees, are dependent upon God for help and healing. With that in mind, Christian counselors do well to resort to prayer frequently during the counseling process. They also do well to keep their Bible in hand and to refer to it often.

12

Counseling Concerning the Well-Being of People

The will of Jehovah for Israel was *shalom*—completeness, soundness, welfare, peace. The coming of the Christ child was attended by a heavenly host saying, "On earth peace, good will toward men" (Luke 2:14, KJV). The early preaching of our Lord included a sermon on "happiness" or "blessedness" (Matt. 5:3–12). God our heavenly Father "causes his sun to rise on the evil and the good, and sends rain on the righteous and the unrighteous" (Matt. 5:45).

Then what is the cause of so much sickness, suffering, and sadness in the world? As we have seen previously, the underlying cause is sin.

From these and related biblical teachings we draw attention to five principles.

First, God desires the well-being of all his creatures.

Second, as long as sin is in the world, its unhappy consequences will be with us. To his very own Jesus said, "In this world you will have trouble" (John 16:33).

Third, the unhappy state of any person, believer or unbeliever, has a dimension related to sin, but not necessarily in an immediate sense. The blindness of a man in Judea was not the result of his sin nor of the sin of his parents (John 9:2–3). Yet illness and death itself occurred among Corinthian Christians because of sin in connection with the Lord's Supper (1 Cor. 11:30).

Fourth, to help better the lot of people does not always entail dealing with the question of sin. Jesus illustrated love for neighbor by reference to a Samaritan who did nothing more or less than dress the wounds of and secure lodging for a robber's victim (Luke 10:25–37). Paul admonished us to "do good to all people, especially to those who belong to the family of believers" (Gal. 6:10).

Fifth, although Christian help comes at the point of need, whatever that need may be, no person is eternally helped until he is brought into right relationship with God through Christ (Acts 4:12).

Not many believers will argue with these principles. Nevertheless, experience shows that it is not easy to maintain them in proper balance in either theory or practice. Current Christian literature, especially of the missionary variety, is replete with arguments concerning questions having to do with holistic mission, priority in mission, development versus evangelism, and whether or not a hungry man can truly hear the gospel. We will not pause to comment further on these very pressing issues. Rather, holding to our five principles, let us see how change in the direction of well-being might be promoted in selected cases by counseling in accordance with the information included in previous chapters.

Case Vignette 1: B. J. (Zaire)

B. J. is a Mbanza from the village of Tipo on the northern edge of the equatorial rain forest of northern Zaire. At the age of twenty he left Tipo to seek employment in Libenge, a commercial center on the Ubangi River some forty miles from his home. He was hired by Missionary

R and proved to be an efficient, conscientious, and cheer-ful worker. He professed faith in Christ and took an in-terest in Bible reading and the activities of the local church.

When B. J.'s father died in the Libenge hospital, Mis-sionary R assisted in transporting the corpse back to Tipo for the funeral. The funeral rites were traditional inas-much as the family members are still animistic spirit wor-shipers. Missionary R was allowed to read from the Gospel of John and make a few comments, however.

After the burial of his father, B. J. returned to Libenge. Soon he became violently ill with malaria. After some days in the hospital his condition improved and he was released. Within a week of his release he received a letter from his relatives in Tipo indicating that he should return to Tipo immediately in order to obtain a medicine known as *nkisi*. Nkisi (which may or may not have medicinal properties) is ordinarily prepared according to a diviner's secret formula and with certain incantations; therefore, the missionary counseled B. J. not to go. He reminded B. J. that God had already used the hospital treatment to begin the recovery process and that, in response to prayer, God would make him completely well if that is in accor-dance with the divine purpose.

Missionary R's counsel went for naught. B. J. returned to his village, stayed for an extended period of time, and ultimately returned to Libenge a different person. He was no longer happy and alert but had become extremely anx-ious. Missionary R surmised that he had become a victim of the spiritually debilitating forces of witchcraft.

Basic Counseling Orientation

Real and perceived universals. Several clans in the area of Tipo (including the clan to which B. J.'s family belongs) were superficially Christianized by Roman Catholic mis-sionaries a generation ago. B. J.'s family remained essen-tially animistic spirit worshipers, however. In that world view there is no distinction between the sacred and the natural. It is incumbent upon Mbanza, for example, to deal with the "real causes" of misfortune, disease, and death. "Not the first spirit but the second spirit is the cause." In other words, one must seek out causes in the spirit, not just the natural, world. Ancestor worship also is imperative for Mbanza animists.

Cultural characteristics. The Mbanza tribe has a collectivistic-dependency culture with an ancestor orientation. It is patrilineal and patrilocal. The death of a husband and father is momentous and traumatic. When a father dies, his brothers assume authority in the family, especially when the family members are comparatively young and not well established.

Individual idiosyncracies. B. J.'s background and understanding were basically those of his family. Although he professed conversion to Christ, his conversion was recent and his Christian understanding can be assumed to have been minimal. We are not informed of his family status except that he was evidently single and still comparatively young. Initially at least, his disposition was pleasant and he was conscientious. However, we can assume that the death of his father and the contracting of malaria occasioned considerable anxiety.

Counseling Universals

A shared world view. Missionary R is a veteran missionary with a command of the language and an understanding of the world view of animists and tribalists. His most concerted studies in this area, however, have occurred subsequent to the case being reviewed here.

A good relationship. Prior to the time in question, Missionary R and B. J. were already parties to both employer-employee and helper-helpee relationships. B. J. might have been expected to accept Missionary R's counsel on the bases of authority and/or obligation if for no other reason. Thus the missionary's role in B. J.'s conversion, his assistance at the time of the death of B. J.'s father, and his help in time of illness all combined to make the counselor-counselee relationship extraordinary. We cannot discount the possibility that B. J. actually wanted to break a relationship which had become too demanding.

The expectation of being helped. This aspect was critical. Missionary R emphasized God's provision in the past and his promises for the future. It is difficult to tell whether B. J. had more hope in the power of the Christian God or the medicine man's nkisi.

An appropriate approach and technique. As far as we know, Missionary R had only a general introduction to counseling approaches and techniques prior to counseling B. J. His account reinforces the conclusion that conscious attention was not given to this aspect of counseling. Considering his personality and general modus operandi, we can assume that Missionary R eschewed a confrontational approach in favor of one that was more pastoral. His approach was basically cognitive and rational, but evidently not dialogical.

Effecting Change

Reflecting on his inability to convince B. J. not to return to Tipo, Missionary R asks, "Why do thousands of Mbanza believers like B. J. disregard the counsel of both African pastors and American missionaries to stay away from diviners and healers and their remedies? Is it because their counsel is not applicable? Is their counsel given in the wrong manner?"

Anyone knowledgeable about the church situation in sub-Saharan tribal Africa can empathize with Missionary R. After many decades of Protestant missionary activity, many churches are still riddled with a kind of sub rosa witchcraft. Before we look at the larger issue, however, let us concentrate on the case before us.

Had he been aware of procedures in Paul Watzlawick's paradigm of change, for example, Missionary R might have been more effective in drawing out B. J.'s understandings and in acquiring a more complete picture. A radical re-framing may have been in order—one which would have gone so far as to lend a certain priority to emotional and social considerations. Missionary R needed to know such things as B. J.'s exact status and role in the new family situation; his (and the family's) understanding of his father's death and his own illness; and who is involved and what approach is taken when the advisability of taking *hospital* medicine is being considered in Tipo. But most of all, Missionary R needed to attempt to bring B. J.'s true *feelings* to the surface— his fears, his sense of obligation, his misgivings with the church, his hopes for the future—and deal with these in prayer for, and counseling with, B. J. After all, in a situation where Christian faith was relatively fresh and untutored, where the church was relatively large but still immature, where societal ties were strong, where cultural conditioning was pagan, and where the missionary counselor was temporary, the emotional pull to Tipo, family, friends, and even the medicine man's nkisi must have been tremendous. In fact, it may well be that B. J. felt that the decision was not his to make.

Concluding Reflections

B. J.'s case reminds us that some macrocosmic adjustments may still be required when it comes to counseling in a collectivistic-dependency culture such as his. The most viable approach may well be a group approach in which the primary role of *both* pastor and missionary is to provide more pertinent and open instruction from the Scripture concerning those forms of magic and witchcraft still evident in the church. Then they can become the catalysts for developing "surrogate family" groups among laypeople within the church—groups which will follow up their instruction by providing belongingness and help. The situation and B. J. allowing, some Christian leader(s) should have accompanied B. J. to Tipo in order to deal biblically, sensitively, and forthrightly with the issue of power because that, in the final analysis, is what this case was all about.

Case Vignette 2: Mr. Y (Malaysia)

Mr. Y is the youngest son of a Chinese family in a village in Malaysia. Not long before he sought counsel his mother had died after an extended illness. His father had died earlier. Although Mr. Y is a Christian, none of his siblings are Christian (although one brother had claimed to be a Christian at one time). Mr. Y taught in an English middle school in his village. He faithfully attended a church pastored by a missionary from England.

When Mr. Y first requested counsel several years ago, he had numerous problems. He was unsure of his teaching job. He was engaged to a non-Christian woman who, according to him, manipulated him into lending her money and repeatedly made him "prove his manhood." He had been suffering from insomnia for some three months and was taking tranquilizers under the direction of a Christian medical doctor. He was unclear concerning his Christian faith and lacked assurance of the forgiveness of sins. On the advice of several Christians he had refused to take part in the funeral rites for his mother and he did not participate in the ongoing ancestor rites that are traditional in Chinese culture. Because of this he was severely criticized by family members. He had sought out the help of several ministers in the area, but their advice differed on important points. Some said he should see a psychiatrist. Some said he just needed rest.

One day when Missionary O (an American) was visiting Mr. Y's missionary-pastor, Mr. Y happened by and was invited in. After proper introductions and tea, the pastor asked Missionary O if he would mind talking to Mr. Y. In the ensuing discussion, Mr. Y was undoubtedly impressed by the missionary's willingness to listen and apparent understanding. After Missionary O returned to his home in a nearby city he received a letter from Mr. Y in which the latter disclosed more of his problems and pleaded for help: "What shall I do medically, psychologically, and spiritually? Please advise me." Thus began a counseling relationship (consisting of correspondence and frequent face-to-face sessions) that lasted for more than a year, until Missionary O returned to the United States on furlough.

Missionary O had been trained in integrity therapy under John W. Drakeford. Early on, therefore, he attempted to apply the principle enshrined in Drakeford's statement that "there is a tacit acknowledgement of the relationship of emotions and conscience in the frequently used expression 'guilt feelings.' Integrity therapy practitioners are quick to point out that it is not 'guilt feelings' but guilt, pure and simple, which is causing the trouble."[1]

Missionary O attempted to help Mr. Y by pinpointing the root causes of Mr. Y's general condition, which he interpreted as a rather severe depression. He rejected Mr. Y's guilt *feelings* and, focusing on guilt per se, explored his relationships with his family, fiancée, and God. He reminded Mr. Y that God has given all of us a conscience and that when we disobey that conscience we are sinning against God. When we cover up sin we lack forgiveness. When we are spiritually ill other types of symptoms may appear. He reminded Mr. Y of the love, goodness, and forgiveness offered by God through Christ. He reminded Mr. Y that only he, with God's help, could make those decisions which would result in positive change. He urged him to stop going from one spiritual counselor to another and to "stick with his own pastor." He advised against taking too many tranquilizers, but nevertheless, to follow his doctor's advice. (His doctor had told Mr. Y that there was nothing wrong with him physically.) Missionary O suggested that it might be well for Mr. Y to seek psychi-

1. John W. Drakeford, *Integrity Therapy: A New Direction in Psychotherapy* (Nashville: Broadman, 1967), p. 24. Quoted in the report of the counselor.

atric help and later was successful in taking him to a psychiatrist. Thereafter, psychiatrist and missionary worked
together, the former utilizing mainly a drug therapy and
the latter supplying spiritual instruction, counseling, and
prayer.

After a year Mr. Y was able to sleep better. He was able
to use prescribed drugs only at night and later did not use
them at all for rather extended periods. His outlook on
life improved. He decided to break his engagement but he
continued to seek his former fiancée's spiritual well-being.
He became more active in his church. In a letter to fur-
loughing Missionary O he indicated that he was improving and asked for continued prayer.

Basic Counseling Orientation

Real and perceived universals. Although a Christian,
Mr. Y was caught between traditional Chinese and Christian understandings. At the heart of his Chinese heritage
was a filial piety intimately linked with ancestor worship
(some would say ancestor reverence).

Cultural characteristics. Missionary O is of the opinion
that the "multicultural mix" of Malaysia makes for a significant difference between the Chinese of that country
and those of Taiwan or even Hong Kong. In respect to the
case before us that difference manifests itself in a more
easygoing attitude toward the changing of one's religion.
Nevertheless, even among Chinese in Malaysia Christianity is still considered to be a foreign religion, the claims
of the ancestors transcend other claims, and the shame
orientation of Chinese culture still holds.

Individual idiosyncracies. Mr. Y's symptoms are not
unfamiliar to cross-cultural Christian workers in that part
of the world. Although his persistence in seeking and
(seemingly) following the advice of Christian counselors
may be considered somewhat unusual in the face of his
general malaise at that time. Stress had been occasioned
by the death of his mother (and, previously, of his father),

the strained relationship with his fiancée, and tension between his Christian faith and his Chinese culture. It is important to remember that both his parents were deceased and that he was the youngest (not the eldest) son. Although his family obligations were still great and well-defined, he had more freedom to act on his own than would have been the case otherwise.

Counseling Universals

A shared world view. Missionary O has a good command of the language, a knowledge of Chinese religion, and a background in counseling and psychology that is well above average. Cognitively and emotionally he was able to identify with Mr. Y.

A good relationship. Here again—probably flowing from Missionary O's spiritual commitment, familiarity with the culture, personal sensitivity, and counseling competence—a good helping relationship was achieved. This was demonstrated by Mr. Y's continuation in the relationship (often at great inconvenience), his willingness to undergo psychiatric treatment at the urging of the missionary (and in spite of a long-standing reluctance), and his continued correspondence with Missionary O.

An expectation of being helped. A combination of faith in God and the Bible (reinforced by the counselor), confidence in the counselor himself, and the physical and emotional results of drug therapy likely combined to give Mr. Y that sense of hope that enabled him to continue therapy and respond affirmatively to counsel. On the other hand, Mr. Y experienced periods of hopelessness when it seemed that he would not improve.

An appropriate approach and technique. Of the various spiritual counselors who tried to help Mr. Y, it is likely that only Missionary O had special training and a well-thought-out counseling approach (Drakeford's integrity therapy). Upon reflection, however, even he now feels that his approach was probably not sufficiently culture-sensitive. Missionary O reports that the psychiatrist involved was Western-trained and basically behavioristic in his orientation.

Effecting Change

In the case before us the Christian counselor used such general techniques as naming and defining the problems. The main thrust of his approach was the attempt to identify Mr. Y's basic problem in terms of guilt and not in terms of the feeling of guilt. This is commendable in the sense that guilt before God is real and must be dealt with realistically. *Guilt* is the problem, not the *feeling* of it. More must be said, however.

Missionary O feels that he was correct in categorizing Mr. Y's condition as some type of depression. He believes that he was correct in calling for psychiatric assistance because he could not ascertain whether the origin of the depression was basically biological or spiritual. At the same time, he also believes that in dealing with the spiritual side of Mr. Y's depression, and due to his training in integrity therapy, he was probably too precipitous in his attempt to identify Mr. Y's "sin" and deal with his guilt.

This analysis is accurate. Also, Missionary O might have found it helpful to gain a better understanding of the psychiatrist's diagnosis and treatment than is indicated in his report. Given his behavioristic orientation, the psychiatrist's diagnostic assessment in terms of the DSM-III multiaxial classification scheme (see pp. 266–67) probably approximated the following:

Axis 1:   Major depression (all criteria are not addressed in the vignette, however)

Axis 2:   No evidence of a personality disorder as such

Axis 3:   No physical disorder

Axis 4:   Psychosocial stressors: bereavement, family and other interpersonal problems
Severity: Moderate—4 (or, Severe—5)

Axis 5:   Highest level of adaptive functioning past year:
          Poor—5

The psychiatrist probably prescribed antidepressants (not just sedatives) almost immediately in order to effect early improvement and afford a more rapid and better response to psychotherapy. He likely viewed Mr. Y's religious convictions (which were the major cause of family stress) in negative terms. Because Missionary O referred his counselee to the psychiatrist in this case, however, we can conjecture that the psychiatrist was content to leave this aspect of Mr. Y's therapy to the missionary. In any case, it is helpful to have a better understanding of psychiatric diagnosis and psychotherapy (when available) than this report evidences.

Furthermore, as sensitive and informed as Missionary O demonstrated himself to be, he still needed to give more attention to the counseling implications of such things as the shame-guilt distinction, the status of the youngest son in a Chinese family, and the decision-making orientation of Chinese such as Mr. Y. Although one might take exception to the advice which resulted in Mr. Y having no part whatsoever in his mother's funeral, nevertheless his refusal to compromise by participating in sacrifices to the ancestors was commendable. In view of the traditional Chinese orientation toward decision-making (reluctance, tentativeness, group dependency), his brother's reversion, and his own perseverance, Mr. Y probably should have had more confirmation than he received (at least initially). The cause of Mr. Y's depression (granted that diagnosis) was likely a consequence of recent and current stresses and the tension between his Christian faith and his Chinese culture. As a matter of fact, shame—not before God, but before family and friends where expectations were so grievously "disregarded"—likely contributed significantly to his condition. Guilt may have had very little to do with it.

Concluding Reflections

The case before us may be a classic case where facility in, and predisposition to, a certain counseling approach overtake cultural sensitivities and actually impede or at least delay effective change. However, the personal qualities and caring attitude of the counselor overshadowed other considerations and encouraged the counselee to continue this counseling relationship until he experienced a positive change. Having considered the variety of "therapists" available to sufferers in Malaysia (see chap. 7), and reflecting on the diabolical practices to which Mr. Y might have fallen prey, we can be grateful that he sought out the caring counsel of one who knew the true God of grace and healing.

13

Counseling Concerning Christian Conversion

The subject of conversion can be expected to be as distasteful in the twentieth century as it was in the first.[1] But, distasteful though it may be to the natural man, God insists upon it as being absolutely essential. Spirit-inspired, Peter challenged his unbelieving contemporaries to "repent . . . and be converted" (Acts 3:19, KJV).

Let us first be clear as to what Christian conversion is. In the New Testament conversion is described by a metaphorical use of the verb *epistrepho*, which means "to turn around, to turn back, to return." The implications are that men are going the wrong way and that they must change direction if they are to be "re-related" to God. This reminds us of Edmund Perry's definition of religion, which takes direct aim at the notion that because there are good elements in the various non-Judeo-Christian faiths they somehow point people in the right direction. He writes that religion is "a generic term comprehending the uni-

1. See Michael Green, *Evangelism in the Early Church* (Grand Rapids: Eerdmans, 1970), p. 144.

353

versal phenomenon of men individually and collectively *being led away from God* [italics added] in manifold ways by diverse claims and systems."[2]

Second, Christians should be clear that conversion is predicated upon the conviction (*elengchos,* John 16:8) of the Holy Spirit and a change of mind (repentance or *metanoia,* Acts 3:19) on the part of the unbeliever. The Holy Spirit is the "Convincer" of sin.

> When he comes, he will convict the world of guilt in regard to sin and righteousness and judgment: in regard to sin, because men do not believe in me; in regard to righteousness, because I am going to the Father, where you can see me no longer; and in regard to judgment, because the prince of this world now stands condemned. [John 16:8–11]

All cross-cultural workers, especially all of those who labor in shame cultures, are aware of the difficulty of convincing people that what happens to them in eternity hinges on what they do with Christ. It is difficult enough to get people to see that "sin is really sin," to say nothing of bringing them to the point where they understand and feel that failure to believe in Christ is the greatest sin of all. That is an almost impossible task. No, it *is* an impossible task apart from the Holy Spirit! He alone can accomplish it!

Again, what about conviction concerning righteousness—what is it, why is it needed, and how is it provided? People all over the world compare themselves with their neighbors. And when they do they measure up quite well because there are usually some neighbors who are concerned with neither mores nor measurements. Only in one place on earth and at one point in history did certain people look at a Neighbor and find a perfect standard of righteousness. What honest citizen of Palestine in the first

2. Edmund Perry, *The Gospel in Dispute: The Relation of Christian Faith to Other Missionary Religions* (Garden City, N.Y.: Doubleday, 1958), p. 88.

third of the first century A.D. could look at Christ and be convinced that he measured up, that his own righteousness was sufficient, that he did not need a righteousness like that of Jesus Christ? But Christ was going away. Who then would convince anyone concerning the right kind of righteousness, his need for it, and God's provision of it? The biblical answer is, "the Helper, the Holy Spirit."

Yet again, what about judgment? Certainly at that point most thinking men of any culture on earth will agree that some kind of judgment somewhere and sometime is in order. Usually there is enough "common guilt" to convince men of that. But notice that our Lord was not speaking of that kind of judgment. He spoke of a judgment that had already taken place at the cross. He spoke of a judgment of Satan, "the ruler of this world." Now who can possibly look at this world objectively and conclude that Satan is a defeated foe; that evil in all its nefarious forms is on the way out; that humble, harmless servants of Jesus are "more than conquerors" through Christ? Only those who are convinced and converted by the Holy Spirit! And our Lord said that the Holy Spirit would accomplish that task.

Third, notice that the Lord Jesus says that the Holy Spirit is sent to convict (*elengxei*) the world of guilt (John 16:8). J. H. Bavinck writes,

> In Homer the verb [*elengchein*] has the meaning of "to bring to shame." It is connected with the word *elengchos* that signifies shame. In later Attic Greek the significance of the term underwent a certain change so that the emphasis fell more upon the conviction of guilt, the demonstration of guilt. It is this latter significance that it has in the New Testament. Its meaning is entirely ethical and religious.[3]

3. J. H. Bavinck, *An Introduction to the Science of Missions*, trans. David Hugh Freeman (Grand Rapids: Baker, 1969), p. 221. For a more extensive discussion, refer to pp. 221–25.

Irrespective of whether the culture of an unconverted counselee reinforces *feelings* of guilt, all men are guilty on three bases. First, all of us are congenital sinners in the sense that we are born into a sinful race (Ps. 51:5). Second, all of us are sinners by choice. We have personally and volitionally sinned (Isa. 53:6; Rom. 3:23). Third, all of us are sinners by the decree of God (Rom. 3:10). Our respective cultures may deny these truths. But our consciences will tend to confirm them. And the Christ-sent Paraclete has been sent to convict us concerning them. When it comes to counseling concerning conversion (and undoubtedly many other needed changes in belief, feelings, and actions) this is crucial. Drakeford is correct. Guilt can be good because it can lead us to embrace the Christ who has paid for our sins.[4]

When it comes to counseling concerning conversion (and undoubtedly many other needed changes in belief, feelings, and actions) this is crucial. Only those who recognize their guilt will in any ultimate sense value the payment made on the cross; only those who value the cross will embrace the Savior; and only those who embrace the Savior will find the ultimate healing.

Case Vignette 1: Mr. S (Bangladesh)

Mr. S was a Muslim teacher in an Islamic school in an average-sized town in Bangladesh. He had been brought up in a traditional Muslim home. He was twenty-eight years of age, married, and had two children. He was well-known and respected in his town. Although a Muslim, he was not really zealous about his faith. He could probably be correctly categorized as a nominal Muslim because, although he participated in public prayers and observed Ramadan and Islamic dietary laws, he was not otherwise active in religious affairs.

Mr. S and his family lived next door to a Christian hos-

4. John W. Drakeford, *Integrity Therapy: A New Direction in Psychotherapy* (Nashville: Broadman, 1967), p. 36.

pital where Missionary B and his wife (who is a medical doctor and a missionary) lived and worked. Day after day when Mr. S went back and forth to his school on his bicycle, Missionary B greeted him warmly.

One day Mr. S invited Missionary B into his home for tea. The missionary had hoped for such an invitation and an opportunity to speak concerning Christ. He was not disappointed. Mr. S had acquired a Bible some months previously and—in addition to the usual questions Muslims entertain concerning the Trinity, Jesus as the Son of God, and fasting—he specifically wanted to discuss two passages of Scripture: the story of Nicodemus and the necessity of a new birth (John 3), and Jesus' words to the effect that whoever loses his life will find it (Matt. 10:39). Thus began a relationship which involved infrequent but amiable visits and some serious discussions concerning the Bible and Christianity.

Mr. S's parental home was located in a village some miles away. When he was walking along a railroad track en route to his parents' home one night, he slipped from a trestle and fell into a creek bed. His foot struck a rock and several bones were broken. He was taken to a Bengali doctor who bandaged his foot and sent him home. The pain was excruciating. Dr. B examined the foot and concluded that only Dr. T, an orthopedic surgeon in a hospital some three days' journey away, would be able to repair the damage. Mr. S did not have sufficient funds, so the missionaries took a collection among themselves and sent him and his nephew to Dr. T. While Mr. S was in the hospital where Dr. T practiced, the Christian staff witnessed to him and gave him a recently translated vernacular New Testament.

Mr. S returned home to convalesce. The bones in his foot had been set but the foot remained very swollen and painful. Day after day he sat on the porch of his home, his foot propped up, his New Testament in his hands. Time after time he called upon the passing Missionary B to stop and discuss the Scriptures.

Missionary B writes,

> That which impressed him most about the Scriptures was
> God's great love. Islam, he said, is a religion of fear and
> law. There was no peace in his heart, but when he read
> the New Testament the words spoke of peace . . . through
> Jesus. One day he made the commitment to Jesus as Savior
> and Lord. I warned him that once he made that commit-
> ment he would no doubt have to face many troubles. . . .
> He might lose his job, his friends would leave him, and in
> general he would be ostracized from the community. He
> said that he was willing to take the risk involved. He
> "stepped out" and began to attend church with us each
> Sunday.

The missionaries took Mr. S to church in their car because he was on crutches and had no transportation other
than his bicycle. During worship service the second Sunday after his profession of faith he spoke up when prayer
was about to be offered and said that he had been reading
in the New Testament that Jesus healed the sick. He asked
for prayer for the complete healing of his foot. Because the
church was quite liturgical, the congregation and its leaders were taken by surprise. But several of the leading
Christians gathered around Mr. S, laid their hands on him,
and began to pray. They were more amazed than he when
the pain immediately subsided and the swelling went down
before their eyes. All rejoiced. Mr. S especially thanked
the Lord Jesus and his fellow Christians over and over
again.

All went well for about a month or so. Then the difficulties began. Neighbors harassed Mr. S and his family.
Fearful of losing face if their son were to remain a Christian, Mr. S's parents pressured him to return to Islam.
Muslim shopkeepers in his community refused to do business with him. He lost his job. To make matters worse,
the church people received Mr. S lukewarmly. And he was
not given a job in the Christian hospital because of the
way this would be interpreted by other Muslims.

Missionary B counseled Mr. S often and over a period of months. The doctrinal questions common to Muslim inquirers and new converts presented minimal difficulty. Moreover, Mr. S remained true to Christ despite persecution. Time and time again the faith of the counselor was challenged by the courage of Mr. S. But up to the hour of the missionary's departure for his homeland, the God who had worked a miracle of healing on behalf of this new member of the divine family had not seen fit to provide him with a job and deliver him from persecution.

Basic Counseling Orientation

Real and perceived universals. Knowledge of the Muslim religion is absolutely essential to counseling its adherents, particularly in regard to conversion.

The value system of Bengalis in general is marked by the ever-present attitude that, if one wants something badly enough, one should pursue it because everything will ultimately work out to one's benefit. All who are party to a decision share responsibility if the situation turns out differently than expected. The only way to be absolved of such responsibility is to avoid being a party (even a silent listener) to it. (This value system and obligation orientation is probably mainly reinforced by the fatalism and sense of brotherhood common to Muslims. A great deal of expertise would be required to ascertain its relative pervasiveness in Bangladesh as over against other Muslim cultures.)

Cultural characteristics. Bangladesh is 85 percent Muslim, but Islam in Bangladesh reportedly differs somewhat from Islam in the Middle East. Perhaps due to the fact that Islam was imposed upon Bengalis by outsiders hundreds of years ago and, more importantly, due to an educational system that exposes them to other ways of thinking, Bengali Muslims usually do not exhibit the extreme forms of iconoclasm that are often found elsewhere. Nevertheless, it is widely believed among Bengali Muslims that to be a good Bengali is to be a Muslim. Conversion is "unthinkable." If one does convert, persecution in the form of social ostracism is invariable.

As in the case among Muslims elsewhere, the sense of brotherhood among Muslims in Bangladesh is very strong—much more so than seems to be the case among Hindu and Christian Bengalis. This lessened sense of brotherhood and mutual helpfulness among Christians is exacerbated for the convert from Islam by a certain suspicion that Muslim converts, being generally aggressive and forward, will "take over" in the church if given an opportunity.

Individual idiosyncracies. Mr. S was a respected person in his society, although somewhat nominal in his Muslim faith. As a teacher he had an enquiring mind. As a respected member of Muslim society he was unique in his willingness to associate openly with an American Christian missionary, in his openness to Christian instruction, and in the depth of his Christian commitment after his conversion. The helpfulness of Christians (particularly missionaries), the healing experience, and especially the working of the Holy Spirit all were factors in his openness and commitment.

Counseling Universals

A shared world view. In the case before us, both counselor and counselee were monotheists, although of vastly different monotheistic persuasions. In addition, Missionary B had had significant exposure to the Islam of Bangladesh and Mr. S had been studying the Bible on his own.

A good relationship. In his report, Missionary B goes to great lengths to emphasize the good relationship that was being built with Mr. S even prior to the counseling period. The fact that the counselee initiated the counseling relationship and that he, as a Muslim, entered that relationship with *questions* rather than *objections* should not be overlooked. Both knew each other's language.

The expectation of being helped. All indications point to the fact that Mr. S anticipated that Missionary B (and other missionaries?) would be able to help him. In fact, this occasioned a great concern on the part of the counselor. To what degree did Mr. S anticipate material help from the mission and missionaries in event he became a Christian?

An appropriate approach and technique. At the time in question, Missionary B professed no special preference for, or proficiency in, one or another counseling approach. On the other hand, he was thoroughly acquainted with Bengali Muslim culture and its ways.

Effecting Change

Let us look at Missionary B's approach to counseling concerning conversion from three perspectives. First, how did he actually go about it? Second, how does he reflect back on his approach? Third, what might we add to his reflections?

Missionary B interacted with Mr. S in much the same way that any knowledgeable missionary might deal with an intelligent inquirer in a situation as sensitive as that which pertains in Bangladesh. He exhibited genuineness and warmth. He respected Mr. S and accepted him as an equal. He depended upon the Scriptures, the Holy Spirit, and prayer. If there was anything unique in this situation it was the rapport between Christian counselor and Muslim counselee and the length to which Missionary B went in order to alert Mr. S to the implications of conversion. Aware of the Bengali tendency to "share blame," he counseled Mr. S very carefully and specifically as to the cost of discipleship in his culture and to the fact that he would have to bear the responsibility for his decision.

Looking back after becoming more acquainted with differentiations of alloplastic/autoplastic and emic/etic change and the various available counseling approaches, Missionary B makes some interesting observations. He now believes that although a more directive counseling approach would generally be expected and accepted in Bengali culture, in the present case his interactional and cognitive approach, and his technique of putting great emphasis on Mr. S's own thinking and responsibility, were appropriate. He feels, however, that he lacked foresight in that he did not involve Bengali church leadership in the counseling process. He should have been the catalyst in building a bridge between Mr. S (and other potential Muslim converts) and a suspicious Christian community.

I would tend to concur with Missionary B's appraisal. But perhaps we should go even further. Almost from the beginning of this counseling relationship Missionary B began to fear that Mr. S either was not giving full consideration to the cost of discipleship or held to the hope that somehow the mission would provide for him and his family. (This hope would not have been completely without foundation, inasmuch as various missions in Bangladesh have attempted to aid new Muslim converts by providing jobs, by selling land to them at little or no interest, or by supporting them in business ventures.) Therefore, Missionary B catalogued the possible consequences of conversion for Mr. S. However, he might have counseled Mr. S in such a way as to reframe the problem by assuming his conversion, exploring solutions that had been tried in Bangladesh and, rejecting those that were unrealistic, charting a new course. In the final analysis, the real solution lay in full acceptance by Mr. S of the position of learner in the church and in a totally new willingness on the part of the Christian church to accept Muslim converts as equal members of the church family and to provide for them in ways indicated by Scripture as God enables them to do so. This points in the direction of a counseling task larger than, and prior to, the counseling task undertaken when Missionary B so wholeheartedly agreed to instruct Mr. S in the Christian faith.

Concluding Reflections

It is the very dilemma which was faced in this case that has occasioned mission strategists such as Phil Parshall to put forward a completely new strategy for reaching

Muslims.[5] Parshall seeks to minimize cultural barriers and to eliminate (insofar as possible) the wrenching of Muslims one by one from their society. Many helpful insights can be gained by studying such proposals, but they offer little help for ministering to Muslim converts like Mr. S who are ready to come to Christ in the face of ostracism and difficulty and before new strategies can be effected.

Case Vignette 2: Mme. O (France)

Mme. O was born shortly after World War II. She was the daughter of working-class French parents. Her parents were nominal Catholics and also members of the Communist Party. They wanted to be assured that she would receive communion and be married in the church eventually. They therefore enrolled her in a catechism class. However, at the age of seven she was informed that Sundays were market days, not for going to church. For some time, Mme. O's parents encouraged her in her school work. She did well, especially in learning the English language. Prior to her last year in high school, however, Mme. O's parents forced her to start work in a factory. Deprived of a healthy diet as a child, Mme. O had never become strong physically. Factory work was very difficult for her.

In order to get away from her unhappy family situation and "to give an expected child a name," Mme. O married. The marriage soon ended in divorce. A second marriage began and ended in the same way. Finally Mme. O was left with three children and severe emotional problems. For several years her second husband cared for the children. She was hospitalized frequently and received treatment from several psychiatrists and psychologists. She experienced a series of ups and downs but was able to secure a fairly responsible position as a translator for an

5. Phil Parshall, *New Paths in Muslim Evangelism: Evangelical Approaches to Contextualization* (Grand Rapids: Baker, 1980).

import company. In a highly competitive job market she feared that she would lose her job. She worked long hours and often skipped lunch in order to keep up with the heavy work load. After work she would return exhausted to her small apartment in a middle-class community in Paris.

A little more than six months prior to the counseling session in view here, a Christian male psychiatric nurse witnessed to Mme. O while she was a patient in a psychiatric hospital. The nurse shared the *Quatre Lois Spirituelles* (a French version of the Four Spiritual Laws), with the result that Mme. O prayed to "receive Christ." Because Mme. O showed an interest in a weekly Bible study and in spiritual things in general, the nurse invited her to attend his church—a comparatively new evangelical church pastored by an American missionary, Pastor K.

After attending services on a fairly regular basis for about three months, Mme. O attended a baptismal service. Impressed, she requested baptism and was assigned to a French laywoman who was to instruct her and prepare her for baptism. The laywoman was soon convinced that Mme. O was not really a Christian, for she had no clear testimony and little understanding of the most elementary Christian doctrines. For her part, Mme. O admitted that she did not know why she wanted to be baptized. She agreed that it would be well to delay baptism until she had more time to study and understand the Bible.

One night Mme. O came to the weekly Bible study and prayer service by public transportation. After the service she asked Pastor K if he would be so kind as to give her a ride home because she had a problem and needed counsel. Knowing her reputation (she had become emotionally dependent upon the male nurse and even fantasized concerning a relationship with him in a way that caused him considerable embarrassment and difficulty), Pastor K said he would take her home but wisely added that he would like to include M. B. (M. B was a retired lay pastor who was known for his prayer ministry and was greatly respected by the congregation.) Mme. O agreed.

After they arrived at her apartment and parked the car, Mme. O told Pastor K of her problem, hesitantly at first but then rapidly and with great emotion.

> Pastor, you know how I miss my children. But my apartment is too small for me. It would be impossible to bring my children here. I have a good job. That is not the problem. But I am so alone.
>
> When I was in the hospital earlier this year I met a man who also has three children. He has a very large home not far from here. Last week I met him again at the department store. He asked me how things were going. One thing led to another. Finally, he invited me to bring my three children and live with him. He said that I could have my own bedroom. We could live together as brother and sister. I would have my children with me and, best of all, I would not be alone.
>
> Pastor, I have been thinking about it seriously. Next Wednesday is the end of the month. If I moved then I could save a month's rent. What should I do? What do you think? Could it work out?

In the back seat M. B prayed silently. Pastor K remembered that he and his family would be leaving for six weeks of Bible camps and vacation the next morning. Even M. B would be leaving in a day or two. How should he respond?

Pastor K began by commending Mme. O for thinking of her children. Counselor and counselee shared something of their mutual concerns occasioned by a pervasive drug culture and other social problems. Mme. O added that her former husband never took the children to church. Eventually, Pastor K spoke of the love of God for the children and for her and recounted the story of salvation. Periodically he asked Mme. O if she really believed what he was saying. Each time, amidst tears, she replied that she did. Drawing the conversation to a close, Pastor K spoke in the following vein:

> Knowing that God wants the very best for you, what do you think God would have you do with your life? I can't make the decision for you. Only you can do that. But I am going to request that before you go to bed tonight you pray and ask the Lord what he wants you to do, ... what he wants you to be. And I promise that I will be praying too. I will pray that God will answer and that you will hear and obey him.

M. B led in prayer and the brief counseling session concluded. All went to their respective homes.

Upon returning to his church some six weeks later, Pastor K was accosted by Mme. O following a Sunday morning service. In her person and attire she was neater than she had been previously. She told him that when she entered her apartment that night and realized that he had not answered her question, she felt hurt and then became angry. Before retiring, however, she decided to pray. First she asked God what he wanted her to do. Then she changed her prayer. She realized that she needed to trust Christ as Savior and make him the Lord of her life. She did so. For the first time in her life the Lord Jesus became real to her. She became a part of the heavenly family. She felt that she need never be lonely again.

By the time that this report was written by Pastor K many months later, Mme. O had become a baptized member of the church. She was still living in her small apartment and did not have her children with her, but they were together almost every weekend. On her own initiative she was leading a regular Bible study for women who had backgrounds and problems similar to her own.

Basic Counseling Orientation

Real and perceived universals. A careful examination of Mme. O's background reveals that an acquaintance with a variety of man and world views had been reflected both in the cases of people who had a profound influence upon her and in her own experience. Her parents had some inclinations toward Roman Catholicism but seem to have basically espoused a naturalistic/materialistic world view. With the exception of one psychiatric nurse, her professional counselors also seem to have taken purely humanistic approaches. Mme. O herself had been involved at various times with the occult, Transcendental Meditation, and Yoga. In a way, Mme. O represents a host of modern men and women who are philosophically, psychologically, and spiritually adrift in the tumultuous sea of a post-Christian, hedonistic society.

Cultural characteristics. Parisian culture is usually characterized as a highly individualistic and independent culture. It is fiercely competitive. The guilt orientation fostered by Roman Catholicism is being eroded (although it should not be disregarded). Women are "liberated." Mme. O's status as a twice-divorced woman in search of still another relationship (inside or outside the bounds of marriage) is not particularly frowned upon. Traditionally, the Roman Catholic Church has provided answers to moral and religious questions through its priests. Still, the French people generally pride themselves on their intellectualism and their ability to make rational decisions on their own. This, along with a kind of popular peer dependency, may be the wave of the future.

Individual idiosyncracies. From her early days Mme. O had been somewhat weak physically and was often subjected to severe emotional strains. By the time she came into contact with Pastor K, various medical doctors, professional counselors, social workers, psychologists, and psychiatrists had worked with her to resolve her problems. In and out of psychiatric and other hospitals, she had probably been helped to some extent because, although filled with anxiety, often depressed, and quite careless concerning her person, she was able to hold an exacting job. Nevertheless, as she put it to Pastor K from the very first, she was a "real case." Not to be overlooked is the fact that she also reported that she has been "sensitive to spiritual things" from the time of her early childhood.

Counseling Universals

A shared world view. Although he is from another culture (the United States), Pastor K is well educated and a part of the same post-Christian generation as Mme. O. Pastor K may not have had a really firm understanding of the occult and the Hindu philosophies that Mme. O had been involved in, but these ideologies do not seem to have had a very strong attraction for Mme. O anyway. Like many of her contemporaries in the Western world, Mme. O viewed them quite pragmatically. She claimed that practicing Yoga (which she learned in a psychiatric hospital) had helped her relax. That was about all.

A good relationship. All of the indications point to a positive counseling relationship between counselor and counselee in this case. However, the relationship was fraught with potential for good or ill, depending on how it was handled. Pastor K wisely involved M. B at the time of the brief counseling session in focus here.

The expectation of being helped. We cannot be sure, but the fact that Mme. O sought counsel from Pastor K likely indicates that she had confidence in his ability to help her. In France this type of problem usually would not be shared with professionals or even family, but only with a close personal friend. Obviously her hope was that the pastor-counselor would reinforce her desire to accept her friend's offer.

An appropriate approach and technique. Depending on their preferences, Mme. O's professional therapists had used various approaches and techniques in dealing with her case. She had undergone psychoanalysis and reported that whatever help this might have been in gaining an understanding of herself, it also left her with resentment, unresolved problems, and depression. She had also been subjected to behavior-modification techniques, but felt that basic problems such as guilt for her past life needed to be dealt with. Pastor K had had some studies in relevant areas, including seminary courses in pastoral counseling and psychology. He was aware of his limitations when it came to counseling someone with a history of mental and psychological difficulties.

Effecting Change

Prior to the brief counseling session in view here, Mme. O had often remarked that she despaired of ever being able to change. Pastor K knew that the basis for a really significant positive change had to be a proper relationship with God. God could "change" her if she would allow him to do so. He also knew that in spite of her personal weaknesses and the pattern of most previously tried therapies (which tended to shift blame to others), Mme. O would have to make up her own mind as to whether or not she would trust and follow Christ. He reports that he consciously avoided being unnecessarily critical and judgmental (because her parents and employer were very critical); that he avoided giving a simplistic answer to all her problems (e.g., "Become a Christian and all will be well"); that he avoided being too directive (because she had to take responsibility for her own decision); and that he attempted to demonstrate the love of God for her.

In this case it is not difficult to further analyze Pastor K's approach in terms of our paradigm of change. Relying on the power of suggestion, he reframed Mme. O's problem in such a way that it became one of relationship to God rather than one of relationship to her friend. Because of the limitation of time (?) Pastor K did this unilaterally. This entailed a certain risk. But perhaps an even greater risk was involved in disregarding the presenting problem and concentrating solely on the need to accept Christ. Where the Bible speaks clearly, Protestant counselors can hardly afford to be less forthright and clear than their Roman Catholic counterparts. And clarity at this point neither detracts from the responsibility of the counselee to make her own decision nor from her need to know and depend on Christ for salvation.

Concluding Reflections

We should not lose sight of the fact that God employed two spiritual counselors to minister to Mme. O. The first one was the psychiatric nurse. He used the Four Spiritual Laws in such a way as to exact what may have been a premature decision from Mme. O. By pressing her to accept Christ before she understood what was involved or had thought about her decision, it may be that she merely responded to *his* earnest desire that she convert. On his part, the nurse may have believed that if she prayed to receive Christ the Holy Spirit would enable her to overcome her difficulties. As it turned out, Mme. O became so emotionally dependent upon him that his family relationships were jeopardized. He left his job and moved to a new area in order to extricate himself from the relationship.

Nevertheless, a sovereign God used the psychiatric nurse to reach Mme. O in spite of the weakness of his approach. It would seem that the nurse's contact with her resulted in her involvement with a Bible-study group and the church. Pastor K therefore had the advantage of meeting Mme. O in the context of the church and was aided in his ministry to her by mature laypersons. In this regard it is rather remarkable that he did not immediately enlist Mme. O's lay helper (and perhaps others) to minister to her during the crucial period of his six-week absence. He was right in insisting that the conversion decision must be Mme. O's if it was to be genuine. But he should have acted upon his knowledge that even in individualistic-independency cultures (if, indeed, French culture in transition can be so categorized), the decision to accept the heavenly Christ needs to be reinforced by practical and undelayed incorporation into his earthly family.

14

Counseling Concerning Growth and the Development of a Christian Lifestyle

God's Word is unequivocal and clear—person gifts are given to the church in order that Christian growth might occur. Paul wrote to an infantile, worldly church at Corinth: "What, after all, is Apollos? And what is Paul? Only servants, through whom you came to believe—as the Lord has assigned to each his task. I planted the seed, Apollos watered it, but God made it grow" (1 Cor. 3:5–6).

To the Ephesians (4:12–16) Paul wrote that apostles, prophets, evangelists, and pastor-teachers were given with definite objectives in mind:

1. "To prepare God's people for works of service"
2. "So that the body of Christ may be built up"
3. "Until we all reach unity in the faith and in the knowledge of the Son of God"
4. "And become mature, attaining to the whole measure of the fullness of Christ"
5. "Then we will no longer be infants . . ."

6. "Instead, . . . we will . . . grow up into him who is the Head . . ."
7. "From him the whole body, . . . grows and builds itself up in love. . . ."

There are many dimensions to the development of a lifestyle that is truly Christian. Growth is both individual and corporate. Individual growth is intellectual, physical, social, and spiritual. Corporate growth is quantitative and qualitative. The cross-cultural counselor encourages and assists growth in others, and grows in the process of encouraging it.

Growth in Individual Christians

This matter of making disciples of all nations means that as Christian workers we are involved with people at crucial points in their life experiences, conversion and baptism being primary examples of this. It also means that we are involved with people in the ongoing process implied in teaching them to observe all things that Christ has commanded (Matt. 28:18–20). James F. Engel focuses on points and process when, from a communicator's perspective, he places stages of development on a "spiritual decision process scale."[1] Howard J. Clinebell, Jr., does the same when, from a counselor's perspective, he sums up Christian counseling in a formula for growth.[2]

Points and process, times of crisis and times of normal development, progression and regression—the development of a Christian lifestyle is not automatic and does not come at a steady rate. A parallel can be seen in quan-

---

1. James F. Engel, *Contemporary Christian Communication: Its Theory and Practice* (Nashville: Nelson, 1979), p. 225. The scale is reprinted on p. 302 of this book.
2. Howard J. Clinebell, Jr., "Growth Counseling," in *Helping People Grow: Practical Approaches to Christian Counseling*, ed. Gary R. Collins (Santa Ana, Calif.: Vision House, 1980), p. 84.

tum theory, according to which atoms or molecules absorb or emit energy not continuously, but in a series of steps. So it is that Christians develop as persons in steps and in response to universal, cultural, and personal challenges.

For example, people everywhere go through a process of physical development from childhood to puberty to adulthood and old age. Obviously, believers in every culture are required to respond to the challenge of these changes in Christian ways. As we have seen, however, the challenges that come with these changes differ according to culture. In many tribal societies the onset of puberty signals the time for marriage. In most technological societies, there is a great gap between the time when young people are physically able to procreate and the time when they are legally and economically ready for marriage. The challenges faced by young peoples in tribal and technological societies, therefore, are very different—so much so that some writers refer to adolescence as an invention of technological societies. Finally, depending on a variety of unique factors, individuals find themselves prepared or unprepared to meet these universal and cultural specifics successfully.

Like the intracultural variety of counseling, cross-cultural counseling becomes a matter of helping individuals respond to the ordinary and extraordinary challenges of life in ways that evidence Christian growth and culminate in a Christian lifestyle. Unlike intracultural counseling, however, cross-cultural counseling takes into account a whole range of challenges that vary with cultural settings as well as individual personalities.

Assisting Growth in Christian Groups

In Ephesians 4:12–16, Paul indicates that not only the individual believer but also the entire body (the church) is to develop and grow. In context, the reference would seem to be to the universal church. But by extension we can apply the passage to local churches and other corporate expressions of the church universal.

As is the case with individuals, religious movements seldom if ever develop at a steady rate over a long period of time. Social tensions and individual behavioral patterns intrude in such a way as to interrupt the process. When change does occur social entropy (analogous to the second law of thermodynamics) tends to set in. Unless corrections are applied, growth is arrested and the movement is in jeopardy.

Eugene A. Nida diagrams this process (see fig. 32).

A movement grows out of a challenge to change at point B. Change accelerates and growth occurs until a crisis is met at point C. If the proper adjustments are made, disintegration and demoralization can be averted. Otherwise, they probably cannot.

Nida points out, for example, that the cultural factors that pertained among the Karens of Burma at the time of the introduction of Christianity favored Christian conversion and the growth of the church. The churches were able to move through the crisis period and, by adopting "a positive attitude toward education and responsibility for community life," build a bridge of adjustment to the outside world while remaining spiritually strong and

FIGURE 32   **The Dynamics of Change in Religious Movements***

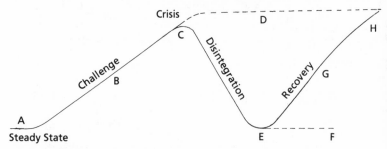

*From "Dynamics of Church Growth" by Eugene A. Nida, in *Church Growth and Christian Mission*, edited by Donald A. McGavran. Copyright © 1965 by Harper and Row.

maintaining growth.[3] On the other hand, early churches in North Africa were demoralized by the opposition of Islam and died out. And in contemporary sub-Saharan Africa many Christian groups that have survived the crises posed by tribal religion and culture have done so by following local prophets and incorporating native practices inimical to biblical Christianity.

Once again we are brought face to face with the need for biblical understanding, enablement by the Holy Spirit, and person-gift ministry. Counselors (whether native or expatriate) who understand social psychology can become instruments of the Holy Spirit in promoting continued growth and vitality in the churches in the same way that those who understand personal psychology can become instruments to aid in the growth of individual Christians.

Case Vignette 1: Mr. and Mrs. A (Hawaii)

Mr. and Mrs. A are Caucasian, in their middle thirties, and the parents of six children. Mr. A is a career man in the American military. At one time Mr. A had attended Bible college and considered the Christian ministry, but increasing family responsibilities kept him in the military. Both husband and wife have been active in the church all their lives. At the time Mrs. A sought counsel, both were attending a rather large church pastored by a "mainlander" who had a background in medical technology, Bible-college training, and one year of pastoral internship before going to the Islands.

While the A family was stationed on another Pacific island, they hired a Micronesian houseboy, T. C. After T. C. made a profession of faith, Mr. and Mrs. A helped him enroll in a Christian college on the mainland.

3. Eugene A. Nida, "Dynamics of Church Growth," in *Church Growth and Christian Mission,* ed. Donald A. McGavran (New York: Harper and Row, 1965), p. 171.

In Hawaii, the A family was visited by T. C., who was en route home for a vacation. According to Mrs. A, during his visit he attempted to seduce both her and her teen-age daughter. The attempts were successfully resisted. But T. C. threatened to have a witch doctor on his native island make a love potion which he would use on Mrs. A and her daughter when he visited them once again during his return trip to the mainland.

A few weeks later the young man did revisit the family. Mrs. A reported that this time he was successful in seducing her while her husband was away. (No sexual relationship with the daughter was reported). Mrs. A became convinced that she was pregnant. Not having had sexual contact with her husband for some seven months, she convinced him to have intercourse with her. In this way she hoped to make her husband think that he was the father of the expected child. Nevertheless, her anxiety increased. What should she do? Seek an abortion? Inform her husband of what actually happened? Let him think he was the father? What would happen if the child turned out to be "unlike" the rest of the family (all of the A family are light-skinned and blond)? Should she contact T. C. at the college?

In great distress and turmoil Mrs. A went to her pastor for counsel. Pastor H gathered the "facts" of the case, tried to reassure Mrs. A, and advised her to go to the medical center for a pregnancy test. The test was positive. Pastor H and Mrs. A agreed to check all the options before involving Mr. A. Pastor H contacted an administrator of the school where T. C. was matriculating so that he might be confronted and counseled. Mrs. A telephoned T. C. directly and asked what he wanted done with the baby. He responded to the effect that he was in no position to rear the child. Besides, if he were to take the child to his native island his potential for Christian ministry would be jeopardized. After considering Scriptures such as Psalm 139:13–16 and Isaiah 49:1–4, Mrs. A and Pastor H ruled out abortion as a Christian option. Pastor H advised Mrs. A that his understanding of genetics led him to believe that in cases of mixed race such as this, the likelihood was that the expected child would be darker than the other children. Adoption was tentatively agreed upon as the best solution.

At this point Mr. A was brought in, the entire situation reviewed, and a final solution agreed upon. Because Mrs. A was obese and might not show her pregnancy very much, nothing was to be said to the children unless it became necessary. At the time of delivery, the child was to be put up for adoption if it proved to be of dark complexion. (Arrangements for this were made with the Department of Social Services.) If the child were of fair complexion, the couple were to rear the child as their own.

When Mr. A took Mrs. A to the hospital for the delivery, he prematurely told the older children that the baby died in childbirth. He had some explaining to do when it turned out that the child was healthy. He was also fair-skinned, blond-haired, and blue-eyed like the other children, so Mr. and Mrs. A abandoned any plans of giving up the child and decided to rear him themselves.

During the counseling process, however, it surfaced that Mrs. A had been the one who seduced the Micronesian and that she had done so repeatedly from the time he was hired some years before. Outwardly at least, Mr. A forgave his remorseful wife. T. C. was counseled and, truly repentant, allowed to continue his studies in the Christian college.

Basic Counseling Orientation

Real and perceived universals. Ostensibly only Christian values and views need be considered here. The phenomenon of the love potion, however, alerts one to the importance of other background information. The resort to aphrodisiac drugs, foods, and potions of various kinds in order to excite sexual desire is nothing new in the history of man, but it is highly questionable and problematic. A love potion prepared by a witch doctor alerts us to Pastor H's need to understand witchcraft as well. Finally, Pastor H's understanding of genetic factors left something to be desired. The baby would not necessarily have been darker than the other children in the family.

Cultural characteristics. Cultures vary widely in their acceptance of children of mixed blood. Hawaiian society could be expected to be very accepting of a dark-skinned child. However, the military normally moves families from place to place and many societies are not nearly so accepting of children of mixed blood. Also, the presence of one child who is different from all others in a family would have been a factor to be reckoned with within the family itself.

Individual idiosyncracies. Of several obvious idiosyncracies in this case, one which is of great significance (but not emphasized in the account) is that Mr. and Mrs. A had not had intercourse for seven months prior to the incident reported here. Mrs. A's obesity, her planned deceit, and the strangeness of some of her explanations also stand out.

Counseling Universals

A shared world view. All of the principals actually shared the Christian world view and espoused biblical authority. Pastor H assumed this and counseled accordingly. However, in reporting that it was later discovered that Mrs. A actually seduced T. C., he enigmatically adds, "I do not believe it was the love potion but the power of positive suggestion [that occasioned the seduction] because when he [T. C.] put the love potion in a letter to the ... daughter, the mother intercepted the mail, smelled the love potion, and refused to allow her daughter to receive the mail."

Nothing is reported which would indicate whether or not counselor and counselee shared the same understanding of the significance of a love potion or of the report that it was prepared by a witch doctor (which may or may not have been the case).

A good relationship. It would appear that a trusting relationship between Mrs. A and Pastor H had been built up over a period of time. She chose to confide in him rather than in someone else. He evidently did not seriously question her version of what had taken place. This proved to be a mistake. Also, private counseling may not occasion the questions in Hawaiian-American culture that it might elsewhere. Even so, one might question the wisdom of one-to-one counseling in this case and especially the exclusion of Mr. A until "options" could be laid out for his consideration.

The expectation of being helped. Mrs. A was desperate, but obviously entertained hope that the problem could be successfully resolved by subterfuge if nothing else. Initial interaction with Pastor H must have confirmed that hope.

An appropriate approach and technique. In retrospect, we see that this aspect of the case was most problematic for several reasons, primarily because the real problem did not surface until much later, although it is distinctly possible that it could have been discovered early on.

Effecting Change

Probably without special forethought Pastor H took a rational approach to counseling which quite neatly follows the Watzlawick paradigm for change: from defining the problem to examining solutions to deciding upon a course of action and implementing it. However, the presenting problem was not the real problem at all. Mrs. A was the seducer. Also, Pastor H now conjectures that the father of the baby was actually Mr. A. Pastor H was too trusting and therefore missed signals which would seem to have dictated a different approach—one that was more probing and perhaps more confrontational (in the vein of Jay E. Adams's nouthetic counseling). From a Christian

point of view, the lifestyle of Mr. and Mrs. A left much
to be desired. Warning signals included such things as
Mrs. A's obesity, her tardiness in exposing T. C., her
planned deceit, and Mr. and Mrs. A's prolonged sexual
abstinence. Mrs. A's problem was that she was guilty of
adultery. Mr. A would seem to have been guilty of neglecting his wife. In this case, Pastor H allowed supposed
ethnic and cultural issues to obstruct his understanding.
From the beginning the presenting problem was a secondary or tertiary problem. Ultimately it was no problem
at all.

Concluding Reflections

It can be argued that this case does not qualify as a case
of *cross-cultural* counseling at all. Both counselor and
counselee were native to white, Anglo-Saxon, Protestant,
North American culture. Even the problem of what to do
with a child of mixed blood did not require resolution.
Admittedly, the case is very marginal. It is included here
because the counselor considered himself to be ministering as a missionary-pastor in a cultural setting which was
very different from his own and working with counselees
whose acculturative, if not enculturative, experiences were
very different from his own. Indeed, it may have been that
his preoccupation with the cultural aspects of the case
(and even a culturally conditioned predisposition to place
the guilt on the Micronesian student rather than on Mrs.
A?) were factors in the incorrect diagnosis.

Case Vignette 2: Mr. S and Miss T (Korea)

Mr. S was one of the leaders in an evangelical student
organization. He was twenty-nine and was not married.
In one of the meetings of the organization, a young woman
stood up to give her testimony. As soon as Mr. S saw her
an inner voice seemed to say that she was the one he was
looking for. Later he found out that she really was not a

born-again Christian. She also belonged to a higher social class than he did. Moreover, he found out that she had been dating a wealthy man for a number of years; that they were planning to marry right after her graduation; and that her graduation was less than six months away.

An all-night Christian meeting with sharing, singing, personal counseling, and Bible teaching to be led by Mr. S was scheduled for Christmas Eve. Miss T was invited to the meeting. Having tried unsuccessfully to persuade her fiancé to come along, she decided to attend without him. That night she came to a saving knowledge of Christ. Throughout the next few months she attempted to persuade her fiancé to receive Christ as well. After several months, she realized that he was not interested at all in her newfound faith and she decided to break their engagement. By that time, however, the families of both of the principals had agreed to the marriage. Miss T encountered severe opposition from both families.

To further complicate matters, within six months of her conversion Mr. S asked Miss T to marry him. When she told her family, Miss T was accused of being a religious fanatic. In fact, her father dealt with her very harshly, even to the point of inflicting physical pain. Her family also attempted to intimidate Mr. S by calling him at work and threatening to employ the secret police to harass him. The irony of the matter was that although Miss T's father was a Confucianist, her mother was a deaconess in a Presbyterian church and often spent whole nights in prayer at the church. At the same time, she secretly sought out a Christian "prophetess" who told her that if her daughter married Mr. S, both of them would be unhappy and their marriage would end in disaster.

In the face of all this, Mr. S continued prayerfully to seek God's will. He became convinced that it was God's will that Miss T and he marry in spite of the opposition and harassment. Miss T agreed. Before proceeding further, however, they decided to visit a Scottish missionary, Missionary W, for counseling.

Missionary W listened to their problem and immediately responded by pointing to Matthew 19:4–5. "Haven't you read," he asked, "that at the beginning the Creator 'made them male and female,' and said, 'For this reason a man will leave his father and mother and be united to his wife, and the two will become one flesh'?" He stressed that both of them were Christians and therefore, if they believed it to be God's will to marry, they could be confident that God would bless their marriage. Christian young people are exhorted to honor and obey their parents, but this command is limited by the phrase *in the Lord* (Eph. 6:1). He emphasized that civil law in Korea now supports the right of young people to marry without their parents' consent once they have reached the age of twenty-four. In the light of all of this he encouraged them to marry if they wanted to despite the opposition of Miss T's parents. Before parting, counselor and counselees had a time of prayer.

The young couple were encouraged by the missionary's counsel. At first they thought of taking his advice and getting married right away. After further reflection and prayer they decided to consult a trusted Korean pastor first to see if he agreed with Missionary W. However, he advised them to be patient and prayerfully wait to see whether Miss T's parents would change their mind. A year or two later Miss T's father consented to meet Mr. S and made a positive evaluation of him. Opposition changed to reluctant acceptance and Mr. S and Miss T were married.

Basic Counseling Orientation

Real and perceived universals. The non-Christian background of this case is primarily that of Confucianism with its emphasis on filial piety, family solidarity, and harmony. The likelihood is that the status and role of the "prophetess" is more like that of a shaman in tribalism than that of a prophetess in the Bible. (There are a number of these prophetesses in the churches in Korea but they seldom are accepted, especially in the established churches.)

Cultural characteristics. A number of cultural factors are relevant to this case. Although the class system was formally abolished in 1894 it remains an important part of the Korean social system. For Miss T to marry someone of a lower social class (Mr. S was from the lower class and she from the upper class), someone with an "inferior" education (Mr. S graduated from a good university but not a prestigious one), and someone who was a "religious fanatic" (Mr. S was a Baptist and a member of an evangelical student organization) was an extremely "shameful" thing in the eyes of her parents. Traditionally in Korea marriages were arranged by parents through the offices of a mediator (*choong-mae-in*). Although the law now allows the principals to marry on their own (if they are more than twenty-four years of age), most Koreans favor an arrangement whereby families arrange for the marriage of their children but leave the final decision to the young couple themselves. Parents usually concentrate on status, health, education, and occupation, whereas young couples tend to concentrate on compatibility. Most all important decisions are still made by the involved group. All of this is in keeping, of course, with an ancestor-oriented collectivistic-dependency culture.

Individual idiosyncracies. As far as we are informed, neither of the counselees brought personal histories or characteristics that bore negatively upon the case. Both demonstrated a commitment to Christ and a desire to do his will.

Counseling Universals

A shared world view. All of the principals in this case (except Miss T's father) held to the Christian world view and accepted the authority of the Bible. The missionary viewed Confucian understandings and values from a very different perspective than that of his counselees and the Korean pastor.

A good relationship. Missionary W's characteristics such as genuineness and warmth were probably not balanced by an empathetic understanding, especially as it related to the reluctance of Miss T to marry in the face of opposition from her parents.

An expectation of being helped. The fact that the counselees decided to resort to another counselor native to Korea indicated a certain hesitancy to accept the counsel of Missionary W. On the other hand, they had an unshakable faith that God's leading would be for their good.

An appropriate approach and technique. The directive approach of Missionary W with his strong dependence on biblical authority was likely not out of keeping with the approach of Korean pastors. However, this approach was probably a factor in preventing Missionary W from gaining a more empathetic appraisal of the whole situation. Moreover, Missionary W should have recommended that Korean church leadership be invited into the counseling situation from the beginning.

Effecting Change

Here is a case where the cultural blinders of the missionary counselor obviously militated against effective cross-cultural counseling. The use of the paradigm of change or of some of the techniques of the more dialogical and relational approaches of Paul Tournier or Clinebell, for example, would have resulted in an increased understanding of the counselees' own understandings and feelings and of Korean culture in general on the part of the cross-cultural counselor. The kind of change to be given priority in this case was alloplastic change—a change in the attitude of Miss T's parents. This change could have been attempted not just to satisfy the parents and aid them spiritually, but also to avoid injuring the Christian cause unnecessarily. The almost invariable local interpretation of a hasty marriage in the face of parental opposition would have been that Christians are disruptive and disrespectful of parents. Change in the parents' attitude did come after an extended period of time. Perhaps it could not have come earlier. And perhaps the missionary could have done little to effect it. But in concert with respected Korean Christian cocounselors he could have tried.

Concluding Reflections

Problem-syndrome cases such as this merit examination in far greater detail that is possible here. From our perspective as Western Christians we can probably identify more readily with Missionary W and his counsel than we can with an approach that keeps a couple who are dedicated to Christ and each other apart for months and even years. And this in deference to the will of parents who do not trust the God of the Bible, who are motivated by considerations of pride and prestige, and who physically abused their own daughter. But we need to be reminded that God is not as impatient as we often are. Nor are many of our Christian brothers and sisters in other lands as impatient as we often are, unless they give overly much credence to counsel that is culturally inappropriate.

15

Counseling Concerning Christian Service

One of the greatest challenges that comes to Christian workers in any cultural context is to reproduce themselves so that the work of Christ may survive their withdrawal from the scene. Whether they be counselors, teachers, pastors, or "simply" Christian laypersons, Paul's charge to Timothy has relevance: "And the things you have heard me say in the presence of many witnesses entrust to reliable men who will also be qualified to teach others" (2 Tim. 2:2). The churches need the special person gifts that the resurrected Christ delights to give to them (Eph. 4:11). The churches also need other kinds of leaders whose service will enable the apostles, prophets, evangelists, and pastor-teachers to concentrate on prayer and a spiritual ministry (Acts 6:1–3). And the churches need people helpers who will build up the body by teaching and admonishing one another "with all wisdom" (Col. 3:16).

Nothing commends the church more than a spiritual leadership. In the pastoral epistles (especially 1 Tim. 3 and Titus 1) the apostle Paul catalogues qualifications for church leaders. There is a sense in which those qualifications can be summed up in two phrases: church leaders must be "above reproach" (1 Tim. 3:2) and "have a good reputation with outsiders" (1 Tim. 3:7). God is desirous that when people inside and outside the church look at Christian leaders they see persons of integrity, people whose service does not dishonor the claims of Christ.

Charles H. Kraft has argued that such requirements for leadership as those indicated in 1 Timothy 3 (above reproach, the husband of one wife, temperate, self-controlled) reflect the expectations of Greco-Roman culture; that the real meaning of the longer list is that people who exhibited these characteristics would be thought of as persons of integrity, self-control, and good will in that culture; and that if we are to have "dynamic equivalent" churches around the world the list would have to be modified in a way that "will communicate these meanings" to the people of the various cultures. By way of illustration, the requirement for being the "husband of one wife" would have to be modified (at least temporarily) among the Kru of Liberia because they believe one cannot trust a man with one wife! Similarly, because of cultural meanings and expectations, church leaders among the Higi of Nigeria should be chosen from the royal social class.[1]

When one traces Kraft's reasoning to its source, one discovers that it stems from a questionable view of the authority of Scripture. And when one examines the yardstick he uses to differentiate that which is cultural and that which is supracultural in the biblical text one discovers that it is fashioned by anthropological evaluations rather than historicogrammatical interpretation.

At the same time, culture *is* important and must not be overlooked. The potentials and pitfalls of counseling

1. Charles H. Kraft, *Christianity in Culture: A Study in Dynamic Biblical Theologizing in Cross-Cultural Perspective* (Maryknoll, N.Y.: Orbis, 1979), pp. 323–25.

concerning Christian service vary significantly from culture to culture. Only the Lord knows how many Christians are serving as person gifts in churches around the world as a result of human counsel apart from a divine call. Only the Lord knows how many have been called and are not serving because they have not been properly counseled or encouraged by their advisers or peers. Many pages could and should be written concerning these matters. We need to be aware of three cautions.

First, biblical qualifications for spiritual leadership should be explicitly emphasized and carefully modeled by the Christian counselor as God gives grace. Paul was very specific in communicating Christ's standards for leadership in the church. But he could also write, "Whatever you have learned or received or heard from me, or *seen in me*—put it into practice" (Phil. 4:9; italics added).

Second, characteristics of leadership peculiar to the counselor's culture should be screened out in the counseling process. Perhaps the greatest error in theory about developing an indigenous church has been the tendency to define and characterize the "three-self" church (self-supporting, self-governing, and self-propagating) in ways which tended toward duplicating the patterns of the Western sending church. Perhaps the greatest error in the attempt to raise up indigenous church leadership lies in the tendency to produce Western-type leaders for non-Western churches. The Madison Avenue, entrepreneurial, choleric type of leader may not square with expectations in the counselee culture. Overreliance on a professional clergy may prove fatal to many churches in the Third World.

Third, attention should be given to capitalizing on potentials and countering the pitfalls of the counselee culture's leadership patterns. (Our case vignettes will serve to illustrate some of these potentials and pitfalls.) Think for a moment of the rather general tendency of Christian workers to counsel almost any promising young convert to commit his or her life to full-time Christian service and to enroll in a Bible school as soon as possible. Counseling in this way may be wise and in order. But more often than not it overlooks significant questions:

What is the potential of mature leaders who already have a means of livelihood to engage in studies designed to aid them in further developing leadership gifts?

What advantages would accrue to encouraging young converts to prove themselves in ways prescribed by the church before embarking upon preparation for full-time ministry?

What pitfalls are inherent in the culturally prescribed expectations that first sons will assume responsibility for the family farm or business, aging parents, and younger siblings; that sponsoring missions and churches will assume responsibility for the placement and success of graduates of their institutions; that girls who are received into Christian schools will be prepared for Christian marriage and provided with acceptable Christian husbands?

Of course, our purpose in bringing these cautions to the Christian cross-cultural counselor is not to encourage capitulation to the counselee's culture in preference to commitment to the lordship of Christ. Rather, it is to promote culture-sensitive counseling in this area so that counseling will be consciously preventative before it becomes necessarily remedial.

Case Vignette 1: Miss F (A Panamanian Student in the U.S.)

Miss F was born into a poor, rural, Roman Catholic family in Panama during the middle 1950s. Her father was thirty-seven years of age when she was born. He was a farmer with very little education. He was coarse in language and lifestyle and drank quite heavily, but he was not notoriously unfaithful to his wife or abusive to his family. Her mother was nineteen years younger than her father but attentive to her family's needs. Miss F was the second oldest of seven children—four sons and three daughters.

After she completed primary and secondary schools, Miss F wanted very much to attend normal school and prepare to teach Indians in remote areas. She knew that education and a career offered the only realistic hope to escape a life of rural poverty. Her father was very much opposed to this. He wanted her to marry and settle in the community. Miss F's mother agreed with her father. So it was against her parents' wishes that Miss F enrolled in normal school and finished three additional years of education.

During this period a young man from a nearby district showed an interest in Miss F. Her father insisted on either marriage or a common-law relationship so she would no longer be his responsibility. Hardly knowing the young man, Miss F yielded to parental pressure and went to live with the young man after being shown purportedly legal papers that attested to their marriage. After three months the young man left. The experience confirmed a fear of men which had been occasioned by some unfortunate experiences at the age of six or seven with male members of Miss F's extended family.

Miss F remained in her home area for a time, but improper advances by her uncle, parental insensitivity, and the traumas associated with extreme poverty caused her to leave. She taught rural Indians for three years and then, at the age of twenty-one, moved to Panama City in hopes of attending the university. Shortly after her arrival she was invited to live with a missionary family. Then one day the sister of an influential Panamanian general recognized her as a former teacher in the school for Indians. A scholarship (covering tuition and books) to a private university was arranged. Miss F began the study of sociology.

Then everything seemed to go wrong. Miss F's grandmother died. She had little money. She was largely alienated from her family. She was too ashamed to confide in her missionary benefactors, but when she broke down and cried hysterically one day they shared the gospel. Miss F trusted Christ and found a measure of relief from her guilt and fears.

During a visit to her hometown she received the attention of another young man, Mr. J. Responding to her resurrected fear and anxiety, he assured her that he was a *simpatizador* (interested in the gospel) and really cared for her. The relationship was alternately one of attraction and rejection. Mr. J was sometimes kind, but he often treated her contemptuously.

Miss F returned to Panama City, was baptized, and matured spiritually. After two years of study at the university she expressed interest in studying the Scriptures and preparing for Christian service as a missionary in her own country. She had good recommendations and was accepted in a Bible institute in the southern part of the United States. Mr. J made a profession of faith and enrolled in the same school. There their relationship continued for a time and was eventually broken off.

In the Bible school Miss F maintained an exemplary record for two years. Then, at the close of her second year news leaked out that a senior student had failed to graduate (graduation was tantamount to a recommendation for Christian ministry) because, even though he had previously been married and abandoned by his wife, he had applied as a single student and had not divulged his true status. Miss F's past flooded back into her mind. She was gripped by a new fear. Would her past become known? Had she really been married when she applied for admission to the school? Would she be refused a diploma and judged unfit for Christian ministry?

During vacation in her native Panama Miss F did her best to locate any existing legal record of her early "marriage." She could find none.

Miss F returned to Bible school for her third year. But she could no longer keep her problems to herself. She confided in a fellow student. Before long other students knew of her problem, and then the administration of the school as well. Miss F was afraid that she would be expelled. She doubted that God could use her because of her past sins. Perhaps those sins were not even forgiven. Her studies began to suffer. Her health became threatened.

Miss F was counseled briefly by a teacher for whom she worked as an assistant and then over a period of time by the president (President H) and the dean of women working in tandem. President H went to great pains to learn all he could about Miss F's past from the missionaries in Panama City and other contacts. He had a number of sessions with Miss F in which he employed some of the techniques and emphases he had learned from William Glasser's reality therapy (reality, responsibility, and right and wrong). The dean of women had more time and was able to follow through with counseling Miss F. (A further advantage of counseling in this way was that Miss F felt freer to share some of the more intimate details of her past with a woman counselor.)

Counseling emphasized that for more than ten years Miss F had lived with the problems of her past guilt without really sharing or resolving them. Now she was at a point where she was being affected spiritually, emotionally, and even physically. Providentially she did not have to analyze and resolve these problems alone. Her counselors were sent by God not simply or primarily as administrators of discipline but as spiritual teachers and helpers. Counselors and counselee together would review Miss F's case realistically and face implications in terms of her relationships with God, other people, and future Christian service. As they came to mutually agreed upon conclusions she would take responsibility to do the right thing as God enabled her.

The counselors assured Miss F that they fully believed she was a true child of God. (Those who knew her in Panama City had witnessed the great change in her life when she was converted. For two years while in school she had given evidence of the fruit of the Spirit.) The counselors then helped sort out problems stemming from her past experiences in terms of their moral, spiritual, legal, and disciplinary aspects and implications.

The moral and spiritual aspects of Miss F's problem were dealt with first. This was not easy. Others must bear the responsibility for many early abuses, although she had to deal with the scars. But what about her early "marriage" and her relationship with Mr. J? The fact was that those relationships occasioned periodic feelings of guilt and unworthiness for Christian service. Considerable discussion left counselors and counselee with unanswered questions as to the degree of her guilt, but certain facts were clear. First, God promises forgiveness when we meet certain conditions (Prov. 28:13; 1 John 1:9). Second, Satan is the "accuser of the brethren" (Rev. 12:10, KJV). Third, she must believe God and not Satan. Forgiveness was hers. The record was clear as far as God is concerned.

The legal aspect of Miss F's problem was dealt with next. If she was legally married in her late teens, that had implications for both the present and the future. Miss F related in detail how she had gone to the government offices where her marriage should have been recorded and found nothing. The counselors took her at her word. The paper she was shown at the time of her "marriage" must not have been genuine. She had not been legally married. To marry "again" would not be adulterous.

When these aspects were settled, there was no difficulty in resolving the issue of discipline as far as the school was concerned. Miss F had not falsified her status on her application, for she was not legally married and was actually single. She was free to continue her studies with the assurance that if she completed them successfully and continued to walk faithfully with the Lord, she would receive her diploma and be recommended for full-time Christian service.

Subsequent to the counseling sessions, Miss F felt a sense of release. She continued her studies with a new sense of dedication. Knowing that problems of this kind are rife in Latin America, she agreed that President H report the facts of her case with a view to helping others.

Basic Counseling Observations

Real and perceived universals. The world view of Latin America generally can be spoken of as that of Christopaganism—a mixture of Roman Catholic/Christian and tribal/animistic ideas and practices. A wide gulf exists between the sacred and secular; a heavy veil separates the "congregation" and the altar. Men and women are the creatures of God but, practically speaking at least, they are not equal. Perhaps the main ingredient of this view (as far as the Spanish heritage is concerned) is the idea of *pundonor* (a point of honor) being rooted in the soul of the individual (especially the male), giving him worth and value. The male establishes his "integrity" or "worth" by controlling and dominating the female. Thus he tends to love her and abuse her. The woman is characterized as subservient, pliable, available, and long-suffering. Authoritarian leaders are everywhere present: in religion the pope and priest, in society the landlord, in government the *caudillo* (boss), and in the family the father.

Cultural characteristics. Great differences exist between broad sections of Latin America (e.g., the more European countries in the south as compared with the mestizo Andean nations (as well as Panama and Mexico) and within nations (e.g., Hispanic as opposed to Portuguese

Brazil). The general views and values already mentioned are shared and expressed in their own ways by rural Panamanians. Sex is considered sinful and debased and therefore is not talked about. At the same time, virility is the proof of manhood. Little distinction is made between marriage ceremonies performed by a priest or magistrate and common-law marriages. There is often a wide disparity between the age of the wife and the husband (as in the case of Miss F's father and mother). Husbands and fathers may be alternately attentive and abusive to their wives and children. Males often take advantage of women and girls, even in their own nuclear and extended families. Understanding and solace are generally found from the mother. Poverty is widespread, as is a sense of fatalism.

Individual idiosyncracies. Miss F was clearly the product of her rural Panamanian culture. As a result of her upbringing and experiences in her childhood and teen-age years, she evidenced psychological scars that were to carry over into her Christian experience. Very early she wanted to extricate herself from the "imprisonment" of her childhood surroundings. Education provided the means of freedom and betterment. But the price of education was alienation from her family and friends. As a third-year Bible school student she was a victim not only of her past, but also of a new culture situation in which she was very insecure and fearful.

Counseling Universals

A shared world view. Even before her conversion, Miss F reacted against many of the ideas and values of her culture, notably fatalism and abject compliance on the part of the female. She was only partially successful in avoiding their implications, however. Even after her conversion she tended to think of sex and marriage in largely negative terms rather than as gifts of God. But by the time she received counseling she had been a Christian for between two and three years and had made some considerable progress in her understanding. She was looking forward to missionary service. Therefore, a knowledge of both Latin American *and* biblical man and world views was essential for counseling. Fortunately, President H has had long experience in Latin America and is widely read in its culture. We are not given any specifics concerning the dean of women.

A good relationship. Because of his position and gender, Miss F was understandably reluctant to confide in President H when it came to certain aspects of her problem. This obstacle was overcome by the inclusion of the dean of women in the counseling process. Both counselors tried to assure Miss F that they were Christian helpers, not just Christian administrators and disciplinarians.

An expectation of being helped. Initially the counselee was extremely reluctant to seek help from anyone outside of her peer group. She looked upon teachers and administrators as disciplinarians rather than counselors. Once this misunderstanding was overcome her Christian faith and (usually) optimistic view of the future seem to have taken over.

An appropriate approach and technique. Cultural patterns would have allowed for a directive and authoritarian counseling approach, especially in the case of a single, female counselee. The personalities of the counselors and counselee as well as the nature of the presenting problem dictated another approach. However, a better acquaintance with Christian counseling materials would have aided the counselors in this regard. The insights drawn from Glasser's reality therapy are not without merit, and have cross-cultural application. But in this case a still deeper appreciation of the cultural system in which Miss F was forced and duped into relationships not to her liking was needed.

Effecting Change

There are several crucial aspects of the positive change effected in the case before us. First, the counselors were successful in reassuring Miss F from the outset, thus gaining her confidence and willingness to confide in them.

Second, the counselors were equipped to understand Miss F's problem from both Latin American and Christian perspectives.

Third, the counselors had the ability to analyze and reframe the presenting problem in such a way as to make the overcoming of it a triumph of faith and even a steppingstone to more effective service.

More must be said, however. Looking back, President H feels that the most vulnerable aspect of counseling in this case was the practical necessity of taking Miss F's word concerning the absence of marriage documents in her home area. Rather, one should point to the seeming inability of the counselors to recognize that Miss F's anxiety stemmed more from her jeopardized status as student and Christian worker than from a feeling of culpability for her early marriage. After all, she did not intend to falsify the record when she registered as a single student. The counseling was evidently successful. But the counselors ran a definite risk in focusing on guilt and in overlooking the still potentially explosive psychological effects of Miss F's childhood experiences. In spite of the counselee's progress, there were cautions that should have been considered with a view to her future well-being and possible missionary or other service.

Concluding Reflections

It is no wonder that Miss F felt abandoned by her family. But even there we can see possible mitigating factors. For one thing, although her mother might have been expected to be more understanding and supportive, she was much younger than Miss F's father. She herself may have felt very threatened. As a future missionary in Panama, Miss F needed encouragement to try to reach her own family. Meanwhile, from the time of her conversion—and even before—the Christian family was her "family" on earth. The responsibility of the Christian family to Miss

F needed to be stressed as much as her responsibility to that family.

Case Vignette 2: Pastor S (South Africa)

Pastor S ministered to a small congregation in a well-populated area of Natal, South Africa. He and his entire congregation were Zulu. This was his first pastorate after completing training in a Bible school. He had been in the church for only a short period when he arrived at the home of Missionary B one day and, after appropriate preliminaries, related the following problem:

> Mfundisi, we were taught at the mission Bible school that the older African pastors are not working in a biblical way. You know each of the older pastors has been preaching in four or five places, and the offerings from those places have been making up their support. Missionary A showed us in the practical theology course that we must not do as they are doing. We are not to "run around like bishops," as he said, but we must stay, each in his own church, every Sunday to build up our people. He showed us too, from the Bible, that the pastor isn't like a chief over his congregation, as the older men have been. The apostle Paul wrote Timothy and Titus that elders were to be chosen in the local churches and that those men should be in leadership with the pastor.
>
> I've tried so hard to do what Missionary A taught us. I seem, however, to have failed completely. I feel very much alone. Our people don't want elders chosen because, they say, none of the members measure up to the Bible's requirements for eldership. They want me to direct the church program myself. Another difficulty is that my congregation is a small one made up of poor people. They are trying to support me but they just can't. Mrs. S has been making dresses to buy the groceries but she's discouraged. There's no provision under the labor laws for a minister of the gospel to do secular work for a second income. Our

children aren't in school because we can't buy books or school uniforms.

[Pastor S was overcome with emotion and could not speak for a few moments. Then he continued.]

Mfundisi, I was so sure God called me to preach, but I just don't see how I can stay in the ministry. What can I do?

Missionary B responded by expressing his personal concern and inviting Pastor S to join him in prayer asking God to give wisdom.

After prayer Missionary B recalled that within a period of eighteen months eight other pastors in the district had left the ministry for the same reason. (Pastor S knew most of them.) He noted that all of them had tried to pastor a single congregation as they had been taught at the Bible school and all left the ministry because their small congregations could not support them adequately. He conjectured that some of them had concluded that the biblical pattern of one congregation and one pastor had failed. He spent considerable time instructing Pastor S concerning the pastoral role and church leadership. He spoke to Pastor S in the following vein:

"Overseeing" the church is a good work (1 Tim. 3:1).

Titus was needed in the young church at Crete in order to provide leadership and appoint others who would provide leadership after his departure, just as Missionary A taught. However, it may be that Titus and also Timothy were more temporary than is the case with Zulu pastors and therefore they were obliged to appoint leaders rather quickly.

Your congregation is likely holding on to the African concept of leadership implied in the proverb, "No two bulls in any one cattle enclosure."

The New Testament seems to make allowance for more than one pattern of church government. The Antioch

church seems to have had a consortium of leadership
made up of prophets and teachers. On the other hand,
there is some evidence that James presided over a
kind of "episcopate" in Jerusalem, according to a recent book by Ralph P. Martin.[2] Like the Zulu people,
Israelites seem to have relied on one leader at the
front.

The Bible makes it clear that we who are leaders are
really servants. Would you say that a chief can be a
servant of his people as he leads them? So would I.
The same is true of the pastor of a congregation.

Diviners, herbalists, and traditional doctors in Zulu society all assume a positive authority. That is one reason why people have confidence in them. You pastors
have the Word of God to proclaim. Should you not
have authority? Do not hesitate to be the leader your
congregation expects you to be.

Think of Pastor N who graduated several years ago and
has pastored the church at Kwa Thema and its branch
churches. This arrangement has had several advantages: lay people have been involved in teaching, the
vitality of the program encourages all, and there has
been more financial support for Pastor N.

The churches have asked some of us missionaries on
the extension committee to help in this sort of out-
reach. One thing we have in mind is to inaugurate
extension schools in which missionaries and pastors
such as yourself can teach leaders of new congregations.

Another plan is to hold retreats for pastors and leaders
in order to encourage spiritual growth and strategy
planning. Howard A. Snyder, for example, points out

2. The reference is to Ralph P. Martin, *The Family and the Fellowship:
New Testament Images of the Church* (Grand Rapids: Eerdmans, 1980),
pp. 66, 110.

that the Bible and history give encouragement to the establishment of smaller growth groups in the church.[3] And according to Phillip M. Steyne, whom you will probably remember, Zionism has this kind of groups, and many have left our congregations to join it as a result.[4] Small growth groups are needed in our congregations. These could become the nuclei of branch churches—all of which could be bound up in the fellowship of the parent church.

If you are going to be home tomorrow I would like to stop by and show you the discipling/church planting program that has been presented to our extension committee; also a Bible-study format for small growth groups.

More important than anything I have so far mentioned are prayer, dependence on God and the power of the gospel, and a burden for unreached people.

Before you and Mrs. S give up the ministry, please pray together concerning the commitment to the type of ministry I have outlined.

The counseling session concluded with prayer and an agreement to meet the next day at Pastor S's home. At that time, or whenever Pastor S and his wife would decide to commit themselves to an effort for church renewal and extension from promises of external funds, Missionary B would divulge that the extension committee had set aside monies to aid in the initial phases of such efforts.

We are not informed as to the ultimate decision of Pastor and Mrs. S.

3. The reference is to Howard A. Snyder, *The Problem of Wineskins: Church Structure in a Technological Age* (Downers Grove, Ill.: Inter-Varsity, 1975).

4. The reference is to Phillip M. Steyne, "The African Zionist Movement," in *Dynamic Religious Movements: Case Studies of Rapidly Growing Religious Movements Around the World,* ed. David J. Hesselgrave (Grand Rapids: Baker, 1978), p. 27.

Basic Counseling Orientation

Real and perceived universals. Counselor and counselee are Christians, of course. But counselors who are well acquainted with the situation in South Africa would be aware of at least two all-important background factors. First, most African pastors are not well trained and ideologically and psychologically still live very close to the traditional African world view. Second, biological needs and needs for security which all Western counselors will acknowledge as basic must be felt by most African Christians in a way which very few Westerners can fully appreciate.

Cultural characteristics. The urban setting very likely means that South African pastors like Pastor S cannot have gardens. Civil laws evidently dictate that pastors are not eligible for employment outside the church. The culture is basically a collectivistic-dependency culture, but this does not militate against authority being invested in one man. As is true in many cultures of this kind, chiefs are past masters at ascertaining the will of people (particularly important people) under them, and ruling accordingly. Learning consists primarily of recalling what the teacher said, not thinking things through for oneself. Racial distinctions are carefully drawn by law and rivalries are deep. But in the case before us both mission and church originate in the United States, not in the state which supports apartheid. The religious scene is characterized by the rise of numerous prophet movements.

Individual idiosyncracies. Pastor S was young. He had a family to support. And he had been instructed by a missionary (occupying a position of authority as a teacher) that *the* biblical pattern for church and pastor is one pastor with a plurality of elders for each congregation. A number of Pastor S's contemporaries were leaving the ministry, a circumstance which must have been a significant factor psychologically and spiritually.

Counseling Universals

A shared world view. Missionary B is a veteran missionary with long experience in South Africa. This fact in itself does not assure us that he was able to adjust to Pastor S's perspective, but his counseling approach provides certain clues which indicate that he was able to draw insights from that perspective. The Bible formed the basis of the faith of both counselor and counselee.

A good relationship. Missionary B was sought out by Pastor S in a time of crisis. (Actually, Missionary B has been called upon to counsel both pastors and younger missionaries on numerous occasions during these recent years of growth and disruption in South African churches and society.)

An expectation of being helped. It is likely that Pastor S hoped to obtain both wise counsel and some kind of material or financial help from Missionary B. This expectation was anticipated on the part of Missionary B and taken into account in his counseling.

An appropriate approach and technique. All cultural signs point toward the directive approach taken by Missionary B. It is also reinforced by the difference in age and experience between counselor and counselee and the long-standing (and only partially justified) paternalistic posture of missions in Africa. The technique of withholding information concerning possible financial support from the extension committee appears to have been wise under the circumstances (although more must be said). Also, the suggestion that counselor and counselee continue their conversation at the home of Pastor S (where he would be on home ground and where Mrs. S would likely be present) was commendable.

Effecting Change

It is hazardous for outsiders, irrespective of their expertise, to comment on this case with a great deal of confidence. It is with some trepidation, therefore, that I suggest that along with everything that was right in Missionary

B's approach, something seems to have been radically wrong. Missionary B's apparent assumption was that Pastor S needed to change his ecclesiology to one that is more biblical and culturally appropriate, and that he needed to make a new commitment to the Christian ministry in dependence upon God (and with a view to a strategy better calculated to provide financial support). There may have been good grounds for this analysis. But was it not incomplete? Was reframing not in order?

It would seem that the change that was required in this case was a *change in the system*. Pastor S would have been the ninth young pastor in the district to leave the ministry. Why? Was something wrong with the understanding and commitment of *all* of the pastors? Should Missionary A (very possibly rather young and inexperienced himself) have been allowed to teach prospective pastors? Is it best to recruit young and relatively untried men for the ministry, train them, and then put them out on their own? Is it reasonable to expect more maturity and sacrifice on the part of new and youthful pastors than on the part of the churches from which they come? Must not churches (and mission) change along with their pastors? In short, is it not true that the situation called for alloplastic and emic change? Could not a missionary of long experience like Missionary B have been a catalyst for that kind of change?

Concluding Reflections

Along with theological and cultural sensitivity, the counseling approach and content of this case vignette quite possibly reveal overly much overt dependence on Western theological and ecclesiastical expertise. More importantly, the larger situation fairly bristles with the results of Western individualistic and paternalistic proclivities. This case should serve as a reminder that, if the church in the Third World is to be well served, effective missionary counseling will usually call for a careful blend of enlightened counseling *and* informed missiology.

Epilogue

If this book has made responsible counseling of the culturally different appear to be a most formidable task, it is because that is so. To *proclaim* the great truths of the gospel across cultural boundaries to audiences large and small, and to proclaim those truths in such a way that they are understandable and persuasive is no small undertaking. But a more generalized understanding of the Christian gospel and the respondents' culture will usually make it possible. To *counsel* across those same cultural boundaries, on the other hand, means that we must be prepared to probe into the experience and make-up of counselees very different from ourselves, and help effect changes in beliefs, feelings, and behavior. A formidable task indeed! And one not to be undertaken lightly!

If this book has revealed something of the complexity of cross-cultural counseling, then, it has not failed in accomplishing at least part of its purpose. If it has also assisted in the surmounting of cultural barriers by providing ways and means of characterizing human universals, identifying cultural differences, and discovering individual uniqueness, it has succeeded in its larger purpose.

More should be written on this important subject. More

will be written. And so the great enterprise of discipling the nations will be encouraged and expedited. But whatever remains to be written and whatever remains to be understood, let us be conscious of our dependence upon the divine Enabler, the Holy Spirit. For him, culture is no barrier.

Bibliography

Abel, T. "Cultural Patterns as They Affect Psychotherapeutic Procedures." *American Journal of Psychotherapy* 10 (October 1956): 728–40.

Adams, Jay E. *The Christian Counselor's Manual.* Phillipsburg, N.J.: Presbyterian and Reformed, 1973.

_____. *Competent to Counsel.* Phillipsburg, N.J.: Presbyterian and Reformed, 1970.

_____. "Nouthetic Counseling." In *Helping People Grow: Practical Approaches to Christian Counseling,* edited by Gary R. Collins, pp. 151–64. Santa Ana, Calif.: Vision House, 1980.

Adeney, Frances. "The Flowering of the Human Potential Movement." *S.C. P. Journal* 5 (Winter 1981–82): 7–18.

Alexander, A. A., Marjorie H. Klein, Milton H. Miller, and Workneh Fikre. "Psychotherapy and the Foreign Student." In *Counseling across Cultures,* rev. ed., edited by Paul P. Pedersen, Juris G. Draguns, Walter J. Lonner, and Joseph E. Trimble, pp. 227–43. Honolulu: The University Press of Hawaii for the East-West Center, 1981.

American Psychiatric Association. *Diagnostic and Statistical Manual of Mental Disorders.* 3d ed. Washington, D.C.: American Psychiatric Association, 1980.

Augustine. *On Christian Doctrine.* Translated by D. W. Robertson, Jr. New York: Liberal Arts, 1958.

407

Bakan, David. "Sigmund Freud and the Jewish Mystical Tradition." *The Christian Scholar* 44 (Fall 1961): 206–22.

Barnouw, Victor. *Culture and Personality.* Homewood, Ill.: Dorsey, 1963.

Bavinck, J. H. *An Introduction to the Science of Missions.* Translated by David Hugh Freeman. Grand Rapids: Baker, 1969.

Benedict, Ruth. *Patterns of Culture.* New York: Penguin, 1934.

Benner, David G. "Psychotherapies: Stalking Their Spiritual Side." *Christianity Today,* 11 December 1981, pp. 32–34.

Berman, Louis. *The Glands Regulating Personality.* Rev. ed. New York: Macmillan, 1928.

Bernard, L. L. *Instinct.* New York: Holt, 1925.

Berne, Eric. "The Cultural Problem: Psychopathology in Tahiti." *American Journal of Psychiatry* 116 (June 1960): 1076–81.

_____. *Games People Play: The Psychology of Human Relationships.* New York: Grove, 1964.

_____. *Principles of Group Treatment.* New York: Grove, 1968.

Berry, J. W., and Walter J. Lonner, eds. *Applied Cross-Cultural Psychology: Selected Papers from the Second International Conference of the International Association for Cross-Cultural Psychology.* Amsterdam: Swets and Zeitlinger, 1975.

Boisen, Anton T. *The Exploration of the Inner World: A Study of Mental Disorder and Religious Experience.* Chicago and New York: Willett, Clark, 1936.

_____. *Religion in Crisis and Custom: A Sociological and Psychological Study.* New York: Harper and Brothers, 1943.

Burton-Bradley, B. G. "Transcultural Psychiatry in Papua New Guinea." *Journal of Cross-Cultural Psychology* 1 (June 1970): 177–83.

Buswell, James O., Jr. *A Systematic Theology of the Christian Religion.* 2 vols. Grand Rapids: Zondervan, 1962.

Carlson, David E. "Relationship Counseling." In *Helping People Grow: Practical Approaches to Christian Counseling,* edited by Gary R. Collins, pp. 31–54. Santa Ana, Calif.: Vision House, 1980.

Carstairs, G. M. "Cultural Elements in the Response to Treatment." In *Transcultural Psychiatry,* edited by A. V. S. de Reuck and Ruth Porter, pp. 169–75. Boston: Little, Brown, 1965.

Chapman, A. H. *Textbook of Clinical Psychiatry: An Interpersonal Approach.* Philadelphia: Lippencott, 1967.

Choi, Philemon Y. W. "The Cross-Cultural Adaptation of a Peer-Counselor Training Program for Hong Kong." Thesis, Trinity Evangelical Divinity School, 1977.

Clements, Forrest E. "Primitive Concepts of Disease." *University of California Publications in American Archaeology and Ethnology* 32 (1932): 185–252.

Clinebell, Howard J., Jr. *Basic Types of Pastoral Counseling: New Resources for Ministries to the Troubled.* Nashville: Abingdon, 1966.

_____. "Growth Counseling." In *Helping People Grow: Practical Approaches to Christian Counseling,* edited by Gary R. Collins, pp. 81–98. Santa Ana, Calif.: Vision House, 1980.

_____. *Growth Counseling: Hope-Centered Methods for Actualizing Human Wholeness.* Nashville: Abingdon, 1979.

Cobb, John R. *The Spirit of a Sound Mind.* Grand Rapids: Zondervan, 1966.

Collins, Gary R. *How to Be a People Helper.* Santa Ana, Calif.: Vision House, 1976.

_____. "Psychology on a New Foundation: A Proposal for the Future." *Journal of Psychology and Theology* 1 (January 1973): 19–27.

_____, ed. *Helping People Grow: Practical Approaches to Christian Counseling.* Santa Ana, Calif.: Vision House, 1980.

Copeland, Elaine J. "Cross-Cultural Counseling and Psychotherapy: A Historical Perspective, Implications for Research and Training." *The Personnel and Guidance Journal* 63 (September 1983): 10–15.

Corey, Gerald, and Marianne Schneider Corey. *Groups: Process and Practice.* Monterey, Calif.: Brooks-Cole, 1977.

Corsini, Raymond, ed. *Current Psychotherapies.* 1st ed. Itasca, Ill.: F. E. Peacock Publishers, 1973.

"Counseling Centre in Hong Kong." *Asian Theological News* 7 (January-March 1981): 18–19.

Dale, Kenneth J. *Circle of Harmony: A Case Study in Popular Japanese Buddhism with Implications for Christian Mission.* Pasadena, Calif.: William Carey Library; Tokyo: Seibunsha, 1975.

Delitzsch, Franz. *Commentary on the Song of Songs and Ecclesiastes.* Translated by M. G. Easton. Grand Rapids: Eerdmans, n.d.

de Reuck, A. V. S., and Ruth Porter, eds. *Transcultural Psychiatry.* Boston: Little, Brown, 1965.

Devereux, George. *Basic Problems of Ethnopsychiatry.* Translated by Basia Miller Gulati. 1970. Chicago: University of Chicago Press, 1980.

Di Loretto, Adolph O. *Comparative Psychotherapy: An Experimental Analysis.* Modern Applications of Psychology series. Chicago: Aldine-Atherton, 1971.

Dohoynes, Henry F., Paul L. Daughty, and Allan R. Holmberg. *Peace Corps Program Impact in the Peruvian Andes.* Cornell Peru Project, Department of Anthropology, Cornell University.

Doob, Leonard W. "The Inconclusive Struggles of Cross-Cultural Psychology." *Journal of Cross-Cultural Psychology* 11 (March 1980): 59–73.

Dooley, Thomas A. *The Edge of Tomorrow.* New York: Farrar, Straus and Cudahy, 1958.

Douglas, J. D., ed. *Let the Earth Hear His Voice.* Minneapolis: World Wide Publications, 1975.

Draguns, Juris G., and L. Phillips. *Culture and Psychotherapy: The Quest for a Relationship.* Morristown, N.J.: General Learning Press, 1972.

Drakeford, John W. "Integrity Therapy." In *Helping People Grow: Practical Approaches to Christian Counseling,* edited by Gary R. Collins, pp. 241–58. Santa Ana, Calif.: Vision House, 1980.

_____. *Integrity Therapy: A New Direction in Psychotherapy.* Nashville: Broadman, 1967.

Dublin, Louis. "Suicide Prevention." In *On the Nature of Suicide,* edited by Edwin S. Schneidman, pp. 43–47. San Francisco: Jossey-Bass, 1969.

Duffie, David. *Psychology and the Christian Religion.* Nashville: Southern Publishing Association, 1968.

Egan, Gerhard. *The Skilled Helper: A Model for Systematic Helping and Interpersonal Relating.* Monterey, Calif.: Brooks-Cole, 1975.

Ehrenberg, Miriam, and Otto Ehrenberg. *The Psychotherapy Maze.* New York: Holt, Rinehart, and Winston, 1977.

Elder, James Lyn. "Pastoral Counseling and the Communication of the Gospel." In *An Introduction to Pastoral Counseling,* edited by Wayne E. Oates, pp. 203–10. Nashville: Broadman, 1959.

Ellis, Albert, and Russell Grieger, with contributors. *Handbook of Rational-Emotive Therapy.* New York: Springer Publishing, 1977.

Engel, James F. *Contemporary Christian Communication: Its Theory and Practice.* Nashville: Nelson, 1979.

Engelsmann, Frank. "Cultural Depression." In *Culture and Psychopathology,* edited by Ihsan al-Issa, pp. 251–74. Baltimore: University Park, 1982.

Erikson, Erik. *Childhood and Society.* 2d ed. New York: Norton, 1963.

Evans, Craig A. " 'Preacher' and 'Preaching': Some Lexical Observations." *Journal of the Evangelical Theological Society* 24 (December 1981): 315–22.

Eysenck, Hans J. "The Effects of Psychotherapy: An Evaluation." *Journal of Consulting Psychology* 16 (August 1952): 319–24.

Eysenck, Hans J., and Eysenck, S. B. G. "Culture and Personality Abnormalities." In *Culture and Psychopathology,* edited by Ihsan al-Issa, pp. 302–14. Baltimore: University Park, 1982.

Festinger, Leon. *A Theory of Cognitive Dissonance.* Evanston, Ill.: Row and Peterson, 1957.

Fiedler, F. E. "The Concept of an Ideal Therapeutic Relationship." *Journal of Consulting Psychology* 14 (June 1950): 239–45.

Finney, Joseph. "*Vai Laaqau* and *Aitu* Healing in a West Polynesian Village." In *Culture-Bound Syndromes, Ethnopsychiatry, and Alternate Therapies,* Mental Health in Asia and the Pacific series, vol. 4, edited by William P. Lebra, pp. 115–29. Honolulu: The University Press of Hawaii for the East-West Center, 1976.

Fishbein, Martin, and Icek Ajzen. *Belief, Attitude, Intention, and Behavior: An Introduction to Theory and Research.* Reading, Mass.: Addison-Wesley, 1975.

Foulks, Edward F., Ronald M. Wintrob, Joseph Westermeyer, and Armando R. Favazza, eds. *Current Perspectives in Cultural Psychiatry.* New York: Spectrum Publications, 1977.

Frank, Jerome D. *Persuasion and Healing: A Comparative Study of Psychotherapy.* Rev. ed. Baltimore: Johns Hopkins Press, 1973.

Freeman, Derek. *Margaret Mead and Samoa: The Making and Unmaking of an Anthropological Myth.* Cambridge, Mass.: Harvard University Press, 1983.

Freer, Sofia, Richard G. Graf, and Paul C. Plaizier. "Interpersonal Perception as a Function of Help-Seeking: A United States-Netherlands Contrast." *Journal of Cross-Cultural Psychology* 10 (March 1979): 101–10.

Freud, Sigmund. *The Future of an Illusion.* Translated by W. D. Robsen-Scott. 1927. New York: Liveright, 1953.

Fromm, Eric. *Man for Himself: An Inquiry into the Psychology of Ethics.* New York: Holt, Rinehart, and Winston, 1947.

Fromm, Eric, and Michael Maccoby. *Social Character in a Mexican Village: A Sociopsychoanalytic Study.* Englewood Cliffs, N. J.: Prentice-Hall, 1970.

Fry, P. S. "The Resistance to Temptation: Inhibitory and Disinhibitory Effects of Models on Children from India and the United States." *Journal of Cross-Cultural Psychology* 6 (June 1975): 189–201.

Glasser, William. *Reality Therapy.* New York: Harper and Row, 1965.

Glick, Paula Brown. "The Attack on and Defense of Margaret Mead." *Royal Anthropological Institute News* 58 (October 1983): 12–14.

Goldenweiser, Alexander A. *Anthropology: An Introduction to Primitive Culture.* New York: F. S. Crofts, 1937.

Goldschmidt, Walter. *Comparative Functionalism.* Berkeley: University of California Press, 1966.

Goldstein, Allen, and Dianne L. Chambliss. "Behavioral Psychotherapy." In *Current Psychotherapies,* 1st ed., edited by Raymond Corsini, pp. 230–72. Itasca, Ill.: F. E. Peacock Publishers, 1973.

Goldstein, Arnold P. "Evaluating Expectance Effects in Cross-Cultural Counseling and Psychotherapy." In *Cross-Cultural Counseling and Psychotherapy,* edited by Anthony J. Marsella and Paul P. Pedersen, pp. 85–101. General Psychology series. New York: Pergamon, 1981.

Gorer, Geoffrey. "The Concept of National Character." In *Personality in Nature, Society, and Culture,* edited by Clyde K. Kluckhohn and Henry A. Murray, pp. 246–59. New York: Knopf, 1948.

Green, Michael. *Evangelism in the Early Church.* Grand Rapids: Eerdmans, 1970.

Griffin, Graeme M. "Pastoral Theology and Pastoral Care Overseas." In *The New Shape of Pastoral Theology: Essays in Honor of Seward Hiltner,* edited by William B. Oglesby, Jr., pp. 49–60. Nashville: Abingdon, 1969.

Gurin, Gerald, Joseph Veroff, and Shiela Feld. *Americans View Their Mental Health.* New York: Basic, 1960.

Guthrie, George M., and David L. Szanton. "Folk Diagnosis and Treatment of Schizophrenia: Bargaining with the Spirits in the Philippines." In *Culture-Bound Syndromes, Ethnopsychiatry, and Alternate Therapies,* Mental Health in Asia and the Pacific series, vol. 4, edited by William P. Lebra, pp. 147–63. Honolulu: The University Press of Hawaii for the East-West Center, 1976.

Hall, Calvin S., and Gardner Lindzey. *Theories of Personality.* New York: Wiley, 1957.

Hammond, D. Corydon, Dean H. Hepworth, and Veon G. Smith. *Improving Therapeutic Communication: A Guide for Developing Effective Techniques.* Social and Behavioral Sciences series. San Francisco: Jossey-Bass, 1977.

Hansen, James C., Richard W. Warner, and Elsie M. Smith. *Group Counseling: Theory and Process.* Chicago: Rand, 1976.

Hapgood, David, and Meridan Bennett. *Agents of Change: A Close Look at the Peace Corps.* Boston: Little, Brown, 1968.

Haring, Douglas G., ed. *Personal Character and Cultural Milieu: A Collection of Readings.* Syracuse: Syracuse University Press, 1949.

Hartog, Joseph, and Gerald Resner. "Concepts and Terminology of Mental Disorders among Malays." *Journal of Cross-Cultural Psychology* 1 (December 1970): 369–81.

Hesselgrave, David J. *Communicating Christ Cross-Culturally: An Introduction to Missionary Communication.* Grand Rapids: Zondervan, 1978.

_____. " 'Gold from Egypt': The Contribution of Rhetoric to Cross-Cultural Communication." *Missiology: An International Review* 4 (October 1976): 83–102.

_____. *Planting Churches Cross-Culturally: A Guide for Home and Foreign Missions.* Grand Rapids: Baker, 1980.

_____, ed. *Dynamic Religious Movements: Case Studies of Rapidly Growing Religious Movements Around the World.* Grand Rapids: Baker, 1978.

Hiebert, Paul G. *Cultural Anthropology.* Philadelphia: Lippincott, 1976.

_____. "The Flaw of the Excluded Middle." *Missiology: An International Review* 10 (January 1982): 35–47.

Hilts, Philip J. "Psychology Welcomes Voodoo: Faith Healers, Spirit Mediums Find New Respect." *The Washington Post,* 21 August 1981, sec. A, p. 2.

Honigmann, John J. *Culture and Personality.* New York: Harper and Row, 1954.

Hseih, Theodore Tin-Yee, Erwin J. Lotsof, and John Shybut. "Internal Versus External Control and Ethnic Group Membership: A Cross-Cultural Comparison." *Journal of Counseling and Clinical Psychology* 33 (1969): 122–24.

Hsu, Francis L. K. *Rugged Individualism Reconsidered: Essays in Psychological Anthropology.* Knoxville: The University of Tennessee Press, 1983.

Hsu, Jing, and Wen-shing Tseng. "Intercultural Psychotherapy." *Archives of General Psychiatry* 27 (November 1972): 700–705.

Inglis, Brian. *The Case for Unorthodox Medicine.* New York: Putnam, 1965.

Irvine, Sid H., and William K. Carroll. "Testing and Awareness across Cultures: Issues in Methodology and History." In *Handbook of Cross-Cultural Psychology: Perspectives,* vol. 2, edited by Harry C. Triandis and Juris G. Draguns, pp. 181–244. Boston: Allyn and Bacon, 1980.

Issa, Ihsan al-, ed. *Culture and Psychopathology.* Baltimore: University Park, 1982.

Jahn, Janheinz. *Muntu: An Outline of the New African Culture.* Translated by Marjorie Greve. New York: Grove, 1961.

Jahoda, Gustav. *Psychology and Anthropology: A Psychological Perspective.* New York: Academic Press, 1982.

——————. "Supernatural Beliefs and Changing Cognitive Structures among Ghanian University Students." *Journal of Cross-Cultural Psychology* 1 (June 1970): 115–30.

Jampolsky, Gerald G. *Love Is Letting Go of Fear.* Toronto: Bantam, 1981.

Janov, Arthur. *Imprints: The Lifelong Effects of the Birth Experience.* New York: Coward-McCann, 1983.

Johnson, Paul E. *Personality and Religion.* New York: Harcourt, Brace, 1933.

Johnson, Walter C. "Depression: Biochemical Abnormality or Spiritual Backsliding?" *Journal of the American Scientific Affiliation* 32 (March 1980): 18–27.

Jung, Carl G. *Modern Man in Search of a Soul.* New York: Harcourt, Brace, 1945.

_____. *Psychological Types.* Translated by H. Goodwin Baynes. London: Routledge and Kegan Paul, 1923.

Kasdorf, Hans. *Christian Conversion in Context.* Scottdale, Pa.: Herald, 1980.

Katz, Martin M. "Evaluating Drug and Other Therapies across Cultures." In *Cross-Cultural Counseling and Psychotherapy,* edited by Anthony J. Marsella and Paul P. Pedersen, pp. 159–73. General Psychology series. New York: Pergamon, 1981.

Kaufmann, Yoram, and Edward C. Whitmont. "Analytical Psychotherapy." In *Current Psychotherapies,* 1st ed., edited by Raymond Corsini, pp. 85–118. Itasca, Ill.: F. E. Peacock Publishers, 1973.

Keesing, Felix M. *Cultural Anthropology: The Science of Custom.* New York: Holt, Rinehart, and Winston, 1958.

Keil, Carl F., and Franz Delitzsch. *Biblical Commentary on the Old Testament.* Vol. 1, *The Pentateuch.* Translated by James Martin. Grand Rapids: Eerdmans, 1968.

Kelley, D. P. *Destroying the Barriers: Receptor Oriented Communication of the Gospel.* Vernon, B. C.: Laurel Publications, 1982.

Kietzman, Dale W., and William A. Smalley. "The Missionary's Role in Culture Change." In *Readings in Missionary Anthropology II,* 2d rev. ed., edited by William A. Smalley, pp. 524–30. Applied Cultural Anthropology series. Pasadena, Calif.: William Carey Library, 1978.

Kiev, Ari, ed. *Magic, Faith, and Healing: Studies in Primitive Psychiatry Today.* New York: Macmillan, 1964.

Kinzie, David, Jin-inn Teoh, and Eng-seong Tan. "Community Health in Malaysia." *American Journal of Psychiatry* 131 (May 1974): 573–77.

_____. "Native Healers in Malaysia." In *Culture-Bound Syndromes, Ethnopsychiatry, and Alternative Therapies,* Mental Health in Asia and the Pacific series, vol. 4, edited by William P. Lebra, pp. 130–46. Honolulu: The University Press of Hawaii for the East-West Center, 1976.

Kittrie, Nicholas N. *The Right to Be Different: Defiance and Enforced Therapy.* Baltimore: Penguin, 1973.

Kluckhohn, Clyde K., and Henry A. Murray, eds. *Personality in Nature, Society, and Culture.* New York: Knopf, 1948.

Kondo, Kyoichi. "The Origin of Morita Therapy." In *Culture-Bound Syndromes, Ethnopsychiatry, and Alternate Therapies,* Mental Health in Asia and the Pacific series, vol. 4, edited by William P. Lebra, pp. 250–53. Honolulu: The University Press of Hawaii for the East-West Center, 1976.

The Koran. Translated by N. J. Dawood. Classics series. Rev. ed. Baltimore: Penguin, 1964.

Koteskey, Ronald L. "Growing Up Too Late, Too Soon: The Invention of Adolescence." *Christianity Today,* 13 March 1981, pp. 24–28.

Kraemer, Hendrik. *The Christian Message in a Non-Christian World.* 3d ed. Grand Rapids: Kregel, 1956.

——————. *The Communication of the Christian Faith.* Philadelphia: Westminster, 1956.

Kraft, Charles H. *Christianity in Culture: A Study in Dynamic Biblical Theologizing in Cross-Cultural Perspective.* Maryknoll, N. Y.: Orbis, 1979.

Kretschmer, Ernst. *Physique and Character.* Translated by W. J. H. Sprott. New York: Harcourt, Brace, 1925.

Kroeber, Alfred L. *Anthropology.* Rev. ed. New York: Harcourt, Brace, 1948.

La Barre, Weston. "Confession as Cathartic Therapy in American Indian Tribes." In *Magic, Faith, and Healing: Studies in Primitive Psychiatry Today,* edited by Ari Kiev, pp. 36–49. New York: Free Press, 1964.

LaHaye, Tim. *The Spirit-Controlled Temperament.* Wheaton: Tyndale, 1966.

Lambo, T. Adeoye. "Schizophrenic and Borderline States." In *Transcultural Psychiatry,* edited by A. V. S. de Reuck and Ruth Porter, pp. 62–74. Boston: Little, Brown, 1965.

Langness, Lewis. "Hysterical Psychoses and Possessions." In *Culture-Bound Syndromes, Ethnopsychiatry, and Alternate Therapies.* Mental Health in Asia and the Pacific series, vol. 4, edited by William P. Lebra, pp. 56–67. Honolulu: The University Press of Hawaii for the East-West Center, 1976.

Lapsley, James N. "Pastoral Theology Past and Present." In *The New Shape of Pastoral Theology: Essays in Honor of Seward Hiltner,* edited by William B. Oglesby, Jr., pp. 31–48. Nashville: Abingdon, 1969.

Lebra, William P., ed. *Culture-Bound Syndromes, Ethnopsychiatry, and Alternate Therapies.* Mental Health Research in Asia and the

Pacific series, vol. 4. Honolulu: The University Press of Hawaii for the East-West Center, 1976.

Leighton, Alexander. "Cultural Change and Psychiatric Disorder." In *Transcultural Psychiatry,* edited by A. V. S. de Reuck and Ruth Porter, pp. 216–27. Boston: Little, Brown, 1965.

Leo, John. "Bursting the South Sea Bubble: An Anthropologist Attacks Margaret Mead's Research in Samoa." *Time,* 14 February 1983, pp. 68–70.

Lewis, C. S. *The Case for Christianity.* 1948. New York: Macmillan, 1962.

_____. *The Weight of Glory and Other Addresses.* New York: Macmillan, 1949.

Lindgren, Henry Clay, and Leonard W. Fisk. *Psychology of Personal Development.* 3d ed. New York: Wiley, 1976.

Lindgren, Henry Clay, and Amelia Tebcherani. "Arab and American Auto- and Heterostereotypes: A Cross-Cultural Study of Empathy." *Journal of Cross-Cultural Psychology* 2 (June 1971): 173–80.

Linton, Ralph. *The Study of Man: An Introduction.* New York: Appleton-Century, 1936.

_____, ed. *The Science of Man in the World Crisis.* 1945. New York: Octagon, 1980.

Lloyd-Jones, D. Martyn. *Spiritual Depression: Its Causes and Cure.* Grand Rapids: Eerdmans, 1965.

Loewen, Jacob A. "Self-Exposure: Bridge to Fellowship." *Practical Anthropology* 12 (March-April 1965): 49–62.

_____. "The Social Context of Guilt and Forgiveness." *Practical Anthropology* 17 (March-April 1970): 80–96.

Lonner, Walter J. "The Search for Psychological Universals." In *Handbook of Cross-Cultural Psychology: Perspectives,* vol. 1, edited by Harry C. Triandis and William W. Lambert, pp. 143–204. Boston: Allyn and Bacon, 1980.

Loudon, J. B. "Social Aspects of Ideas about Treatment." In *Transcultural Psychiatry,* edited by A. V. S. de Reuck and Ruth Porter, pp. 137–60. Boston: Little, Brown, 1965.

Lubin, Gerald I., and C. H. Paulsen, eds. *Piagetian Theory and Its Implications for the Helping Professions. Proceedings of the Eighth Interdisciplinary Conferences,* vol. 2. Cosponsored by University Affiliated Program, Children's Hospital of Los Angeles and the

University of Southern California Schools of Education and Religion, 1979.

Luzbetak, Louis. *The Church and Cultures.* Techny, Ill.: Divine Word Publications, 1963.

Maier, Henry W. "Piagetian Principles Applied to the Beginning Phase in Professional Helping." In *Proceedings of the Seventh Interdisciplinary Conference,* vol. 1, pp. 1–13. Cosponsored by the University Affiliated Program, Children's Hospital of Los Angeles and the University of Southern California Schools of Education and Religion, 1979.

Malinowski, Bronislaw. *The Father in Primitive Psychology.* 1927. New York: Norton, 1966.

Margetts, E. L. "Methods of Psychiatric Treatment in Africa." In *Transcultural Psychiatry,* edited by A. V. S. de Reuck and Ruth Porter, pp. 268–93. Boston: Little, Brown, 1965.

Marsella, Anthony J. "Depressive Experience and Disorder across Cultures." In *Handbook of Cross-Cultural Psychology: Perspectives,* vol. 6, edited by Harry C. Triandis and Juris G. Draguns, pp. 237–91. Boston: Allyn and Bacon, Inc., 1981.

Marsella, Anthony J., and Junko Tanaka-Matsumi. "Cross-Cultural Variations in the Phenomenological Experience of Depression." *Journal of Cross-Cultural Psychology* 7 (December 1976): 379–93.

Marsella, Anthony J., and Paul P. Pedersen, eds. *Cross-Cultural Counseling and Psychotherapy.* General Psychology series. New York: Pergamon, 1981.

Martin, Ralph P. *The Family and the Fellowship: New Testament Images of the Church.* Grand Rapids: Eerdmans, 1980.

Marx, Melvin W., and William A. Hillix. *Systems and Theories in Psychology.* 3d ed. New York: McGraw-Hill, 1979.

Maslow, Abraham H. *Motivation and Personality.* 2d ed. New York: Harper and Row, 1970.

May, Rollo. *Psychology and the Human Dilemma.* New York: Van Nostrand Reinhold, 1966.

Mayers, Marvin K. *Christianity Confronts Culture: A Strategy for Cross-Cultural Evangelism.* Contemporary Evangelical Perspectives series. Grand Rapids: Zondervan, 1973.

McGavran, Donald A. *The Clash Between Christianity and Cultures.* Washington, D.C.: Canon, 1974.

_____. *Understanding Church Growth*. Grand Rapids: Eerdmans, 1970.

_____, ed. *Church Growth and Christian Mission*. New York: Harper and Row, 1965.

McNeill, J. T. *A History of the Cure of Souls*. New York: Harper and Row, 1965.

Mead, Margaret. *Coming of Age in Samoa*. New York: Morrow, 1928.

_____. *Sex and Temperament in Three Primitive Societies*. New York: Morrow, 1935.

Meade, Robert D. "The Center for Cross-Cultural Research." *Journal of Cross-Cultural Psychology* 1 (March 1970): v–vi.

_____. "Future Time Perspectives of Americans and Subcultures in India." *Journal of Cross-Cultural Psychology* 3 (March 1972): 93–99.

Meadows, P. "The Cure of Souls and the Winds of Change." *Psychoanalytic Review* 55, no. 3 (1968): 491–504.

Meier, Paul B., Frank B. Minirth, and Frank B. Wichern. *Introduction to Psychology and Counseling: Christian Perspectives and Applications*. Grand Rapids: Baker, 1982.

Menninger, Karl. *Theory of Psychoanalytic Technique*. New York: Harper and Row, 1958.

Montgomery, John. *Principalities and Powers: A New Look at the World of the Occult*. Minneapolis: Bethany Fellowship, 1973.

Morley, Peter, and Roy Wallis, eds. *Culture and Curing: Anthropological Perspectives on Traditional Medical Beliefs and Practices*. Contemporary Community Health series. Pittsburgh: University of Pittsburgh Press, 1979.

Mowrer, O. Hobart. *The New Group Therapy*. New York: Van Nostrand Reinhold, 1964.

Mowrer, O. Hobart, et al. *Integrity Groups: The Loss and Recovery of Community*. Urbana: Integrity Groups, 1974.

Mucchielli, Roger. *Introduction to Structural Psychology*. Translated by Charles L. Markmann. New York: Funk and Wagnalls, 1970.

Munroe, Robert L., and Ruth H. Munroe. "Perspectives Suggested by the Anthropological Data." In *Handbook of Cross-Cultural Psychology: Perspectives*, vol. 1, edited by Harry C. Triandis and William W. Lambert, pp. 253–319. Boston: Allyn and Bacon, 1980.

Murase, Takao. "Naikan Therapy." In *Culture-Bound Syndromes, Ethnopsychiatry, and Alternate Therapies.* Mental Health in Asia and the Pacific series, vol. 4, edited by William P. Lebra, pp. 259–69. Honolulu: The University Press of Hawaii for the East-West Center, 1976.

Murdock, George P. "The Common Denominator in Cultures." In *The Science of Man in the World Crisis,* edited by Ralph Linton, pp. 123–42. 1945. New York: Octagon, 1980.

Murdock, George P., et al. *Outline of Cultural Materials.* 4th rev. New York: Taplinger, 1961.

Murphy, Jane. "Psychotherapeutic Aspects of Shamanism on St. Lawrence Island, Alaska." In *Magic, Faith, and Healing: Studies in Primitive Psychiatry Today,* edited by Ari Kiev, pp. 58–83. New York: Free Press, 1964.

Murphy, Jane, and Alexander Leighton, eds., *Approaches to Cross-Cultural Psychiatry.* Ithaca, N.Y.: Cornell University Press, 1965.

Narramore, Clyde M. *The Psychology of Counseling.* Grand Rapids: Zondervan, 1960.

Neill, Stephen C. *Christian Faith and Other Faiths: The Christian Dialogue with Other Religions.* 2d ed. London and New York: Oxford University Press, 1970.

Nevius, John L. *Demon Possession.* 8th ed. Grand Rapids: Kregel, 1968.

Nida, Eugene A. "Communication of the Gospel to Latin America." In *Readings in Missionary Anthropology II,* 2d rev. ed., edited by William A. Smalley, pp. 627–38. Applied Cultural Anthropology series. Pasadena, Calif.: William Carey Library, 1978.

——————. "Dynamics of Church Growth." In *Church Growth and Christian Mission,* edited by Donald A. McGavran, pp. 190–92. New York: Harper and Row, 1965.

Oates, Wayne E., ed. *An Introduction to Pastoral Counseling.* Nashville: Broadman, 1959.

Oglesby, William B., Jr., ed. *The New Shape of Pastoral Theology: Essays in Honor of Seward Hiltner.* Nashville: Abingdon, 1969.

Olson, Bruce. *For This Cross I'll Kill You.* Carol Stream, Ill.: Creation House, 1973.

Opler, Marvin K. *Culture, Psychology, and Human Values: The Method and Values of a Social Psychiatry.* Springfield, Ill.: Charles C. Thomas, 1956.

Opler, Morris E. "Themes as Dynamic Forces in Culture." *American Journal of Sociology* 51 (September 1945): 198–206.

Osborne, Grant R. "Contextualization: A Hermeneutical Approach." Paper presented at the Third Consultation of Theology and Mission, Trinity Evangelical Divinity School, Deerfield, Ill., 18–20 March 1982.

Parshall, Phil. *New Paths in Muslim Evangelism: Evangelical Approaches to Contextualization.* Grand Rapids: Baker, 1980.

Parsons, Anne. *Belief, Magic, and Anomie.* New York: Free Press, 1969.

Patterson, C. H. *Relationship Counseling and Psychotherapy.* New York: Harper and Row, 1974.

Pattison, E. Mansell. "A Theoretical-Empirical Base for Social System Therapy." In *Current Perspectives in Cultural Psychiatry,* edited by Edward F. Foulks, Ronald M. Wintrob, Joseph Westermeyer, and Armando R. Favazza, pp. 217–53. New York: Spectrum Publications, 1977.

Paul, Gordon L. *Insight versus Desensitization in Psychotherapy: An Experiment in Anxiety Reduction.* Stanford: Stanford University Press, 1966.

Pedersen, Paul P., Walter J. Lonner, and Juris G. Draguns, eds. *Counseling across Cultures.* 1st ed. Honolulu: The University Press of Hawaii for the East-West Center, 1976.

Pedersen, Paul P., Juris G. Draguns, Walter J. Lonner, and Joseph E. Trimble, eds. *Counseling across Cultures.* Honolulu: The University Press of Hawaii for the East-West Center, 1981.

Perry, Edmund. *The Gospel in Dispute: The Relation of Christian Faith to Other Missionary Religions.* Garden City, N. Y.: Doubleday, 1958.

Prince, Raymond. "Indigenous Yoruba Psychiatry." In *Magic, Faith, and Healing: Studies in Primitive Psychiatry Today,* edited by Ari Kiev, pp. 84–120. New York: Free Press, 1964.

_____. "Variations in Psychotherapeutic Procedures." In *Handbook of Cross-Cultural Psychology, Perspectives,* vol. 6, edited by Harry C. Triandis and Juris G. Draguns, pp. 291–349. Boston: Allyn and Bacon, 1981.

Proceedings of the ISS Twenty-Fifth Anniversary Conference. Development of Societies: The Next Seventy-Five Years. Boston: Martinus Nijhoff, 1979.

Queen, Stuart A., and Robert W. Habenstein. *The Family in Various Cultures.* 4th ed. New York: Lippencott, 1974.

Redfield, Robert. *The Primitive World and Its Transformations.* Ithaca, N. Y.: Cornell University Press, 1957.

Rogers, Carl R. "Interpersonal Relationships: Year 2000." *Journal of Applied Behavioral Science* 4 (July/August/September 1968): 265–80.

_____. *On Becoming a Person: A Therapist's View of Psychotherapy.* Boston: Houghton Mifflin, 1961.

Rogers, Carl R., and Barry Stevens. *Person to Person: The Problem of Being Human, a New Trend in Psychology.* Lafayette, Calif.: Real People, 1967.

Rogers, Clement F. *An Introduction to the Study of Pastoral Theology.* Oxford: Clarendon, 1912.

Rogers, Everett M., and Floyd F. Shoemaker. *Communication of Innovation.* New York: Free Press, 1971.

Rosen, G. *Madness in Society: Chapters in the Historical Sociology of Mental Illness.* Chicago: University of Chicago Press, 1980.

Ruesch, Jurgen, and Gregory Bateson. *Communication: The Social Matrix of Psychiatry.* New York: Norton, 1951.

Saler, Benson. "Religious Conversion and Self-Aggrandizement: A Guatemala Case." *Practical Anthropology* 12 (May-June 1965): 107–14.

Schneidman, Edwin S., ed. *On the Nature of Suicide.* San Francisco: Jossey-Bass, 1969.

Scroggie, W. Graham. *Know Your Bible: A Brief Introduction to the Scriptures.* 2 vols. London: Pickering and Inglis, 1940.

Segall, Marshall H. *Cross-Cultural Psychology: Human Behavior in Global Perspective.* Monterey, Calif.: Brooks-Cole, 1979.

Shapira, Ariella, and Judy L. Todd. "U.S. and British Self-Disclosure, Anxiety, Empathy, and Attitudes to Psychotherapy." *Journal of Cross-Cultural Psychology* 5 (September 1974): 364–69.

Sheldon, W. H., with the collaboration of S. S. Stevens and W. B. Tucker. *The Varieties of Human Physique: An Introduction to Constitutional Psychology.* 1940. New York: Coward-McCann, 1983.

Skinner, B. F. *Beyond Freedom and Dignity.* Toronto: Bantam, 1972.

Smalley, William A., ed. *Readings in Missionary Anthropology II.* 2d rev. ed. Pasadena, Calif.: William Carey Library, 1978.

_____. "Some Questions about Missionary Medicine." *Practical Anthropology* 6 (November-December 1959): 90–95.

Snyder, Howard A. *The Problem of Wineskins: Church Structure in a Technological Age.* Downers Grove, Ill.: Inter-Varsity, 1975.

Spindler, George D., ed. *The Making of Psychological Anthropology.* Berkeley: University of California Press, 1978.

Spiro, Melford, ed. *Burmese Supernaturalism.* Englewood Cliffs, N. J.: Prentice-Hall, 1967.

Spitzer, Robert L., Andrew E. Skodol, Mirian Gibbon, and Janet B. W. Williams. *DSM-III Case Book: A Learning Companion to "The Diagnostic and Statistical Manual of Mental Disorders."* New York: American Psychiatric Association, 1981.

Steyne, Phillip M. "The African Zionist Movement." In *Dynamic Religious Movements: Case Studies of Rapidly Growing Religious Movements Around the World,* edited by David J. Hesselgrave, pp. 19–40. Grand Rapids: Baker, 1978.

Strouse, Jean. "Freud without Myths." *Newsweek,* 29 October 1979, pp. 97–98.

Strupp, H. "On the Basic Ingredients of Psychotherapy." *Journal of Consulting and Clinical Psychology* 41 (August 1973): 1–8.

Sue, Derald W. *Counseling the Culturally Different.* New York: Wiley, 1981.

Sulloway, Frank J. *Freud, Biologist of the Mind: Beyond the Psychoanalytic Legend.* New York: Basic, 1979.

Sundberg, Norman D. "Research and Research Hypotheses about Effectiveness in Intercultural Counseling." In *Counseling across Cultures,* rev. ed., edited by Paul P. Pedersen, Juris G. Draguns, Walter J. Lonner, and Joseph E. Trimble, pp. 304–42. Honolulu: The University Press of Hawaii for the East-West Center, 1976.

_____. "Toward Research Evaluating Intercultural Counseling." In *Counseling across Cultures,* 1st ed., edited by Paul P. Pedersen, Walter J. Lonner, and Juris G. Draguns, pp. 139–69. Honolulu: The University Press of Hawaii for the East-West Center, 1976.

Textor, Robert B., ed. *Cultural Frontiers of the Peace Corps.* Cambridge, Mass.: The M.I.T. Press, 1966.

Thayer, Joseph H. *Thayer's Greek-English Lexicon of the New Testament.* New York: American Book Co., 1889.

Torrey, E. Fuller. *The Mind Game: Witch Doctors and Psychiatrists.* New York: Emerson Hall, 1972.

Tournier, Paul. *The Healing of Persons.* Translated by Edwin Hudson. New York: Harper and Row, 1965.

Townsend, John Marshall. *Cultural Conceptions and Mental Illness: A Comparison of Germany and America.* Chicago: University of Chicago Press, 1978.

Triandis, Harry C., gen. ed. *Handbook of Cross-Cultural Psychology: Perspectives.* 6 vols. Boston: Allyn and Bacon, 1980–83.

Trobisch, Walter. *I Loved a Girl: Young Africans Speak.* New York: Harper and Row, 1965.

_____. *My Wife Made Me a Polygamist.* Rev. ed. Downers Grove, Ill.: Inter-Varsity, 1971.

Tseng, Wen-Shing. "Folk Psychotherapy in Taiwan." In *Culture-Bound Syndromes, Ethnopsychiatry, and Alternate Therapies,* Mental Health in Asia and the Pacific series, vol. 4, edited by William P. Lebra, pp. 164–78. Honolulu: The University Press of Hawaii for the East-West Center, 1976.

Turnbull, Colin M. *Africa and Change.* New York: Knopf, 1973.

UNESCO Statistical Yearbook 1981. Dunstable, England: United Nations Educational, Scientific, and Cultural Organization, 1981.

Unger, Merrill F. *Biblical Demonology.* 6th ed. Wheaton: Scripture Press Foundation, 1965.

Van Til, Henry R. *The Calvinistic Concept of Culture.* Grand Rapids: Baker, 1959.

Vine, W. E. *An Expository Dictionary of New Testament Words.* Westwood, N.J.: Revell, 1940.

Vitz, Paul C. *Psychology as Religion: The Cult of Self-Worship.* Grand Rapids: Eerdmans, 1977.

Vontress, Clement E. "Racial and Ethnic Barriers in Counseling," In *Counseling across Cultures,* rev. ed. edited by Paul P. Pedersen, Juris G. Draguns, Walter J. Lonner, and Joseph E. Trimble, pp. 87–107. Honolulu: The University Press of Hawaii for the East-West Center, 1981.

Walz, Gary R., and Libby Benjamin, eds. *Transcultural Counseling: Needs, Programs, and Techniques.* New Vistas in Counseling series, vol. 7. New York: Human Sciences, 1978.

Watzlawick, Paul, John H. Weakland, and Richard Fisch. *Change: Principles of Problem Formation and Problem Resolution.* New York: Norton, 1974.

Waxler, Nancy E. "Social Change and Psychiatric Illness in Ceylon: Traditional and Modern Concepts of Disease and Treatment." In

Culture-Bound Syndromes, Ethnopsychiatry, and Alternate Therapies. Mental Health in Asia and the Pacific series, vol. 4, edited by William P. Lebra, pp. 222–40. Honolulu: The University Press of Hawaii for the East-West Center, 1976.

Welter, Paul. *How to Help a Friend.* Wheaton: Tyndale, 1978.

Whiting, J. W. M., and Child, Irvin L. *Child Training and Personality: A Cross-Cultural Study.* New Haven: Yale University Press, 1953.

Wilson, R. Ward. "God's Image in Mankind: The Essence of Human Nature." Mimeographed manuscript, n.d.

Winter, Ralph D. "The Highest Priority: Cross-Cultural Evangelism." In *Let the Earth Hear His Voice,* edited by J. D. Douglas, pp. 213–41. Minneapolis: World Wide Publications, 1975.

Wintrob, Ronald M., and Youngsook Kim Harvey. "The Self-Awareness Factor in Intercultural Psychology: Some Personal Reflections." In *Counseling across Cultures,* rev. ed., edited by Paul P. Pedersen, Juris G. Draguns, Walter J. Lonner, and Joseph E. Trimble, pp. 108–32. Honolulu: The University Press of Hawaii for the East-West Center, 1981.

Wittek, Raymond A. "Woman Charged in Murder Was Given Weekend Passes." *Staten Island Advance,* 19 March 1983, sec. A, p. 5.

Wittkower, E. D., with the assistance of Hsien Rin. "Recent Developments in Transcultural Psychology." In *Transcultural Psychiatry,* edited by A. V. S. de Reuck and Ruth Porter, pp. 4–17. Boston: Little, Brown, 1965.

Wohl, Julian. "Intercultural Psychotherapy: Issues, Questions, and Reflections." In *Counseling across Cultures,* rev. ed., edited by Paul P. Pedersen, Juris G. Draguns, Walter J. Lonner, and Joseph E. Trimble, pp. 133–62. Honolulu: The University Press of Hawaii for the East-West Center, 1981.

Yamamoto, Joe. "An Asian View of the Future of Cultural Psychiatry." In *Current Perspectives in Cultural Psychiatry,* edited by Edward F. Foulks, Ronald M. Wintrob, Joseph Westermeyer, and Armando R. Favazza, pp. 209–15. New York: Spectrum Publications, 1977.

Yap, P. M. "Phenomenology of Affective Disorder in Chinese and Other Cultures." In *Transcultural Psychiatry,* edited by A. V. S. de Reuck and Ruth Porter, pp. 84–107. Boston: Little, Brown, 1965.

Zilboorg, Gregory. *A History of Medical Psychology.* New York: Norton, 1941.

Index of Subjects

Acculturation, 35, 238
Adam, 98, 168, 169, 170
Adopter categories, 263–64
Alcoholics Anonymous, 83
Alloplastic change, 319–20, 384, 404
Altered states, 125
Amani Counselling Center (Nairobi), 140
Analytic therapies, 77
Ancestor worship, ancestor reverence, 224, 232, 343, 346, 348
Animistic world view, 162–63, 176–77, 342–43, 394
Anxiety, 131
Arica, 37, 162
Augustine, 25, 50, 113
Autoplastic change, 319–20

Behavior interpretation, 66
Behaviorism, 37, 158–59
Behavior modification, 70–71, 78
Behavior therapy, 70–71, 77, 90–91
Bethani Fellowship Resources (Nigeria), 141
Bilaterality, 319
Biofeedback, 37
Bonding, 30

Breakthrough Counseling Centre (Hong Kong), 139–40
Bride price, 224, 247–49
Brief counseling, 324–26, 331–35
Buddha, 43
Buddhism, 52

Christian (biblical) world view, 166–75
Churches Counseling Service (Singapore), 138
Client-centered therapy, 69–70, 78, 181, 330
Clinical Pastoral Education (CPE) movement, 27–28, 92–94, 107
Cognitive dissonance, 30
Collectivistic-dependency culture, 213–17, 236, 249, 286, 298–99, 343, 345, 383, 402
Community counseling, 87
Conditioning theory, 70–71, 77–78
Confucianist–Taoist world view, 164–65, 176, 236, 336, 381–85
Confucius, 43, 164, 207
Congruence, 70
Consultant management groups, 84
Contingent-reinforcement learning, 77–78

Index of Authors and Theorists

431

Index of Scripture

Genesis

1:26–27—166
1:28—228
1:31—169, 280
2:7—167
2:24—250
2:25—171
3—280
3:8–11—171
3:14–19—228
3:15—280
3:19—280
6:6–7—228
8:21–9:17—228

Exodus

18:19—104

2 Chronicles

25:16—104

Proverbs

11:14—104
15:22—104
28:13—393

Psalms

139:13–16—376

Ecclesiastes

12:13–14—283

Isaiah

1:26—104
49:1–4—376

Jeremiah

17:9—285

Matthew

5:3–12—340
5:45—340
10:36—317, 318
10:39—335, 357
19:4–5—382
22:37–40—281
25:41—283
26:41—19
28:18–20—229, 372
28:19—49

Mark

15:43—104

Luke

2:14—340
9:23—287
10:25–37—341
10:36—286
23:50—104

John

1:17—281
3—357
4:21—174
7:7—281
9:2–3—241, 341
15:13—287
16:8—242, 354, 355
16:8–11—354
16:33—340

Acts

1:8—32
3:19—353, 354
4:12—341

435